WESTFIELD PUBLICATIONS
IN MEDIEVAL STUDIES

The Poetry of Arnórr jarlaskáld

WESTFIELD PUBLICATIONS
IN
MEDIEVAL STUDIES

Volume 8

CENTRE FOR MEDIEVAL
AND RENAISSANCE STUDIES
QUEEN MARY AND WESTFIELD COLLEGE
UNIVERSITY OF LONDON
1998

The Poetry of Arnórr jarlaskáld

An Edition and Study

Diana Whaley

CENTRE FOR MEDIEVAL
AND RENAISSANCE STUDIES
QUEEN MARY AND WESTFIELD COLLEGE
UNIVERSITY OF LONDON
1998

BREPOLS

The printing of this book is made possible by a gift to the
University of Cambridge in memory of
Dorothea Coke, Skjaeret, 1951,
and by a grant from the Sponsorship Fund of the
University of Newcastle upon Tyne.

Printed in Belgium
D/1998/0095/33
ISBN 2-503-50663-1

Contents

Preface ix

Maps: Places and Peoples Named in Arnórr's Verses xiii

1. Scandinavia and the Baltic xiii
2. The British Isles xiv

Note on Abbreviations and Conventions xv

Part One: Introduction

Chapter One. Sources for Arnórr's Verses: Prose Works and Manuscripts 3

I Introduction 3
II *Separate Óláfs saga helga* 5
III *Heimskringla* 9
IV *Morkinskinna* 12
V *Fagrskinna* 13
VI *Hulda-Hrokkinskinna* 14
VII *Flateyjarbók* 15
VIII *Orkneyinga saga* 17
IX *Knýtlinga saga* 19
X *Snorra Edda* 20
XI *The Grammatical Treatises* 23

Chapter Two. Reconstructing the Poems of Arnórr 25

I Authorship 25
II Reconstruction of the major poems 26
A. Assignment of verses to individual poems 27
B. Ordering of verses 30
III Fragments 33
IV Verses outside the canon 36

Chapter Three. The Life of Arnórr Þórðarson jarlaskáld 41

I Youth in Iceland 41
II Departure abroad 43
III Years in the Orkneys 43
IV Audience at the Norwegian court 44
V Later years 46

Chapter Four. Subject-Matter and its Presentation 49

I Heroes and their deeds 49
II The four main *drápur* 51
A. *Hrynhenda* 51
B. *Magnússdrápa* 53
C. *Þorfinnsdrápa* 53
D. *Haraldsdrápa* 54
III Traditional motifs 55
A. List of motifs 55
B. Specimen analysis: motifs in *Þorfinnsdrápa* 17 58
IV The Christian element 62

Chapter Five. Diction 65

I Introduction 65
II Everyday words 67
III Poeticisms 68
A. Variety 68
B. Formal elaboration 70
C. Descriptive quality 70
D. Mythological, legendary and historical allusions 73
IV Rare and unique words 76

Chapter Six. Metre 79

I *Dróttkvætt* and *hrynhent* in Arnórr's work 79
II Metrical rules 80
III Stress patterns in Arnórr's *dróttkvætt* lines 85
IV Stress patterns in Arnórr's *hrynhent* lines 92
V Assonance 94

Part Two: Text

Presentation of the Text 101

I Outline 101
II The Edited Text 103
III The Diplomatic Text 106
IV The Critical Apparatus 108

Edited Text, with Translation 113

Rǫgnvaldsdrápa 113
Hrynhenda 113
Magnússdrápa 118
Þorfinnsdrápa 123
Haraldsdrápa 128
Fragments 133

Diplomatic Text and Commentary 137

Rǫgnvaldsdrápa 137
Hrynhenda 142
Magnússdrápa 182
Þorfinnsdrápa 220
Haraldsdrápa 268
Fragments 301

Appendices 317

A. Tables showing distribution of Arnórr's verses in MSS 317
B. Comparison of present edition with Finnur Jónsson's in *Skjaldedigtning* A 325
C. Careers of Arnórr's heroes: chronological and bibliographical list 331

Bibliography, with Abbreviations 337

A. Manuscripts, facsimiles and editions 337
B. Printed works: primary sources and secondary literature 343
C. Note on further bibliography 359

Index 361

Preface

GREAT progress has been made in skaldic studies during the last two decades, with the appearance of important books by Gabriel Turville-Petre, Gert Kreutzer, Roberta Frank, Klaus von See, Bjarne Fidjestøl, Edith Marold, Hans Kuhn, Margaret Clunies Ross and Russell Poole, as well as numerous articles on individual topics. This presentation of the work of Arnórr Þórðarson jarlaskáld grows from a conviction, shared with these authors, that skaldic poetry need no longer be regarded as a cultural curiosity well suited to linguistic and textual analysis but only barely worth attention as literature. Increasingly, its complexities are appreciated as products of deliberate and exuberant artistry, rather than of the perversity of skalds or skaldic metres.

This book differs from its immediate predecessors, which are anthologies, surveys, or else studies of particular aspects of skaldic art, in being focussed on a single skald; the exception is Krause's study of Eyvindr skáldaspillir (1990). It hence also reflects the belief that in the work of a given skald the meeting of tradition with individual and period taste produces a particular stamp which well repays examination.

The corpus of Arnórr jarlaskáld's surviving work is, relative to that of many skalds, large and well preserved. It comprises almost six hundred lines, mainly composed in praise of Scandinavian rulers who flourished in the mid eleventh century: Magnús Óláfsson inn góði 'the Good' and Haraldr Sigurðarson, later harðráði 'Hard-ruler', kings of Norway, and Þorfinnr Sigurðarson and Rǫgnvaldr Brúsason, earls of Orkney, whose patronage is commemorated in Arnórr's nickname.

Arnórr no doubt inherited his verbal facility from his poet father Þórðr Kolbeinsson, and learned poetic technique from him during his youth in Iceland in the second and third decades of the eleventh century. Once abroad, he may well have been stimulated to exercise his skill to the full by competition with many other Icelandic skalds who flourished contemporaneously at the Norwegian court. The extant work of these men, and notably of Þjóðólfr Arnórsson, provides valuable material for comparison with Arnórr's, although unfortunately space permits only fleeting comparisons within this book.

Arnórr was composing only decades after the Christian faith had been formally established in western Scandinavia. Hallfreðr vandræðaskáld, Sigvatr Þórðarson and others had already expressed Christian sentiments in their court poetry, but the use of these was still a matter of personal choice rather than convention. By incorporating Christian allusions, therefore, Arnórr anticipates the tendency for later skalds increasingly to use their medium for hagiographical or devotional composition as opposed to purely secular panegyric.

Arnórr's poetry is serious in character, though wit too is to be found. Many of his most striking verses evince a taste for effulgent praise and graphic, even grotesque, description. Arnórr inherits a fully developed skaldic tradition of oral panegyric, with its characteristic subject-matter, diction, syntax and metre. His command of his medium permits him to strike away from the most well-established traditions, as when he introduces prayers or similes into his verses or when he casts an encomium in the new *hrynhent* metre; but for the most part he works through established conventions, ranging freely in his choice and arrangement of words between the plain and the esoteric or elaborate. When he does use the more arcane skaldic devices, such as extended kennings or intricate clause arrangements, he seems to be prompted by a delight in verbal display and in the complex associations of words rather than by a desire to mystify. He may challenge the intellect and imagination of his audience but, like his contemporaries, he does not cultivate the extreme obscurity found in some earlier skaldic poetry, for example the *Þórsdrápa* of Eilífr Goðrúnarson.

Arnórr's poetry has not until now been published separately, but it has been edited as part of longer works. The collections of his poetry in Vigfusson and Powell's *Corpus Poeticum Boreale* II (1883) and in Finnur Jónsson's *Skjaldedigtning* I B (1912) suffer from somewhat reckless editorial emendation. E. A. Kock, especially by challenging Finnur Jónsson's assumptions about skaldic style, produced a more conservative edition of the skaldic corpus (*Skaldediktningen*, 1946–49), and the editors of the relevant sagas in the Íslenzk Fornrit series have often thrown light on textual points in verses by examining them in their prose contexts.

Part Two of this book contains the canon of Arnórr's surviving work in both diplomatic (or strictly, semi-diplomatic) and edited form, with a translation, commentary and other materials necessary to the establishment of the text. I hope that this might prove not only a serviceable edition in its own right, but also a modest contribution to the re-editing of the skaldic corpus as a whole, which has long been seen as an urgent need (see Jón Helgason 1950, Fidjestøl 1985), and which at the time of writing promises to become a reality. The explanatory materials in Part Two have been devised on the assumption that users of this book will already have some considerable familiarity with Old Icelandic, and some acquaintance with skaldic practice (to which Turville-Petre 1976 and Frank 1978 are excellent introductions). The conventions and layout adopted throughout Part Two are explained on pp. 101–12.

The six introductory chapters in Part One concern the manuscript sources of Arnórr's verses, the reconstruction of the poems, the life of Arnórr, and literary aspects of his poetry. Because of limitations on space, much less than full justice is done to certain topics, such as the historical background (summarily covered by a chronological and bibliographical list in Appendix C), or the relations between Arnórr's work and other early Norse-Icelandic poetry. Material on Christian and pagan elements, and on the arrangement of clauses within the metrical lines, has already been published in my articles of 1982–83 and 1983 (see Bibliography B, under Edwards), and is not duplicated here.

The present book has a frustratingly long history, publication being much delayed through unavoidable practical difficulties, and only selective updating has been possible during the protracted phase 'in press'. I am glad, however, to express my thanks for help given along the way. I would, indeed, like to begin with the pre-history of my skaldic work by thanking John McKinnell for fostering my undergraduate enthusiasm for Norse, and for giving me a kindly push in the right (that is, north-westerly) direction on graduation. My attraction to skaldic studies was encouraged in various ways by Paul Bibire, the late Gabriel Turville-Petre and the late David Evans. My greatest debt, however, is to Ursula Dronke, who supervised the preparation of the first incarnation of this book as an Oxford doctoral thesis, and who lavished on it more hours of patient and creative consideration than I dare count up. It is also a pleasure to thank Richard Perkins and Joan Turville-Petre, examiners of the thesis, for valuable suggestions, and Peter Foote for advice generously given at a later stage; also Hans Bekker-Nielsen. The staff of the Arnamagnæan Institute and Dictionary in Copenhagen kindly provided awkward photographic extracts of manuscripts, assistance during a visit in spring 1977, and helpful responses to written queries at various times; and numerous other friends and colleagues have provided guidance on specific matters. I am aware, nevertheless, that in an enterprise like this one, that touches on many different areas of expertise, philological and otherwise, there are bound to be faults of omission and commission, and these of course are my sole responsibility.

I offer sincere thanks to the staff of Brepols and the Editorial Board of Westfield Publications in Medieval Studies, especially to Brian Place, Peter Orton and Felicity Rash for their selfless and skilful handling of a technically difficult production. The onerous task of typing the work onto floppy disk and proof-reading the result was eased by some cheerful and patient help from Elisabeth Simms and Sara Rowe; I also thank Ann Rooke for producing final versions of the maps.

Since skaldic study is hardly a remunerative occupation, I also have practical debts to record. I am grateful to the Principal and Fellows of St Hilda's College, Oxford, for their award of a Randall-MacIver Junior Research Fellowship which provided financial support for twelve months in 1977–78. Much more recently, the University of Newcastle upon Tyne provided a most generous sum from its Sponsorship Fund, which, together with a grant from the Dorothea Coke Fund in the University of Cambridge, enabled production costs to be met. I am pleased to record my heartfelt gratitude to the managers of both funds.

Finally, all my endeavours have been carried out against a background of tolerance, love and encouragement from my family, and I would like to pay tribute especially to my mother's support during years of what must have seemed like perpetual studenthood.

Diana Whaley
University of Newcastle upon Tyne

Note: Names in brackets do not occur in the text of Arnórr's poetry
Lower case italics indicate peoples

Note: Names in brackets do not occur in the text of Arnórr's poetry

Note on Abbreviations and Conventions

A. Poetry of Arnórr

Frag:	Fragment
Hdr:	Haraldsdrápa
Hryn:	Hrynhenda
Mdr:	Magnússdrápa
Rdr:	Rǫgnvaldsdrápa
Þdr:	Þorfinnsdrápa

B. Other Norse-Icelandic Poetry

All other references to skaldic and Eddaic poetry follow the style of *Lexicon Poeticum* (*LP*); abbreviated references to poetry are expanded in the Index.

Skaldic poetry is quoted from the edited texts in the 'B' volumes of Finnur Jónsson's *Den norsk-islandske Skjaldedigtning* (*Skjald*), hence, e. g., 'Hfr 3, 26' designates verse 26 of Hallfreðr's *erfidrápa* 'memorial poem' for Óláfr Tryggvason (his third poem in *Skjald*). '*Ht* 102' refers to verse 102 of Snorri Sturluson's *Háttatal*.

Eddaic poetry is quoted from the Neckel-Kuhn edition of the *Edda*, 1962. References take the same form as for skaldic poetry, e. g. *Vsp* 57 refers to verse 57 of *Vǫluspá*.

Note: Abbreviations referring to manuscripts are incorporated in Chapter One and in Bibliography A; those referring to printed works (prose texts and secondary literature) are in Bibliography B.

C. Grammatical and Other Terms

acc.	accusative
adj.	adjective
dat.	dative
em.	emendation
esp.	especially
f./fem.	feminine
gen.	genitive
Gmc	Germanic
hap. leg.	hapax legomenon
lit.	literally
M. Lat.	Medieval Latin
m./masc.	masculine
Mod. Icel.	Modern Icelandic
MS	manuscript
n./neut.	neuter
nom.	nominative
OE	Old English
OHG	Old High German
O. Icel.	Old Icelandic
ON	Old Norse
p. p.	past participle
pl.	plural
pres. part.	present participle
sing.	singular
subj.	subjunctive
s. v.	sub voce
v. l.	varia lectio

D. Treatment of Names

Names of countries are given in English, as, generally, are other place-names for which a standard English form exists, such as Jutland or Pentland Firth. Other place-names are kept in their Old Icelandic form, with modern equivalents in the appropriate language at their first appearance. Personal names, including some such as those of Danish kings or English earls, are also given primarily in their Old Icelandic form.

PART ONE

INTRODUCTION

1

Sources for Arnórr's Verses: Prose Works and Manuscripts

I Introduction

ARNÓRR jarlaskáld's poems share the fate of most skaldic panegyrics: they are preserved on vellum or paper not in a continuous, complete form but as fragments cited here and there in prose works, to authenticate the narrative in sagas on historical subjects or to illustrate points in treatises on poetics or grammar.[1] The *drápur* of Arnórr — *Rǫgnvaldsdrápa (Rdr), Hrynhenda (Hryn), Magnússdrápa (Mdr), Þorfinnsdrápa (Þdr)* and *Haraldsdrápa (Hdr)* — are not merely the artificial creations of editors, for we know their names from ON sources and can in most cases assign verses to them with some confidence;[2] but to gain an idea of the complete poems we must rely on reconstructions made from more or less incomplete collections of fragments. The present chapter concerns the sources from which these scattered fragments are assembled.

Of the extant MSS which are of textual value for Arnórr's verses the oldest are vellum codices such as Morkinskinna, from the latter half of the thirteenth century — two centuries after Arnórr's death — and the youngest are paper MSS from the seventeenth and eighteenth centuries. In numerical terms, the richest MS sources for Arnórr's verses are Flateyjarbók (108 helmings or half-strophes),[3] Hrokkinskinna (83 helmings) and Hulda (68 helmings).

[1] For general discussions of the rôle of verses within sagas, see Wolf 1965 and Bjarni Einarsson 1974.

[2] The title *Haraldsdrápa* is not found in ON sources, but is inferred from the mention of an *erfidrápa* (memorial poem) for Haraldr (see Chapter Two, II).

[3] The anglicised form of ON *helmingr*, literally 'half', is used throughout.

In assessing the value of MSS as sources for the text in the present work, their age, their interrelations, their physical state of preservation and the quality of their readings have all been considered. The MSS I have used are for the most part the same as those which provide the text and critical apparatus in Finnur Jónsson's *Den norsk-islandske Skjaldedigtning* (henceforth *Skjald*), A I 332–54. The differences between my presentation of the MSS and Finnur's, together with the differences in the editorial reconstruction of the poems (and hence in the numbering of the verses) are listed in Appendix B.

The MSS which contain texts of Arnórr's verses are so numerous that it is not possible to give a paleographic and orthographic description of each one. The following brief notes on the provenance, date, condition and textual relations of the prose works and their MSS are confined to what is relevant to Arnórr's poetry. They are drawn mainly from catalogues of MS collections,[4] from the editions and studies mentioned throughout this chapter and listed in Bibliography A, and from articles contained in *Kulturhistorisk leksikon for nordisk middelalder* (*KLNM*, 1956–78). Where the dating of a MS is disputed, that given in the *Registre* to *Ordbog over det norrøne prosasprog* (1989) is adopted.

Throughout the notes, some MSS are listed which are not used in the edition in Part Two of this book, but which are significant within the textual history of the work in question. The entries for these are bracketed, with headings in normal rather than bold type. It should also be explained that in this chapter and elsewhere, I italicise names such as *Morkinskinna* (*Msk*) and *Flateyjarbók* (*Flat*) when speaking of the work, i. e. the content of the MS, but use roman type when the MS itself is the primary focus of comment. It has to be admitted that the distinction is not always easy to maintain.

The MSS are listed in tabular form in Appendix A, so that it may be seen at a glance which of Arnórr's verses appear in each MS. Both there and in the notes below attention is drawn to verses which are lacking in a MS whose text otherwise matches that of other MSS of the same work at the relevant points. In other cases where a verse is lacking in a MS, it may be assumed that the MS is defective or that its text is generally condensed in comparison with that of other MSS.

[4] Kålund 1888–94 for Arnamagnæan MSS, Kålund 1900 for other MSS originally or still held in Copenhagen, and Gödel 1897–1900 for Stockholm MSS.

The MSS are grouped below and in Appendix A according to the works they contain. Snorri Sturluson's 'Separate' *Óláfs saga helga (Ólsh(Sep))* is discussed first, then the encyclopaedic works, *Heimskringla (Hkr)*, *Morkinskinna (Msk)*, *Fagrskinna (Fsk)*, *Hulda-Hrokkinskinna (H-Hr)* and *Flateyjarbók (Flat)*, then *Orkneyinga saga (Orkns)* and *Knýtlinga saga (Knýtls)*, and finally the non-historical works, *Snorra Edda (SnE)* and the *Third* and *Fourth Grammatical Treatises* (*Third GrT* and *Fourth GrT)*.

II Separate Óláfs saga helga

Snorri Sturluson's separate saga of Óláfr Haraldsson inn helgi (d. 1030) is believed to have been written c. 1220–30 (so Holtsmark 1967, 549). Snorri clearly had *Orkns* among his written sources. There is no clear evidence that he used *Fsk* in his saga of Óláfr helgi, as he did in his other sagas of kings (Bjarni Einarsson, *Ágrip* 1984, cxxv–cxxvii). Fifteen helmings by Arnórr are quoted in the saga (see Appendix A, Table 1) and, apart from *Hdr* 5, all of them appear in passages which describe either events and characters in the Orkneys or the career of Magnús Óláfsson.

O. A. Johnsen and Jón Helgason, in their classic edition of 1941, included detailed discussion of the MSS and their relations. They grouped the MSS into three main classes (pp. 1091–1121, esp. 1097 and 1107–9), and those which have value for the text of Arnórr's poetry are listed here within these classes, with the best MS of each class first. The stemmata for classes 'A' and 'C' (below) are based on those in the 1941 edition, pp. 1103 and 1112 respectively, where it is stressed that there may be more lost intermediate stages than the diagrams show. The stemmata for this, as for other prose works, will be a reasonable guide to the textual relations of the verse quotations, although it cannot necessarily be assumed in every case that the transmission of the verses follows an identical path to that of the prose.

'A' Class	'B' Class	'C' Class
2	61 (Þdr 5b, Hdr 5)	4
75a	68	61 (remainder)
321		75b
325V (Þdr 5b,21, Hdr 5)		325V (remainder)
325VI (Mdr 1,2,10, Hryn 5–7)		325VII

Bœjarbók, preserved in 73	Bb (Rdr 1, Hdr 5)
	Flat
	Th

Notes: (i) AM 325XI 2e is omitted here, although it is in Johnsen and Helgason's list of 'A' MSS, and 325XI 2f is similarly omitted from the 'C' MSS. They are discussed instead with the *Heimskringla* MSS, since Johnsen and Helgason state that 'fragmentene i 325 IX og XI må regnes for å være Heimskringla-håndskrifter' (*Ólsh(Sep)* 1941, 1119); Jonna Louis-Jensen regards 325XI, 2 as a hybrid (1977, 32).

(ii) 61 and 325V are of dual class. '(Remainder)' indicates that Arnórr's verses, apart from those already detailed under 'A' or 'B', appear in the part of the MS which belongs to the 'C' class. 325VI belongs partly to the 'A' class and Bb partly to the 'C' class, but otherwise they do not wholly correspond with any of the three classes.

'A' Class Manuscripts

*A, the presumed lost original, has some textual errors and secondary readings which are not found in the other classes.[5] In the stemma below, asterisks indicate lost MSS, and brackets indicate MSS which have not supplied readings for the critical apparatus in the present edition.

2: Holm Perg. 4o nr 2. Icelandic; latter half of 13th century. Printed as the main MS in the 1941 edition; facsimile also available — see Bibliography A. Has *Ólsh(Sep)* complete, and hence contains 15 helmings by Arnórr.

75a: AM 75a fol. Icelandic; c. 1300. Defective. Contains 4 helmings by Arnórr.

321: AM 321 4o. A paper copy of 75, made by the priest Halldór Jónsson of Reykholt in the 17th century, when the text of 75 was more complete than it is now. Contains *Rdr* 1 and *Mdr* 10 beyond the verses which 75 preserves, and its readings for these two verses (but for no others) are used in the critical apparatus.

325V: AM 325V 4o. Icelandic; beginning of 14th century. Contains 15 helmings by Arnórr.

[5] An example from *Hryn* 6 is given by Johnsen and Helgason, *Ólsh(Sep)* 1941, 1103, under 'S. 615, vers 189[1]'.

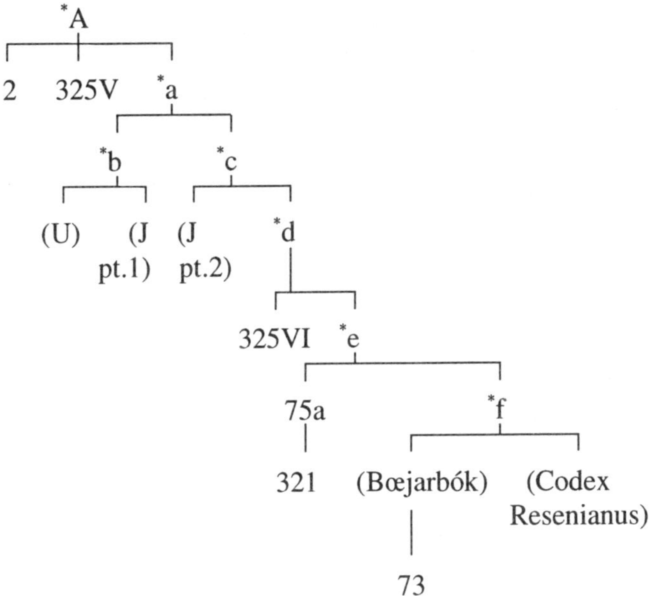

325VI: AM 325VI 4o. Icelandic; latter half of 14th century. Three main hands. Well written, though now in bad condition. Has 13 helmings by Arnórr.

(Bœjarbók á Rauðasandi was an Icelandic codex containing an interpolated version of *Ólsh(Sep)*. Only 4 leaves of it remain (AM 73b, containing no verses by Arnórr), but there are paper copies. Of these only one both contains verses by Arnórr and is reasonably faithful to its original:)

73: AM 73a fol. Beginning of 18th century. Hands of three Icelandic copyists. *Rdr* 1 and *Mdr* 10 come at points in the text at which Bœjarbók had lacunae, and have been copied from the 325V text, so that the 73 readings for these verses do not have independent value and are omitted from the apparatus in the present edition. The main text of 73 preserves the orthography of Bœjarbók, although not without errors; it contains 15 helmings by Arnórr.

‘B’ Class Manuscripts

Apart from some fragments which contain no verse by Arnórr, 61 and 68 are the only members of the class. They derive from a common original, but independently and possibly with lost intermediate stages, since they so often differ in wording (*Ólsh(Sep)* 1941, 1108).

61: AM 61 fol. Icelandic; c. 1350–75 to fol. 109v; c. 1400–50 thereafter. For specimen facsimile and edition, see Bibliography A. More than one hand. 61 has 14 helmings by Arnórr, all but 3 of them in the younger part of the MS. *Þdr* 21 and its introduction do not appear in ch. 89 as they do in other MSS of the saga, although 61's text otherwise corresponds with theirs at that point.

68: AM 68 fol. Icelandic; first half of 14th century. For specimen facsimile, see Bibliography A. Same hand as MS R of *SnE*. Defective. Contains 3 helmings by Arnórr. Ch. 89 lacks *Þdr* 21, as in 61.

‘C’ Class Manuscripts

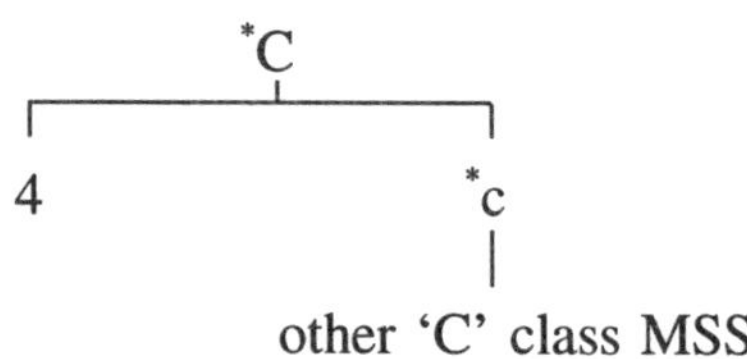

4: Holm Perg. 4o nr 4. Icelandic; c. 1320–40. Many lacunae. It often has a reading — probably the original one — in common with MSS of other classes, while other ‘C’ MSS have a secondary variant.[6] Contains 13 helmings by Arnórr.

61: AM 61 fol. The MS belongs partly to the ‘C’ class, partly to ‘B’, and has been listed above.

75b: AM 75b fol. Icelandic; c. 1325–50. Fragment, in clear regular hand, but in poor condition. Contains 2 helmings by Arnórr.

325V: AM 325V 4o. Partly ‘C’, partly ‘A’; listed above.

[6] Among the examples is one from *Hryn* 7: see *Ólsh(Sep)* 1941, 1112, under ‘S. 615, vers 189[7]’.

325VII: AM 325VII 4o. Icelandic, but with Norwegian influence on orthography; latter half of 13th century — oldest MS after 2. Two hands; first characterised by archaic phonological features. Some damage. Contains 12 helmings by Arnórr. *Mdr* 10 is lacking because of the defective state of the MS, but *Þdr* 5b and its introduction are absent from a text otherwise complete at the relevant point.

Bb: Bergsbók, Holm Perg. fol. nr 1. Icelandic; c. 1400–25. For facsimile, see Bibliography A. Two main hands. Contains 15 helmings by Arnórr.

Flat: Flateyjarbók. This great codex contains a text of *Ólsh(Sep)*, but it is treated separately below since it also covers other works containing Arnórr's poetry.

Th: Tómasskinna, GKS 1008 fol. Icelandic; c. 1400 to fol. 78v, thereafter latter half of 15th century. For facsimile, see Bibliography A. Three hands. There are a great many nonsensical readings, not least in the text of Arnórr's poetry, of which the codex contains 15 helmings.

III Heimskringla

For editions, see Bibliography A, pp. 338–39.[7] Snorri Sturluson's *Hkr* contains a Prologue and sixteen sagas of Norwegian kings, including three which between them contain 41 helmings by Arnórr (see Table 2, p. 319): those of Óláfr Haraldsson inn helgi (4 helmings), Magnús Óláfsson inn góði (30 helmings) and Haraldr Sigurðarson inn harðráði (7 helmings).[8]

The view of Sigurður Nordal has been generally accepted, that *Ólsh(Hkr)* is a shortened and reworked version of *Ólsh(Sep)*, completed c. 1230 (1914, 166–204; Whaley 1991, 52). Some material found in *Ólsh(Sep)*, including miracles of St Óláfr, has been transferred to the saga of Magnús góði in *Hkr*. The transferred text also includes *Hryn* 5 and 6a, and *Mdr* 1, 2 and 10.

[7] Bjarni Aðalbjarnarson gives brief descriptions of the MSS and their history in *Hkr* 1941–51, III, but no information on graphic or orthographic features. Finnur Jónsson gives summary information of this kind in *Hkr* 1893–1901, III.

[8] *Ólsh* is in *Hkr* 1941–51, II, *Magns* and *Hars* in *Hkr* 1941–51, III. *Óláfs saga kyrra* in *Hkr*, unlike the versions of this saga in *Msk*, *Fsk* and *H-Hr*, does not contain Arnórr's *Þdr* 3. Instead, Stúfr 1 is cited.

Snorri's sources for his sagas of Magnús Óláfsson and his successors included versions of *Msk*, *Fsk* and *Orkns*.

The MSS of *Hkr* divide into two main groups: the 'Kringla' or 'x' group and the 'Jöfraskinna' or 'y' group. This is made clear in the stemma tentatively presented by Bjarni Aðalbjarnarson (*Heimskringla* 1941–51, III, xciv).[9] My only alteration is to place in brackets the MSS which do not supply texts of Arnórr's poetry, and to mark lost stages in the transmission of the text by asterisks.

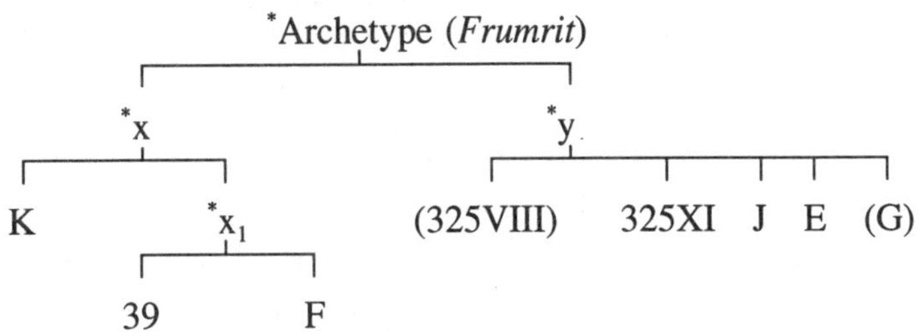

Kringla group Manuscripts

(Kringla was an Icelandic codex of an estimated 180–200 leaves. The *terminus ad quem* is c. 1270, so that there is at most a gap of forty years between Snorri's original text and the MS. Except for a single leaf which contains no verse by Arnórr (Lbs Frag 82, National Library of Iceland), Kringla itself was destroyed by the fire which ravaged Copenhagen in 1728, but it survives in paper copies made before that date:)

K: AM (35), 36 and 63 fol. End of 17th century. Hand of Ásgeir Jónsson. MS 36 contains *Ólsh(Hkr)*; 63 contains the sagas of kings from Magnús góði to Magnús Erlingsson. The copy is for the most part carefully made, although there are occasional errors and omissions. MS 63 is the most valuable part of the transcript for Arnórr's poetry. K preserves 41 helmings by Arnórr. Other copies of Kringla, by Ásgeir and by Jón Eggertsson, are less accurate and are not used in the present edition.

[9] Jonna Louis-Jensen (1977, 36), while acknowledging the value of Bjarni's stemma, stresses that, since so few of the *Hkr* MSS contain the entire work, a more realistic picture would be given by a series of separate stemmata.

F: Codex Frisianus or Fríssbók, AM 45 fol. Icelandic, but perhaps written for a Norwegian; early 14th century. For facsimile and edition, see Bibliography A. Preserves the first and third parts of *Hkr*, but not *Ólsh*, presumably because whoever commissioned the writing of the MS already owned a copy of *Ólsh(Sep)*. F has an antecedent MS in common with 39 (below), which was not identical with K. F as a copy is inferior to 39, and the text has been altered, either deliberately or through carelessness, in many places. F contains 36 helmings by Arnórr, since it lacks the *Ólsh* verses and the helming *Mdr* 14. The text which surrounds *Mdr* 14 in other *Hkr* MSS is present, and only the verse and its introduction are missing.

39: AM 39 fol. Icelandic; c. 1300. 43 vellum leaves. The first 10 leaves have defective and difficult text from the first part of *Hkr*. The remainder extend, almost continuously, from *Ólsh(Hkr)* ch. 245 to *Haraldssona saga* ch. 2. Clear script; orthography in some ways conservative. MS 39 is the closest of the extant texts to K. It contains 33 helmings by Arnórr.

Jöfraskinna group Manuscripts

(Jöfraskinna 'Princes' vellum' was written in the first half of the 14th century, and is of disputed provenance (see Louis-Jensen 1977, 22–23). The MS was in the fire of 1728, so only four leaves survive (Holm Perg. fol. nr 9, II, containing no verse by Arnórr), but two paper copies had been made before this:

J1: AM 37 fol. ends at ch. 74 of *Ólsh* and so contains no verse by Arnórr.)

J2: AM 38 fol. End of the 17th century. Hand of Ásgeir Jónsson. The orthography is not quite faithful to the original, and there are sometimes arbitrary alterations. Contains 37 helmings by Arnórr. *Hdr* 5 is lacking from an otherwise full text.

47: Eirspennill 'Brass clasp', AM 47 fol. Provenance disputed (Louis-Jensen 1977, 22–23); c. 1300–25. For edition, see Bibliography A. Two hands. Begins at ch. 239 of *Ólsh(Hkr)* (and hence does not contain *Hdr* 5) and runs to the end of *Hkr*. 47 is considered to give the best text in this group (e. g. Bjarni Aðalbjarnarson, *Hkr* 1941–51, III, xciv). Contains the same helmings by Arnórr as J2.

325XI 2e: AM 325XI 4o, fragment 2e. Latter half of 13th century; provenance not known. Covers, complete or incomplete, chs 79 and 81–82 of *Ólsh(Sep)*, but the fragment is so brief that it is not immediately clear whether it belongs to the Separate or the *Hkr* recension (see p. 6). Contains only *Þdr* 5b by Arnórr.

325XI 2f: AM 325XI 4o, fragment 2f. Latter half of 14th century. As in the case of fragment 2e, the recension is difficult to ascertain. Contains only *Hdr* 5.

IV Morkinskinna

See Bibliography A for edition and facsimile. Dating is difficult, but the compilation is generally believed to have been made c. 1220 or earlier, in Iceland (Jónas Kristjánsson 1988, 161). It probably covered the lives of Norwegian kings 1035–1177, but the surviving, defective, copy, ends at 1157. There are close affinities between *Msk* as it now stands and *Orkns* and *Hkr*, although the precise relationship between the three is not beyond doubt.[10]

The extant version of *Msk* is not the original one. It has been expanded by the addition of *þættir* and extra verses (Finnur Jónsson 1927, 185), as is proved by comparison with *Flat* and other texts which have clearly used an older version of *Msk*. But already in the original *Msk* skaldic poetry must have abounded. In the extant text there are 273 citations of full strophes or helmings.

Msk: Morkinskinna 'Rotten vellum', GKS 1009 fol. Icelandic; c. 1275. Now 37 vellum leaves. There are lacunae, and parts are otherwise damaged, but much is easily legible. A lacuna of six leaves near the beginning of the saga of Magnús means that for 39 helmings of Arnórr (*Hryn* 8–10, 13 and 15, and *Mdr* 1–2, 4–12a and 13–18) we have the text of *Msk* not in the same recension as the extant MS but only in the one copied in *Flat*. In sections where both *Flat* and *Msk* are extant, there is some significant textual variation, and this is registered in my critical apparatus to Arnórr's verses in Part Two, but the content is essentially the same, so that for general purposes the two texts can be considered together.

[10] *Msk* 1932, xii–xiii; Bjarni Aðalbjarnarson 1936, esp. 151–52; Hødnebø 1966, 705.

The *Msk* MS contains 33 helmings by Arnórr, all of which are quoted in the sagas of Magnús and Haraldr except for *Þdr* 3, which occurs in *Óláfs saga kyrra*.

V Fagrskinna

For editions, see Bibliography A. *Fsk* is believed to have been composed in Norway, by an Icelander or Norwegian, between 1220 and 1240, and probably in the 1220s (Bjarni Einarsson, *Ágrip* 1984, cxxiv, cxxvii–cxxxi and references there). The work covers the history of Norway's kings, from Halfdan svarti in the ninth century to 1177, the reign of Magnús Erlingsson. The treatment is mainly summary, but some episodes are recounted quite fully.

The chapters of *Fsk* which contain poetry by Arnórr — those concerning Magnús, Haraldr and Óláfr kyrri — are greatly indebted to a lost **Msk*, an earlier recension than the preserved one, and one which was not so heavily interpolated.[11] On the other hand, it seems that the author of *Fsk* has altered and shortened the *Msk* text, omitting, among other things, some skaldic verse (Louis-Jensen 1977, 70 and n. 16).

The MSS fall into two main groups, as the following stemma shows. The possibility should be allowed that there are further lost stages between the archetype and Fsk A and B.

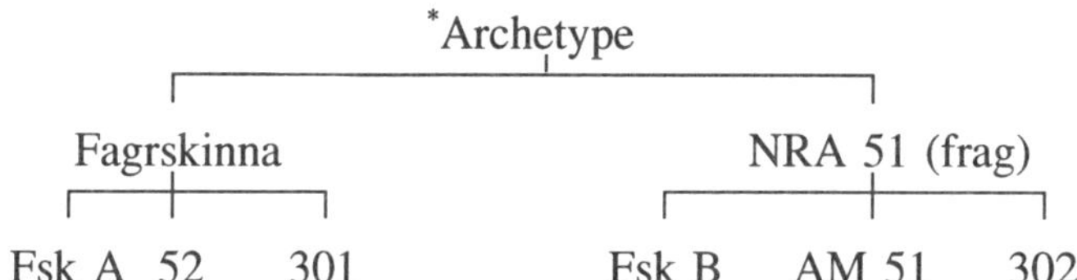

Group A Manuscripts

(Fagrskinna 'Fair vellum' was a Norwegian codex from the first half of the 14th century. It was destroyed in the fire of 1728 but three copies had been made before that by Ásgeir Jónsson. Two of them,

[11] See Bjarni Einarsson, *Ágrip* 1984, ci and references; Jakobsen 1968, esp. 56–57.

AM 52 fol. and AM 301 4o, are inferior copies, and only the following is used in the present edition:)

Fsk A: AM 303 4o. End of 17th century. Contains 16 helmings by Arnórr. *Mdr* 10b, 14, 16 and 18b, which are quoted in Fsk B, are lacking from an otherwise complete text in Fsk A.

Group B Manuscripts

Again, the original was burned in the fire of 1728. A fragment survives (Det norske Riksarkiv nr 51) whose script and orthography suggest it was written in the mid 13th century, i. e. very soon after the composition of the work. On the other hand, there were already many lacunae when it was copied c. 1700. The following copy is used for the 'B' readings (AM 51 fol. and AM 302 4o being poorer copies):

Fsk B: UB 371 fol. (Universitetsbiblioteket, Oslo). Circa 1700. A generally careful copy by Ásgeir Jónsson. Contains 14 helmings by Arnórr.

VI Hulda-Hrokkinskinna

For edition, see Bibliography A. The compilation was probably made some time after 1280 (Louis-Jensen 1977, 1). It covers the sagas of reigns from Magnús góði to Magnús Erlingsson, i. e. 1035–1177. For the sagas of Magnús góði and Haraldr harðráði, *Msk* was the main source, apparently in a version expanded from the original by various *þættir* and verses. The relations between *Msk*, *Flat* and *H-Hr* are seen in the following stemma, which is a simplified version of that presented by Jonna Louis-Jensen (1977, 194). Lost MSS are marked by asterisks. 'Msk2' is the archetype of the extant *Msk*, and of the other descendants of *Msk*.

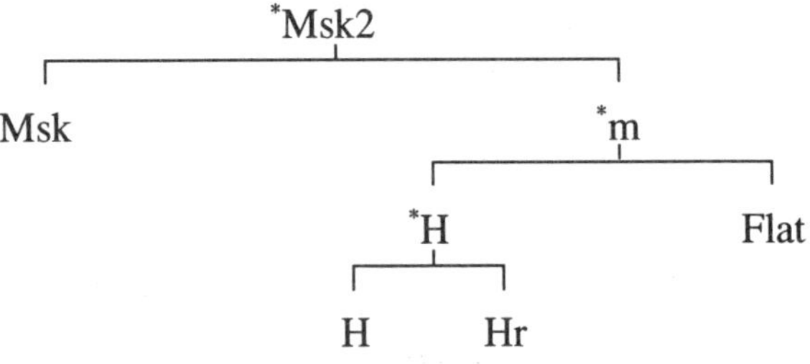

A text of *Hkr* belonging to the Jöfraskinna group was also used, especially in the latter part of the compilation.

The text of the verses in *H-Hr* is on the whole poor. In some cases the corruption probably derives from a corrupt exemplar, while in others it is the result of faulty copying or deliberate alteration. As Louis-Jensen points out, the compiler based his alterations on inadequate knowledge of poetic diction and form (1977, 152–55).

H: Hulda 'The Hidden One', AM 66 fol. Icelandic; 14th century, probably the third quarter (Louis-Jensen 1977, 7 and 14). For facsimile, see Bibliography A. Mostly in a good, clear hand with consistent orthography. The early chapters of the saga of Magnús góði are missing, and with them 7 full strophes and a helming by Arnórr. However, 69 helmings are preserved, all of them in the sagas of Magnús and Haraldr, except for *Þdr* 3 in that of Óláfr kyrri.

Hr: Hrokkinskinna 'Wrinkled vellum', GKS 1010 fol. First half of 15th century. A sister MS to H. The scribe modernises somewhat, and is often careless. The main value of Hr is that it supplies the opening of *Magnúss saga*, missing from H, and with it 15 helmings by Arnórr. It thus preserves 84 helmings by Arnórr, and for *Hryn* 4 and *Mdr* 3 it is the sole MS.

VII Flateyjarbók

See Bibliography A for edition and facsimile.[12] The compilation is of sagas, *þættir*, genealogies and poems. It includes sagas of Óláfr Tryggvason and Óláfr helgi. For *Ólsh* the exemplar was a text of Snorri's separate saga closely related to AM 61 fol. Sagas of Magnús and Haraldr were not originally included in the compilation, probably because Jón Hákonarson, who commissioned the writing of the MS, already owned a MS of them, namely Hulda (Louis-Jensen 1977, 70–72). The two sagas (which interlock so much that they are barely separable) have been copied onto an additional 23 leaves, written about 100 years later than the bulk of the codex. The exemplar was a text of *Msk*, not the extant defective MS but a sister MS to it — probably the same one as used, at one remove, in *H-Hr* (see stemma

[12] On the content and history of the manuscript, see Finnur Jónsson 1927, 139–90 and Johnsen and Helgason in *Ólsh(Sep)* 1941, 1026–34.

above, and Louis-Jensen 1977, 70–72). The copy in *Flat* contains some modernised forms, and there are several errors caused by faulty reading. *Flat* is the only vellum MS that contains *Orkns* almost complete. This is not written out continuously, but is scattered throughout the sagas of the two Olafs. (The relevant parts for Arnórr's verses are *Flat* II 176–82 and 404–519.)

Flat:[13] **Flateyjarbók, GKS 1005 fol.** Icelandic; c. 1387–95, with later 15th-century additions. Two main hands, those of Jón Þórðarson and Magnús Þórhallsson. Because of its range of contents, the quantity of Arnórr's verse that the compilation contains is exceptionally great: 108 helmings. It has 11 of the 15 helmings which are found in full texts of *Ólsh(Sep)*. Of these only *Þdr* 21 and *Hdr* 5 occur in the part of *Flat* which belongs to the *Ólsh(Sep)* recensions, while the remainder fall within the saga of Magnús and *Orkns*. The sagas of Magnús and Haraldr in *Flat* contain in all 71 helmings by Arnórr, for as well as supplying the 39 helmings missing from *Msk* and enumerated under that heading, they contain 32 helmings for which *Msk* also has a text. The *Orkns* verses by Arnórr, listed below, are all present in *Flat*, except for *Þdr* 2 and 18. Since *Þdr* 18 is preserved only in the verse collection in 702 (see below), it is not possible to tell whether it was included in the original saga, but *Þdr* 2 is lacking from an otherwise full text. *Þdr* 19 and 22 are both quoted twice in *Flat*, in chs 32 and 56 of the saga (= *Flat* II 422 and 440). In neither place are they integrated into a narrative, and the same is true of *Frag* 2, quoted in ch. 56. *Flat* is numerically the richest source for the verses in *Orkns*, but for quality of readings, 325IIIb, 332 and 702 must be given priority (with the exception of *Þdr* 20).

[13] For brevity, I use the siglum 'Fl' when referring to the MS in the lists of sources and in the critical apparatus in Part Two.

VIII Orkneyinga Saga

For editions, see Bibliography A, pp. 340–41.[14] The extant version of the saga is believed to date from c. 1230, but an earlier version is thought to have been composed by c. 1200 (Nordal, *Orkneyinga saga* 1913–16, v; Finnbogi Guðmundsson 1967, 700). The existence of this is implied by references to *Jarla sögur/saga* in *Flat* III 270, *Fsk* p. 201, and Snorri's *Ólsh(Sep)* p. 255 and *Ólsh(Hkr)* ch. 103, p. 173. The saga covers the history of Orkney and its jarls for more than three centuries, ending in the original version c. 1171 (Finnbogi Guðmundsson, *Orkns* 1965, lxxviii and xc). *Orkns* was probably written by an Icelander who had lived some years in the islands and was familiar with their geography and traditions.

The value of *Orkns* for the study of Arnórr's poetry is that it preserves most of the extant *Þdr* (the most important single poem in the saga). It contains 14 whole strophes and 3 helmings from *Þdr*, as well as *Frags* 1–3 and *Rdr* 1 — a total of 38 helmings (see further Table 4, p. 321).

The extant MSS of *Orkns* are believed to descend from a common original which, together with its immediate descendant, has perished. The stemma below, based on that presented by Finnbogi Guðmundsson, makes this clear (*Orkns* 1965, cxxvi). Lost MSS are indicated by asterisks, MSS which do not contain verse by Arnórr are set in brackets, and MSS irrelevant to the transmission of Arnórr's verse are omitted. The broken lines indicate sources which are of value for the poetry but not for the continuous prose text: 702 and its derivative 762 preserve texts of full strophes, while *LR* (only available in an early printed version) and 48m supply readings almost exclusively for individual words.

The MSS are presented here in what the stemma suggests to be the most coherent order.

325III: AM 325IIIb 4o. Icelandic; c. 1300. One leaf. Of the MSS which contain verse by Arnórr, this is the closest to the archetype. Contains 4 helmings.

[14] Finnbogi Guðmundsson's edition of 1965 contains notes on the history and content of the MSS, but not on orthography. Sigurður Nordal's of 1913–16 supplied details of the orthography and abbreviations in the vellum MSS.

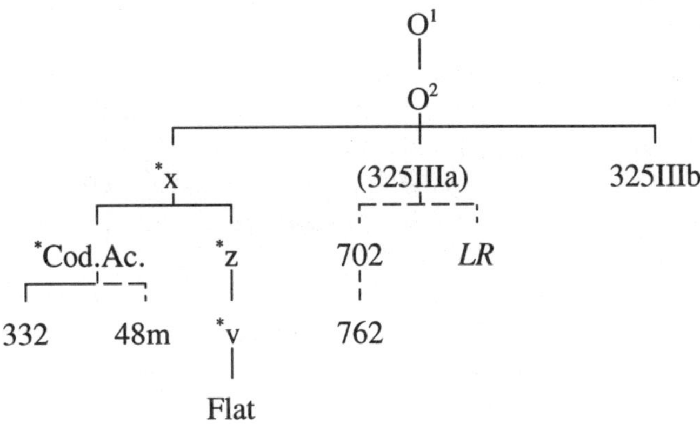

(325IIIa: AM 325IIIa 4o. Icelandic; c. 1300–50. Two vellum leaves. The extant fragment contains none of Arnórr's verse, but extracts from the MS had been made when it was in a more complete state:)

702: Isl. R. 702 4o. (Universitetsbiblioteket, Uppsala). Hand of Magnús Ólafsson (1573–1636). A collection of verses from various sources, including *Egils saga*, *Ragnars saga loðbrókar* and *Orkns*. Those from *Orkns* are introduced by prose extracts from the saga, often in summary form, and are sometimes followed by explanatory comments. 702 contains 24 helmings by Arnórr, including *Þdr* 18, for which it is the only significant MS.

(AM 762 4o contains selections by Magnús Ólafsson from the verses in 702, especially those from *Orkns*. The prose comments have been rendered into Danish. MS 762 thus has no independent value. (It was used in place of 702 by Finnur Jónsson in *Skjald* A.))

LR: Specimen Lexici Runici. Published by Ole Worm in Copenhagen in 1650, this too is largely the work of Magnús Ólafsson. It is a glossary of words and phrases culled from several sources. The greatest number is from *Grettis saga*, but there are over 100 entries from *Orkns*,[15] including some which are of value for the text of *Þdr* 11, 13 and 17. The orthography of the MSS is not reproduced.

[15] Faulkes 1964, esp. 92–94; Finnbogi Guðmundsson, *Orkns* 1965, cxi–cxii.

(Codex Academicus (Cod. Ac.) was a vellum MS which burned in the fire of 1728. Ólafur Halldórsson has shown that it dated from the latter half of the 13th century and was probably written by an Icelander (1964, 154–55). It now survives in the following incomplete forms:)

332: AM 332 4o. Circa 1700; hand of Ásgeir Jónsson. The original orthography is not followed exactly, but the copy is considered reliable in most other respects. (See further Ólafur Halldórsson 1964, 131–32.) It supplies the Cod. Ac. text for four fragments of the saga, and includes 7 strophes from Arnórr's *Þdr* and 2 helmings.

48m: Marginal notes to AM 48 fol. (See Ólafur Halldórsson 1964, 132 and 145–50.) 48 is a copy by Ásgeir Jónsson of parts of *Flat.* It thus has no independent textual value; but Ásgeir wrote in the margin additions and corrections which were clearly taken from Cod. Ac., and these I designate 48m. Most consist of isolated words or phrases, but *Þdr* 2 is written out in full.

Flat: Flateyjarbók: see the separate section above (VII).

IX Knýtlinga Saga

For editions, see Bibliography A, p. 341. Óláfr Þórðarson hvítaskáld (d. 1259), nephew of Snorri Sturluson, is named as source for some of the saga's content, and it is quite likely that he is in fact the author (Bjarni Guðnason, *Danakonunga sögur* 1982, clxxix–clxxxiv). As a synoptic history of the kings of Denmark, *Knýtls* is of small value for the preservation of Arnórr's verses. Only 3 helmings are quoted — *Hryn* 14b and 15 — and there are other texts for these.

When paper MSS are included, the MSS are quite numerous. They are customarily divided into groups 'A' and 'B'.

Group 'A'

The 'A' recension is more complete than 'B', which only begins at ch. 22 of the saga (the chapter in which the *Hryn* verses are cited) and appears to have a shortened version of the original text in some places. The 'A' text was preserved in 'Codex Academicus', an Icelandic MS of c. 1300 which perished in the fire of 1728.

(AM 18 fol. is a copy of the lost codex, made c. 1700 by Árni Magnússon. Chs 3–82 are now missing, so that there is no text of Arnórr's verses.)

20d: AM 20d fol. Early 18th century. Partly written by Árni Magnússon, copying from AM 18 fol. when that MS was complete. It covers *Knýtls* chs 1–27, and contains all 3 helmings quoted from Arnórr in the saga.

873: NKS 873 4o. 18th century. Hand of Jón Vídalín. Copied from AM 18 fol. when complete, it contains the 3 helmings by Arnórr.

Group 'B'

Again the vellum original has not survived.

1005: AM 1005 4o. First half of 17th century. Probably a copy of the lost 'B'. Contains the saga complete from ch. 22 onwards.[16] Contains only the helming *Hryn* 14b. *Hryn* 15 and its prose introduction are lacking although 1005's text at the relevant point otherwise corresponds with that of 20d and 873.

X Snorra Edda

See Bibliography A, pp. 341–42 for editions. This 'text-book for skalds' is named *Edda* and ascribed to Snorri Sturluson in the oldest extant MS, U. The work must have been begun c. 1220, but when it was completed is unknown. It comprises four parts: *Prologus*, *Gylfaginning*, *Skáldskaparmál* and *Háttatal*. *Skáldskaparmál* 'Language of Poetry', a presentation of kennings and *ókennd heiti*, contains some 411 citations from 70 skalds, and most of these are isolated helmings or couplets, although some poems, including Bragi's *Ragnarsdrápa* and Þjóðólfr's *Haustlǫng*, are quoted at length.

On the evidence of *SnE*, Snorri knew in whole or part each of the extant *drápur* by Arnórr. Between them, the extant MSS of *Skáldskaparmál* contain a total of 80 different lines by Arnórr (see Table 6), and *Þdr* 15 appears twice in MSS R and T. A further 14½ lines are preserved in the two supplementary treatments of poetic

[16] Finnur Jónsson used the readings of KBS Papp. 4o nr 41 in the apparatus to *Hryn* 14 in *Skjald* A, but since 41 is a copy of 1005 (Petersens and Olson, *Sǫgur Danakonunga* 1919–25, xix and xxv) it has no independent value.

diction known as 'Orms Eddu-Brot' and 'Laufás-Edda' and found in MSS W and 743, respectively (see further below).

Principal MSS[17]

Three vellum MSS (R, U and W) and one paper MS (T) have a complete or near-complete text of *SnE*. The relations between these have been much disputed, but it is clear that R, W and T form a group while the briefer text of U belongs to a different branch of tradition, and may follow an early version of Snorri's own.

R: Codex Regius, GKS 2367 4o. Icelandic; first half of 14th century. For facsimile, see Bibliography A. Of the *SnE* MSS, R, together with T, contains the largest number of verses by Arnórr: 18 helmings and 3 couplets.

T: Codex Trajectinus, 1374 Cod. MS, Universiteitsbibliotheek, Utrecht. For edition and specimen facsimile, see Bibliography A. Circa 1595. Contains *SnE* almost complete. Orthography partly follows the exemplar — which is thought to date from the later 13th century — but blends this with late 16th-century usage. T preserves exactly the same verses as R.

U: De la Gardie 11, Universitetsbiblioteket, Uppsala. For facsimile, see Bibliography A. Icelandic; c. 1300–25. Some verses are lacking which are found in R, T, and often in other MSS of *SnE*, including 3 helmings by Arnórr: *Hryn* 12a, *Mdr* 2b and *Þdr* 12. The surrounding prose passages are also absent. A fourth helming, on the other hand, has been omitted from an otherwise complete text, for *Þdr* 15 is quoted twice in R and T, but in U only once — presumably to avoid duplication. U, then, has a total of 15 helmings and 3 couplets by Arnórr.

W: Codex Wormianus, or Ormsbók, AM 242 fol. For facsimile and edition, see Bibliography A. Icelandic; c. 1350. W's text of *SnE* lacks the final part of *Skáldskaparmál*, and with it six helmings and a couplet by Arnórr which are in R and T; but on the other hand it contains the additional verses *Hryn* 6a and 16a. These appear in the so-called 'Orms Eddu-Brot', a three-page text derived from *Skáldskaparmál* which is peculiar to W; see

[17] Volume III of *SnE(Arnamagn)*, 1848–87, contains an account of the manuscripts, of which that in Finnur Jónsson's 1931 edition is essentially a summary. Also useful is Faulkes 1988, xxix–xxxiii.

Bibliography for edition. (For the *Grammatical Treatises* in W see below.)

Fragmentary texts

743: AM 743 4o. 17th century. Hand of Ketill Jörundsson. One of several MSS — textually the best as far as Arnórr's verse is concerned [18] — of a version of *SnE* made by Magnús Ólafsson of Laufás (1573–1636). Commonly called *Laufás-Edda*, its second part contains kennings and *heiti* gathered from W and at least one other MS of *SnE* and set in alphabetical order of subject, with verse illustrations. (See Bibliography A for editions.) The importance of *Laufás-Edda* for Arnórr's poetry is that it alone preserves *Frags* 4 and 9 and the half-line *Frag* 11 — a total of 6½ lines.[19]

748: AM 748 Ib 4o. For facsimile and edition see Bibliography A. Icelandic; c. 1300–25. Of Arnórr's verse it contains 8 helmings, 4 couplets and a single line, all of which occur within *Skáldskaparmál* except for 7 lines in the *Third GrT* (see below).

748II: AM 748 II 4o. (Formerly catalogued as AM 1eβ fol. and designated 1eβ in *Skjald.*) For facsimile and edition see Bibliography A. Icelandic; c. 1400. In good condition. Contains 9 helmings and one couplet by Arnórr.

757: AM 757a 4o. For edition, see Bibliography A. Icelandic; c. 1400. In poor condition. Contains most of *Skáldskaparmál*, in a shortened text descended from that found in AM 748 I, and preserves 9 helmings and 4 couplets by Arnórr. 757 is unique among MSS of *SnE* in having a two-line citation from *Þdr* 5.

[18] Cf. Jón Helgason 1966, 175; *SnE* (Faulkes 1979) p. 53.

[19] Other verses preserved in MSS of *Laufás-Edda* are *Hryn* 6a, *Mdr* 12b, 17b and 19, *Þdr* 1, 2, 4, 14 and 22a, and *Hdr* 17, but the readings for these either replicate those of W or are clearly erroneous, with a few exceptions which are mentioned in footnotes in Part Two. Three mistaken attributions to Arnórr in *Laufás-Edda* are discussed on pp. 36–38 below.

XI The Grammatical Treatises

See Bibliography A for editions. The *Third GrT* and *Fourth GrT* to some extent share the aim of *SnE*: to revive interest in, and knowledge of, skaldic poetry.

Although the author of *Third GrT* is not named, it is customarily ascribed to Óláfr Þórðarson hvítaskáld (d. 1259). It is in two parts: (i) *Málfræðarinnar grundvöllr*, a discussion of the basics of spelling and grammar, and (ii) *Málskrúðsfræði* (a modern name), a section on stylistics for which the chief model was the part of Donatus's *Ars Maior* known as 'Barbarismus'. Where Donatus used Latin poetry as illustrative material, Óláfr substitutes skaldic verses, thus preserving several which would otherwise have been lost (see Gísli Sigurðsson 1994). This applies to three of the four fragments by Arnórr which *Third GrT* contains: the couplets *Hryn* 1 and 2, and the single line which I designate *Frag* 10. The fourth fragment, *Hryn* 3/3–4, is also found in the sagas of Magnús góði. *Third GrT* thus preserves a total of 7 lines by Arnórr.

Fourth GrT was probably written c. 1340–50 (Holtsmark 1960, 418). It deals with *colores rhetoricæ* and forms a continuation to *Third GrT*. The author is not known but has been guessed to be Bergr Sokkason (d. c. 1350). Like the author of the *Third GrT*, he based his work on Latin writings, and used skaldic verses — some apparently of his own composing — to illustrate. Of Arnórr's work only *Hryn* 3/3–4 is quoted.

The vellum MSS also contain all or part of *SnE*, and have already been discussed under that heading. For *Third GrT* the relevant MSS are W, 748, and 757, which ends at ch. 11 and therefore lacks most of Arnórr's lines. For *Fourth GrT* W is the sole MS.

2

Reconstructing the Poems of Arnórr[1]

I Authorship

THE VERSES which are given in the present work as the corpus of Arnórr's poetry are, with only two exceptions, attributed to Arnórr in at least one prose source. Often the lines are cited with an explicit introduction such as *Svá segir Arnórr* or *Sem kvað Arnórr*. The name is variously given as *Arnórr*, *Arnórr jarlaskáld* or, as in the introduction to *Mdr* 18 in *Flat*, *Arnor skalld* (normalised *Arnórr skáld*).[2] The tag, *Þetta kuad Arni jallaskalld* which introduces *Hdr* 14 in *Flat* is just one slip beside many accurate renderings of the poet's name in the same work. In many cases the attribution to Arnórr is implied, though no less clear for that: the citation simply follows another verse by Arnórr without a break, or with the heading, *Ok enn kvað hann*, or, *Ok enn*.

Only two strophes, *Þdr* 19 and *Frag* 2, have no named author, and they so obviously concern the battle of Rauðabjǫrg (Roberry, Orkney, on which see pp. 43–44) and so intensely express the skald's distress over the strife between the 'jarls, my dear friends' (*jarlar, ástmenn órir*) that there can be little doubt that Arnórr is their maker.

[1] The canon of Arnórr's poetry is presented in Vigfússon and Powell's *Corpus Poeticum Boreale* (*CPB*) II 184–98, in the Arnamagnæan edition of *Snorra Edda* (*SnE(Arnamagn)*) III 559–75, in Finnur Jónsson's *Den norsk-islandske Skjaldedigtning* (*Skjald*) A I 332–54, B I 305–27, and in E. A. Kock's revision of *Skjald*, *Den norsk-isländska Skaldediktningen*, I 155–65. In *SnE(Arnamagn)* the poems are reconstructed but only the first line of each verse is printed. The reconstruction was the work of Finnur Jónsson, and it was reproduced with little change in *Skjald* and in Kock's re-edition.

[2] In quoting from ON prose works I reproduce the text of the printed editions, in some of which the MS orthography is preserved while in others it is normalised.

For seven verses, the prose sources preserve conflicting traditions about authorship.[3] *Hryn* 12 is ascribed in *SnE* (all MSS) to the skald 'Markús', whereas in *Hkr* it is attributed, no doubt correctly, to 'Arnórr jarlaskáld'. *Hryn* 20 is also ascribed to Markús in the *SnE* MS 748. These attributions to Markús are understandable, since Markús Skeggjason did compose a *hrynhent* poem, in memory of the Danish king Eiríkr Sveinsson (Erik Ejegod, d. 1103). But *Hryn* 12 and 20 can hardly belong to that poem since, being an *erfidrápa*, it contains no apostrophes to the hero, whereas there are three in *Hryn* 12 and one in *Hryn* 20, and they are common in other parts of Arnórr's *Hryn*.

Þdr 4 is attributed to 'Ragnarr' in the paper MS T of *SnE*, but to Arnórr in the four vellum MSS of *SnE* in which the verse is found; and 'Ormr jarlaskáld' is credited with *Þdr* 15 in one of its two appearances in MS T, but 'Arnórr' in its second appearance in the same MS, and in all other MSS of *SnE*. *Hdr* 7 is attributed in MS Hr to 'Steinn', but in its more reliable sister MS H and in Msk and Flat to Arnórr. The reading of Hr is clearly a case of dittography, since a verse by Steinn Herdísarson is quoted only a few lines earlier.

The remaining two disputed verses are both quoted within the same context. *Flat* credits 'Skúli' with *Mdr* 4, and with *Hryn* 8, which is introduced, *Og enn kuad hann*. In Hr, meanwhile, *Hryn* 8 is introduced, *Svâ segir Arnórr í Hrúnhendu* and then the words, *Þess getr ok í Magnúsardrápu* introduce *Mdr* 4. *Mdr* 4 is also quoted in *Fsk*, and ascribed to Arnórr. The attributions to Skúli can hardly be taken seriously. Skúli Illugason is mentioned in *Skáldatal* 'List of Poets' as a poet of Knútr inn helgi Sveinsson, king of Denmark in the 1080s (*SnE(Arnamagn)* III 258 and 267), but nothing survives of his work. Otherwise, the only skald of that name was Skúli Þorsteinsson, grandson of Egill Skallagrímsson. He died in 1040 (Wood 1964, 175), and there is no reason to think he composed about Magnús.

II Reconstruction of the Major Poems

Since Arnórr's poems are preserved as scattered fragments, they must be reconstructed, and although much of the reconstruction can be made with some degree of certainty, there is (and always will be)

[3] A further eight verses which are almost certainly the work of other skalds but which are attributed in one of their MSS to Arnórr are discussed in section IV below.

much scope for doubt and debate. This becomes evident when, for example, Guðbrandur Vigfússon's arrangement of *Þdr* in *CPB* II 194–97 is compared with Finnur Jónsson's in *SnE (Arnamagn)* III 568–70 and *Skjald* A I 343–48, B I 316–21 (which is retained by Kock in his *Skaldediktningen*). There are several points of difference between my own reconstruction of the corpus and that found in *Skjald*, and these are listed in Appendix B. My conclusions also differ in some particulars from those of Bjarne Fidjestøl (1982, esp. 127–32 and 172), despite my respect for his arguments. Space does not permit a detailed verse-by-verse rationale of my reconstruction (for which, see Edwards 1979, ch. II), but the principles on which it is based are outlined here. I begin with the criteria for relating verses to specific poems, then consider the ordering of the verses within each poem.

A. Assignment of verses to individual poems

1. Compositions of Arnórr

In restoring the verses as nearly as possible to their original places, an important starting-point is the range of poems which tradition assigns to Arnórr.

The names *Hrynhenda* (and variants)[4], *Magnússdrápa* (or *Magnúsardrápa*), *Rǫgnvaldsdrápa* and *Þorfinnsdrápa* all appear in ON works, usually in statements of the pattern *Enn kvað Arnórr í Rǫgnvaldsdrápu* which precede verse quotations. Arnórr is also credited with a *Blágagladrápa* 'Poem of the Dark Geese', which he is said to have recited for Haraldr Sigurðarson on the same occasion as he declaimed *Hryn* (see, e. g., *Msk* p. 118). The poem's subject-matter must have been Haraldr's career up to, at the latest, 1046, but, with the possible exception of *Frag* 5 (section III below), none of Arnórr's extant verses covers this material, unless the editors of *CPB* (II 191–93) were right to divide the 'Haraldr' verses between two poems, one an *erfidrápa* devoted entirely to Haraldr's last campaign. This division is presumably based on a handful of readings which would suggest that the verses about events before 1066 were addressed to a living prince. There are 2nd sing. verbs in *Hdr* 2 and

[4] The title appears variously as *hrynhenda* (H), *hrunhenda* (Hr), *hryneande* (*Ólsh(Sep)* MSS except 2, which reads *i hermandiNi*) and *Magnvs drapa* (*Third GrT* and *Knýtls*).

3 (with 3rd sing. vv. ll.); in v. 3 *buðlungr* (v. l. *buðlung*) could be an apostrophe, and in v. 5 there is present-tense praise: *sa er fremstr er* (v. l. *var*) *manna*. In the absence of other and less equivocal evidence, however, it is preferable to assume that only a single, memorial, poem about Haraldr survives (so also Fidjestøl 1982, 131).

The *erfidrápa* about Haraldr Sigurðarson inn harðráði is mentioned, but not directly named, in the prose introductions to *Hdr* 14 and (still further from a specific title) to *Hdr* 5. Throughout this book the title *Haraldsdrápa* (*Hdr*) is used, after the model of the remaining *erfidrápur*.

From the existence of *Frag* 6, a prayer for 'Hermundr', we can postulate a *Hermundardrápa* (or *Hermundarflokkr)*, and there was probably also a *Gellisdrápa*, for *Laxdœla saga* ch. 78, p. 229 records the tradition that Arnórr composed an *erfidrápa* about Gellir Þorkelsson (died 1073). The possibility that *Frag* 7 comes from this *drápa* is considered in section III below.

If *Skáldatal* is to be believed, Arnórr was skald to two further royal patrons: Knútr inn ríki Sveinsson (d. 1035) and Óláfr kyrri (d. 1093).[5] One of Arnórr's extant helmings (*Frag* 4) might well have been composed in praise of Knútr (see section III below); but the association with Óláfr kyrri finds virtually no support (see Context to *Þdr* 3 in Part Two and Fidjestøl 1982, 127).

2. *Prose evidence on individual verses*

Explicit introductions such as *Enn kvað Arnórr í Rǫgnvaldsdrápu*, which identify certain verses as coming from certain poems, are only available for a minority of verses. To these may be added verses which follow on closely within the same prose passage with introductions such as *Ok enn svá*, and which therefore may be thought to belong to the same poem. The majority, however, are introduced by unspecific tags such as *Sem Arnórr kvað*, and in these cases we need to turn to the wider contexts in prose works. When, for instance, the rather impressionistic battle-verse *Hdr* 12 is cited in connection with a campaign fought by Haraldr, there is little choice but to assume that it comes from a poem about Haraldr.

[5] Arnórr is named as a poet of Knútr in both MSS of *Skáldatal* (AM 761 4o and 'U', De la Gardie 11), printed in *SnE(Arnamagn)* III 258 and 267, but as a poet of Óláfr in MS U only.

3. Internal evidence

Especially useful for verses not ascribed to particular poems in their prose introduction is the evidence of details of content such as personal or place names which can be used to identify the hero or the event, and hence the poem. Thus *Hryn* 11 and 12 are plausibly connected with Magnús Óláfsson, and hence with *Hryn*, because they concern an attack on the Wends at Jóm (modern Wollin).[6] Similarly, *Hryn* 9 and 16 are associated with Magnús by the naming of the ship Visundr (see Commentary to *Hryn* 9/4).

More difficult are the verses concerning events in Orkney and North Britain which involved both jarls, Þorfinnr and Rǫgnvaldr, either as comrades or enemies, and which could belong to a poem for either of them. However, since some of these contain pointers towards Þorfinnr, and since he was, according to *Orkns* chs 22–24, pp. 56–62, much more prominent in military campaigns, it seems reasonable to assign the doubtful cases to *Þdr*.

Metre and style (including diction and clause arrangement) are generally less reliable touchstones since, although Arnórr's *drápur* each have their individual character, they are too uniform in respect of specific metrical or stylistic features for these to be decisive criteria. An obvious exception is the distinctive *hrynhent* metre which immediately differentiates the two encomia for Magnús, *Hryn* and *Mdr*, and there are a few contexts where an individual image or item of vocabulary provides a clue. Further, I believe that an item of diction in *Mdr* 19, whose membership of *Mdr* has been thought uncertain (see Fidjestøl 1982, 130 and 1984, 245), is an important pointer. This strophe, preserved only in *SnE*, praises a young, unnamed and (in all but one MS) deceased *skjǫldungr* 'ruler'. The Danish associations of this term, and its use four times in *Hryn* to apostrophise Magnús, including the similar paean in *Hryn* 20, support the supposition that the verse does indeed belong to the *Mdr*. This in turn implies that the *Mdr* is an *erfidrápa*; and further hints of this are the calls to retainers (*Mdr* 1 and perhaps *Mdr* 18) and the absence of apostrophes.

[6] External authority for Magnús's leadership of this attack is provided by Adam of Bremen, p. 137, scholion 56 (57); see also *Icelandic Annals* pp. 17, 58, 108, 317 and 469.

B. Ordering of verses

1. Structure of other skaldic poems

Some notion of the characteristic arrangement of form and content in a skaldic poem can be gained from the better-preserved skaldic compositions (most of which postdate Arnórr's work), and from the terminology used by the skalds (surveyed in Kreutzer 1977, 207–14).

As far as we know, Arnórr cast all his panegyrics in the noble form of the *drápa*. This probably tended to be longer than the *flokkr*, literally 'group', although it was not necessarily so.[7] Its main distinguishing feature was the refrain or *stef*, and indeed it has been suggested that *drápa* etymologically means *kvæði drepit stefjum* 'a poem set with refrains'.[8] The *stef*, at least in *drápur* from Arnórr's time, usually contained lofty and rather vague praise of the hero. Certain of Arnórr's extant verses, especially *Hryn* 20, *Mdr* 19 and *Þdr* 12, may have been *stef*, but none is traditionally labelled as such.

A *drápa* could have more than one *stef* — as many as six, if the title *Sexstefja* is to be taken at its face value — [9] or the same one could be used throughout. There are two *stef* in Egill's *Hǫfuðlausn* (tenth century), in *Leiðarvísan* (twelfth century) and in Árni Jónsson's *Guðmundardrápa* (fourteenth century).[10] The length of the *stef* varied from two to four lines, and these were either incorporated as a unit into a strophe, often forming the second helming, or else dispersed

[7] The two terms appear, and are clearly differentiated, in v. 34 of Hallar-Steinn's *Rekstefja* (12th century). See further Kreutzer 1977, 87–88.

[8] So Sigurður Nordal 1931–32, 144–49, esp. 148; cf. Sveinbjörn Egilsson's gloss *carmen intercalatum* for the word *drápa*, 1860, s. v. The *stef* is not, however, an indispensable feature of the *drápa*: there is a reference to *drapan steflavsa* in Snorri's commentary to *Háttatal (SnE* p. 213), and Haukr Valdísarson's *Íslendingadrápa* provides an example of a *drápa* which appears never to have had a refrain. For further observations on the *stef* see Hellberg 1981, Fidjestøl 1982, 182–90, and Kuhn 1983, 212–14.

[9] This is the name given, in *Ólsh(Sep)* p. 580 and *Magns(H-Hr)* p. 129, to Þjóðólfr Arnórsson's mighty encomium for Haraldr Sigurðarson. Only one identifiable *stef* now remains.

[10] Finnur Jónsson's dating of poems in *Skjald* is followed here and elsewhere, unless specified otherwise.

line by line over two or more strophes (*klofastef* 'split refain' or *rekstef* 'chased, inlaid refrain').[11]

The appearance of the *stef* at intervals throughout the *drápa* marks off the strophes into groups named *stefjamél* 'refrain section(s)',[12] a term we know in the first instance from Arnórr jarlaskáld himself, for his *Hryn* 11 actually declares itself to be the opening of such a section, with the words, *Heyra skalt ... í stefjaméli* 'You shall hear ... in a refrain section'. Snorri (*SnE* p. 244) says that the *stefjamél* may be as numerous as the skald wishes, but preferably of the same length.

Collectively, the *stefjamél* formed the weighty core of the poem in which individual feats of the hero were presented, probably in chronological order. Sigvatr Þórðarson's *Víkingarvísur*, although not forming a *drápa*, clearly exemplify such ordering, and other examples of the poetic enumeration of battles and place-names are to hand (Fidjestøl 1982, 213–17, who uses the terms *orrostnatal* and *stadnamndikt*). Flanking the *stefjamél* were an exordium, for which *upphaf* may or may not be an ancient technical term,[13] and a conclusion known as the *slœmr*. The two outer sections, often identical in length, glorified the hero in general terms, and sometimes alluded to the occasion of the poem's composition. The skald very often heralded his poem with a call for a hearing such as *hljóðs bið'k* and a statement to the effect that he was declaiming, or about to declaim, his praise-poem.[14] Arnórr's *Þegi seimbrotar* 'Gold-breakers be silent' (*Mdr* 1), *Nú hykk ... segja ... ýtum* 'Now I mean to tell men' (*Þdr* 1) and the parallel *Nú hykk ... segja* in *Mdr* 1 clearly belong to this convention. *Mdr* 1 seems to be a fusion of the exordium with the start of the first *stefjamél*, helming 1b beginning the narrative of Magnús's journey from the east.

[11] Hallar-Steinn himself calls his poem *Rekstefja* (*Rst* 1).

[12] *Stefjabalkr* appears to be a synonymous term (see Kreutzer 1977, 210–11), although Tate distinguishes between the *stefjabalkr*, the whole centre section of a poem throughout which *stef* occur, and the *stefjamél* which, if there is more than one *stef*, are subordinate units, each marked off by a different *stef* (1978, esp. p. 31).

[13] E. g. in Ótt 1, 1, *Jǫfurr heyri upphaf ... bragar míns*; Kreutzer, 1977, 207, seems to take it so.

[14] The motif *Hljóðs bið'k* is discussed in Wood 1960; see also Kreutzer 1977, 266-71.

A rare feature which appears no less than five times in Arnórr's *erfidrápur* is a prayer for the deceased hero (in *Rdr* 3, *Þdr* 22 and 23, *Hdr* 17 and *Frag* 6). These prayers should probably be placed at the end of the poem, just as the account of Þorfinnr's career in *Orkns* ch. 32, p. 83 is brought to a close with *Þdr* 22, which includes a brief prayer for his soul. Another possibility is that they functioned as refrains, as in *Stúfsdrápa* (c. 1067), in which the *klofastef* expresses a wish that Haraldr's soul may have a dwelling-place with Christ.

2. Order of verses in prose narratives

This type of evidence is particularly useful when two or more verses appear in fairly close succession so that it seems likely that the compiler is quoting a sequence directly from a poem that he knows in full, and then building up his narrative around it (or else using pre-existing prose links). An example is the sequence *Þdr* 5–11, which forms the kernel of the account in *Orkns* ch. 20, pp. 43–51, of Þorfinnr's campaign against 'Karl Hundason' and the Scots.

3. Chronology or internal logic of content

The factual content of some strophes can be used to fit them into a chronology of episodes in the life of the hero. Ideally, the chronology is established from a variety of independent historical sources, but often it is the sagas in which the verses appear that are the sole source for chronology so that there is an overlap between this kind of evidence and that of (2) above. (Chronological summaries of the lives of Arnórr's heroes are given in Appendix C.)

Where two or more verses refer to the same episode, the internal logic of their content is an important guide. A simple instance of this is found near the beginning of *Mdr*, where vv. 6 and 7 amplify and enact Magnús's vow to 'possess Denmark' (*Danmǫrk eiga*) in *Mdr* 5, and therefore certainly follow it. Two slightly more complex cases, in which I depart from the ordering adopted by Finnur Jónsson, deserve mention here.

The four verses *Mdr* 12–15 all appear to describe the battle of Helganes, despite the contrary evidence of *Flat* (see the Prose Contexts for *Mdr* 12, 14 and 15 in Part Two). The internal ordering of this group varies in the prose works so that the best guide is the content. Verse 12 describes battle being joined, and includes the preliminary words:

Vítt hef'k heyrt at heiti	I have heard it is called broad
Helganes ...	Helganes ...,

which suggest that it was the opening verse of a *stefjamél* devoted to Helganes. Verse 15 depicts the human wreckage of the battle and is undoubtedly the last of the set. Of the remaining two verses 13 describes Magnús hurling spears and relentlessly wielding his sword, and 14 celebrates the success gained by this onslaught — the capture of enemy ships — so that 13–14 seems the most logical order. (The reverse order is adopted in *Skjald.*)

In the case of *Hdr* 11, 12 and 13 I have, tentatively, allowed the order suggested by the internal logic to override that indicated by the prose context. The verses appear in the order 12, 11, 13 in the sagas of Haraldr (and in *Skjald*), but they are separated not only by prose passages but also by citations from other skalds. Verse 12 evinces regret that the prince's *ofrausn* '(?)excess of pride' caused his death, v. 11 contains praise of his valour in battle, and v. 13 tells of his fall and the loyalty of the *liðsmenn* who survived him. The sequence of ideas is thus smoother if v. 11, which concerns the living Haraldr, is placed before vv. 12 and 13, which speak of his death, and this is the arrangement tentatively adopted in the present work.

Mdr 12, cited above, illustrates the kind of verbal indicators that may suggest a strophe's position relative to others on the same theme. Other such phrases include *Nemi drótt* 'Let liegemen mark' (*Þdr* 15) or *Síðan vas þat's ...* 'Later it happened ...' (*Hryn* 9), which probably signal the beginning of a new stage in the narrative, and *Heyra skalt ... í stefjaméli* 'You shall hear ... in a refrain-section' (*Hryn* 11).

A further feature which might help in the process of ordering verses is stylistic. Concatenation of verses by lexical repetition or metrical carry-over has been observed by Chase in twelfth-century skaldic poems (1985) and in earlier work, for instance verses by Þjóðólfr Arnórsson, by Poole (1991, 69–70). Traces of concatenation can be found in Arnórr's surviving work, e. g. the repetition of *Skjǫldungr* as the first word of *Hryn* 12 and 13, but not on a scale sufficient to base decisions about ordering on it.

III Fragments

My category of 'Fragments' is large compared with Finnur Jónsson's '*Vers af ubestemmelige digte, samt én lausavísa*' in *Skjald.* In four cases I dissent from Finnur's assignment of a verse to a particular poem, while in others I have suggestions, either new, or old ones worth reviving, about possible assignments. For these reasons I include here a brief discussion of the individual fragments. *Frag* 6 is identifiable but is included here because of its extreme brevity.

Apart from the three strophes from *Orkns* which I designate *Frags* 1, 2 and 3, all the fragments appear only in *SnE* (including the *Laufás-Edda*) or the *Third GrT*, and hence are unattached to any historical narrative. In no case do the introductory words specify to which poem or to which hero the lines belong.

***Fragment* 1** has all the appearance of a freestanding occasional verse (*lausavísa*), with its present and future tense verbs, its relatively prosaic word-order within each clause,[15] its strong lyrical element, and its complete sense. According to *Orkns* ch. 26 (pp. 66–67), it was composed during a lull in the battle off Rauðabjǫrg between the jarls Þorfinnr and Rǫgnvaldr.

***Fragments* 2 and 3**. The topic is again the battle of Rauðabjǫrg. It has been assumed that these two verses belong to *Þdr* (*SnE(Arnamagn)* III 570 and *Skjald*), but in *Frag* 2 the words:

Ek em, síz ýtar hnekkðu	I am loth, since men thwarted
jarla sætt, es ek vætti ...	the jarls' truce, as I foresaw ...
hegju tr*au*ðr at segja	to speak of events

sound as though they were composed at the time of the events rather than twenty years later, and the possibility should be kept open that the verse is a *lausavísa*.

As for *Frag* 3, it has a regretful, speculative tone unlike that of the verses which certainly belong to *Þdr*. It is suggested in the Commentary that the strophe refers to Rǫgnvaldr Brúsason. If this is so, the sentiments expressed — that, but for the treachery of others, Rǫgnvaldr would have been victorious — would read strangely in the midst of an encomium about the actual victor, Þorfinnr. It is possible that *Frag* 3 is either a *lausavísa* or a verse from a poem about Rǫgnvaldr, but the extant fragments of *Rdr* are so exiguous that they give no clear idea of its original scope and subject-matter.

***Fragment* 4**. As suggested in the Commentary to this helming, the *Danir* and the *Skǫ́nungar* are probably the same body of men, and

[15] Cf. Edwards 1983, 145.

hann their sovereign — the most likely candidate being Knútr inn ríki. Arnórr implies that he was present at the court in question. The other main possibility is that the helming comes from *Mdr*,[16] and refers to a visit by Arnórr to Magnús when he was holding court in Denmark. But if so, *Skǫ́nungar* would be an ill-judged designation for the Danes since the men of Skáney (Skåne) often supported Sveinn Ulfsson against Magnús, and Magnús is described as 'baleful to Scanians' (*ballr Skǫ́nungum*) in *Mdr* 14.

***Fragment* 5**. The hero of this fragment is pictured sailing out warships and staining them with blood to the benefit of the raven. Such a picture would fit any of the Viking heroes of Arnórr's panegyrics — Haraldr, Magnús, Rǫgnvaldr or Þorfinnr; but the verse is cast in the present tense, and hence cannot belong to *Hdr*, *Mdr*, *Rdr* or *Þdr*, all of which are memorial poems. It could perhaps come from the lost *Blágagladrápa* 'Poem of the Dark Geese [? Ravens]' for Haraldr.

***Fragment* 6** is a two-line prayer which Snorri attributes to Arnórr. It happily includes the name Hermundr and so can be assumed to be a remnant of a memorial poem for the Icelander Hermundr Illugason (on whom, see p. 46).

***Fragment* 7** is a helming in *hrynhent* metre about the judgement of men by God and St Michael. Because of its concentrated theological matter it seems unlikely to belong to the *Hrynhenda* for Magnús Óláfsson, but it could come from a poem about the archangel Michael, or from a *lausavísa*. The editors of *CPB* (II 184) propose that the helming refers to 'a painting or hangings on which the Last Judgement is figured' and belongs to a poem for Gellir Þorkelsson. This is quite plausible, in the light of the statement of *Laxdœla saga* that Gellir 'had a very fine church built at Helgafell, as Arnórr jarlaskáld testifies in the memorial poem he composed for Gellir, and he speaks clearly about this' (ch. 78, p. 229). One is reminded of the *Húsdrápa* of Ulfr Uggason (c. 985), in which the skald describes scenes on the walls of Óláfr pái's new homestead at Hjarðarholt.

***Fragment* 8**, a picturesque helming describing an off-shore battle, is, together with *Frag* 10, taken in *SnE(Arnamagn)* III 572 and *Skjald* to be part of the *erfidrápa* for Haraldr; but it would be equally

[16] This is suggested in *SnE(Arnamagn)* III 567–68. The verse is there assumed, without further explanation, to refer to the strife with Sveinn Ulfsson, but to be corrupt.

compatible with Arnórr's description of the battle off Helganes in *Mdr*, of the battles at Dýrnes (Deerness) or Rauðabjǫrg in *Þdr*, or of Haraldr's encounters with Sveinn Ulfsson.

***Fragment* 9** is so brief and so textually difficult that to assign it to a poem would be mere guesswork. The picture of bones scattered on the sea-shore is reminiscent of Arnórr's vision of floating bodies and corpse-strewn beaches in *Mdr* 15, but nothing else indicates that the two have any connection.

***Fragment* 10** is the single line *sumar hvern frekum erni* 'every summer to the greedy eagle'. The statement when complete was presumably that a prince fed (or feeds) the eagle every summer. Such a statement could equally well apply to Magnús, Þorfinnr, Haraldr or some other ruler.

***Fragment* 11** is the half-line *foldar fiðr* 'plumage of the earth [grass]'. It is clearly impossible to recover the context from which this kenning has been detached.

IV Verses outside the Canon

A couplet preserved only in the *Laufás-Edda* MSS, and published from AM 742 4o and Thott 1496 4o (Royal Library, Copenhagen) by Jón Helgason (1966, 177–78), is attributed to Arnórr. It is cited to illustrate the use of Sýr as an appellation for Freyja, and reads (in AM 742, with edited text in parallel):

Sæll er sÿr-hallar	Sæll es Sýr-hallar
seïda beïn-reïdar.	seiða bein-reið*ir*.

If the couplet is syntactically complete, MS *sÿr-hallar seïda beïn-reïdar* probably form a kenning, nom. sing. masc. in form, with *Sæll es* as its predicate. I cannot improve on Jón Helgason's interpretation, to which this paragraph is heavily indebted. *Sýr-hǫll* must mean 'hall of Freyja', and Freyja's hall was named Folkvangr (*Grí* 14). *Folkvangr* in turn could be a 'shield' kenning conforming to the established formula 'land of battle' (Meissner 1921, 169). The '(coal-) fish' (*seiðr*) of the shield is a sword (cf. Meissner 1921, 154), and the one who directly (*bein-*) brandishes it (*reiðir*, incorporating a slight emendation to the suffix) is a warrior. Hence, literally, 'Fortunate is the straight-wielder of the fish of Freyja's hall [shield→swords→warrior]'.

The possibility that this is a genuine verse of Arnórr cannot be ruled out, but there are important grounds for scepticism. The verse is not among the core material common to most MSS of *Laufás-Edda*, and these in general contain much of unknown origin and of doubtful attribution. AM 742 4o and Thott 1496, moreover, may not have independent value but may have obtained their common supplementary verses from closely related exemplars (Jón Helgason 1966, 175). The attribution is also stylistically dubious. The punning obscurity of the *ofljóst* expression *Sýr-hǫll* = Folkvangr = *folkvangr* = 'shield' is unlike anything else in Arnórr's known work, as is the defiantly anti-naturalistic image of sword as fish. Lastly, the *haðarlag* metre, with its five-syllable line, is not otherwise used by Arnórr. The couplet will always remain a problem case, but these seem to me sufficient grounds for excluding the couplet from the edited text in Part Two.

There are five verses which are ascribed in a majority of MSS to skalds other than Arnórr, but for which Arnórr is named as author in a single MS. I have little hesitation in omitting these five from the canon of Arnórr's poetry since in every case the content and / or style of the verse tells against this attribution, as well as the weight of MS evidence.

A single example will suffice. The Uppsala MS of *SnE* credits Arnórr with a four-line fragment, while MSS R, T, 748, 748II and 757 assign it to Þorkell hamarskáld (*SnE* p. 185):

Mér réð senda	The descendant of heroes
of svalan ægi	sent to me
Vǫlsunga niðr	across the chill ocean
vápn gollbúit.	a gold-adorned weapon.

(Text from *Skjald* B I 409; cf. *Skjald* A I 439.)

The fragment is in *fornyrðislag*, but we have no other evidence that Arnórr ever composed panegyrics or *lausavísur* in this metre; nor does the detail of a royal gift being sent by sea agree with anything we know of Arnórr's career (though it does not disagree). The prose context to the verse suggests that it is wrongly attributed to Arnórr, for it is immediately preceded in *SnE* by *Hryn* 20, which is introduced by the words, *sem Arnor q(vað)*. This evidently led the scribe of U (or of an exemplar to U) into the mistaken repetition of the name when quoting the next verse fragment.

The remaining four verses which, for similar reasons, cannot be considered part of the canon are the following:

Skald and Verse (References to *Skjald*)	Prose Source(s)	MS Attributions
Óttarr svarti, Óláfsdrápa sœnska v. 3 (A I 289; B I 267)	SnE pp. 181–82	U to Arnórr; other 4 SnE MSS to Óttarr
Óttarr svarti, Hǫfuðlausn v. 19b (A I 296; B I 272)	Fsk p. 159 Ólsh(Hkr) ch. 102 Ólsh(Sep) p. 254 Orkns ch. 19, p. 41 SnE p. 185	U to Arnórr; all others to Óttarr
Óttarr svarti, Knútsdrápa v. 11b (A I 298; B I 275)	Fsk p. 165 Ólsh(Hkr) ch. 150 Ólsh(Sep) pp. 437–38 SnE p. 148 SnE p. 167	T to Arnórr (SnE p. 167); T to Óttarr (SnE p. 148); all others to Óttarr.
Rǫgnvaldr kali, lausavísa 7 (A I 506; B I 409)	SnE(Svb.Eg.) p. 234[17] Orkns ch. 85, p. 195	743 to Arnórr; 332 and Fl to Rǫgnvaldr

There are, moreover, two fragments that are assigned to Arnórr in at least one MS, without his name being specified:

(i) The helming in praise of 'Ingi's brother' printed as v. 4 of Bǫðvarr balti's *Sigurðardrápa* in *Skjald* (A I 505; B I 478) follows Arnórr's *Mdr* 19 and *Þdr* 22 in *SnE* p. 113. *Mdr* 19 is introduced, *Sva q(vað) ArnoR iarlaskald*, and *Þdr* 22, *Ok enn sem hann q(vað)*. The third verse is then ascribed in MSS R and 757 to 'Kolli', and to Bǫðvarr balti in U; but W and its derivatives in *Laufás-Edda* omit any introductory words, thus implying Arnórr's authorship, while T explicitly introduces it, *Ok enn sem hann kvað*, with *hann* referring back to Arnórr.

(ii) Þjóð A 1, 21 (*Skjald* A I 366, B I 337) is ascribed to Þjóðólfr (Arnórsson) in the *Hkr* MSS K, F, J2, 39 and 47, and in MSS H and

[17] The fragment is preserved in various MSS of *Laufás-Edda*; see *SnE* (Faulkes 1979) pp. 279 and 357 and nn.

Hr; but in Flat it follows immediately on Arnórr's *Mdr* 13, which is introduced, *Sem Arnor segir*, so that the implication is that Arnórr also composed Þjóð A 1, 21. Again, the evidence of the other MSS and of the verse itself shows beyond reasonable doubt that the attribution to Arnórr is erroneous.

3

The Life of Arnórr Þórðarson jarlaskáld[1]

THERE is no *Arnórs saga jarlaskálds* as there are sagas of the earlier skalds Egill, Kormákr and Hallfreðr; nor does Arnórr figure prominently in the sagas of Norwegian kings, as do Sigvatr Þórðarson and others. Indeed, it may be said that in more than one sense Arnórr was no hero; rather he was a serious-minded, moderate man who disliked conflict, and who was remembered not for his own deeds, but for his praise of others.

The bare outline of Arnórr's life can be tentatively reconstructed from a variety of sources — certain of the *Íslendingasögur*, the compilations of *konungasögur* in *Msk, Flat* and *H-Hr*, *Orkns* and *Skáldatal* — and some idea of his character can be gleaned from these and from his poetry. As for the details of the incidents in which Arnórr appears, they doubtless owe much to popular or literary fiction, which makes them more entertaining as story but less reliable as history.

I Youth in Iceland (after 1011)

Arnórr was brought up at Hítarnes, a prosperous farm on the west coast of Iceland, not far south of the lovely peninsula Snæfellsnes. His father Þórðr Kolbeinsson was born in 974,[2] and was himself a skald, from whose work parts of two poems in praise of Eiríkr jarl Hákonarson survive, as well as a single strophe from a poem about Gunnlaugr ormstunga, and a dozen *lausavísur*. Þórðr figures prominently in *Bjarnar saga Hítdœlakappa*, which begins with the

[1] A sketch of Arnórr's life is also available in Hollander 1942, 99–104 and 108–9.

[2] So Sigurður Nordal and Guðni Jónsson, eds., *Borgfirðinga sǫgur* 1938, lxxxvii.

story of Þórðr's rivalry with Bjǫrn Hítdœlakappi for the hand of Oddný eykyndill Þorkelsdóttir, and the deceit by which he finally won her. The couple married in or about 1010,[3] and are said in the saga to have had five sons and three daughters (ch. 6, p. 125). Arnórr, Kolbeinn and Kolli are the only ones of Þórðr's children named there. Kolli was probably the youngest of the three, for he was believed by Bjǫrn Hítdœlakappi to be his own son (ch. 21, pp. 171–72), and Bjǫrn was abroad during the early years of the marriage between Þórðr and Oddný. Kolbeinn may have been the eldest son, since he bore the name of his grandfather, and if so, Arnórr could not have been born before 1012; if Arnórr was the eldest, and if the saga tradition merits credence on these points, a date as early as 1011 is possible.

Two incidents from Arnórr's youth are narrated in the *Íslendingasögur*. In *Grettis saga* ch. 60 (pp. 194–97) Þórðr Kolbeinsson, under pressure from his neighbours in the Mýrar district, sends his son Arnórr out with a band of men against the outlawed Grettir, who has been preying on the stock of the neighbourhood farms. Grettir, with two companions, takes up position on a point of land stretching into a river which was thereafter called Grettisoddi. By the time Arnórr and company arrive, Grettir has successfully repelled two bands of attackers, killing ten men and maiming or mortally wounding five others. Understandably, Arnórr decides not to engage: 'Arnórr did not wish to put himself in danger, and he won a strong reproach from his father and many others. Men consider that he was no great fighter (*engi garpr*).'

According to the chronology of the saga, Arnórr would have been eleven or twelve at this time,[4] which makes it somewhat incredible that he should have been involved in the intended attack, let alone leader of it. However, the saga's chronology is highly questionable (see Nordal 1938, 12–17), and the incident may have taken place years later. In either case the story may be true in so far as it reveals a peace-loving trait in Arnórr's character.

Hatred of discord is again revealed in an episode recounted in *Bjarnar saga* ch. 23 (pp. 174–75). At a horse-meet at Fagrskógr,

[3] *Borgfirðinga sogur* 1938, lxxxvii. Their marriage appears to have been in summer (*Bjarnar saga* ch. 5, p. 123).

[4] Grettir is reckoned to have been raiding the Mýrar area in the years 1021–24 (Guðni Jónsson, ed., *Grettis saga* 1936, lxv). The Mýramenn's attack takes place at the beginning of Grettir's third winter there, i. e. 1023.

the perennial rivals Þórðr Kolbeinsson and Bjǫrn Hítdœlakappi cynically amuse themselves by exchanging verses in praise of one another's wives. When Þórðr asks his sons Arnórr and Kolli how they have liked the entertainment, Arnórr is distinctly disapproving: 'I certainly don't like it; such things are not pleasing.' His scruples are not shared by his brother Kolli: 'I don't see it like that: it seems to me a fair deal if verse answers verse.'

II Departure Abroad (? after 1031)

Arnórr was probably in his early twenties when he first went abroad. He is named in *Skáldatal* (pp. 258 and 267) among the skalds of King Knútr inn ríki, and, as suggested on pp. 34–35, *Frag* 4 may be in praise of him. Knútr died in England in 1035, so that if Arnórr did compose poetry for him, he must have left Iceland in or before that year.

Arnórr himself indicates that his voyages were undertaken primarily or partly in the interests of trade when he declares (in *Hryn* 1):

Kljúfa lét'k í kaupfǫr dúfu	I made my bark cleave the billow
knarra minn við borð en stinnu.	with its firm strakes on a trading voyage.

III Years in the Orkneys (before 1045)

Arnórr's own words suggest that he spent the early part of his adult life in the Orkney islands, during the joint rule of the jarls Þorfinnr Sigurðarson and Rǫgnvaldr Brúsason. He was married to a relative of the jarls, for he speaks in a verse which Snorri quotes from *Rǫgnvaldsdrápa* (*Rdr* 2) of his marriage-tie with the jarl. There were at least two sons by the marriage, for Arnórr refers to 'my young sons' in his lament for Þorfinnr (*Þdr* 4, c. 1065).

Þdr 3 shows that Arnórr held an honoured position at Þorfinnr's court for several years, and the relatively detailed presentation of events in *Þorfinnsdrápa*, which spans the mid 1020s to the mid 1040s, bears witness to an intimate knowledge of Orcadian events. In two battles — one at Vatnsfjǫrðr (Loch Vatten) in Skye (c. 1036) and another between the jarls Þorfinnr and Rǫgnvaldr at Rauðabjǫrg (Roberry) in the Pentland Firth (c. 1044) — Arnórr actually took part in the fighting. This is clear from *Þdr* 13 and 20.

Arnórr's intimation that he was present at Rauðabjǫrg is supplemented by the prose account in *Orkns* ch. 26 (p. 66). It is told there that Þorfinnr, when his ship comes under attack, commands it to be cut loose from the rest of his fleet and rowed to land. The slain and wounded are put ashore, and so too is Arnórr: 'Þorfinnr ordered Arnórr jarlaskáld from the ship. He was in the jarl's company and very dear to him (*í kærleikum míklum*).' According to the saga it is now that he utters the *lausavísa Frag* 1.

Rǫgnvaldr survived the battle of Rauðabjǫrg, but not the feud with Þorfinnr, by whose men he was killed c. 1045. Arnórr composed a memorial poem for him of which a mere ten lines survive. There is no evidence about Arnórr's contacts with the Orkneys after this time, for his memorial poem for Þorfinnr (died c. 1065) throws no light on this point, and does not specifically describe any events from the last twenty years of Þorfinnr's life.

IV Audience at the Norwegian Court (1045 or 1046)

It seems that Arnórr left the Orkneys, either temporarily or permanently, after the death of Rǫgnvaldr, for he appears at the Norwegian court during the joint reign of Magnús Óláfsson and his uncle Haraldr Sigurðarson (c. 1045–46). The tale of Arnórr's appearance there is told in *Msk, Flat* and *H-Hr*.[5] It is an entertaining anecdote which is too artfully written to be credited as a verbatim report of Arnórr's exchange with the monarchs, but it may well have some truth as a reflection of the characters of the men involved.

The skald who emerges from the tale is a confident and quick-witted individualist. Arnórr has, according to the story, already won the nickname 'jarlaskáld' and a high reputation, for when the kings, at their meat, learn that he has come and has composed poems about both of them, they summon him straightway. Arnórr is down at the harbour tarring his ship but, without pausing to clean his hands, strides to the royal hall and enters with an imperious, 'Give way to the kings' skald'. After greeting the two kings with the resoundingly poetical *Heilir allvalldar baþir*, he achieves a diplomatic stroke by declaring

[5] *Msk* pp. 116–18; *Flat* III 321–23; *Hars(H-Hr)* pp. 195–98. It is printed under the editorial title of *Arnórs þáttr jarlaskálds* in *Íslendinga sögur* ed. Guðni Jónsson, XII 167–71.

that he will recite the poem for Magnús first. Magnús is satisfied at this, while the jealous and testy Haraldr is pacified by Arnórr's explanation that 'it is said that young people are impatient'.

Arnórr begins to declaim *Hrynhenda* and, after introductory strophes about the jarls 'west across the sea' and his own voyages (which call forth an impatient remark from Haraldr) launches into ringing praise of Magnús, beginning, 'Magnús, hear a mighty poem' (*Magnús, hlýð til máttigs óðar, Hryn* 3). Haraldr, presumably provoked by the line 'Every prince is far below you' (*Hverr gramr es þér stóru verri*), interrupts to protest, 'praise this king as you please ... but do not criticise other kings'. Later in the recitation Haraldr, a connoisseur of skaldic verse, cannot conceal his admiration: 'This man composes very forcefully, and I don't know where he will get to' ('*Allacafliga yrkir sia maþr. oc eigi veit ec hvar cømr*').[6] He declares that *Hrynhenda* will be recited as long as Scandinavia is peopled, and doubtless this is a realistic, if dramatised, account of the effect the poem had on its first hearers.

As for the poem which Arnórr then recites in praise of Haraldr, the *Blágagladrápa* 'Poem of the Dark Geese [? Ravens]', Haraldr is said to prophesy that it will soon fall out of memory; and indeed there is no certain trace of it in the written sources. It is nevertheless called, rather conventionally, 'a good poem' (*gott qveþi*) by the author of the anecdote,[7] and Haraldr considers it worthy of the reward of a gold-chased spear. Arnórr in gratitude promises Haraldr a memorial poem if he outlives the king.

Magnús rewards Arnórr with a golden ring which the skald fixes on the spear and raises aloft as he strides down the hall, declaring, 'high shall be borne both kings' gifts'. Magnús adds to his gift a trading vessel with cargo, and becomes a close friend of the skald (*oc gerþiz mikill astvþar vinr hans*).

It seems likely that, if Arnórr did indeed become intimate with king Magnús, he may have remained in Norway for several months.

[6] V. l. *hvar staðar nemr* 'where he will stop', Hr.

[7] Cf., for example, *Hallfreðar saga* ch. 6, p. 155, where Óláfr Tryggvason calls the *drápa* in his honour *gott kvæði*; Hallfreðr's *Uppreistardrápa* (now lost) is described in the same way in the saga-writer's own voice (ch. 9, p. 178).

Certainly the fact that he composed another, *dróttkvætt*, poem for Magnús after his death in 1046 or 1047[8] might support this surmise.

V Later Years (c. 1046 – after 1073)

The Norse prose sources provide no clue as to Arnórr's whereabouts in the last decades of his life. The relatively good preservation of Arnórr's poetry might suggest that he made his home in Iceland during his later years, and the only other factual evidence we have — the fact that certain poems were composed — is for the most part compatible with this theory.

Chronologically the next poem in the canon after the *dróttkvætt Magnússdrápa* is the memorial *drápa* for 'Hermundr', of which only a couplet survives. The only influential Hermundr of the mid eleventh century for whom this poem could have been made is the son of Illugi and brother of Gunnlaugr ormstunga, on whom Arnórr's father Þórðr Kolbeinsson had, as already mentioned, composed a *drápa*. Hermundr, one of the confederates of *Bandamanna saga*, died c. 1055,[9] and this might suggest that Arnórr was in Iceland for at least part of the 1050s.

Arnórr is reported to have composed a *drápa* for another prominent Icelander, Gellir Þorkelsson, who also figures in *Bandamanna saga*,[10] and the possibility that *Frag* 7 is a remnant of this was discussed on p. 35. Gellir died in Denmark in 1073 as he was returning from a pilgrimage to Rome, and if Arnórr did compose in his memory, this would indicate not only that Arnórr was alive about 1073, but probably also that he was resident in Iceland at the time, for while the doings of Norwegian kings would be reported and much discussed in Iceland, it is less likely that, if Arnórr were abroad, there would be enough information and enough stimulus for him to compose about Icelanders.

The remaining poems by Arnórr — the memorial poem for Þorfinnr jarl (died c. 1065), the memorial poem for Haraldr

[8] 1047 is the traditional date (Icelandic Annals pp. 17, 58, 108, 250 and 318). Ólafia Einarsdóttir, however, argues persuasively that 1046 is the correct date (1964, 199–213).

[9] On Hermundr, see Magerøy 1957, 154–55; on the date of his death, see Guðbrandur Vigfússon 1853–56, 441.

[10] On Gellir, see Magerøy 1957, 156–57.

Sigurðarson (d. 1066) and a poem, now lost, if it ever existed, for Óláfr kyrri (d. 1093) — throw no further light on the later part of Arnórr's life.

4

Subject-Matter and its Presentation

SINCE both the subject-matter of skaldic encomiastic poetry and its style are highly conventionalised, it is only after close examination that the character of an individual poem or poet emerges. The following chapters are devoted to features of the content and style of Arnórr's poetry which, if not unique in themselves, combine to give his work a character of its own.

In the present chapter, section I briefly characterises the principal themes and their presentation in the poetry, section II compares the presentation of the subject-matter in the four main *drápur* of Arnórr — *Hrynhenda, Magnússdrápa, Þorfinnsdrápa* and *Haraldsdrápa* — and section III, composed of an analytical list of motifs and a specimen study of one strophe, illustrates the interplay of tradition and innovation in Arnórr's choice and handling of subject-matter. It is from the list of motifs and from the synoptic headings to the verses in the normalised texts (in Part Two) that the full range of subject-matter in Arnórr's poetry can best be seen. Finally, Arnórr's Christian utterances, an important aspect of his art concerning both subject-matter and presentation, are briefly discussed in section IV.

I Heroes and their Deeds

Almost all of Arnórr's verses share the purpose of recording and glorifying the deeds of a contemporary Norse ruler, and since the ideal ruler of the eleventh century was pre-eminent especially in war and seafaring, it is fitting that these should be the main themes of the poetry. Further, skaldic tradition furnished the poet with a rich store of images and vocabulary touching these themes which enabled him to suggest that the deeds of the present continued or outshone the glories of the past.

Largely because of this shared purpose and firm poetic tradition, the various heroes of Arnórr's poems are not sharply individualised. Unflinching valour is the attribute constantly singled out for praise. Nevertheless, other prized qualities appear, sometimes encapsulated in the form of kennings such as *auðgjafi* 'wealth-giver' or *hlenna dolgr* 'foe of thieves', sometimes more directly stated in the form of adjectives. Magnús Óláfsson is described as handsome *(fríðr)*, wise *(drjúgspakr)*, generous *(mildr)*, popular *(elska þjóðir ... Hryn* 19) and just *(réttr)*.[1] Of Haraldr Sigurðarson and Rǫgnvaldr Brúsason, both described by prose writers as handsome men,[2] Arnórr's extant verse gives no physical description, but Haraldr is characterised as *fljótmæltr* 'swift-spoken' and *harðgeðr* 'stern-spirited' (cf. his nickname *harðráði*, although not recorded until the thirteenth century),[3] and Rǫgnvaldr as *herþarfr*, which may mean 'beneficent to troops', and *snjallr* 'wise, quick'. Arnórr's other Orcadian lord, Þorfinnr, is presented as tall *(hǫ́r)*, handsome *(fríðr)* and ruthless *(slíðrhugaðr)*. The claim of good looks is contradicted by the prose tradition and may be poetic flattery;[4] the other two attributes are mentioned in prose.

It was suggested above (p. 31) that the historical kernel of each *drápa* — which is largely devoted to warfare or seafaring — has chronological order as its organising principle. Some episodes in the overall chronological scheme are themselves coherent narrative units, for example *Mdr* 1b–4, in which Magnús Óláfsson's return from Garðar (N.W. Russia) is traced, but more often each scene or moment of action is presented individually, so that the overall effect is cumulative rather than strictly linear. Indeed, certain of the battle verses, for instance *Þdr* 7b and *Hdr* 3b, take up the skaldic option of

[1] Snorri Sturluson describes Magnús as *meðalmaðr á vǫxt, réttleitr ok ljósleitr, ljóss á hár, snjallmæltr ok skjótráðr, skǫrunglyndr, inn mildasti af fé, hermaðr mikill ok inn vápndjarfasti. Allra konunga var hann vinsælstr, bæði lofuðu hann vinir ok óvinir* (*Hars(Hkr)* ch. 30, p. 107).

[2] Haraldr is *fríðr maðr ok tíguligr, bleikhárr ok bleikt skegg ok langa kanpa, nǫkkuru brúnin ǫnnur ofar en ǫnnur* (*Hars(Hkr)* ch. 99, p. 19). Rǫgnvaldr is *allra manna fríðastr, hárit mikit ok gult sem silki* (*Orkns* ch. 19, p. 41).

[3] Turville-Petre 1968, 3; Bjarni Aðalbjarnarson, ed., *Hkr* 1941–51, III, xxxix, n. 1.

[4] *Hann var manna mestr ok sterkastr, ljótr, svartr á hár, skarpleitr ok nefmikill ok nǫkkut skolbrúnn* (*Orkns* ch. 20, p. 43).

intercalating clauses to produce a lively enactment of the simultaneous actions which make up the melée of battle.[5]

The individual threads which make up the descriptive or narrative fabric range from reports that a battle was fought or a journey made (perhaps at a specified time or place), through more precise statements that one side outnumbered the other or that certain weapons were used, to graphic details such as helmeted men taking their places at the oars or flame running over the foreheads of slain warriors.

Poet and audience usually seem to stand as spectators to the events, viewing them either in the middle-distance or at closer range. But occasionally the skald declares his own involvement, which may be physical (his part in a battle) or emotional (his relationship with his patron or his grief at his death).

On the other hand, the skald can distance himself (and us) from the events and provide a frame for them by drawing attention to the poem itself, and his own artistry in composing and delivering it.[6] Devices used by Arnórr include the traditional 'call for a hearing' (as in *Hryn* 3, *Magnús, hlýð til máttigs óðar*, 'Magnús, hear a mighty poem') and the heralding of a new surge of verse (as in *Hryn* 14, *Nú mun kvæðit aukask* 'Now will the poem swell'). The skald also punctuates his detailed description of specific events with generalised exclamations of praise (as in *Mdr* 18, *Ert gat hilmir hjarta* 'a spirited heart the sovereign got').

II The Four Main *Drápur*

A. *Hrynhenda*

Even by skaldic standards, *Hryn* is a magnificently effusive poem, and it stands out from the remainder of Arnórr's work especially because of its distinctive metre and because it is addressed to a living prince. Magnús Óláfsson's deeds are celebrated mainly through second person verbs, and he is repeatedly apostrophised with titles such as *Hǫrða dróttinn, hilmis kundr* or *skjǫldungr*.

[5] See further Edwards 1983 II, 164–71; also Lindow 1982, which interestingly probes the truism that skaldic verse is essentially non-narrative.

[6] On the professional self-consciousness of the skalds see Clover 1978; also Fidjestøl 1982, 210–12 and 221–27.

The overall subject-matter resembles that of the *dróttkvætt* poems, and we witness the capture of enemy ships or the firing of enemy homes, corpses lying in heaps or the raven shaking his bloody feathers after feasting on carrion. Of the fighting itself, however, there is little close-up description. We are not told, for instance, that 'swords bit' or 'blades were reddened' as in the remaining three *drápur*. As for factual detail, some of the events are precisely located *(umb Stafangr norðan,* v. 10; *sunnr at Jómi,* v. 12), but many of the place-names introduced are rather general *(sœnskar byggðir,* v. 5; *Danaveldi,* v. 10), and there are scarcely any indications of time.

In presenting the voyages of Magnús west from Russia and south to Denmark, Arnórr produces seafaring descriptions which surpass those of earlier skalds (though he may have been encouraged by his father Þórðr Kolbeinsson's example: see Fidjestøl 1982, 208). Particularly in vv. 4 and 10 we can note precise nautical terms which sharpen the picture of a storm-tossed ship, and an effect of movement is gained by the use of short clauses in combination with the strong trochaic pulse and straightforward word-order which distinguish *Hryn.*

It is within the context of seafaring, too, that Arnórr's praise of his patron is most effulgent. In vv. 10 and 17 Arnórr flatters Magnús by praising his ship, saying that its gilded ornament is like blazing fire or like the sun racing up into the firmament; and in v. 18 he adds to this dazzling aureole the implication of divine favour when he says that it seems to men, watching Magnús's ship, as though it were attended by a host of angels.

The beauty of these images is all the more remarkable when one reflects how seldom simile is used by the skalds, for of Arnórr's predecessors only Hallfreðr (if indeed he is the author of the *lausavísur* ascribed to him) used this figure very fully.[7] It is also in *Hryn* that Arnórr's most notable metaphor occurs *(Hryn* 3): *haukr réttr estu, Hǫrða dróttinn* 'a just hawk you are, Hordalanders' lord'.

[7] See Hfr *Lv* 24, where Hallfreðr compares his lady to a gilded vessel; or Hfr *Lv* 15 and 16, where she is likened to a swan but her lumbering husband to a fulmar stuffed with herring. Other skalds make fleeting comparisons, e. g. Eyvindr skáldaspillir, who says that his hero's sword pierced armour *sem í vatn brygði* 'as though it were slashed through water' (*Hák* 5). Fidjestøl observes that, from Arnórr onwards, what similes do occur often concern seafaring, a theme which the skalds characteristically portray with more naturalism than battle (1982, 208–9).

B. *Magnússdrápa*

The *dróttkvætt* poem *Mdr* celebrates the same hero and essentially the same events as *Hryn*. It is curious that Arnórr should have covered the same ground twice, and that the metrical innovation should come in the first version (Fidjestøl 1984, 245), but this is the case if, as seems probable, *Mdr* is a memorial poem (see further ch. 2, p. 29). There are many stylistic similarities between the two (Fidjestøl 1984, 245–49), yet there are also differences of presentation. These can be seen by comparing the treatment of the battle off Helganes in the two poems (*Hryn* 15 and *Mdr* 12–15). The site of the battle is named in both, but only in *Mdr* is there any indication of time (*røkr ǫndurt* 'at twilight's approach'; *haustnǫ́tt gegnum* 'through the autumn night'). In both poems the capture of enemy ships is reported, and a carrion-beast comes to prey on the slain, but only in *Mdr* are the actions which precede victory described: among other details, Magnús is seen hurling spears at enemy helmets and ruthlessly swinging his sword.

Although *Mdr* comes closer than *Hryn* to being a chronicle of events, some of its verses are noteworthy for their graphic, even grotesque, description. The ravening wolf is vividly pictured in vv. 8 and 15, and almost the whole of v. 11 describes a wolf trying to scale a huge pile of bodies. The wolf is here designated by an unusually elaborate kenning, and this reflects the general character of *Mdr*, in which kennings are used rather more extravagantly than in Arnórr's other poems.

In *Mdr* as it is preserved, only vv. 18b and 19 contain generalised praise of the hero, and, after the first helming, the skald rarely refers to himself or to the progress of the poem.

C. *Þorfinnsdrápa*

The special characteristics of *Þdr* spring from the close bond which held between Arnórr and the jarls of Orkney. This is clear from the four (presumed) extant fragments of the exordium — v. 1 with its blend of personal lament with exuberant heralding of the encomium, vv. 2 and 3 with their reminiscences of winter drinking scenes, and v. 4 with its (now obscure) references to deep sorrow and the skald's own sons.

Arnórr was present at two, at least, of the battles he commemorates (Vatnsfjǫrðr and Rauðabjǫrg) and, although *Þdr* was composed some twenty years after the events, his descriptions of these and other battles are exceptionally vigorous, packed with short clauses which depict flying missiles, biting swords and streaming blood.

Arnórr's portrayal of the battle between his two lords at Rauðabjǫrg reflects the anguish with which he recalls it. His emotional involvement in the battle is plainly stated in v. 20a, and it is evident in v. 19 from the choice of vocabulary, and in v. 20b from the sharpness of focus and the almost obsessive repetition as Arnórr enumerates three points on the ship against which blood spurts.

Many of the details in the battle-descriptions of *Þdr* could have been supplied by the eye of imagination, but there is also much of a more factual nature which is clearly the word of an eye-witness or of one who had access to first-hand reports. Thus place-names are numerous, and more precisely local than in the other *drápur* (e.g. *Torfnes, fyr Ekkjal sunnan,* v. 9). *Þdr* is, further, the only poem in which Arnórr specifies the day of the week on which a battle was fought (*mánadagr,* v. 9; *fría morginn,* v. 13), and the only one in which numbers of ships are given (*fimm snekkjur, ellifu skeiðar,* v. 6).

The hero of *Þdr* is usually in the forefront of the battle scenes, advancing his standard, reddening his sword or capturing enemies. Þorfinnr is lauded in general terms in vv. 2, 12, 15 and 21, and in v. 22 Arnórr declares that the great cataclysm will beset the world before a jarl finer than Þorfinnr will be born in the Orkneys. This strophe also includes a brief prayer for Þorfinnr, and a twofold prayer is found in *Þdr* 23.

D. *Haraldsdrápa*

Hdr is the latest and in some ways the least interesting of Arnórr's major poems. In *Þdr* Arnórr's personal interest in events which are long past brings them vividly before his eyes and ours; but one gains no such sense of immediacy from *Hdr*, and this accords with the fact that we know of no link between Arnórr and the Norwegian court during the reign of Haraldr.

In many instances adjectives ornament otherwise plain contexts. Compounds such as *folksnarr* 'battle-swift' or *fljótmæltr* 'swift-spoken' abound, and some of them are rare and obscure (see Commentary to *togfúsa* Hdr 8/6, *hlítstyggr* 11/4). A particularly effective use of a graphic adjective in v. 8 is noted on pp. 77–78.

Often, too, it appears that Arnórr has drawn upon heroic cliché in order to fill out his matter, as when the hero advances 'glad under gold-reddened helmet' (v. 3), or when his men desire no quarter, choosing rather to fall with their slain lord (v. 13).

Elsewhere, what the poem lacks in flamboyance is made up in laconic understatement, as when Arnórr describes Haraldr's ruthless suppression of the Uplanders (v. 6):

heit dvínuðu Heina;	the threats of the Heinir fell away;
hyrr gerði þá kyrra.	fire made them quiet.

Generalised assertions of Haraldr's greatness supplement the praise of his individual triumphs. Such eulogy occupies two whole strophes and a helming (vv. 14–16) and appears sporadically elsewhere, often in the form of subordinate clauses such as *þess's fremstr vas manna* 'of him who was foremost of men' (v. 5).

One helming (v. 17) is a personal prayer for Haraldr, but, this apart, the skald's voice is heard little in the extant *Hdr.* No introductory lines or comments on the progress of the poem have survived, and almost the only personal touch is in v. 15, where Arnórr rhetorically declares himself 'in the dark', unable to conceive who could achieve more than Haraldr.

III Traditional Motifs

By far the greater part of Arnórr's poetry is composed of variations on basic motifs which are found elsewhere in the skaldic corpus. The range of motifs used by Arnórr is illustrated here.

A. List of Motifs

1. Warfare

The hero —

- makes a vow / threatening speech
- gives orders to his men
- advances into battle
- strikes terror into the enemy
- shows no fear
- casts off armour
- hurls weapons

wields / reddens his sword
shows no mercy to the enemy / pays them out
routs the enemy
piles up the dead
feeds the creatures of battle
burns buildings / corpses
wins victory / fame / territory
defends his land
dies

The hero's men —
are in the minority
advance
serve their lord well
fail their lord
rout the enemy
feed the creatures of battle
fall beside their leader

The enemy —
advance
feel fear
flee
fall

The battle:
Armies advance
Battle is joined at the place called ...
Banners sway / flutter
Stones are hurled
Spears / arrows fly
Swords are swung
Swords sing
Weapons bite / are reddened
Shields are shattered
Armour is pierced
Blood flows
The slain lie on the field
The creatures of battle come / cry out
The creatures of battle feast on carrion

2. Seafaring

The hero shows no fear of the sea
Men embark
Ships are launched from the rollers
The wind speeds the ship
The ship plunges / shivers
The hero keeps his ships out at sea
A voyage is completed

3. Sea-battle

Ships move into the attack
Ships are cleared / captured
Blood splashes the ship
Blood colours the waves

4. The hero — general praise

The hero was only ... years old when ...
None has achieved such deeds so young
The hero has no equal
The hero is powerful
The hero provides matter for verse

5. The skald

'I call for a hearing'
'I make verses'
'The poem grows'
'I tell men about ...'
'I know / have heard about ...'
'I praise my patron'
'I repay my patron's generosity'
'I mourn for my patron's death'
'I pray for my patron's soul'

While Arnórr's poems are in large measure formed, mosaic-like, from familiar motifs, there is an intermixture of more novel content. The first four half-strophes of *Þdr*, for example, have a quite individual stamp, as suggested above. Even the battle scenes, which especially lend themselves to stereotype, contain some fresh ideas. In *Mdr* 13, for instance, Arnórr pictures sparks flying from spear-points, and in *Þdr* 18 he refers to the dawning light which makes battle possible, and evokes the sound of horns blaring between the strongholds. I have found none of these details in earlier skaldic battle poetry.[8] The following section illustrates further the blend of conventionality and novelty in the content of Arnórr's poetry by means of comparisons with poetry by his predecessors and contemporaries.

B. Specimen Analysis: Motifs in *Þorfinnsdrápa* 17

The numbers set above the text are those assigned to the motifs in the discussion which follows.

-----------1---------------	
Stǫng bar jarl at Engla	The jarl bore his standard onto the
----1---- -------3---------	
ættgrund, en rauð stundu	native soil of the English, and straightway
---------2------------------	
— vé bað vísi knýja —	— the leader called for banners to advance —
--------3-----------	
verðung ara tungu.	his liegemen reddened the eagle's tongue.
---4----- ------5------	
Hyrr óx, hallir þurru,	Flame grew, halls shrank;
------------6------------	
herdrótt rak þar flótta;	the war-band drove men to flight there;
-------------7--------------	
eim hratt, en laust ljóma,	the foe of branches flung out smoke, and
-----------7------------	
limdolgr, náar himni.	hurled light against the sky.

[8] The closest parallel to the image of sparks flying from weapons is that of swords giving off light, as in *Upp skulum órum sverðum ... glitra* 'We shall make our swords gleam aloft', Eg *Lv* 6. *Dagr's upp kominn*, which precedes rallying calls in *Bjarkamál in fornu*, is an inexact parallel to the idea of light enabling battle.

1. The hero carries a standard ashore (*Stǫng bar jarl at Engla | ættgrund*)

There are several other skaldic contexts in which an advance of standards is pictured, but none, to my knowledge, shows standards being carried ashore. Compare Þjóð A 4, 4 (c. 1044):

Nú taka Norðmenn knýja ...	Now the Norwegians start to advance
... Magnús merki.	Magnús's standards.

An early picture of troops advancing from ships, with shields rather than standards, is found in Bragi's *Ragnarsdrápa* 11.

2. The hero calls for standards to be advanced (*vé bað vísi knýja*)

There is no precise parallel, but see the quotation from Þjóðólfr above. For a hero giving orders for an attack compare also *Vell* 24 (c. 986):

Hlym-Narfi bað hverfa	The Narfi of the clash of the
hlífar flagðs ...	shield-ogress [axe→battle→warrior][9]
... at landi.	called on them to turn towards the land.

3. Liegemen redden the eagle's tongue (*en rauð stundu verðung ... ara tungu*)

Here a novel, if not visually very compelling, turn is given to the familiar image of warriors feeding, or reddening, carrion birds or beasts.[10] Earlier skalds speak of the raven's (or eagle's) beak or 'whiskers' being reddened in blood. Both are apparently (for the text is difficult, with various rival MS readings) mentioned by Egill in the same verse, *Hfl* 11 (c. 936):[11]

[9] In glossing extended kennings I first give the meaning of the enclosed kenning and then that of the enclosing kenning. Thus in the present example 'shield-ogress' (*hlífar flagðs*) means 'axe', the 'clash' (*hlymr*) of the axe is 'battle', and the 'god' (Narfi, a son of Loki) of battle is a warrior.

[10] See Fidjestøl 1982, 200–24 on 'likdyr-motivet'.

[11] The dating of *Hǫfuðlausn* is also difficult; its authenticity has been questioned, e.g. by Jón Helgason (1969) and Baldur Hafstað (1994, 19; cf. also Kristján Árnason 1994).

órut blóðsvanar	not lacking in blood were
benmǫs granar ...	the wound-gull's [raven's] whiskers;
en oddbreki	and the point-billow [blood]
gnúði hrafni	roared against the raven's
á hǫfuðstafni;	head-prow [beak];

and Arnórr's kenning *ulfa ferðar tungurjóðr* gives a compressed image of a warrior reddening the tongues of a wolf-pack (*Hryn* 5), but I know of no other context in which it is a bird's tongue that is stained with blood.

4. Fire grows (*Hyrr óx*)

Compare Atli (c. 1070):

... eisur vaxa ...	flames grow,
... gim geisar.	fire rages.

Both this motif and that of smoke and light mounting against the sky (no. 7 below) are paralleled in the *Edda*. Compare *Vsp* 57:

geisar eimi við aldrnara,[12]	smoke rages with the life-nourisher [? fire];
leicr hár hiti við himin siálfan;	towering flame sports against the very sky;

and, from an Eddaic fragment in *Vǫlsunga saga*:

Eldr nam at œsaz, ...	Fire began to swell,
ok hár logi við himni gnæfa.	and towering flame to rise up against the sky.[13]

5. Buildings are burnt (*hallir þurru*)

Fidjestøl notes the parallel between Arnórr's *Hyrr óx, hallir þurru* and *Hyrr sveimaði, hallir þurru* (Gísl 1, 5, early 12th century) in the course of a review of 'burning' motifs (1982, 204–6). The use of *þurru*, literally 'decreased', also finds an approximate semantic parallel in Jórunn 1: *Hús lutu ... fyr eisum* 'Houses bowed down before the flames' (early 10th century). Compare also the Eddaic *Akv* 42: *Forn timbr fello* 'The ancient timbers fell' (referring to a building

[12] V. l. *oc aldrnari* in Hauksbók and *SnE* MSS.

[13] Printed in *Edda* (1962 edition), I 322.

on fire). The contrast of mounting flame and falling buildings (motifs 4 and 5) is also made in Þ Sær 1, though not so tersely and pointedly as in Arnórr's verse.

6. The war-band routs the enemy (*herdrótt rak þar flótta*)

Reka flótta 'to pursue the fleeing, to put to flight' is very common in ON battle descriptions, both verse and prose. One simple example will suffice: Ótt 3, 7 (1026): *þú rakt flótta* 'you [Knútr] put them to flight'.

7. Smoke and light are cast up against the sky (*eim hratt, en laust ljóma, | limdolgr, náar himni*)[14]

Bjǫrn krepphendi's line *limsorg náar himni* (B krepp 5) may be a direct reminiscence of Arnórr's,[15] but otherwise the closest parallels to this picture are found in the *Edda* (see motif 4 above), and Arnórr's 'fire' kenning *limdolgr*, literally 'foe of branches', resembles *sviga læ* 'bane of twigs' in *Vsp* 52. In other skaldic verses smoke and red-hot embers are said to be thrown upwards, though not specifically against the sky: see, e.g., Þjóð A 4, 2 and Valg 2.

Because of limitations of space it is unfortunately not possible to present more fully the resemblances in imagery and wording between Arnórr's poetry and that of other skalds, nor to consider whether these are coincidental or caused by direct influence. (There is some discussion of individual points in the Commentary in Part Two.) This question has been discussed by Jan de Vries in his article 'Über Arnórr Jarlaskáld' (1952). The author presents the relevant material with care and convincingly points to links with Hallfreðr vandræðaskáld, Sigvatr Þórðarson, Þjóðólfr Arnórsson and others, although he is occasionally, in my opinion, too ready to assume imitation on the part of Arnórr. The influence of Arnórr's poetry on later skalds is especially clear in the *hrynhent* panegyrics by Markús Skeggjason (c. 1104) and by Sturla Þórðarson (c. 1262; not discussed by de Vries).

[14] For explanation of the form *náar*, as of other textual points, see Commentary.

[15] Fidjestøl remarks on the fact that Bjǫrn's reminiscence of Arnórr's Orcadian verse occurs within a description of Magnús berfœttr's successes in the Hebrides (1982, 205).

As for Eddaic poetry, the images of cataclysm in *Þdr* 22 indicate that Arnórr knew some earlier apocalyptic poetry, and the verbal similarities with *Vǫluspá* noted above and in the Commentary to *Þdr* 22 suggest that Arnórr consciously imitated that poem, in order that the solemn beauty of its tones should resound in his own elegy. There are also resemblances with *Helgakviða Hundingsbana* I, the first, though not the earliest in date of composition, of the Eddaic 'Helgi lays', and Alexander Bugge in 1914 argued that the lay is a symbolic poem celebrating the deeds of Magnús Óláfsson, and that Arnórr is its creator.[16] In the first part of his article on the subject Bugge invoked historical circumstances in an attempt to demonstrate parallels between the careers of Helgi and Magnús, but many of his points are too general to be demonstrably more than coincidental and others are flawed by inaccuracy or overstatement.[17] The remainder of Bugge's thesis rests on verbal parallels (especially in kennings) between Arnórr's work and the Helgi lay, and wider stylistic resemblances such as the presence of simile and graphic sea-description. In my view the similarities with Arnórr's work are not close or numerous enough to prove more than that the author of the *Helgakviða* was familiar with skaldic poetry.

IV The Christian Element

To include prayers and other Christian material in skaldic encomia was not unprecedented in Arnórr's time — models were to hand in the work of Hallfreðr, Sigvatr and others — yet the quantity and range of Arnórr's Christian allusions make them a notable feature of his poetry (see Edwards 1982–83 and, for a broader survey, Fidjestøl 1989).

Five verses by Arnórr (*Rdr* 3, *Þdr* 22 and 23, *Hdr* 17 and *Frag* 6) contain petitions for the soul of the hero, three of them framed around the verb *hjalpa*, and in *Hdr* 16b the outer clause is a clear

[16] Hollander (1963, 140–41) inclined to accept Bugge's view, but it has been ignored by most other writers on *H Hund* I and its origins.

[17] To give a single instance, Bugge states that Magnús Óláfsson fought Knútr and his sons and was victorious (1914, 362), but in fact Knútr died before Magnús returned to Norway, his son Sveinn fled from Norway, apparently without a struggle, soon after Magnús's arrival, and it is doubtful whether Magnús ever fought Knútr's other sons Haraldr and Hǫrða-Knútr.

avowal that heaven has received the hero.[18] A still more specific and concentrated piece of doctrine is found in *Frag* 7 on the judgement of mankind by God and St Michael, which in its surviving form is independent of any encomiastic context (though see p. 35). This is the earliest skaldic reference to the archangel Michael (discounting the word *Míkálsmessa* in O kík 1,1, c. 1046).[19]

As well as introducing more or less self-contained Christian allusions, Arnórr occasionally gives a Christian tint to inherited panegyric conventions. Thus, his prayer in *Hdr* 17 is uttered in gratitude for a gift, just as whole poems (among them Bragi's *Ragnarsdrápa*) had been composed to requite a gift. In his praise of Magnús góði Arnórr is especially lavish with Christian colouring. He portrays Magnús's victory against the Wends (*heiðit folk)* as a conquest of evil, divinely assisted (*Mdr* 8 and 10 and probably *Hryn* 13; see Commentary to *Hryn* 13/6); and divine favour is again implied by the flamboyant imagery of *Hryn* 18, which includes one of the earliest Scandinavian references to angels, and by the laudatory topos in *Hryn* 19.

The striking eschatalogical signs of *Þdr* 22 include some, such as the sun turning black, that are reminiscent of the Book of Revelation, but none that can be identified as belonging unambiguously to either the Christian apocalypse or the pagan Ragnarǫk. Arnórr's poetry is also quite generously furnished with allusions to pagan myth, but in my view they have no religious significance, and instead belong purely to the level of poetic diction. They are consequently discussed in the following chapter.

18 Compare Þórarinn loftunga's affirmation about Óláfr Haraldsson in *Glælognskviða* 4 (c. 1032).

19 For further discussion of this theme and of the verse, see Edwards 1982–83, 40–41.

5

Diction

I Introduction

THE SKALDS' inherited vocabulary not only comprised everyday words, technical terms, proper names and traditional poeticisms or *heiti* (some of these more or less figurative), but also contained time-honoured and still fertile patterns for further word formation, and of all these Arnórr made effective use. In discussing so rich a subject as the diction of Arnórr's poetry, one can only hope to suggest, by selected examples, the skald's resourcefulness and his sensitivity to the particular associations of individual words. (Words and phrases of especial interest are also noted in the Commentary in Part Two.)

For the purposes of this discussion Arnórr's poems are treated as a group rather than individually, for their particular characters owe less to their diction than, for example, their word-order. In relation to their length, *Mdr* and *Hdr* contain more adjectives than *Hryn* or *Þdr*. *Mdr* is also relatively rich in kennings, while in *Hdr* they are fewer and plainer than elsewhere; but otherwise the differences between the four main *drápur* are not striking.

A distinction is made in this chapter between everyday words and poeticisms. The 'poeticisms' include firstly words which, on the evidence of the lexicons, seldom or never occur in prose, especially *heiti* such as *marr* 'sea' and kennings such as *skýrann* 'cloud-hall [sky]', and secondly words whose meaning when used in poetry differs from that when used in prose, such as *helmingr* 'war-band' ('half' in prose). To discuss separately the everyday and the poetic is convenient, but, given the lack of direct evidence for eleventh-century prose usage and the limited nature of our knowledge of ON vocabulary generally, the distinction between the two can in some cases only be tentative.

Since the kennings constitute the most variegated and most distinctively 'skaldic' element in Arnórr's diction, they are the focus of much of the following discussion, and an informal definition is therefore necessary.

The kenning has been variously defined and categorised by scholars of ON and OE,[1] but most have agreed that it is a periphrasis which denotes a nominal concept (such as 'man', 'sword' or 'gold') which in prose would be expressed by a single noun. It has two parts, both substantival: a base word and a determinant. The determinant is in the genitive case or else is the first element of a compound. In Arnórr's kenning *ǫrva hríð* '(snow-)storm of arrows [battle]', the determinant is *ǫrva* 'of arrows' and in *hrælǫg* 'corpse-sea [blood]' it is *hræ* 'corpse'. The two elements are juxtaposed according to certain stereotyped patterns, for instance 'warrior' can be denoted by any god's name, with any word for 'battle' or 'weapon' as determinant, e. g. *rimmu Yggr* 'Óðinn of battle / battle-tumult'.

The determinant, and occasionally the base word, may itself be a kenning, so that three elements are involved (*tvíkennt* 'doubled kenning') or more (*rekit*, lit. 'driven, chased'; both terms in *SnE* p. 215). Thus Arnórr's *hrosta brim* 'surf of brewing mash [ale]' is joined to a further determinant, *Alfǫður* 'All-father's, Óðinn's' to form the *tvíkennt* conceit *Alfǫður hrosta brim* 'All-father's mash-surf [poetry]'.

In many kennings the base word is metaphorical, for if it is taken in its literal sense, it is quite incompatible with the meaning of the kenning as a whole. Thus battle (*ǫrva hríð*) is not a storm (*hríð*) in the ordinary sense, nor is ale (*hrosta brim*) surf or sea (*brim*). In my own, fairly broad, view of the kenning, metaphor is not a defining feature but rather a useful means of distinguishing types within the kenning system.[2]

[1] See, e. g., Meissner 1921; Fidjestøl 1974, with Hallberg 1978 and Fidjestøl 1979 as sequels; Turville-Petre 1976, xlv–lix; Amory 1982; Marold 1983, 24–36; Engster 1983, esp. 23–25; and Gurevich 1994. Fidjestøl and Amory apply linguistic theory to the investigation of kennings. Further definitions and references are given in Frank 1985, 163–64, while post-1985 contributions to the study of skaldic diction include Clunies Ross 1987, Amory 1988, Malm 1990, Smirnickaja 1992 and Gurevitsj 1993.

[2] This approach is akin to that of Meissner 1921 and Marold 1983. The view that all true kennings are based on metaphor is found as early as the 13th century, in the *Third GrT* of Óláfr hvítaskáld (p. 104). Among 20th-century scholars who maintain a similar view is Brodeur (1952, esp. 142). Snorri's position is not entirely clear, but he seems to include non-metaphorical figures among the kennings (Clunies Ross

The highly stereotyped nature of the kenning, and the metrical constraints on the choice of kenning elements, raise the question whether individual kennings contribute particular effects (such as visual images, mythological or political allusions) to their poetic contexts, or whether they are mere substitutions — albeit formally ornate ones — for ordinary nouns. Undoubtedly kennings of all types occur, in skaldic verse at large and in Arnórr's in particular, but, as pointed out below and in the Commentary in Part Two, at least some of Arnórr's kennings are appropriate and effective in context.

II Everyday Words

Over half of Arnórr's nouns and most of his adjectives and verbs are also recorded in ON prose. Some of these were doubtless used because only a commonplace word would fit the formal patterning of rhythm or assonance in the verse, or because the skald wished to express a concept (such as *kló* 'claw', *fría morginn* 'Friday morning', *rauðr* 'red' or *valda* 'to cause') for which no specifically poetic term suggested itself; but they were probably used also because Arnórr does not cultivate extreme obscurity (as also in other areas such as word-order: see Edwards 1983, esp. 153).

Few items in Arnórr's 'everyday' stock are noticeably over-worked. *Ungr* might be so labelled, for it occurs in *Hryn* 7, *Mdr* 2, 17 and 19, and *Þdr* 9, as well as being compounded in *barnungr* in *Mdr* 7 and used in the comparative form *œri* in *Hryn* 8 and *Þdr* 5, although the stress on the youth of his dauntless heroes is justified. The description of land as 'broad' is, to judge from *LP*, a cliché, but Arnórr just stops short of excess in its use.[3] Similarly, 'high' is an established epithet for fire, but Arnórr quickens the convention by using the superlative, *hæstr hyrjar ljómi* 'towering / highest blaze of fire' in *Hryn* 12.

The intrinsically plain *hæstr* is again put to good use in *Hryn* 6, where Arnórr reminds Magnús, *Austan komt með allra hæstum ... œgishjalmi* 'From the east you came with highest of all ... helm of terror'. The adjective so placed wittily endues the figurative

1987, esp. 62–69).

[3] *Fyr víðu Vestlandi, Mdr* 9; *vítt Helganes, Mdr* 12; *í virki breiðu, Hryn* 12; *at breiðu Jótlandi, Mdr* 6.

ægishjalmr with the force of the concrete. Again, the simple colour terms 'bright' and 'black' are used to fine effect when opposed as the rhyming pair of *Þdr* 22/1, *Bjǫrt verðr sól at svartri* 'Bright sun to swart will turn'. The stark, doom-laden imagery is continued in the next line, *Søkkr fold í mar døkkvan* 'Earth will sink in the dark ocean'. Further examples include the colour terms in *Frag* 8 and the verb *hǫggva* 'hack' in *Þdr* 20a.

Frequently, the timely introduction of an everyday word lends particularity to a descriptive context, and *Hryn* 4 illustrates this well. This fine strophe contains not a single kenning and at the most three *heiti* (*skjǫldungr* 'king, prince', *vǫndr* 'mast' and the emendation *varta* '?prow'), but it effects a compelling picture of a storm-tossed ship largely by means of nautical terms, graphic epithets and forceful verbs. In *Hryn* 10, another seafaring verse, vividness is again achieved by particularity, and in Arnórr's picture of the battle in the Pentland Firth in *Þdr* 20b, the scene becomes all the more immediate when we are told that it was against the *saumfǫr* 'nail-row', the *skjaldrim* 'shield-rail' and the *skokkr* 'decking' that the blood spurted.

III Poeticisms

A. Variety

Much of the vocabulary of the skalds, simply by its remoteness from everyday speech, imparts a ceremonious tone to an encomium and dignifies the people or things commemorated there. It also enables constantly-recurring concepts to be expressed in constantly-varied terms. Arnórr's resourcefulness in this respect can be illustrated from a single group of *heiti*. 'Sword' is expressed fourteen times by a *heiti* in his poetry, and there are nine different ones: *brandr* '?blade / fire-brand', *hjǫrr* 'sword', *hneitir* 'striker', *járn* 'iron one', *malmr* 'metal one', *skelkingr* '?fearsome one', *skúfr* 'tasselled one', *stál* 'steel one' and *tyrfingr* '?wooden-hafted one'.[4] Arnórr's *heiti* for 'sea / wave', 'ship' and 'battle' are similarly varied. In the case of some concepts where there is less variety, this probably reflects a narrower choice of traditional vocabulary. 'Land', for example, is designated by a *heiti*

[4] On *skelkingr*, *skúfr* and *tyrfingr*, see Commentary to *Þdr* 5/2, *Hdr* 3/5 and *Hdr* 2/3 respectively.

nine times by Arnórr, but only three different *heiti* (*fold*, *grund* and *láð*) are used; and this tallies with the fact that it is less well represented in the *þulur* than any of the concepts mentioned above, and with the fact that many of the *jarðar heiti*, such as *brekka*, literally 'slope', or *hváll*, literally 'copse, hill' (*Þul* IV æ 2), would have been unsuitable for the sense 'territory' that Arnórr required.[5]

The variety produced by the *heiti* is eclipsed by that of the kennings. Arnórr's poetry contains about one hundred and fifty kennings (over one hundred and sixty if kennings enclosed within *tvíkennt* or *rekit* kennings are counted separately), and, like his contemporary Þjóðólfr Arnórsson, he uses more, and more adventurous, kennings than is usual among skalds of the mid and late eleventh century. The extant poetry of Valgarðr á Velli and Halli stirði, for example, suggests that they were extremely sparing in their use of the figure.

The kenning, with its bipartite structure, gave the skald ample scope to show his resourcefulness in the choice of referent (such as 'man / prince / warrior', 'ship' or the rarer 'mind / thought', 'silver', 'wind' or 'winter'), the choice of formula (such as 'god of battle' meaning 'warrior' or 'slayer of the snake' meaning 'winter'), and in the choice of individual words to fill the formula. In *foldar fiðr* 'plumage of the earth', hence 'grass' (*Frag* 11), for instance, Arnórr produces a unique variation on the rare formula 'hair of the earth'.[6]

Another variable is the relationship between the kenning, particularly its base word, and the person or thing to which it refers, that is, the degree to which it is literal or figurative.[7] Individual skalds differ considerably in their preferences here; Arnórr's taste is catholic. Over half of his kennings are transparent expressions of relationship such as *Áleifs sonr* or *Hjalta dróttinn*, in which the words have their literal meaning, or 'agent noun' kennings such as *eggrjóðandi* 'edge-reddener' or *hrafngrennir* 'raven-feeder', in which

[5] Terms for 'land' occurring in pagan eulogies are listed by Malmros (1994, 539–40).

[6] Meissner (1921, 89) cites only five kennings for 'grass' from the whole skaldic corpus (he does not include Arnórr's *foldar fiðr*).

[7] Einar Ól. Sveinsson made a fourfold classification of kennings chiefly on the basis of the metaphorical or non-metaphorical character of the base word (1947). For alternative approaches to classification, see, e. g., Noreen 1921, 4–6, Mohr 1933, esp. 16–18 and 21, and references in n. 1 above.

the words are used with mild synecdoche, picturing one highly specialised activity in order to suggest the wider concept 'warrior'. But Arnórr is also lavish in his use of more esoteric kennings, such as the metaphorical 'sky' kenning *sólar hjalmr* 'sun's helmet' or the personified 'fire' kenning *hallar bani* 'killer of the hall'.

B. Formal elaboration

Compounds and phrases, longer and metrically heavier than simplices, are a particularly fruitful way of varying and ornamenting the poetic expression. Arnórr's fondness for using existing compounds and fashioning new ones is shown not least by his adjectives. Discounting formations with *ó-* or *-ligr*, there are over fifty compound adjectives in his poetry, i. e. one every twelve lines of verse (compared with one every seventeen lines in Þjóðólfr's verse). More than half of these, such as *bǫðsnarr* / *folksnarr* 'battle-swift', or *geðfrœkn* 'mind-bold', refer to valour or strength, and contribute to the sustained paeans of praise for the warrior-heroes. They conform to ancient and widespread patterns and they may appear familiar even if, like the examples cited, they are not actually attested elsewhere. Their elements were probably chosen as much for their aptness to complete patterns of rhythm or assonance as for their precise meaning. (Examples of more enterprising compound adjectives are given in section IV below.)

Arnórr's taste for formal elaboration is further demonstrated by his kennings. He frequently adorns the basic two-part pattern by adding epithets (as in *rammþing Glamma* 'Glammi's mighty encounter [battle]' or *lituðr hramma aldins, ótams varðrúnar viggs* 'stainer of the claws of the troll-wife's old, untamed steed [wolf→warrior]) or by using the *tvíkennt* or *rekit* varieties, again illustrated by *lituðr hramma* ... Arnórr's poetry contains well over a dozen of these extended kennings, and while they are not necessarily mystifying, they demand a high degree of intellectual participation from the audience and reward with a corresponding satisfaction — perhaps akin to that of solving a riddle or crossword puzzle.

C. Descriptive quality

Many of the poeticisms used by Arnórr bring to life in our imagination certain aspects, often visual, of the object or person designated. Thus, among the *heiti* for 'sea', *flóð* evokes an image of the sea particularly in its swelling, surging moods since its non-poetic sense is 'flood, deluge' or 'flood-tide', as also does *grœðir* since it has obvious etymological links with *grœða* 'to make grow', *gróði* 'increase, swell, flood', etc. Similarly, *járn* 'sword' literally means 'iron' and *þrima* 'battle' literally 'din, thunder'.

How consciously Arnórr chose these words cannot usually be discovered, but the rarity of some of his *heiti* (see section IV of this chapter) suggests conscious design in at least some instances, as does his exploitation of the metaphorical element in the 'ship' names *naðr* and *Visundr*. *Naðr* (literally 'serpent', mostly in poetry) for 'ship' reproduces the pun implicit in the more common *dreki* 'dragon (ship)', and is wittily combined with the verb *skríða* — a verb frequently predicated to both ships and snakes (see *LP*) — to evoke an image of a smoothly gliding dragon-prowed ship in *Hdr* 2, *naðrs borð skriðu norðan*. Compare also *rendi Visundr norðan*, 'Bison charged from the north' in *Hryn* 9 (Visundr here being a proper name).

Of the kennings, a majority appear to be newly composed, albeit according to inherited patterns, and here Arnórr's wit and imagination are more easily demonstrated. *Hjǫrdynr* 'sword-clash', for instance, conveys the savage confusion of battle by concentrating on its tumultuous sound, and that this is not a chance effect is shown by Arnórr's other kennings for 'battle', most of which are of the same descriptive kind. Words for 'storm' (twelve examples) or for 'noise' (seven examples) are especially favoured as base words, and almost all of these well convey the thunderous commotion of battle, the only exception being *þeyr* 'thawing wind' in *hjǫrþeyr*. The skald could, according to the conventions, have chosen words such as *skúr* 'shower', *galdr* 'spell', *rǫdd* 'voice' or *sǫngr* 'song' which are somewhat weak and artificial terms for the roar of battle, but in fact he chose the more forceful and imaginatively apt ones. A further point of interest here is that a comparable image is to be found among Arnórr's verbs. In *Hdr* 9 *dynja* 'resound, rush', which is most often predicated to subjects such as earth, rain and fire, suggests a comparison with the dinning rush of elemental forces when Arnórr applies it to the flight of the enemy at the battle of Fulford.

The sensitivity with which Arnórr fashions his kennings is further illustrated by two expressions for 'ship', *élmarr* 'blizzard- / storm-steed' and *œðiveðrs elgjar* 'elks of the raging gale', which give a vivid impression of a ship charging like an animal through stormy seas. Meissner lists thirty different kennings for 'ship' with *marr* 'horse' as base word, and fourteen with *elgr* 'elk' (1921, 211 and 218–19 respectively). But in each group it is only Arnórr's examples (*élmarr* and *œðiveðrs elgjar*) that have 'storm' or 'gale' as the determinant, the others being mainly 'sea', 'sea-king', or words for part of the ship, and there are no other sure examples of 'ship' kennings with determinant meaning 'wind' or 'weather', other than *byr* 'favouring wind, breeze'. This suggests that Arnórr introduced the 'storm / gale' words into his kennings consciously and imaginatively, and this is confirmed by the poetic contexts in which they occur. *Œðiveðrs elgjar*, for example, appears in a helming in which the phrases *á skelfðan grœði* 'on the tossing swell' and *und drifnu tjaldi* 'under spray-drenched awnings' reinforce the image of a tumultuous storm (*Hryn* 16a):

Ótti, kunnuð elgjum hætta	Terror of seized gold, you expertly
œðiveðrs á skelfðan grœði,	risk elks of the raging gale on the
fengins golls, eða fœðið ella	tossing swell, or else you pass
flestan aldr und drifnu tjaldi.	the most part of your life under spray-drenched awnings.

There are further indications that Arnórr often fashioned his kennings thoughtfully so that they would fit their particular context. It is noticeable, for example, that four of the kennings which portray the hero in the role of providing the beasts of battle with blood or carrion — *ulfa ferðar tungurjóðr* 'tongue-reddener of the wolf-pack' etc. — are concentrated in *Hryn* 5 to 7, a sequence of strophes which celebrate the triumphant return to Norway of the ten-year-old Magnús Óláfsson. In these kennings the skald is apostrophising the mature Magnús, a seasoned warrior, but they also further his aim of presenting the boy king in the light of a conquering hero, for they create an aura of martial glory, although in fact no battles are fought.

The kennings discussed above are typical of Arnórr's usual technique in so far as they serve to emphasise or illuminate the subject-matter of the poetry. Thus in *œðiveðrs elgjar* the context leads us to dwell on the image of the ships at sea, not on the secondary image of 'elks'. However, Arnórr does very occasionally use the device that Snorri calls *nýgørving*, literally 'new creation, innovation' (*SnE* pp. 121 and 217), to achieve the opposite effect: the secondary image contained in the base word of the kenning is reinforced by the surrounding words (often another kenning) and enjoyed for its own sake, so that the imagination is temporarily deflected from the primary subject-matter. The clearest example is in *Hryn* 18, *Mildingr rennir Meita hlíðir sævar skíði* 'The ruler makes the ski of the ocean skim Meiti's slopes'. The 'slopes of Meiti' are the sea and the 'ski of the ocean' is the ship. Omitting the determinants from the kennings, we read *Mildingr rennir hlíðir skíði* 'The ruler makes the ski skim the slopes'. Thus we have simultaneously an image of a king skiing across snowy hills and one of a king speeding his ship across the waves.

Similarly, in the final couplet of *Mdr* 12 it seems that the image of a rain-storm, as well as that of a battle, was vividly before Arnórr's eye. In the *rekit* expression *rógskýja rýgjar regn* 'rain of the ogress of strife-clouds [shields→axe→battle]' the secondary image of 'rain' in the base word is highlighted by being juxtaposed with 'cloud', and the predicate *helt ... haustnǫtt gegnum* 'kept up through the autumn night' invests the downpour as well as the battle with the chill, dark atmosphere of the autumn night.

D. Mythological, legendary and historical allusions

The diction (especially kennings) used by Arnórr and exemplified above is frequently based on poetic comparisons drawn originally from nature, as when a battle is pictured as a storm or a ship as an animal; but it can also take the imagination beyond the present, natural world. In particular, the many kennings and *heiti* that contain mythological, legendary and historical names impart a certain lustre to the referent — be it battle, a weapon or a prince — by linking the present with glories of the more or less remote, and more or less imaginary, past. The mythological allusions are considered first.

Arnórr's poetry contains six kennings for 'God', almost all of which refer to Him, with varying elaboration, as 'lord of heaven', e. g. *sóltjalda stillir*, literally 'ruler of the sun's awnings' *Rdr* 3, or *himins skapvǫrðr* 'heaven's shaping guardian', *Mdr* 10. The remaining examples are in *Hryn* 18, *Hdr* 17, and *Frags* 6 and 7. The Christian allusions in Arnórr's poetry are, however, not confined to single words or phrases, and therefore have been discussed in Chapter Four on subject-matter and its presentation.

The pagan allusions are of a quite different nature — fossilised items of poetic diction rather than tokens of belief, and hence they properly belong in the present discussion. Within the 'pagan' layer in Arnórr's work it may be useful to distinguish three types of reference, even if the boundaries between them cannot always be drawn with certainty: (i) allusions to mythical narratives, (ii) mythical names not necessarily related to particular narratives, and (iii) items which may be common nouns and / or may refer to mythical personages.

The first category includes the kennings *erfiði Austra* 'Austri's toil' and *Ymis hauss* 'Ymir's skull', which evoke the creation myth in which the sky is fashioned from the giant Ymir's skull and held aloft at its corners by the dwarves Norðri, Suðri, Austri and Vestri (*SnE* p. 15).[8] It also includes the 'poetry' kenning *Alfǫður hrosta brim* 'All-father's mash-surf', which refers to Óðinn's possession of the mead of poetry (on which, see Frank 1981 and Davidson 1983, 418–47). All three kennings are of a rare enough type to suggest that they are used with positive intent, and the intent in the case of the 'sky' kennings, I believe, is to add an antique and grandiose air to already sweeping praises. The 'poetry' kenning is wittily juxtaposed with references to literal drinking in the opening of *Þdr*. There is, then, ample poetic justification for the inclusion of such references, and no reason at all to suspect Arnórr of having any genuine belief in pagan conceptions.

The second category of mythical names includes three 'warrior' kennings: *rimmu Yggr* 'Óðinn of battle', *gǫndlar Njǫrðr* 'Njǫrðr of battle' and *unnar Baldr* 'Baldr of the sword' (based on an emendation, see Commentary to *Þdr* 14/1 and 14/3). In these the gods' names seem to be arbitrary and interchangeable, mere counters within the kenning formula '"god" of "battle / weapon" = "warrior"'. Similarly, *Miðgarðr* 'earth, the middle enclosure' in *Hdr* 16, although a vestige of the pagan world-picture, probably has little or no mythical import. Hel, in *Mdr* 10 *Hel klauf hausa fǫlva* 'Hel clove pallid skulls', does have a punning mythical reference to the realm of the dead and the goddess of that realm, and this is pointed up by the juxtaposition of the word with 'heaven' and 'earth' (*himins; jǫrðu*), but its primary significance is as the name of Magnús Óláfsson's battle-axe.

Still further from profound mythical significance are the members of the third category — terms such as *hlǫkk*, *gǫndul* and *hildr* which mean 'battle' but perhaps also 'valkyrie', and *bára*, *dúfa*, *kolga* and

[8] These and a further three 'heaven / sky' kennings by Arnórr which encapsulate natural images rather than myth, and are embedded in kennings for 'God' (*Rdr* 3, *Frags* 6 and 7) are quoted in *Skáldskaparmál*, *SnE* pp. 113–15, and are interestingly discussed in that context by Clunies Ross, 1987, 135–37. A further non-mythical example is in *Þdr* 5.

unnr which mean ‘sea / wave’ but which Snorri also names among the nine daughters of the sea-deities Rǫn and Ægir (*SnE* pp. 116 and 175, *bára* not mentioned p. 175). If Arnórr intended these as anything more than common nouns, he must have been playing upon his audience’s knowledge and expectations, for he does nothing to encourage a sense of personification. In his use of *ægir* ‘sea’, on the other hand, there is a strong hint of personification, encouraging thought of the sea-god himself, when Þorfinnr is said to contend against him (*bægja við ægi*, *Þdr* 15).

To summarise so far, the pagan-derived diction in Arnórr’s work belongs to the form of the poetry, not its content. Like the allusions to legend, it lends grandeur and variety, and reminds the skald’s audience of his and their illustrious predecessors, but its use cannot be regarded as religious in intention or effect.

Turning to the legendary allusions, we find again that some of these are to shadowy figures such as the ‘sea-kings’ Endill, Glammi or Meiti, whose names can have conveyed little more than an aura of antique splendour. It is also doubtful whether *bragningr*, *ǫðlingr*, *dǫglingr* and *siklingr*, all *heiti* for ‘prince’, would have evoked recollections of the royal ancestors Bragi, Auði, Dagr or Sigarr with whom Snorri links them.[9] Other *heiti*, however, recall well-remembered heroes such as Hǫgni, Sigurðr (via the term *vǫlsungr*, which Arnórr uses in *Hdr* 14/1 in the general sense ‘prince’ or ‘hero’),[10] or Buðli, father of Atli (in the ‘prince’ term *buðlungr*).

The allusions are sometimes pointedly historical rather than legendary. The kenning *Eydana meiðir* ‘harmer of Isle-Danes’ is set in the midst of *Hdr* 6, a helming which portrays Haraldr harðráði ruthlessly subduing the men of Upplǫnd, and it acts as a concise and timely reminder of a previous phase in the king’s career, when he attempted to subdue the populace of the Danish islands. Further examples are noted in the Commentary (e.g. *Þdr* 5/7, *Einars hlýri*, and *Hdr* 17/3, *Girkja vǫrðr ok Garða*).

Similarly, among the *heiti* for ‘sword’, *hneitir* literally means ‘striker, wounder’. It occurs in Einarr Skúlason’s *Geisli* (v. 43) as the name of Óláfr helgi’s sword, and it is likely that Arnórr intends a

[9] *SnE* p. 183; cf. de Vries on these words, *bragningr* under *bragnar*.

[10] The only other record of this sense is in Sturl 4, 30.

hinting reference to that when he uses the word in connection with Óláfr's son Magnús in *Mdr* 1 and 13.

To conclude this section, and to illustrate the enriching effects of legendary allusions in context, we may take *Hryn* 9b, where the description of Magnús's company is endued with splendour not only by reference to dark-age heroes (*Gjúka ættar klæði*, see Commentary) but also by reference to the exotic and the excellent in *girzkum malmi* and *Peitu hjalma*. The verb *hræðask*, a rare historic present,[11] also increases the vividness of the scene:

Samnask bað til hverrar hǫmlu	He urged to rally at every rowlock
— hræðask menn við ættar klæði	— men fear the garments of Gjúki's
Gjúka; þótti gǫfugt eiki	offspring; splendid seemed the bark
girzkum malmi — Peitu hjalma.	with its Russian metal — helmets of Poitou.

IV Rare and Unique Words

Arnórr shows great resource in introducing different words to express the same concept; but not at the price of extreme obscurity. Of his *heiti*, for example, fewer than a dozen are rare, if 'rare' words are defined as those for which *LP* has fewer than four entries, discounting citations from *þulur* and from Arnórr himself. They include *áll* 'sea-current, sea', *fúra* '(fir) ship' and *tyrfingr* 'sword', all of which occur in a *þula* and one or two other poetic contexts, and the 'sword' *heiti skelkingr* and *skúfr*, only recorded in *þulur* (and the latter is slightly doubtful since the MS spellings are *skofr* and *stufr*). If *gautar* is correctly taken as a *heiti* for 'men' and *þing* as a *heiti* for 'battle', they each have only one sure parallel (see Commentary to *Hdr* 8/3 and *Hryn* 5/7).

When Arnórr introduces a rare or unique word into his poetry, it is probably more with the intention of impressing his audience than of baffling them. The *hapax legomena*, which include adjectives such as *forhraustr* 'outstanding in valour' or *rógǫrr* 'strife-quick' and kennings or kenning elements such as *limdolgr* 'foe of branches [fire]' or *angrtælir* 'grief-beguiler', may in many cases be the creations of

[11] Arnórr also employs the historic present in the graphic *Mdr* 15, and in *Hryn* 11 and *Hdr* 15. Åkerblom maintained that there were no certain examples of the 'historic present' in the strict sense in *dróttkvætt* up to 1100 (1917, esp. 313) but, as Poole has amply demonstrated (1991, 24–56), it is more common than Åkerblom thought.

Arnórr himself, but they are based on familiar patterns of word-formation, especially compounding but also derivation, and are for the most part self-explanatory. This can be illustrated from the nouns (other than kennings), among which there are seven nonce-words. Four are compounds, and of these *armhrauð* 'arm-ornament', if it is the correct reading in the difficult *Frag* 4/3 (see Commentary), is of particular interest, for the second element *-hrauð* is unique in Norse. The remaining three compounds, *auðvinr*, *óskepna* and *ættgrund*, contain no obscure elements and are readily comprehensible: *auðvinr*, literally 'wealth-friend', is paralleled by *auðgjafi* 'wealth-giver', *hnossvinr* 'jewel-friend' and the adjective *auðmildr* 'generous with riches'; *óskepna* 'monstrous, unnatural thing' resembles *óskǫp* 'unnatural event(s)', *óskapligr* 'unnatural' and *skepna* 'creature';[12] *ættgrund* resembles *áttjǫrð*, *ættland* and *ættleifð*, all 'native land, patrimony'.

The three unique simplices are all formations in *-i*, and again all resemble well-attested words: with *afreki* 'hero' compare *afrek* '(heroic) deed', *afreka* 'achieve', *afreksmaðr* 'champion' and *afraki*, which appears among the *konunga heiti*; with *knarri* 'ship' compare *knǫrr* '(trading) vessel'; and with *typpi* 'mast-head' compare the synonymous *toppr*. *Typpi* is a fine instance of Arnórr's verbal wit. It can be assumed to share with its cognate *toppr* the senses 'top, knob, masthead' (as in *siglutoppr*, literally 'sail-top', *Þul* IV z 6; *Maríu saga* p. 789) and 'forelock', and Arnórr, in his phrase *élmars typpi*, literally 'tops of the blizzard-steeds [of the ships]' evokes both of these so that the images of ship and steed are both made more vivid.

That Arnórr at his best invents words that are strikingly apt in context is further illustrated by *allnǿttfǫrull* 'ever prowling by night' in *Mdr* 11.[13] The epithet qualifies an elaborate kenning for 'wolf', and contributes to the heavy intricacy of the verse which so well enacts the wolf's laborious but vain attempts to climb the heap of slain. Similar artistry is revealed in *Hdr* 8, in which the sensuous

[12] Records of similar forms from the modern period include '*óskepia* vel *óskepni*', meaning 'monster', in Björn Halldórsson 1814, s. v., and *óskepi* and *óskapnaður*, both 'monster, formless thing' (*óskepi* also means 'chaos') in Blöndal 1920–24; the 1963 Supplement offers an occurrence of *óskepna* itself, meaning 'monster'.

[13] Cf. perhaps *síðfǫrull* 'out, abroad late' which, however, is not recorded before Arnórr's time, and the personal name Nǿttfari.

richness of the near-unique adjective *glóðheitr* is admirably drawn out by its context:

Fell at fundi stillis	Down flowed, at the ruler's conflict,
— framm óðu vé — móða	— standards stormed forth — upon wearied
(ámt fló grjót) á gauta	men (dark stones flew)
glóðheitr ofan sveiti.	ember-hot blood.

Glóð- suggests both brightness and heat, so that there is a dramatic contrast between the glowing blood and the exhausted passivity of the warriors. At the same time the brightness of the blood is set off against the dark stones (*ámt grjót*). See further Commentary to *Hdr* 8.[14]

To summarise, Arnórr's poetry contains a rich array of kennings which range from the self-evident (*Áleifs sonr*, *Hjalta dróttinn*, *eggrjóðandi*) to the riddling and the rare (*sólar hjalmr* or *Austra erfiði* 'sky', *foldar fiðr* 'grass'). All kennings, by their formal complexity and their indirectness of meaning, dignify the verses and the deeds they celebrate, but many of Arnórr's kennings transcend the level of stereotyped verbal ornament and function as poetic images (*élmarr* 'ship', literally 'blizzard-steed', *rógskýja rýgjar regn* 'battle', literally 'rain of the ogress of strife-clouds'). That Arnórr fashioned his kennings with conscious care for their individual meanings is suggested not least by his elegant fusion of the 'ship' kenning *æðiveðrs elgjar* 'elks of the raging gale' with the surrounding description of storm-tossed seas.

The nouns (other than kennings), adjectives and verbs in Arnórr's poetry, although less exotic than the kennings, bear witness both to his resourcefulness in using his inherited vocabulary, everyday or esoteric, and adding to it by his own coinages, and to his imaginative skill in choosing particularised or forceful words to enrich his descriptions.

[14] For further compound adjectives that are interesting or unusual, see *Mdr* 5/1 *afkarlig*, *Mdr* 10/2 *ódæsinn*, *Mdr* 13/2 *drjúgspakr*, *Mdr* 16/2 *arflógandi*, *Hdr* 2/8 *hrafnþarfr*, *Hdr* 4/6 *fljótmæltr*, *Hdr* 8/6 *togfúss*, *Frag* 3/5 *ílendr*, *Frag* 5/2 *sælútr*, *Frag* 8/4 *grandaukinn*, and Commentary to these.

6

Metre

ARNÓRR is a skilful user of inherited forms, but also something of a pioneer. The present chapter, after a preliminary section, outlines the metrical rules governing Arnórr's poetry, characterises his particular operation of those rules, and examines some aspects of the relationship between metrical features and literary and syntactic ones.

I *Dróttkvætt* and *Hrynhent* in Arnórr's Work

Of the 581½ lines which comprise the canon of Arnórr's work, 451 are composed in *dróttkvætt* 'court metre'. The isolated single line which I designate Fragment 10 was, as the presence of an *aðalhending* and lack of an alliterating pair show, an even line. The remaining lines are in *hrynhenda* (*hrynhendr háttr* or *hrynhent*) 'flowing metre', and all but four of these belong to the great encomium for Magnús Óláfsson which takes its name from the metre.[1] Whereas the *dróttkvætt* is very well known to us from many fine poems dating as far back as the ninth century, Arnórr's *Hrynhenda* is the earliest extant praise-poem in that metre, and it may have been Arnórr who introduced it into Scandinavia. Until 1981 the six-line fragment of *Hafgerðingadrápa* 'Tidal-Wave Poem', attributed to a Hebridean Christian sailing to Greenland aboard an Icelandic vessel, had customarily been dated c. 1000 and hence regarded as the earliest specimen of *hrynhent*; but Jakob Benediktsson argued convincingly, if not conclusively, that the poem may have been composed in the latter half of the eleventh century.

[1] The poem and its metre are interestingly discussed in Fidjestøl 1984, esp. 249–55.

It must therefore remain an open question whether or not Arnórr is the creator of the *hrynhent* metre. In either case, Arnórr's mastery of form in the *Hryn* is certainly his most important contribution to the formal development of skaldic poetry. After Arnórr's time the metre is used for secular or semi-secular panegyrics such as Markús Skeggjason's *Eiríksdrápa* (c. 1104) and for *drápur* by Óláfr hvítaskáld and Sturla Þórðarson in the early thirteenth century, as well as for specifically Christian praises, including Gamli kanóki's *Jóansdrápa* in the twelfth century and several works in the fourteenth, notably Eysteinn Ásgrímsson's *Lilja*.

The *hrynhent* metre is clearly a development of the *dróttkvætt*. It has a norm of eight syllables and four stresses per line compared with six syllables and three stresses per *dróttkvætt* line, but is based on identical patterns of rhythm and assonance. Except where otherwise stated, therefore, the metrical rules summarised below apply to both metres. There is also, however, a possibility that *hrynhent* is influenced, directly or indirectly, by Latin hymns, or, as maintained by Hallvard Lie, metrical prayers, in trochaic tetrameter, of which a classic instance is:

ýmnum dícat túrba frátrum
ýmnum cántus pérsonet ...
(Heusler 1925–29, I 305, Lie 1952, 82–89, Foote 1984, 252–53).

II Metrical Rules[2]

Arnórr's *dróttkvætt* and *hrynhent* verses share with most of the skaldic corpus a metre in which strongly stressed syllables, more weakly stressed and completely unstressed syllables are disposed according to certain recurrent patterns. The fully stressed syllables frequently carry alliteration, which is also placed according to a limited number of patterns. In these respects the metre resembles that of Eddaic and virtually all other early Germanic poetry. It differs, however, in that it is syllable-counting, has an invariable cadence to the line, and has

[2] Lucid outlines of the rules of ON metre are given in Turville-Petre 1976, xviii–xx (on *dróttkvætt*) and xxii–xxxiii (on *hrynhent*), and by von See, 1967, esp. 3–16 and 37–52; more expansive is Kuhn 1983. An important critique of Kuhn is Gade 1989, and see Gade 1995 (which appeared after this chapter had been completed); another recent approach to skaldic metre is Kristján Árnason 1991.

internal rhyme. Whereas the earliest known specimens of *dróttkvætt*, from the end of the ninth century, show some metrical flexibility, especially in the use of internal rhyme and the placing of alliteration, the poetry of Arnórr and his contemporaries shows almost complete conformity to certain rules, which therefore can be readily stated. The following notational conventions will be used.

´	main (full) stress
`	secondary (half) stress
x	unstressed element
|	caesura
–	long syllable
⏑	short syllable
⏑⏑	resolution, as in drăpă
‿	elision, as in Nóregi‿at

(The notions of 'main stress', 'secondary stress' and 'unstress' conceal rather more subtle distinctions, but are adequate to present purposes.)

The metre is essentially syllable-counting, in the sense that the number of syllables per metrical line is limited; stress and length of syllable also play a crucial part. Most *dróttkvætt* lines consist of six syllables, most *hrynhent* of eight; but two syllables, the first of which is short, may be 'resolved', standing in place of one long syllable. An example, with resolution in the first stressed position, is (*Þdr* 8/1):

Þrima vas þvígit skemmri ⏑́⏑ x –́ x –́ x .

With resolution in the first unstressed position (*Þdr* 7/5):

Stall drapa — strengir gullu –́ ⏑x⏑ –́ x –́ x .

Apparently superfluous syllables may in other cases be discounted by assuming elision of vowels, e. g. *dýrr Nóregi‿at stýra*, *Mdr* 7/4, or by assuming that scribes of manuscripts have produced non-original syllables, inserting pronouns or replacing short forms by longer alternatives. The practice of removing these as part of a 'normalisation' process is less widely approved now than formerly (e. g. Fidjestøl 1985, 78), and it is perhaps time for it to be thoroughly reviewed, but until this has been done it seems reasonable to continue the practice (see further pp. 104–5, Presentation of the Text).

The close of the line is necessarily filled by a trochee (´ x) in *dróttkvætt*, and in *hrynhent* by two trochees, the first stress of which may be on a long or short syllable. In the remainder of the line various rhythmic patterns are formed by combining the three grades of stress in falling (higher-to-lower), rising (lower-to-higher) or blended patterns. Trochaic rhythms are especially common. A majority of lines contain three full stresses, but secondary stresses regularly supplement these in certain types of line. Eduard Sievers classified *dróttkvætt* lines (along with other early Germanic lines) on the basis of the various stress patterns, and the resulting 'Five-Type' system, although by no means beyond criticism, remains the most practicable and widely-used system for description (Sievers 1893, esp. 31–36, 98–105).[3] It has been refined for *dróttkvætt* poetry in a lifetime of publications by Hans Kuhn, culminating in *Das Dróttkvætt* (1983), and the work of Sievers and Kuhn is the main foundation for the present discussion. Even when the same basic system is used, however, there is room for rival analyses of individual lines or even groups of lines, and I have tried to identify the main problem cases in the discussion, as well as specifying my scansions of all the lines towards the end of section III below. The five principal types, illustrated from Arnórr's *dróttkvætt* poetry, are:

A	–́ x –́ x –́ x, e. g. glœddi eldr af oddum	Mdr 13/3
B	x –́ x –́ –́ x, e. g. at frammi í gný grimmum	Mdr 5/5 (with elision)
C	x –́ ⏓́ x –́ x, e. g. í hjalmþrimu, hilmir	Hdr 11/3
D	–́ –́ ⏓̀ x –́ x, e. g. Upplendinga brendi	Hdr 5/2
E	–́ –̀ x –́ –́ x, e. g. rógskýja helt rýgjar	Mdr 12/7

An important sub-group within the A type comprises the 'A2k' lines, where 'k' indicates *kurz* 'short'. E. g:

Mdr 8/8 allfrekr bani hallar –́ –̀ ⏑́ x –́ x .

[3] The other main system, proposed by Heusler (1925–29, I 167–201), is highly complex and has not been widely adopted.

The second main stress falls on a short syllable (*ba*- in the example), but in compensation for this the second syllable is secondarily stressed instead of unstressed. Within the D type an important sub-type is D4, _́ _́ x _̀ _́ x, which is not represented in Arnórr's *dróttkvætt* corpus, unless such a line as *Mdr* 15/6 belongs here, but it is found in *Hryn* 15/4, *viðr Helganes blóðugt fiðri.*

While the Five-Type classification of metrical lines, and some of its premisses (for instance, that all *dróttkvætt* lines have three main stresses)[4] are open to challenge, most of the remaining features of versification are generally accepted: they are established by observation and in many cases are spelt out by Snorri Sturluson in his commentary to *Háttatal*.

The metrical lines are joined in pairs (*vísufjǫrðungar*) by alliteration. Two alliterating sounds (the *stuðlar* 'supports' or 'props') occur in the odd line of the pair and one (the *hǫfuðstafr* 'main post') on the first syllable of the even line. A vowel is considered to alliterate with any other vowel, and with *j*, but consonants must alliterate with identical sounds. The groups *sk, sp* and *st* count as single units and generally cannot alliterate with each other or with *s* alone or in other combinations. It is generally accepted that the alliterating syllables coincide with main stresses.

The system of internal rhyme (*hendingar* '?catches, links', cf. verb *henda* 'catch') is, like alliteration, based on an alternation of odd and even lines, although in this case the two lines of a pair are not joined by a common assonating sound. The *hendingar* most frequently coincide with full stresses, but often too with secondary stresses. Whether they can fall on unstressed syllables is debatable, as explained below. The second part of the rhyming pair falls on the last stressed syllable of the line, i. e. the penult. The even line carries full rhyme (*aðalhending* 'chief rhyme'), consisting of like vowel and consonant(s), e. g. *mægð : frægðar* in *Rdr* 2/4, or occasionally just of

[4] In lines such as *Hdr* 12/5, *sá's aldrigi aldins*, for example, the second syllable of *aldrigi* 'never' is, according to standard metrical theory, fully stressed, yielding a C line, but since the syllable is phonetically and semantically light, this analysis, with its assumption of three full stresses, might be considered artificial. Similarly, in *Mdr* 10/5, *þá's umb skapt — en skipti*, the relative adverb *þá's* 'as, when' (which takes no part in the assonance) must be assumed to be fully stressed in order for the line to match a recognised type (A). On the other hand, just such a pattern is proven by the alliteration in *Hdr* 11/5, *þar's til þengils hersa.*

syllable-final vowel. The odd line carries half-rhyme (*skothending*, whose literal meaning is elusive) consisting of like consonant(s), e. g. *glœdd- : odd* in *Mdr* 13/3. The odd line may optionally contain an *aðalhending* instead of a *skothending*.

Many or most lines are divided by a clear syntactic break or caesura (Kuhn 1929, 1983 §§34, 56, 66; challenged by Hollander, 1953, 196–97 and Gade 1988), which falls between the two *stuðlar* in odd lines and normally between the two rhyming syllables in both odd and even lines. E. g. (verb | object in *Mdr* 2/7):

> bǫ́ru | brimlogs rýri 'bore the surf-fire's diminisher',

or (clause | clause in *Þdr* 7/6):

> stál beit, | en rann sveiti 'steel bit, and gore flowed'.

In a dozen or more lines by Arnórr, however, the concept of the caesura is not useful, since the first and last words of the metrical line are syntactically more closely related to each other than to the middle word(s), or for some other reason. In *Mdr* 14/1, for instance:

> Skeiðr tók Bjarnar bróður 'took the ships of Bjǫrn's brother',

a caesura between the two *stuðlar* would separate two parts of the same kenning.

The strophe (*vísa*) is of eight lines. However, half-strophes or helmings (*helmingar*) are metrically and, with few exceptions, syntactically, self-contained, and they are often preserved in isolation. Out of the 57 complete strophes by Arnórr still extant, 7 are syntactic units, in which line 5 opens with a conjunction introducing a subordinate clause.[5]

The *hrynhent* metre needs little comment, since, as already stated, it is based on the same principles as the *dróttkvætt*. In this metre the line is expanded, typically containing eight syllables and four main stresses. The third foot always takes the form –́ x or ⏑́ x.

[5] The strophes are *Mdr* 5, 10 and 11, *Þdr* 22, *Hdr* 11 and 12, and *Frag* 3.

III Stress Patterns in Arnórr's *Dróttkvætt* Lines

Since the cadence of the metrical line is always a trochee, it is by examining the preceding four or five syllables that the rhythmic preferences of a skald can be discovered. The majority of Arnórr's *dróttkvætt* lines are standard A lines (–́ x –́ x –́ x) or A2k (–́ –̀ ⏑́ x –́ x). The two groups jointly comprise 293 lines, i. e. 65% of the *dróttkvætt* corpus. 170 are odd lines (i. e. 75.5% of all odd lines), 123 even (i. e. 54.4% of even). In about one sixth of these cases (some 29 odd, 16 even lines), the main stresses fall, as normal, on long syllables, but the 'unstressed' fourth position, or more rarely the second, is also occupied by a long syllable which is either the second element of a nominal compound (noun, proper name, adjective or numeral) or an independent monosyllabic nominal, and which elsewhere would frequently carry full or secondary stress. An example is *Skjaldborg raufsk, en skúfar, Hdr* 3/5. Nevertheless, the weight of these syllables is not metrically significant (as it is in A2k lines), and they do not carry internal rhyme, so that they are best treated as 'heavy unstresses', and the lines counted as standard A type (so Kuhn 1983, §42), rather than being treated as a separate sub-category with secondary stress in addition to the two main stresses in the first four syllables (so Sievers 1893, 33 and 103). In any case, the syllables with 'heavy unstress' belong to a continuum of phonetic, grammatical and semantic types, including long derivational syllables such as *(varn)endr*, *(kon)ungr* or *(mild)ingr,* finite verbs such as *slítr*, and less weighty derivational syllables such as *-ug(r)/ -ig(r)*. If *-borg* in *Hdr* 3/5 were treated as a secondary stress, it would be difficult to decide which, if any, of these syllable-types should also be so treated (Kuhn 1983, §42).

The A2k lines are a different case, since here the secondary stress is metrically significant, compensating for the second full stress falling on a short syllable. Only 1 of Arnórr's odd lines is A2k, but 55 even, so that they constitute 12.4% of his *dróttkvætt* corpus.

The trochaic movement of the A lines, especially the 192 (42.6% of the *dróttkvætt* corpus) which contain no secondarily stressed or heavy unstressed syllables, is swift and regular. It often points up moments of resolute action in the hero's career, e. g. *Þdr* 13/5:

Þjóð bar skjótt af skeiðum 'the crew carried swiftly from the ships';

or *Þdr* 17/3:

vé bað vísi knýja 'the leader called for banners to advance',

and the effect is particularly noticeable when there is an unbroken succession of trochaic lines. There are chains of 7 A or A2k lines in the action-filled *Þdr* 13 and *Hdr* 2, and shorter chains are frequent elsewhere in Arnórr's *dróttkvætt* corpus, though they are perhaps not prevalent enough to suggest that this was positively cultivated.[6]

The effect of the trochaic lines is especially vigorous when they contain strongly stressed verbs, as happens in over 100 cases, half of which have the verb in line-initial position, e.g:

Mdr 10/1 Óð með øxi breiða
Hdr 9/5 Dunðu jarlar undan.[7]

Lines with an iambic or rising stress pattern in the first two, or even first four, syllables (Sievers' B and C types, x _́ x _́ _́ x and x _́ ⏑́ x _́ x respectively) can occur only as odd lines, since every even line begins with a stressed and alliterating syllable, and they account for only a tiny proportion of Arnórr's *dróttkvætt* lines. According to my analysis, there are 6 definite cases of B lines (i. e. 2.7% of odd lines), and 5 of C (2.2% of odd lines). The clearest cases, such as the examples given above (p. 82), open with an unambiguously unstressed element — a preposition preceding its noun (*Hdr* 11/3), a relative pronoun such as *sá's* (in *Hdr* 12/5, 14/3), or a conjunction such as *at* or *ef* (which in *Mdr* 5/5 and 11/5, and in *Frag* 3/5, links the two helmings of a strophe). Four B lines (*Rdr* 2/1, *Þdr* 4/1, 15/1 and 16/5) begin with a finite, or, in the difficult *Þdr* 4/1, probably non-finite, verb which could be fully stressed or unstressed, e. g. *Rdr* 2/1:

Réð Heita konr hleyti _́ _̀ x _́ _́ x or x _́ x _́ _́ x .

[6] J. Stephens: '*Dróttkvætt* creates its own metre in which falling rhythm predominates without ruling' (1971, 85). Heusler, on the other hand, emphasised the abundance of non-trochaic rhythms in *dróttkvætt* verse (1925–29, I 298).

[7] The verbal fillings characteristic of the various types of metrical line are examined in J. Turville-Petre 1969 and Kuhn 1983, ch. III; also Fidjestøl 1984, 251–52.

These could therefore be E or B lines; but the patterns of internal rhyme and the word-classes which occupy the syllables favour B rather than E.

A more difficult group, which has to be left with 'either/or' status, comprises lines which could be taken as C or D. The interpretation of these, as of others discussed in this section, is a general problem of skaldic metrics, not specific to Arnórr's poetry. His examples are:

Mdr 1/1 Nú hykk rjóðanda reiðu
Mdr 1/3 — þegi seimbrotar — segja
Mdr 1/5 Vasat ellifu allra
Mdr 8/3 sveið ófǫ́m at Jómi
Mdr 17/3 lét fullhugaðr falla
Þdr 1/1 Nú hykk slíðrhugaðs segja
Þdr 1/3 (þýtr Alfǫður) ýtum
Þdr 22/3 brestr erfiði Austra
Hdr 16/5 Hefr afreka en øfra
Frag 6/1 Hjalp, dýrr konungr, dýrum
Frag 8/1 Svalg áttbogi ylgjar.

Resolution of a short-stemmed disyllable in *Mdr* 1/3 and *Mdr* 1/5, and shortening of *Nú hykk* into *nu hykk* or *nú'kk* (Sievers 1893, 57) in *Mdr* 1/1 and *Þdr* 1/1 is assumed. In all 11 cases the alliteration falls on syllables 2 and 5 (or 3 and 6 where there is resolution of 1–2). The verbal filling always consists of a finite verb in syllable 1 or 1–2 resolved plus, in syllables 2–4 or 3–5, a trisyllabic nominal (noun, adjective, numeral) or an equivalent noun phrase (attributive adjective + noun, in *Frag* 6/1, or disyllabic nominal + preposition, in *Mdr* 8/3). Syllable 3 (4 where there is resolution) is short in all except *Mdr* 1/1 and *Mdr* 8/3. Since finite verbs are frequently found both unstressed and stressed, and since the normal stress pattern for a trisyllabic word or word group would be ´ ` x , with the possibility of ´ ´ x in some circumstances, these lines could reasonably be interpreted either as C (x –́ ⏓́ x –́ x) or D (–́ –́ ⏓̀ x –́ x). In favour of C are the verbal fillings, and the placement of the alliteration, both of which correspond better with Kuhn's description of the C lines (§60a) than that of the D odd lines (§61), although such descriptions can be self-fulfilling. *Mdr* 1/3, *Þdr* 1/3, *Þdr* 22/3 and *Frag* 8/1 belong to a sub-group which Kuhn sees as C, specifically 'Ck^{3}' lines, and designates the 'brestr' type, after Arnórr's *Þdr* 22/3, *brestr erfiði Austra* (1969 and 1983, §§36, 60a, 130), in which the opening verb forms the first part of the hending (*þegi: segja* etc.). However, under this analysis the syllable on which the *hending* falls is assumed to be unstressed, which may be seen as *a priori* unlikely, and which indeed only otherwise occurs in another problem group, of which Sigvatr's *hlýð mínum brag, meiðir* is the classic example (there are no examples in Arnórr). Kuhn takes the 'hlýð' lines as B, but they could be D4 or E (1983, §60).[8] Further, to interpret these eleven odd lines as C is to detach them from structurally identical even lines whose alliteration, inescapably on the first syllable, shows to be D lines, e. g. *Hdr* 3/6, *skaut hoddglǫtuðr oddum* (cf. also *Hdr* 10/4, 14/2).[9] It may be possible to make distinctions within the group of eleven lines: for instance, the negated copula *vasat* in *Mdr* 1/5 may well be unstressed, and hence the line C rather than D; while in *Mdr* 1/1, 1/3 and *Þdr* 1/1, the poetic context (announcing praise and calling for silence) might suggest that the line begins with resolute full stress and is therefore D. However, it seems most reasonable to regard the whole set as of uncertain type. Their rhythmic status must have been obvious when the poems were declaimed, but it may be one of the points which is now beyond recovery.

The remaining lines (Sievers' D and E types) share with the A lines a strongly stressed first syllable, but, in addition to the three main stresses, contain a secondary stress so that the movement is less bouncing, more weighty. Arnórr's *dróttkvætt* poetry contains 23 D lines (5.1% of the *dróttkvætt* corpus), of which all but one are even lines. E lines constitute exactly 25% of the corpus: there are 32 odd lines (i. e. 14.2% of odd lines) and 81 even (35.8% of even). The figures for E lines include a few 'doubtfuls'. In particular, *Mdr* 15/6, *vann Áleifs sonr bannat* could alternatively be D4, and *Þdr* 17/6 *herdrótt rak þar flótta* could be A. Alternation between the regular pulse of the A lines and the heavier and more irregular movement of the D or E lines is a major factor in the characteristically 'choppy' feel of *dróttkvætt* verses. Compound nouns and adjectives are

[8] Fidjestøl (1985, 72) also seems doubtful about Kuhn's treatment of the 'brestr' and 'hlýð' groups.

[9] In a similar way, comparison of *hlýð mínum brag, meiðir* with even lines such as *rann eldr of sjǫt manna*, *Hdr* 1/2, might suggest E rather than B.

particularly common in D and E, so that the lines are frequently descriptive and, in the case of the usually verb-less D lines, rather static. E lines, however, frequently portray action, and in fact they contain finite verbs rather more often than A lines do.

The following is a complete list of Arnórr's *dróttkvætt* lines, classified according to metrical type. The scansions are based on my edited text. In some cases alternative analyses, reflecting other textual or metrical interpretations, are possible.

Analysis of Arnórr's *dróttkvætt* lines

A lines: Rdr 1/1, 1/3, 2/3. Mdr 1/4, 1/8, 2/1, 2/3, 2/5, 3/2, 3/7, 4/1, 4/5, 4/7, 5/3, 5/7, 6/1, 6/3, 6/5, 6/7, 7/1, 7/3, 7/5, 7/6, 7/7, 8/1, 8/5, 8/6, 9/3, 10/1, 10/3, 10/5, 10/7, 11/1, 11/2, 11/7, 12/1, 12/2, 12/3, 13/1, 13/3, 13/4, 13/5, 13/6, 13/7, 14/1, 14/3, 14/4, 15/2, 15/3, 15/5, 15/7, 16/3, 17/1, 17/5, 17/7, 18/1, 18/3, 18/5, 18/7, 19/3. Þdr 3/3, 4/3, 5/1, 5/2, 5/5, 5/7, 6/1, 6/3, 6/7, 7/2, 7/3, 7/5, 7/7, 7/8, 8/1, 8/2, 8/3, 8/7, 9/5, 9/6, 9/7, 10/1, 10/2, 10/4, 10/6, 10/7, 11/1, 11/3, 11/6, 11/7, 12/1, 12/4, 13/2, 13/4, 13/5, 13/7, 14/1, 14/2, 14/3, 15/3, 16/1, 16/3, 16/8, 17/1, 17/3, 17/5, 18/1, 18/2, 18/3, 18/7, 19/2, 19/3, 19/4, 19/5, 19/7, 19/8, 20/3, 20/8, 21/2, 21/3, 22/1, 22/4, 22/5, 23/3. Hdr 1/1, 1/3, 2/2, 2/3, 3/1, 3/3, 3/7, 4/1, 4/3, 4/7, 4/8, 5/1, 5/3, 5/4, 5/5, 5/6, 6/1, 7/1, 7/3, 8/1, 8/3, 8/5, 8/7, 8/8, 9/3, 9/5, 9/8, 10/2, 10/3, 10/6, 10/7, 10/8, 11/1, 11/5, 11/6, 11/7, 12/2, 12/3, 12/4, 12/7, 13/1, 13/3, 13/4, 13/5, 14/1, 15/1, 15/2, 15/3, 15/6, 15/7, 16/3, 16/7, 16/8, 17/1, 17/2, 17/3. Frag 1/1, 1/5, 2/1, 2/2, 2/4, 2/5, 2/8, 3/3, 3/7, 4/1, 8/3, 9/1.

Ah lines (A with heavy unstress): Mdr 1/7, 2/7, 3/1, 3/3, 4/3, 5/8, 7/2, 8/7, 11/3, 12/8. Þdr 2/4, 3/1, 5/3, 6/4, 8/5, 9/2, 9/4, 9/8, 12/3, 13/1, 13/3, 16/7, 18/5, 20/2, 20/6, 20/7. Hdr 2/4, 2/6, 2/7, 3/5, 4/5, 9/1, 9/7, 10/5, 12/1, 13/8, 14/4, 15/5, 15/8, 16/1. Frag 1/7, 1/8, 2/7, 4/3, 5/3.

A2k lines (A with heavy unstress balancing light stress): Rdr 1/4. Mdr 1/6, 2/4, 3/4, 3/6, 4/4, 4/8, 6/4, 6/6, 8/2, 8/8, 9/2, 10/6, 10/8, 11/4, 11/8, 12/6, 15/8, 17/2, 17/6, 18/4, 18/6, 19/4. Þdr 3/4, 4/2, 4/4, 5/4, 6/2, 7/4, 8/8, 11/4, 12/2, 13/6, 14/4, 15/2, 16/4, 17/4, 17/8, 18/4, 22/8. Hdr 2/5, 2/8, 3/2, 3/4, 4/6, 8/4, 11/2, 12/6, 13/2. Frag 1/4, 2/6, 3/4, 3/6, 4/2, 9/2, 10.

B lines: Rdr 2/1. Mdr 5/5. Þdr 4/1, 15/1, 16/5. Hdr 14/3.

C lines: Mdr 11/5, Hdr 11/3, 12/5, 13/7. Frag 3/5.

C/D lines: Mdr 1/1, 1/3, 1/5, 8/3, 17/3. Þdr 1/1, 1/3, 22/3. Hdr 16/5. Frag 6/1, 8/1.

D lines: Rdr 1/2. Mdr 2/2, 2/6, 4/2, 7/4, 11/6, 13/8, 14/2, 16/2, 17/8. Þdr 3/2, 6/8, 20/4, Hdr 3/6, 5/2, 5/8, 6/2, 6/3, 10/4, 11/8, 14/2, 16/6. Frag 4/4.

E lines: Rdr 2/2, 2/4, 3/1, 3/2. Mdr 1/2, 2/8, 3/5, 3/8, 4/6, 5/1, 5/2, 5/4, 5/6, 6/2, 6/8, 7/8, 8/4, 9/1, 9/4, 10/2, 10/4, 12/4, 12/5, 12/7, 13/2, 15/1, 15/4, 15/6, 16/1, 16/4, 17/4, 18/2, 18/8, 19/1, 19/2. Þdr 1/2, 1/4, 2/1, 2/2, 2/3, 5/6, 5/8, 6/5, 6/6, 7/1, 7/6, 8/4, 8/6, 9/1, 9/3, 10/3, 10/5, 10/8, 11/2, 11/5, 11/8, 13/8, 15/4, 16/2, 16/6, 17/2, 17/6, 17/7, 18/6, 18/8, 19/1, 19/6, 20/1, 20/5, 21/1, 21/4, 22/2, 22/6, 22/7, 23/1, 23/2, 23/4. Hdr 1/2, 1/4, 2/1, 3/8, 4/2, 4/4, 5/7, 6/4, 7/2, 7/4, 8/2, 8/6, 9/2, 9/4, 9/6, 10/1, 11/4, 12/8, 13/6, 15/4, 16/2, 16/4, 17/4. Frag 1/2, 1/3, 1/6, 2/3, 3/1, 3/2, 3/8, 5/1, 5/2, 5/4, 6/2, 8/2, 8/4.

The distribution of line-types in Arnórr's *dróttkvætt* poetry is shown in the following table.

Metrical types in *dróttkvætt* poems of Arnórr

O = Odd lines, E = Even lines, T = Total; / means that this line-type cannot occur in even lines.

	RDR			MDR			ÞDR			HDR			FRAGS			TOTAL			
Type	O	E	T	O	E	T	O	E	T	O	E	T	O	E	T	O	E	T	
A	3	0	3	46	11	57	43	21	64	39	17	56	9	3	12	140	52	192	
Ah	0	0	0	7	3	10	9	7	16	9	5	14	4	1	5	29	16	45	
A2k	0	1	1	0	22	22	0	17	17	1	8	9	0	7	7	1	55	56	
(TOTAL A	3	1	4	53	36	89	52	45	97	49	30	79	13	11	24	170	123	293	)
B	1	/	1	1	/	1	3	/	3	1	/	1	0	/	0	6	/	6	
C	0	/	0	1	/	1	0	/	0	3	/	3	1	/	1	5	/	5	
C/D	0	/	0	5	/	5	3	/	3	1	/	1	2	/	2	11	/	11	
D	0	1	1	0	9	9	0	3	3	1	8	9	0	1	1	1	22	23	
E	1	3	4	8	23	31	16	26	42	3	20	23	4	9	13	32	81	113	
TOTAL	5	5	10	68	68	136	74	74	148	58	58	116	20	21	41	225	226	451	

Metrical types in *dróttkvætt* poems of Arnórr: percentage equivalents of above

Percentages are reckoned to the nearest whole %, so that some apparent inaccuracies result, and misrepresentation especially of low numbers. (0) in fact represents 0.4%, rounded down to the nearest %.

	RDR			MDR			ÞDR			HDR			FRAGS			TOTAL		
Type	O	E	T	O	E	T	O	E	T	O	E	T	O	E	T	O	E	T
A	60	0	30	68	16	42	58	28	43	67	29	48	45	14	29	62	23	43
Ah	0	0	0	10	4	7	12	10	11	16	9	12	20	5	12	13	7	10
A2k	0	20	10	0	32	16	0	23	12	2	14	8	0	33	17	(0)	24	12
(TOTAL A	60	20	40	78	53	65	70	61	66	85	52	68	65	53	59	76	54	65)
B	20	/	10	2	/	1	4	/	2	2	/	1	0	/	0	3	/	1
C	0	/	0	2	/	1	0	/	0	5	/	3	5	/	2	2	/	1
C/D	0	/	0	7	/	4	4	/	2	2	/	1	10	/	5	5	/	2
D	0	20	10	0	13	7	0	4	2	2	14	8	0	5	2	(0)	10	5
E	20	60	40	12	34	23	22	35	28	5	35	20	20	43	32	14	36	25
TOTAL:	100 for each column																	

As the table shows, the relative frequency of the various line-types remains fairly consistent across the three main *dróttkvætt* poems, *Magnússdrápa, Þorfinnsdrápa* and *Haraldsdrápa*. A lines are always two or three times more common than the next most numerous, E, and the remaining types taken together never account for more than 12.1% of the total. The minority types are particularly rare in *Þdr*, and E correspondingly more frequent. Points of detail such as the fact that *Hdr* contains 3 out of the 6 certain cases of C, and the only examples of A2k and D in odd lines, are interesting, but involve such small numbers that it would rash to attach great significance to them.

Earlier studies of the metrical practice of skalds by Sievers, Hollander and Kuhn[10] are not directly comparable either with each other or with my figures for Arnórr. However, they do tend to reveal approximately the same frequencies for the various line-types and to

[10] Sievers on Sigvatr Þórðarson, 1893, 102–3, Hollander on a sample of skaldic poetry, 1953, 193–95, and Kuhn on the odd lines of the *dróttkvætt* corpus to 1200, 1983, §§58–65.

suggest that the uniform character of the metre in Arnórr's three main *dróttkvætt* poems, as well as some features such as the sharp difference in the use of odd and even lines, are determined less by the unvarying personal preferences of the skald than by the linguistic and prosodic forms with which he worked.

Proportions of line-types may not be particular to Arnórr or his age, but the detailed manifestations of the underlying types are in at least two instances typical of the eleventh century. The use of 'heavy unstressed' syllables in A lines seems to have been fashionable in the years 1030–66, and is conceivably influenced by Old English verse (Kuhn 1983, §42). The 'brestr' type of C/D line came into use c. 1010 and had its heyday in the mid eleventh century (Kuhn 1983, §60a); and the placing of a stressed, long-stemmed verb at the beginning of a line, as in *Óð með øxi breiða, Mdr* 10/1, is more common in the eleventh and twelfth centuries than earlier (J. Turville-Petre 1969, 343; Kuhn 1969, 408–10). Another innovation into skaldic practice, though one already attested in ninth- and tenth-century verse, is the placing of alliteration in the fourth and fifth syllables of odd lines in the subgroups which Kuhn designates A3, XB and XE. An example is *Mdr* 3/5, *Nótt beið ok dag dróttins*. There are twelve further examples of this placing in Arnórr's *dróttkvætt* verse, eight of them in *Þdr*. All are B or E lines.[11]

IV Stress Patterns in Arnórr's *Hrynhent* Lines

The *hrynhent* lines follow essentially the same patterns as the *dróttkvætt*, but in each case the line is longer by one foot — the third foot — , which always has the stress-pattern ´ x, although the stressed syllable may be long or short. A typical A line is:

Hryn 3/3 yppa rǫ́ðumk yðru kappi   _́ x _́ x _́ x _́ x ,

and an E line:

Hryn 15/6 jarl vissi sik foldar missa   _́ _̀ x _́ _́ x _́ x .

[11] *Mdr* 5/5, 9/1; *Þdr* 4/1, 7/1, 9/3, 15/1, 16/5, 17/7, 20/5, 22/7; *Hdr* 14/3; *Frag* 2/3.

The second half of the line is therefore invariably trochaic, and in the first half, too, trochaic rhythms are strikingly prevalent in early *hrynhent* verse (all six lines of the *Hafgerðingadrápa* are trochaic), a fact which seems to support the theory, mentioned above, of influence from Latin hymns or metrical prayers, which were octosyllabic and strongly trochaic.

Out of Arnórr's 130 *hrynhent* lines, the overwhelming majority are A type. The A2k subtype with secondary stress does not occur, and even the A lines with heavy unstressed syllables mentioned in connection with *dróttkvætt* amount to little more than a dozen. There is therefore little disturbance of the rhythmic alternation of stress and unstress. Lines with iambic openings (i. e. B and C types) do not occur, and there is only one example of D (*Hryn* 15/4, D4) and two of E (*Hryn* 13/2 and 15/6). A further three lines, *Hryn* 3/5, 3/6 and 14/7, may be either A with heavy unstress or E. *Hryn* 3/6 in particular can reasonably be scanned as E: *hverr gramr es þér stóru verri* ´̲ `̲ x ´̲ ´̲ x ´̲ x, but perhaps even here the overwhelmingly trochaic rhythm of the poem suggests a reading with strong stress on the copula *es*, hence an A line with heavy unstress on *gramr*. The rhythmic regularity of the poem is (as Fidjestøl observes, 1984, 250) partly achieved by the near-total avoidance of words of three or four syllables with secondary stress on the second. The sole instance is the necessary place-name Skotborgarǫ in *Hryn* 13/2.

Arnórr's successors developed the *hrynhent* by making fuller use of the variety of metrical patterns. Heusler examined the first two feet (usually four syllables) of *hrynhent* odd lines and reckoned that in Arnórr's work only 2.4% have non-trochaic rhythms. (This tallies with my analysis, if the doubtful lines are A not E.) The proportion of non-trochaic lines rises, Heusler found, to 14% in the *Eiríksdrápa* of Markús Skeggjason, and to 17% in four religious poems which also belong to the twelfth century. With Óláfr hvítaskáld (c. 1240) they reach 30%, only to fall again in the fourteenth century (1925–29, I 303).

Arnórr's *hrynhent* verses, then, are rhythmically less flexible than later *hrynhent* verses and his own *dróttkvætt* poetry, and some, for example *Hryn* 11 and 12, verge on monotony, but on the other hand the pulse can be used to powerful effect. The insistent rhythms of *Hryn* 3:

Magnús, hlýð til máttigs óðar;	Magnús, hear a mighty poem;
manngi veit ek fremra annan;	I know no other more excelling;

produce a commanding ring perfectly suited to the opening of a royal panegyric, and well deserving of the term *hrynhenda* 'flowing metre'. Similarly, the first three lines of *Hryn* 4b, each purely trochaic and each partitioned at the same point into two clauses, the second of which begins with *en*, are resoundingly expressive of the beating of the waves and the plunging advance of the ship:

Vafðir lítt, en vendir bifðusk;	You wavered little, but masts shuddered;
v*art*a hrǫkk, en niðr nam søkkva;	the prow jolted, and started to plunge;
geystisk hlýr, en hristi bára,	the bows surged on, and the billow,
hrími stokkin, búnar grímur.	flecked with rime, shook the adorned figure-heads.

(The highlighting of the verbs by means of internal rhyme and alliteration also increases the dynamic effect.)

V Assonance

The pattern of alliteration and internal rhyme is almost perfectly regular throughout Arnórr's poetry (both *dróttkvætt* and *hrynhent*, which from here on are discussed together) as it stands in the MSS. The five cases where it is not so are mentioned in the Commentary (*Hryn* 4/4, *Hryn* 17/3, *Hryn* 18/3, *Þdr* 13/7 and *Frag* 2/1). Where there is reason to think textual corruption possible and a contextually and metrically satisfactory emendation is to hand, I have emended, but in *Hryn* 18/3 and *Þdr* 13/7 there seems insufficient reason for this, so the possibility remains open that Arnórr very occasionally permitted himself metrical inexactitude.

Despite the apparent rigidity of the skaldic conventions regarding assonance, there are certain variables which a skald may exploit. For instance, it is permissable for the *skothendingar* to contain vowels or diphthongs which are unlike not only in quality but also in quantity, e. g. *Hryn* 10/3 *fastligr : geystri* or *Mdr* 7/7 *bráskat* : *þroski*, but there are only some sixteen examples of this in the whole corpus, which suggests that Arnórr sought a high degree of similarity of phonetic structure in his assonating syllables. (The proportion of *skothendingar* with unequal vowel length is greater in the verses of Þjóðólfr Arnórsson.)

Another variable is the use of consonantal or vocalic alliteration. Consonantal alliteration, being formed by sounds which are identical rather than merely alike, strikes the ear more immediately than vocalic alliteration, and probably more forcibly, since a sequence of consonant and vowel is articulated with a powerful release of sound, by contrast with the unrestricted flow of sound in a vowel (e. g. Trubetzkoy 1969, 94).[12] Thus in *Hryn* 7:

skildir stǫkk með skœðan þokka	the shield-provider of the ship's prow
skeiðar brands fyr þér ór landi	bolted with baleful thought before you from the land,

the explosive *k* of the alliterating *skildir* — *skœðan* — *skeiðar brands* chimes with, and is reinforced by, the *k* of the half-rhyme *stǫkk* : *þokka*, and is well suited to express the rapidity with which Sveinn Alfífuson (the *skildir skeiðar brands*) flees the land, and the malice he feels for Magnús (*þér* in the couplet). Throughout the corpus of Arnórr's verse, vocalic alliteration occurs approximately once in every four couplets; there is little variation between the four major *drápur*. Arnórr's lines frequently contain more assonance than the rules require — *aðalhendingar* in odd lines where only *skothendingar* are necessary, as well as more casual internal rhymes or alliterating syllables which extend or supplement the principal assonances. In the 290 odd lines of Arnórr's poetry there are some 50 *aðalhendingar*, including 17 rhymes of *a* : *ǫ* or *á* : *ǫ́*, which count, as elsewhere in the skaldic corpus up to the twelfth century, as *aðalhendingar* since these pairs also occur in even lines, though less frequently (8 instances; see Hreinn Benediktsson 1963 and Anderson 1973). The proportions (*aðalhendingar* in 17.2% of odd lines when *a* : *ǫ* long and short are included) perhaps suggest that Arnórr permitted, rather than deliberately cultivating, these, but they do sometimes have striking local effect. The verses about Þorfinnr's skirmishes with the Scots are, for instance, particularly rich in examples of extra assonance, which seem to give special power to the exultation over the jarl's bloody victories. *Þdr* 7a contains four *aðalhendingar*, while in *Þdr* 9b *sungu*

[12] Flasdieck (1950, 277) referred to words with initial vowel as belonging to 'the weakest, "auxiliary" group of the dynamic scale'. He supported the view that alliterating initial vowels in Germanic poetry were preceded by a glottal stop which was itself the necessary homophonous device.

— *sunnan* supplements the main alliterative sequence on *þ* in the first couplet. If a chance effect, this is a felicitous one, for the repeated *s* almost mimics the whistling or 'singing' of the swords. Similarly, in *Þdr* 8a *skemmri* and *skjótt*, each of which belongs to a *hending*, alliterate together, adding an extra resonance to the 'official' alliteration of *þrima* — *þvígit* — *þat*. Moreover, the *aðalhendingar* in lines 2 and 4 are both on the same syllable (*skjótt* : *spjótum, dróttinn* : *flótta*), and line 3 echoes the *t* further (*mætr* : *neyti*).

The pattern of metrical stress in Arnórr's poetry overwhelmingly corresponds with, and heightens, that assumed for the spoken prose language, and it is emphasised by the alliteration and to a lesser extent by the internal rhyme. Over half of the syllables that carry alliterating or rhyming sounds belong to nouns, and this tallies with the fact that it is nouns which are most often stressed in spoken prose (as well as with the fact that skaldic verse, like other early Germanic poetry, is strongly noun-dominated). Nearly one quarter of alliterating syllables belong to adjectives, and the remainder to adverbs (including the negative *eigi*), finite verbs, non-finite verbs, pronouns and numerals, in descending order of frequency. A very small minority (two or three cases each) belong to 'grammatical words': relative pronouns or relative adverbs (*hinn's, sá's, þar's*), conjunctions (*áðr* (twice) or *áðr an*), prepositions (*viðr, millum*) and demonstrative articles (*þeirar, þess*)[13]. That the disyllabic words (*millum, þeirar*) carry stress and alliteration is natural, but the other cases of stressed grammatical words are monosyllabic, and furthermore add nothing to the poetic effect of the couplets in which they stand, e. g. *Hryn* 15/3–4:

valgammr skók í vápna rimmu	the corpse-vulture ruffled in the roar of weapons
viðr Helganes blóðugt fiðri.	at Helganes his bloody plumage.

In such cases the skald may be suspected of altering the natural emphasis of the language in the interests of metre, not meaning.

Much the same proportions are found among the rhyming syllables, although syllables belonging to verbs (finite and non-finite) are noticeably more frequent here than in alliteration (this corresponds with the findings of Hollander, 1949, 275–76), and those belonging to

[13] The verses concerned are: *Hryn* 15/4, *Mdr* 14/3, *Þdr* 4/3, 18/1, 22/5, *Hdr* 4/7, 5/6, 9/3, 10/3, 11/5.

nouns are correspondingly fewer, though they still account for half of the total. The most striking difference between the placing of alliteration and of rhyme, however, concerns the second elements of nominal and adjectival compounds. These do not take part in Arnórr's alliteration, except in *Hryn* 14/1, *Hefnir, fenguð yrkisefni*, where the second element of the compound, preceded by a completely unstressed inflexional syllable, naturally bears full stress. In rhyme, however, secondarily stressed elements are freely used, e. g. *gunnbráðr : háði*, *Rdr* 1/4, or *sóltjalda : Rǫgnvaldi*, *Rdr* 3/2. In some ways, therefore, the system of *hendingar*, a specifically skaldic feature of the prosody, departs farther from the hierarchy of emphasis in the everyday language than alliteration does; though it should be mentioned that participation of grammatical words in rhyme is still more rare than in alliteration.[14]

A celebrated feature of skaldic poetry is the comparative freedom of its word-order. Within the helming, clauses may be segmented and set discontinuously in more or less complex patterns, and within individual clauses the ordering of words may depart dramatically from that encountered in the prose language. In this aspect of his art Arnórr characteristically blends moderation with expressive virtuosity, and I have attempted to illustrate this elsewhere (Edwards 1983, II). Here my concern is with the rôle assonance plays in clarifying or obscuring the syntactic relations between words.

In over half of the 290 couplets in Arnórr's poetry the *hǫfuðstafr* and both *stuðlar* belong to the same clause, and in several of these couplet and clause are co-terminous (this is especially frequent in *Mdr*), or the three alliterating syllables mark the boundary of an independent clause. An example of the latter is *Hryn* 9/3–4:

skíði vas þá skriðar of auðit	the ski of the prop was then granted
skorðu; rendi Visundr norðan.	swift motion; Bison charged from the north.

In such cases as these the alliterating staves demarcate and support the syntactic structure. Where the syntactic unit is longer than a couplet, however, this is not necessarily so. In *Mdr* 5/7–8, for example, the alliteration does little to guide comprehension. It will be noted that in the couplet above two of the alliterating words, *skíði* (dat. sing.) and *skorðu* (gen. sing.) form a kenning, 'ski of the ship's prop [ship]'.

[14] *Hryn* 15/4, *Þdr* 4/3, *Hdr* 9/3, 10/3, 11/5.

This is one of some twenty examples of couplets in which two alliterating syllables belong to the same kenning; and there are nearly fifty instances of pairs of adjective-and-noun (including base words of kennings), and a further forty of such pairs as subject-and-verb, verb-and-object, possessive genitive-and-noun or grammatically parallel adjectives. In at least a dozen couplets, all three alliterating syllables are syntactically close, e. g. *Mdr* 5/5–6, *í gný grimmum / grafnings* 'in the cruel clash of the graven shield' (adjective-and-kenning). Thus it is quite common in Arnórr's verses (over 40% of couplets) for the alliteration to set in strong relief two words which are very closely linked in the syntax. This may be no more than the natural product of the linguistic and metrical forms, and contrary instances could be quoted, in which the alliterating words are either syntactically unconnected or else only loosely connected, e. g. *Hdr* 1/1–2, where *rauð, rýrt* and *rann* all belong to different clauses, but that is an extreme case and not representative: the general effect of the alliteration in Arnórr's poetry is to clarify, rather than obscure, the syntactic structure of the lines.

The rôle of internal rhyme is different. The *hendingar* fall on words which belong to the same clause in approximately two-thirds of Arnórr's lines, but they relatively seldom emphasise the link between elements of the same kenning, or between other tight syntactic units such as adjective-and-noun. There are instances of this, such as *Mdr* 6/2, *snarfengjan bar þengil* 'carried the quick-acting lord', or *Hdr* 6/2, *reiðr Eydana meiðir* 'wrathful harmer of Isle-Danes'; but one cannot in general regard the internal rhyme as a means of illuminating syntactic structure.

PART TWO

TEXT

Presentation of the Text

I Outline

The poems are given in their supposed chronological order of composition, beginning with *Rǫgnvaldsdrápa*; the miscellaneous fragments are placed last. Each poem is presented in the following format, the details of which are given in sections II to IV below.

Edited text with translation

Edited (normalised and emended) texts of the whole corpus are, for easy consultation, placed together on pp. 113–35. Each poem is presented as a continuous reading text, reconstructed in accordance with the principles proposed in Chapter Two. The verses are grouped under general headings (e. g. 'Exordium', 'Return to Norway') which may suggest the possible structure of the original poem. The individual verses also have synoptic headings.

The text is that of the best MS available, with variant readings from other MSS silently incorporated where necessary. Emendations, i. e. readings which occur in no MS, are italicised. The orthography is 'normalised' in order to make reading easier and to recapture as closely as possible the linguistic forms of Arnórr's time.

Parallel with the text is an English translation, which is designed to convey first the meaning of the original and second something of its style, as far as is possible without straining the English to the point of incomprehensibility. Thus the arrangement of words and clauses is preserved where possible, but the intricacies of the original word-order and the syntactic differences between the two languages mean that the translation can seldom be truly parallel. Similarly, I make informal use of alliteration, but do not attempt to reproduce the original patterns of rhythm or internal rhyme. Some of the English vocabulary chosen is archaic or 'poetic', in an attempt to suggest the variety and the peculiarly poetic flavour of the original.

Diplomatic text and commentary

This a verse-by-verse study, presenting among other things all the MS evidence required for the establishment of the text, and discussion of the interpretations on which the edited text rests.

Under the heading **Sources** the relevant printed works and MSS are listed. For *Fagrskinna*, *Heimskringla*, *Knýtlinga saga* and *Orkneyinga saga* references are to the editions in the Íslenzk Fornrit series, but the earlier editions listed in the Bibliography should be consulted for fuller textual information. The first MS to be listed is in each case the main MS for the verse, selected on the basis of its textual history and of the quality of its readings, in general and in the verse in question. Folio numbers are indicated, except that for Flateyjarbók (Fl) the numbers refer to columns.

The **Context** is a summary of the prose passage(s) within which the verse is preserved, including the introductory words, where these are of particular interest (i. e. fuller than routine tags such as *sem Arnórr segir*).

The **Diplomatic text** is printed unemended from the main MS, and alongside it the **Edited text**, reproduced from the continuous reading text in order to show clearly what editorial decisions have been made.[1]

The **Prose order** is set below: the edited text, with the words re-ordered as though in prose. This is admittedly an artificial construct which does poor justice to the original, producing awkwardnesses which are not apparent in the poetic lines and forcing elements such as adverbials or apostrophes to be assigned to a single clause, whereas in the original they may qualify more than one clause, or indeed the whole helming (see Edwards 1983, 171–73 on cases of *apo koinou*). The Prose order is nevertheless a useful aid that enables the syntactic arrangement of the verse as I construe it to be seen at a glance. Emendations are again italicised and readings adopted from MSS other than the main MS are incorporated.

A **Translation** accompanies the Prose order, following its word-order as closely as is reasonable. In other respects it is virtually identical with the translation included in the continuous reading text.

[1] I am pleased to acknowledge here that the adoption of this format was influenced by the layout of the text in Davidson 1983. I am also grateful to Mr P. J. Frankis for providing a 'reader response' to a number of alternative layouts.

Kennings are explained in square brackets, as are references to particular persons, where this is necessary. Where no explanation is given it can be assumed that terms for warriors, heroes or rulers refer to the main hero of the *drápa* in question.

The (Critical) **Apparatus** contains all variant readings which are of potential significance.

The **Commentary** concerns points of interest or difficulty in the vocabulary, syntax or subject-matter of the text. Variant readings are evaluated, except for those which are clearly nonsensical or which the sum of the MS evidence shows beyond reasonable doubt to be scribal errors or alterations. Words and phrases under discussion are given in the MS orthography in the headings (e. g. 3/4 *iqvęþi flioto*), but thereafter in normalised orthography, except where the MS spelling as such is under discussion. In considering textual cruces I am indebted to discussions by previous scholars, but my references to these are not exhaustive, for editorial conjectures which are particularly ill-supported are not mentioned. Explanations of standard points of grammar are not routinely given in the Commentary, since this has been considered unnecessary for the likely readership of the book. By the same token, it is hoped that the Commentary and other materials in Part Two will furnish enough guidance to any problematic items of vocabulary, while other items will be familiar or readily checked in the standard lexicons, making a formal Glossary unnecessary.

II The Edited Text

The normalised orthography adopted here, and in the Prose Order versions of the verses that derive from it, is that used by most earlier editors of poetry of the same period (e. g. by Finnur Jónsson in *Skjald* B, E. A. Kock in *Skaldediktningen* and the editors of Íslenzk Fornrit). It is difficult to establish the appropriate spelling in certain cases where phonological alternatives exist, e. g. *Áleifr/Óláfr* or *morgunn/morginn*, but I have attempted to give a text as nearly possible authentic for the eleventh century. Individual choices of form are based on the evidence of skaldic versification (especially rhymes by Arnórr and other eleventh-century skalds) and of runic inscriptions and early MS spellings, and on the information yielded by the standard grammars (especially that of Noreen, 1923) about the etymology of words and their development in ON. Where in doubt about the appropriate spelling of a word, I have chosen to err on the side of the more archaic form. Points of particular interest are noted in the Commentary.

Certain questions of normalisation arise repeatedly throughout the text, and the conventions I have adopted in these cases are outlined here.

A. Superfluous syllables in MS text

Several of Arnórr's *dróttkvætt* lines, as they stand in the MSS, contain seven instead of the usual six syllables, and some *hrynhent* lines have nine instead of the usual eight. In many of these lines 'resolution' can be assumed to be present (see p. 81); but there are many which cannot be scanned thus, and these contain words and phrases for which there is a possible variation in pronunciation between contracted, monosyllabic forms, and longer, disyllabic forms (or between disyllabic and trisyllabic respectively). Examples are *hykk / hygg ek* 'I think', *gervik / gervi ek* 'I do', *fyr / fyrir* 'before, in front of' and *svát / svá at* 'so that'. Scholars in the last century, notably Eduard Sievers, sought to demonstrate that the contracted forms (*fyr* etc.) were favoured by the skalds of the tenth to twelfth centuries, and that the longer forms (*fyrir* etc.) which abound in the MSS were introduced by scribes when the verses were committed to writing from c. 1200 onwards (1878, 449–514).

The licence of using contracted forms is sanctioned by Snorri, who refers to it as *bragarmál* (*SnE* p. 219), and the evidence of skaldic metre certainly favours the almost universal restoration of contracted forms in certain categories of words and phrases, while in others it appears that skalds of the eleventh century used both longer and shorter variants at need.

In my edited text I restore the shorter, contracted form where the evidence (especially from Arnórr) is decisively in favour of this, and mark the contraction where possible by an apostrophe. For example, the subordinating conjunction *at* 'that', following an adverb, is always contracted, hence *svá't*, *þótt* and *því't*, as in *Mdr* 11/7 — *ǫld lá vítt — þótt vildi* (the MS here reads *þott*, not *þo at*). Similarly the prepositions usually written *fyrir*, *undir* and *yfir* in the MSS and the verb *hefi(r)* 'has' are always contracted (respectively *fyr*, *und*, *of* and *hef(r)*).

On the other hand, there are cases where longer, uncontracted forms are demanded by the metre. Thus the copula *es* (MS *er*) is syllabic in 5 cases, e. g. *Hryn* 3/6 *hverr gramr es þér stóru verri*, but contracted in 5 other cases, e. g. *Hdr* 15/1 *myrkt's, hverr meira orkar*. Similarly, the enclitic *ek* 'I', *þú / tu* 'you', and *es* (MSS *er*) 'who, which' (relative particle) or 'as, when' (conjunction) occur in both contracted and uncontracted forms.

B. Normalisation of MS spellings

(a) MSS *er*, relative particle and conjunction. Normalised *es* (contracted *'s*) is established by the internal rhyme in *Hdr* 11/5: *þar's* [v. l. *þá's*] *til þengils hersa* (Sievers 1878, 497; he includes some possible examples of *er* from the 11th century).

(b) MSS *er(t)* 'is, are', 3rd and 2nd sing. pres. verb. Normalised *es(t)*, also infin. *vesa* and past *vas(t)*, are required since the *-r-* forms do not appear until the mid 12th century (Sievers 1878, 492; Noreen 1923, §498, anm. 6 and §532, anm. 1).

(c) MSS *kuðr/kunnr, maðr/mannr, saðr/sannr* and *suðr/sunnr*. It appears from the rhymes *Hryn* 13/7 *kunnr : runnin* and *Þdr* 5/8 *mannr: -ranni* that *-nnr* not *-ðr* was the form used by the skald in these words, and it has been levelled throughout the edited text.

(d) MSS *-lld-/-ld-* and *-nnd-/-nd-* in the past tense of weak verbs: normalised *-ld-* and *-nd-*. The past of verbs such as *fylla* and *spenna* etymologically has a geminate consonant, so *fylldi, spenndi* etc. But such forms as these rhyme in Arnórr's verse on words containing *-ld-* and *-nd-* (e. g. *hendr : spendi*), but not on *-ll-* and *-nn-*, so that it seems legitimate to assume that shortening of *ll, nn* before *d* had already taken place by Arnórr's time.

(e) MSS *-lð-/-ld-* and *-nð-/-nd-*: normalised *ld* and *nd*. It is usually maintained that *ð* following a long root syllable ending in *l/n* had changed to *d* by Arnórr's time,[2] and this spelling is used in the edited text, e. g. *deildisk* but (after a short root syllable) *dunði*.[3]

(f) MSS *of/um*: normalised *of*. *Um*, developed from *umb*, is very common as preposition and expletive particle in all Icelandic MSS but

[2] On this change, see Celander 1906, Noreen 1923, §238, 1, b, and Jakob Benediktsson 1960.

[3] The oldest Icelandic MSS have no trace of the change *ð>d* after *l/n* in words with an original short root syllable (such as *dunðu, valði* or *synð*), and the evidence of skaldic rhymes suggests that it did not take place in Icelandic until c. 1300 (so Celander 1906, 43–44 and 60).

the earliest; but *of* is the appropriate form for Icelandic up to the 12th century and is restored in the edited text, e. g. *Hryn* 12/1 (as a preposition): *fórt of óþjóð eldi* 'you advanced through the evil folk with flame' and in *Hryn* 11/7 (as an expletive particle): *flaustum varð þá flóð of ristit* 'by ships the flood was cloven then'. The only exception to this is that *um*, in the spelling *umb*,[4] has been retained when the context requires a preposition with the distinct sense 'about, around' (referring to space, not time), since *um(b)* had this function even in early Icelandic.[5] An example, from *Hdr* 13, is:

køru ...	they chose
umb folksnaran fylki	around their battle-keen captain
falla liðsmenn allir.	to fall, all the liegemen.

The preposition *of* in the sense 'over, above' is often represented in the MSS by *yfir*, as mentioned above.

III The Diplomatic Text

This is based on a fresh reading of the relevant MSS, where necessary using ultraviolet light. It aims to be faithful to the MS renderings of the verses, within reason, i. e. within the constraints of what is typographically possible, and what is necessary to the establishment of Arnórr's text. Insofar as the reproduction of the MSS is slightly less than exact, therefore, the text may be regarded as semi-diplomatic rather than fully diplomatic.

Lineation

The verses are set out as metrical lines in my text even when written continuously, as though prose, in the main MS.

[4] *Umb* is the appropriate form for the 11th century. See, e. g., Noreen 1923, §278, anm. 1.

[5] For extended discussions of *of* and *um(b)* in ON, see Kuhn 1929, Foote 1955, and Fidjestøl 1989.

Punctuation

Most vellum MSS have a stop or other punctuation mark at the close of each strophe or half-strophe. I print a final stop even where none is present in the main MS. No other punctuation is used.

Orthography and word division

The orthography of the MSS is reproduced, except that variant forms of the same letter are not reproduced, so that, e. g., printed *r* represents MS *r* and *r* rotunda (similar in shape to an Arabic 2), and printed *av* and *aa* represent these letters written separately or as a ligature.

Some pairs of graphs are not clearly differentiated in certain MSS, e. g. *u* and *v* or upper and lower case *S* / *s*, but I follow the MSS as accurately as possible. The same is true of word divisions.

Diacritics

Accent signs over vowels, e. g. *á, í,* are reproduced, since these have phonological significance in some MSS. Neither the dot over *y* nor the diagonal flourish over *u* used by some scribes is reproduced, since not phonologically significant. Printed *i* is used to represent its dotless counterpart in MSS.

Abbreviations

These are given in expanded form, and are marked by italicisation. In expanding an abbreviated form I have been guided by the unabbreviated spelling of the word in the same MS or, failing that, by the spelling of the MS in general. In cases where it has not been possible to determine whether *f* with superscript vertical flourish (f̍) represents *fyr, fir, fyrir*, or *firir*, I use *fyrir* as the expanded form.

Scribal corrections

Where a scribe has corrected himself by means of deletion marks, superscript letters, etc., I give the second, corrected form without comment.

IV The Critical Apparatus

A. Selection of variants

I seek to give all the variant readings which are of significance for the textual criticism of Arnórr's poetry, and the general principles of selection are set out in section A1 below. Where I have departed from these principles it has been in the direction of giving more, rather than fewer, variants, and the commonest reasons for doing so are outlined in section A2. In section C the practical application of the general principles is illustrated: the full MS texts for *Rdr* 1 are presented in parallel, and can be compared with the critical apparatus that has been drawn from them (pp. 110–11).

1. General principles

(a) Purely orthographic variants are not noted, e. g. for *Rdr* 1/3 the entry 'niørdr 4, 61, 325V, 325VII, Bb (or mordr), Th, 332, Fl' covers five different spellings, *niørdr*, *níordr*, *niordr*, *niorðr* and *niavrdr*, since all the vowel symbols have the same value in the orthography of the MSS concerned, representing the reflex of Gmc *e*, with breaking and *u*-mutation, and *d/ð* are likewise equivalent.

(b) Variants routinely produced by phonetic change are not noted, since the MS spellings so often reflect the linguistic features proper to the time and place at which the MS was written, rather than those of the composition of the poem, e. g. *ec/eg*, *hlaut/laut* or *hriðir/riðir*.

(c) By-forms of the same word or phrase are not noted, e. g. *enn/inn/hinn* or *giǫrva/gerva*.

(d) Morphological variants are not noted, e. g. *kunnit/kunnut* 'know, can' (2nd pl. pres.).

(e) Numerals such as '.x.' or 'iiii' are not noted if the word is spelt in full in the main MS; but if the main MS has a numeral only, variants with the word fully spelt are included in the apparatus, e. g. in *Rdr* 1/3 the main MS has '.x.', and *tíu* is included in the apparatus, but in *Hryn* 14/5 where the main MS has *fiorar* the variant 'iiii' is not included.

2. Departures from the principles: cases where more variants may be given

(a) Where there exists the possibility of confusion between two words which are phonologically similar, but not identical. In *Hryn* 5/2, for instance, the main MS has *yGr* and v. l. *ygr* is included in the apparatus, since (i) *Yggr* 'Óðinn, Terrible One' and (ii) *ýgr* 'fierce' both exist.

(b) Where a rare word or name is involved, e. g. in *Frag* 7/1 where main MS *Mikáll* and v. l. *Mikiall* are both given.

(c) Where there is any uncertainty about the identity of a variant. As a case in point: in *Hryn* 10/4 Fl has *fyrris*, where all others, including the main MS K, have *fyris*. The use of double or single consonant spellings is erratic in Fl, so that it is not certain whether the same or a different reading is at hand here.

(d) Where the spelling of a word could be of interest, as in *Hryn* 11/2 *hylmis/hilmís*, where the spelling adopted in the edited text differs from that of the main MS.

B. Presentation of variants

The same conventions are followed in the critical apparatus as in the diplomatic text (see pp. 106–7), with the addition of the following in the case of omitted or illegible words.

(a) Where a MS, by comparison with others of the same recension, lacks a word or words and is not physically damaged, this is shown by, e. g., '**bygðir]** om. W' ('om.' for 'omitted').

(b) In a few cases where a reading is unclear because of poor calligraphy rather than damage to the MS, this is shown by a question mark; e. g. '**hélug]** heilug J2(?), 47' indicates that *heilug* is clear in 47 but not in J2.

(c) Where part of a word is illegible because of a tear, rubbing or fading in the MS, it is shown by an ellipsis (...). The number of dots does not indicate the possible number of letters missing.

(d) Where a whole word or line is illegible this is shown by, e. g., '**hæstan]** illeg. 757'.

C. Specimen of critical apparatus: *Rǫgnvaldsdrápa* 1.

The full text from all relevant MSS is shown here. The text and apparatus drawn from these readings may be compared on pp. 137–38.

2	Deilldiz af sva alldin
4	Deilldiz af s*va* at alldin
61	Deilldiz af þviat alld*ri*
321	deilldiz af sem alldin
325V	Deilldiz af sva at alld*ri*
325VII	Dæilldiz af sua at alldun
Bb	Deilldizt af sva at alldri
Th	Deilldizt af s*er*i alld*ri*
325III	Deilðiz af sem alldin
332	Deildiz af sva at aldin
702	Deilldiz af sva at alld*ir*
Fl	Dæilldízst af suo at alld*ir*
(48m)	(alldin)
2	el g*ra*fni*n*ga þelar
4	el grafninga þelar
61	els g*ra*fninga þelar
321	el grafninga þelaz
325V	iel g*ar*fıııga þelar
325VII	el g*ra*mninga þelar
Bb	ęl g*ra*mnínga þęlar
Th	el g*ra*fni*n*ga þelar
325III	æl grafningia þælar
332	el gramni*n*ga þelar
702	el g*ra*fninga hvela
Fl	el grafni*n*ga þelar
(48m)	(gramninga)
2	gavndlar ıııoðr í gavrþv*m*
4	gavn*n*dlar niørdr igǿrdum
61	guɴlar níordr igaurdv*m*
321	gaundlar ar i gaurdum
325V	guɴaʀ niorðr i gavrdv*m*
325VII	gavndlar niavrdr i gavrdu*m*
Bb	gȯnlar ıııordr i gavrdvm

Th	gunlar niordr j gaurdu*m*
325III	gvNar vorðr igavrðvm
332	guN*ar* niorðr i gorðum
702	Gun*n*ar vòrdr i gòrdu*m*
Fl	gun*n*ar níordr j górdu
2	gvNbraþr .x. háþi
4	gun*n*bradr .x. haðe
61	gun*n*bradr tíu haadi
321	gun*n*bradr tio hadi
325V	gvn*n*braðr tiu haði
325VII	gunb*r*aþr tiu haðe
Bb	gun*n*brad .x. hadi
Th	gun*n*bradr tiv hadí
325III	gun*n*braðr tiv haði
332	gun*n*braþr x hadi
702	gim*m*bradr x hädi
Fl	gun*n*bradr tíu hade.

Edited Text, with Translation

Rǫgnvaldsdrápa

1. *Ten battles are fought in Garðar*

Deildisk af svá't aldin
él grafninga þélar
gǫndlar Njǫrðr í Gǫrðum
gunnbráðr tíu háði.

It so fell out that ten ancient
snow-storms of the graven shields' rasp
the Njǫrðr of battle, hasty in war,
brought about in Garðar.

2. *Arnórr gains renown through marriage into the jarl's family*

Réð Heita konr hleyti
herþarfr við mik gerva;
styrk lét oss of orkat
jarls mægð af því frægðar.

Heiti's scion, beneficent to hosts,
made a marriage-alliance with me;
because of that the strong brother-bond
with the jarl brought me renown.

3. *Prayer for Rǫgnvaldr*

Sannr stillir, hjalp snjǫllum,
sóltjalda, Rǫgnvaldi.

True ruler of the sun's awnings,
help the prudent Rǫgnvaldr.

Hrynhenda

Exordium

1. *Arnórr's trading voyage*

Kljúfa lét'k í kaupfǫr dúfu
knarra minn við borð en stinnu.

I made my bark cleave the billow
with its firm strakes on a trading voyage.

2. *Rowing in rough seas*

Seinkun varð, þá's hlébarðs hanka
hnika*ði* ǫ́r en ljóta bára.

There was drag, as the foul breaker
drove against the oar of the cleat-bear.

3. *Call for a hearing; general praise of Magnús*

Magnús, hlýð til máttigs óðar; manngi veit ek fremra annan; yppa rǿðumk yðru kappi, Jóta gramr, í kvæði fljótu. Haukr réttr estu, Hǫrða dróttinn; hverr gramr es þér stóru verri; meiri verði þinn an þeira þrifnuðr allr, unz himinn rifnar.	Magnús, hear a mighty poem; I know no other is more excelling; I mean to raise up your prowess, prince of Jutes, in a swift-running song. A just hawk you are, Hordalanders' lord; every prince is far below you; may your whole success surpass theirs, until the sky is riven.

Magnús's return to Norway

4. *Voyage west over the Baltic; rough seas*

Herskip vannt af harða stinnum hlunni geyst í Salt et Eystra; skjǫldungr, stétt á skǫrum hvéldan skeiðar húf með girzku *rei*ði. Vafðir lítt, en vendir bifðusk; v*art*a hrǫkk, en niðr nam søkkva; geystisk hlýr, en hrist*i* bára, hrími stokkin, búnar grímur.	War-ships you made from the most firm launcher to speed into the Eastern Salt; king, you boarded the ship's hull, curved by its jointed planks, and with Russian tackle. You wavered little, but masts shuddered; the prow jolted, and started to plunge; the bows surged on, and the billow, flecked with rime, shook the adorned figure-heads.

5. *March across Sweden; Swedes join Magnús's force*

Rauðar bǫ́ruð randir síðan, rimmu Yggr, of sœnskar byggðir; eigi gaztu liðskost lágan; landsfolk sótti þér til handa.	Next you carried scarlet targes, battle-Óðinn, through Swedish settlements; no mean pick of troops you gained; the men of the land put themselves in your hands.
Austan þurðuð, ulfa ferðar ǫldum kunnr, með hvíta skjǫldu, tungurjóðr, til tírar þinga teknir menn, ok dǫrr en reknu.	From the east you swept, wolf-pack's tongue-reddener, with white shields, renowned to peoples, men chosen for glorious encounters, and with chased spears.

6. *Magnús arrives in Þrœndalǫg; his enemies are in terror*

Austan komt með allra hæstum, Yggjar mǫ́s, í þrœnzkar byggðir, fiðrirjóðr, — en fjandmenn yðra falma kvǫ́ðu — œgishjalmi. Breiðask vissu, blágamms fœðir benja kolgu, yðrir dolgar — hræddir urðu fjǫrvi at forða fjandmenn þínir — vesǫld sína.	From the east you came with highest of all helm of terror, to the Þrœndalǫg settlements, feather-reddener of Óðinn's gull, and your foemen were said to falter. Your enemies knew, feeder of the swart vulture of wound-surf, that their wretchedness — in fear your foemen were forced to save their lives — was growing.

7. *Magnús's rival [Sveinn Alfífuson] is forced to flee*

Ungan frá'k þik, eyðir, þrøngva,
ulfa gráðar, þeira ráði;
skildir stǫkk með skœðan þokka
skeiðar brands fyr þér ór landi.

I have heard that, young, you constrained,
queller of wolves' greed, their course;
the shield-provider of the ship's prow bolted
with baleful thought before you from the land.

8. *Magnús, still a youth, gains Norway*

Eignask namtu óðal þegna,
allan Nóreg, gotna spjalli;
manngi ryðr þér mildingr annarr,
Mœra gramr, til landa œr*i*.

You came to win the estates of liegemen,
all of Norway, counseller of men;
no other monarch will clear himself lands,
King of the Mœrir, younger than you.

Expedition to Denmark

9. *Magnús launches a large fleet south; splendour of his ship and troops.*

Síðan vas þat's sunnr með láði
siklingr ýtti flota miklum;
skíði vas þá skriðar of auðit
skorðu; rendi Visundr norðan.
Samnask bað til hverrar hǫmlu
— hræðask menn við ættar klæði
Gjúka; þótti gǫfugt eiki
girzkum malmi — Peitu hjalma.

Later it happened that south along the coast
the sovereign launched a great fleet;
the ski of the ship's prop was then granted
swift motion; Bison charged from the north.
He urged to rally at every rowlock
— men fear the garments of Gjúki's
offspring; splendid seemed the bark
with its Russian metal — helmets of Poitou.

10. *Rough voyage past Stavanger to Denmark; splendour of the ship*

Ljótu dreif á lypting útan
lauðri — bifðisk goll et rauða;
fastligr hneigði fúru geystri
fýris garmr — ok skeiðar stýri.
Stirðum helzt umb Stafangr norðan
stǫlum — bifðusk fyrir álar;
uppi glóðu élmars typpi
eldi glík — í Danaveldi.

Foul surf surged in against the
poop — the red gold shuddered;
powerful, the fir-tree's hound pitched the rushing
ship of fir — and the galley's helm.
Sturdy prows you steered from the north
by Stavanger — currents foamed in front;
mast-heads of the storm-steed glowed aloft
like fire — to the realm of the Danes.

Campaign against the Wends

11. *Magnús launches a huge fleet against the Wends; the skald announces a new section*

Heyra skalt, hvé herskjǫld bǫ́ruð,	You shall hear how you carried the war-shield,
hilmis kundr, til Venða grundar	ruler's kinsman, to the land of the Wends
— heppinn drótt af hlunni sléttum	— well-starred, you dragged from the smooth launcher
hélug bǫrð — í stefjaméli.	rime-spread prows — in a refrain-section.
Aldri frá'k — en, vísi, valdið	Never have I heard — and, prince, you cause
Venða sorg — at dǫglingr spenði	grief for the Wends — of a sovereign steering
(flaustum varð þá flóð of ristit)	(by keels the flood was cloven then)
fleiri skip til óðals þeira.	more ships against their patrimony.

12. *Magnús subdues the men of Jóm by fire*

Skjǫldungr, fórt of óþjóð eldi;	King, you fared through the evil tribe with flame;
auðit vas þá flotnum dauða;	fated then was death to men;
hæstan kynduð, hlenna þrýstir,	crusher of thieves, you kindled a towering
hyrjar ljóma sunnr at Jómi.	blaze of fire south at Jóm.
Hvergi þorði hallir varða	No wise dared they halls defend,
heiðit folk í virki breiðu;	the heathen host in the broad stronghold;
buðlungr, unnuð borgarmǫnnum	royal one, you wrought in the townsmen,
bjǫrtum eldi stalldræp hjǫrtu.	by bright flame, terror-struck hearts.

13. *Magnús defeats a superior force near the Skotborg river [Hlýrskógsheiðr]*

Skjǫldungr, lézt við skíra valdit	King, you caused by the gleaming
Skotborgarǫ́ Venða sorgum;	Skotborg river griefs to come upon the Wends;
yngvi, vas sá frægr, es fenguð,	sovereign, that, your success, was famed,
fǫrnuðr þinn, við helming minna.	which you won with the smaller troop.
Vári, lá þar valkǫstr hæri,	Defender, renowned to men, a corpse-pile lay there higher
— vas þér sigr skapaðr grams ens digra —	— victory of the stout lord was fated to you —
virðum kunn*r*, an víða runnin	than the clan of wolves, run from far and wide,
varga ætt of klífa mætti.	could scale.

War against Sveinn Ulfsson

14. *Magnús's deeds provide matter for verse; he fights four battles in one season*

Hefnir, fenguð yrkisefni,
Áleifs; gervi'k slíkt at mǫlum;
Hlakkar lætr þú hrælǫg drekka
hauka; nú mun kvæðit aukask.
Fjórar hefr þú, randa rýrir
reyrar setrs, á einum vetri
— allvaldr, estu ofvægr kallaðr —
ǫrva hríðir frœkn of gǫrvar.

Avenger of Óláfr, you furnished matter
for verse; I fashion such deeds into words;
hawks of Hlǫkk you allow to quaff
the corpse-sea; now will the poem swell.
Hewer of the shield-reed's home,
you have, in a single season,
— all-ruler, you are called invincible —
four arrow-blizzards daring performed.

15. *Glorious battle off Helganes; Magnús wins land and ships from the jarl*

Keppinn vannt, þat's æ mun uppi,
Yggjar veðr, meðan heimrinn byggvisk;
valgammr skók í vápna rimmu
viðr Helganes blóðugt fiðri.
Yngvi fekktu ǫll með hringum
— jarl vissi sik foldar missa —
þjóðum kunnr, (en þú tókt síðan)
þeira flaust (við sigri meira).

Thrustful, you fought a wind-storm of Yggr
which will ever be extolled while the world is peopled;
the corpse-vulture ruffled in the roar of weapons
at Helganes his bloody plumage.
Sovereign, you seized every single
— the viceroy felt his loss of land —
galley of theirs, renowned to men,
and then you gained a greater victory.

General Praise

16. *Magnús the seafarer*

Ótti, kunnuð elgjum hætta
œðiveðrs á skelfðan grœði,
fengins golls, eða fœðið ella
flestan aldr und drifnu tjaldi.

Terror of seized gold, you expertly
risk elks of the raging gale on the
tossing swell, or else you pass
the most part of your life under spray-drenched awnings.

Glíkan berr þik hvǫssum hauki,
hollvinr minn, í lypting innan
— aldri skríðr und fylki fríðra
farligt eiki — Visundr snarla.

Bison carries you, like a keen hawk,
my true friend, inside the poop
— never shall glide with finer prince aboard
a goodly oak — swiftly.

17. *Magnús's fame and courage; glory of his fleet*

Eigi létuð, jǫfra bági,
yðru nafni mannkyn hafna;
hvártki flýrðu, hlenna *rýr*ir,
hyr né malm í broddi styrjar.

You did not allow, subduer of lords,
the race of men to neglect your name;
you flee neither, destroyer of thieves,
fire nor steel in the forefront of battle.

Hlunna es, sem rǫðull renni,
reiðar búningr, upp í heiði,
— hrósa'k því es herskip glæsir
hlenna dolgr — eða vitar brenni.

The array of the chariot of launchers is as though
the sun were racing up in the bright sky,
— this I praise, how his warships he adorns,
the foe of thieves — or beacons flaring.

18. *Glory of Magnús's fleet*

Mǫnnum lízk, es mildingr rennir
Meita hlíðir sævar skíði,
unnir jafnt sem ósamt renni
engla fylki himna þengils.

It seems to men, as the ruler makes
the ski of the ocean skim Meiti's slopes,
just as though skimming the waves with him
were the angel-host of the skies' prince.

19. *Magnús's popularity; fame of his retainers*

Eyðendr fregn'k at elska þjóðir
— inndrótt þín es hǫfð at minnum —
grœði lostins goði et næsta
geima vals í þessum heimi.

I hear that men love him who clears
— your personal troop is held in memory —
the steed of the ocean, lashed by the surge,
next after God in this world.

20. *Magnús is for ever unsurpassed*

Skjǫldungr, mun þér annarr aldri
œðri gramr und sólu fœðask.

King, never will another lord,
loftier than you, be born under the sun.

Magnússdrápa

Exordium; Magnús's return to Norway

1. *The skald announces his encomium; Magnús is ten years old when he sails from Russia*

Nú hykk rjóðanda reiðu
rógǫrs, því't veit'k gǫrva,
— þegi seimbrotar — segja
seggjum hneitis eggja.
Vasat ellifu allra
ormsetrs hati vetra,
hraustr þá's herskip glæsti
Hǫrða vinr ór Gǫrðum.

Now I mean to tell men, for
fully I know it, of the career of the
strife-quick — gold-breakers be silent —
reddener of the sword's edges.
Not fully eleven winters was
the hater of the reptile's home
when, dauntless, the friend of
Hordalanders arrayed warships to leave Garðar.

2. *Magnús musters his fine troops and sails to Sigtún*

Þing bauð út enn ungi
eggrjóðandi þjóðum;
fim bar hirð til hǫmlu
hervæðr ara bræðis.
Salt skar húfi héltum
hraustr þjóðkonungr austan;
bǫru brimlogs rýri
brún veðr at Sigtúnum.

The young reddener of edges
summoned men to the muster;
lively, the eagle-feeder's troop
went in war-garb to the oar-loops.
The dauntless high-king clove the salt
with rime-spread hull from the east;
sharp gales bore the surf-fire's
diminisher towards Sigtún.

3. *Landed in Sweden, Magnús is eager to march west; Norwegians desire his protection.*

Gekk á *Svíþjóð* søkkvi
Sveins, es fremð vann eina;
fýstisk Áleifs austan
afkart sonar hjarta.
Nǫtt beið ok dag dróttins
dygg ferð Jaðarbyggva;
fýst bað gra*m* í geystu
gífrs veðr*i* sér hlífa.

The queller of Sveinn, who wrought
nothing but triumph, marched into Sweden;
urging westwards was the
prodigious heart of Óláfr's son.
Night and day the worthy host
of Jaðarr-men awaited their liege;
urgently, in their troubled she-troll's
gale, they begged the prince to protect them.

4. *Sveinn [Alfífuson] flees from Magnús's anger; Magnús quickly recovers his patrimony.*

Flýði fylkir reiði
framr þjóðkonungs ramma;
stǫkk fyr auðvin okkrum
armsvells hati, gellir.
Létat Nóregs njóta
nýtr þengill gram lengi;
hann rak Svein af sínum
sókndjarfr fǫðurarfi.

The audacious leader fled the
mighty fury of the high-king;
he bolted from our treasure-friend,
the hater of arm-ice, the howler.
The doughty prince did not let
the lord enjoy Norway for long;
he drove, daring in attack,
Sveinn from his father's legacy.

Expedition to Denmark

5. *Magnús vows to possess Denmark or die*

Afkarlig varð jarla
orðgnótt, sú's hlaut dróttinn;
fylgði efnð því's ylgjar
angrtælir réð mæla:
at framm í gný grimmum
grafnings und kló hrafni
fúss lézk falla ræsir
feigr eða Danmǫrk eiga.

Prodigious was the lordly wealth of
words, with which the liege was endowed;
his deeds matched what the beguiler
of the she-wolf's dolour did say:
that ahead in the cruel clash of the
graven shield under the raven's claw
the prince said glad he would drop,
doomed, or else possess Denmark.

6. *Voyage south; Magnús is welcomed on landing in Jutland*

Segja mun'k, hvé Sygna
snarfengjan bar þengil
hallr ok hrími sollinn
hléborðs visundr norðan.
Setti bjóðr at breiðu
brynþings — fetilstinga
fús tók old við œsi —
Jótlandi, gramr, branda.

I will tell how it carried the
quick-acting lord of the Sygnir,
listing and encrusted with rime,
the bison of the lee-side from the north.
The convenor of the corselet-meet beached
on broad Jutland, — eager, folk received
the impeller of sword-belt stabbers —
the fierce prince, his prows.

7. *Magnús, still a youth, gains Denmark*

Náði siklingr síðan
snjallr ok Danmork allri
— mǿttr óx drengja dróttins —
dýrr Nóregi at stýra.
Engr hefr annarr þengill
áðr svá gnógu láði
— bráskat bragnings þroski —
barnungr und sik þrungit.

Then the excellent prince attained,
daring, the whole of Denmark
— the strength of the warriors' liege waxed —
to rule, as well as Norway.
No other lord before has
thrust such ample lands,
— the sovereign's manhood did not fail —
whilst a stripling, under his sway.

Campaign against the Wends (1)

8. *Magnús defeats the Wends and burns their corpses at Jóm*

Vann, þá's Venðr of minnir,
vápnhríð konungr síðan;
sveið ófǿm at Jómi
illvirkja hræ stillir.
Búk dró bráðla steikðan
blóðugr vargr af glóðum;
rann á óskírð enni
allfrekr bani hallar.

Then worked the king a weapon-
blizzard, which Wends remember;
the ruler singed not a few
wrong-doers' corpses at Jóm.
A body swift-roasted the bloody
wolf dragged from the embers;
darted on unbaptised brows
the most ravenous death of the hall.

Battle at Ré

9. *Magnús fights eagerly at Ré, by Vestland*

Fúss lét á Ré ræsir
rammþing háit Glamma;
valska rauð fyr víðu
Vestlandi gramr branda.

Eager at Ré the ruler set in
motion Glammi's mighty encounter;
Frankish blades off wide
Vestland the ruler reddened.

Campaign against the Wends (2)

10. *Magnús wields his axe [at Hlýrskógsheiðr]; God ordains the outcome*

Óð með øxi breiða	Stormed forth with broad axe
ódæsinn framm ræsir	the strenuous ruler
— varð umb hilmi Hǫrða	— there arose round the Hordalanders' lord
hjǫrdynr — ok varp brynju,	a sword-clash — and cast off his byrnie,
þá's umb skapt — en skipti	as round the shaft — and heaven's
skapvǫrðr himins jǫrðu;	shaping guardian allotted earth;
Hel klauf hausa fǫlva —	Hel clove pallid skulls —
hendr tvær jǫfurr spendi.	both hands the hero clenched.

11. *Magnús piles up his slain enemies; the skald praises him*

Svá hlóð siklingr hǫ́van	The sovereign, swift-moving, heaped up
snarr af ulfa barri	a corpse-mound of wolves' barley
— hrósa'k hugfulls vísa —	— I praise the life of the mettlesome
hrækǫst — fir*a* ævi,	liege of men — so high
at áleggjar Yggja*r*	that the steed of the river-limb-Óðinn's
allnǫ́ttfǫrull máttit	spouse, ever prowling by night,
— ǫld lá vítt — þótt vildi,	— men were strewn widely — could not
vífs marr yfir klífa.	scale it, though he longed to.

War against Sveinn Ulfsson (1): Battle off Helganes

12. *Magnús disables enemy ships at Helganes; battle is joined by night*

Vítt hef'k heyrt at heiti	I have heard it is called broad
Helganes, þar's elgi	Helganes, where many elks
vágs enn víða frægi	of the wave the wide-famed
vargteitir hrauð marga.	wolf-cheerer stripped.
Røkr ǫndurt bað randir	At twilight's approach the tree of
reggbúss saman leggja;	the ship called for shields to be set together;
rógskýja helt rýgjar	the rain of the ogress of strife-clouds
regni haustnǫ́tt gegnum.	kept up through the autumn night.

13. *Magnús fights heroically with spear and sword*

Dǫrr lét drengja harri	Spears the warriors' liege, ever
drjúgspakr af þrek fljúga	wise, made by his strength fly,
— glœddi eldr af oddum —	— flame sparked from spear-heads —
almi skept á hjalma.	hafted with elm, at helmets.
Létat hilmir hneiti	The lord did not allow
Hǫgna veðr í gǫgnum	throughout the wind-storm of Hǫgni

— jǫrn flugu þykkt sem þyrnir —	— iron flew thick as thorns —
þél harðara sparðan.	his sword, firmer than a file, to be spared.

14. *Magnús captures Sveinn's fleet*

Skeiðr tók Bjarnar bróður	Longships of Bjǫrn's brother
ballr Skǫ́nungum allar	he, baleful to Scanians, seized
— þjóð røri þeirar tíðar	— men rowed up at the right
þingat — gramr með hringum.	moment — the monarch, every one.

15. *Corpses of Sveinn's men are seen on the Jutland coast; wolf and eagle feast*

Sveins manna rekr sunnan	Sandy corpses of Sveinn's men
sǫndug lík at strǫndum;	from the south are cast ashore;
vítt sér ǫld fyr útan	folk see far and wide off
Jótland, hvar hræ fljóta.	Jutland where bodies float.
Vitnir dregr ór vatni	The wolf drags from the water
— vann Áleifs sonr bannat —	a heap of the slain; Óláfr's son
(búk slítr vargr í víkum)	(the wolf tears a corpse in the creeks)
valkǫst — ara fǫstu.	made fasting forbidden for the eagle.

War against Sveinn Ulfsson (2): Sequel to Helganes

16. *Magnús attacks Skáney*

Uppgǫngu vann yngvi	An assault ashore, mighty enough,
arflógandi gnóga;	the wealth-squandering sovereign launched;
gerði hilmir Hǫrða	the Hordalanders' prince caused a
hjǫrþey á Skáneyju.	thawing wind of swords on Skáney.

17. *Magnús punishes the Danes by slaughter in Falstr*

Svik réð eigi eklu	Not scantly did the all-ruler
allvaldr Dǫnum gjalda;	repay the Danes for their deceit;
lét fullhugaðr falla	high-mettled, the monarch made fall
Falstrbyggva lið tyggi.	the troop of Falstr-men.
Hlóð — en hǫla tœðu	He raised up, — and richly
hirðmenn ara grenni —	retainers served the eagle-feeder —
auðar þorn fyr ǫrnu	the thorn-tree of treasure, for eagles,
ungr valkǫstu þunga.	young as he was, heavy heaps of slain.

18. *Punitive attack on Fjón; the skald acclaims Magnús's prowess when young*

Enn rauð frǫ́n á Fjóni	Further, he reddened on Fjón
— fold sótti gramr dróttar;	— the retinue's lord attacked the land;

ráns galt herr frá hǫ́num —	the people paid dear for robbing him —
hringserks lituðr merki.	the painter of the mail-coat, bright banners.
Minnisk ǫld, hverr annan	Let men recall which troop-commander has,
jafnþarfr blǫ́um hrafni	equally generous to the swart raven,
— ert gat hilmir hjarta —	— a spirited heart the sovereign got —
herskyldir tøg fyldi.	lived out his second decade.

General praise

19. *Magnús's bounty and magnificence forever unequalled*

Ungr skjǫldungr stígr aldri	Never will a young king so bounteous
jafnmildr á við skildan	board a shield-hung bark
— þess vas grams — und gǫmlum	beneath the ancient — ample was
— gnóg rausn — Ymis hausi.	that lord's glory — skull of Ymir.

Þorfinnsdrápa

Exordium

1. *The skald announces his encomium and mourns the jarl*

Nú hykk slíðrhugaðs segja	Now I mean to tell men
— síð léttir mér stríða —	— not soon will my anguish lighten;
(þýtr Alfǫður) ýtum	All-father's mash-surf roars —
jarls kostu (brim hrosta).	of the fell-hearted jarl's excellence.

2. *Þorfinnr drinks ale through the winter; his bounty*

Orms felli drakk allan	Through all the serpent's slayer he,
alkostigr fen hrosta	surpassing, drank the swamp of malt,
— rausn drýgði þá ræsir —	— the ruler exercised bounty then —
Rǫgnvalds niðr í gǫgnum.	the scion of Rǫgnvaldr.

3. *Arnórr's position at court; Þorfinnr drinks ale*

Hét'k, þá's hvern vetr sǫ́tum	I called, as each winter I sat
hrafns verðgjafa, jafnan	facing the raven's feast-giver, always
— líð drakk gramr — á góðar,	— the lord drank ale — to the stalwart
gagnvert, skipa sagnir.	ships' companies.

4. *Arnórr's sons share in his mourning for Þorfinnr*

Bera sýn of mik mínir	My young sons begin to bear for me
morðkends taka enda	at the death of the battle-skilled

þess of þengils sessa
þung mein synir ungir.

bench-mate of the monarch,
manifest, heavy sorrows.

Start of Þorfinnr's warfaring career

5. *Þorfinnr proves himself when fourteen years old*

Hilmir rauð í hjalma
hreggi skelkings eggjar;
fór, áðr fimmtán væri,
fetrjóðr hugins, vetra.
Gǫrr lézk grund at verja,
geðfrœkn, ok til sœkja
œri Einars hlýra
engr mannr und skýranni.

The ruler reddened in storm
of helmets the sword's edges;
he set forth before he was fifteen
winters, the raven's foot-reddener.
Ready to guard his realm,
mind-bold, and mount attacks
has no man younger than Einarr's brother
declared himself, under the cloud-hall.

War against Karl and the Scots

6. *Þorfinnr triumphs over Karl's larger fleet off Dýrnes*

Endr hykk Karli kendu
kyndóm jǫfur brynju
— land vasa lofðungs kundar
laust — fyr Dýrnes austan.
Fimm snekkjum réð frammi
flugstyggr við hug dyggvan
rausnarmannr at ræsis,
reiðr, ellifu skeiðum.

Once, I believe, the hero taught Karl
the monstrous verdict of the mail-coat
— the realm of the ruler's son was not
for the taking — east off Dýrnes.
Five long-ships he steered forth,
flight-shunning, with doughty heart,
the angered man of splendour
against the lord's eleven galleys.

7. *Scots fall at sea; weapons do their work; Þorfinnr is fearless.*

At lǫgðu skip skatnar
skilit; fell herr á þiljur;
svǫ́mu jǫ́rn í ǫ́mu
óðhǫrð Skota blóði.
Stall drapa — strengir gullu;
stál beit, en rann sveiti;
broddr fló; bifðusk oddar
bjartir — þengils hjarta.

Men steered ships to the attack
decisively; troops slumped to the decking;
iron blades, rage-hard, swam
in the dark blood of Scots.
No terror struck — bow-strings shrilled;
steel bit, and gore flowed;
spear-head flew; shining sword-points
quivered — the ruler's heart.

8. *Þorfinnr routs the enemy; he wins victory south of Sandvík*

Þrima vas þvígit skemmri;
þat vas skjótt, at spjótum
mætr við minna neyti
minn dróttinn rak flótta.

The battle was none the briefer for that;
it happened swiftly that with spears
and a smaller company my precious
liege put them to flight.

Gall, áðr grams menn fellu,
gunnmǫ́r of her sǫ́rum;
hann vá sigr fyr sunnan
Sandvík; ruðu branda.

Screamed the battle-gull, before the lord's men fell,
above the wounded war-band;
he won victory south of
Sandvík; they reddened swords.

9. *Þorfinnr, still young, joins battle on a Monday at Torfnes, south of the Ekkjall*

Ulfs tuggu rauð eggjar,
eitt þar's Torfnes heitir,
— ungr olli því þengill —
(þat vas mánadag) fránar.
Sungu þar, til þinga,
þunn fyr Ekkjall sunnan,
sverð, es siklingr barðisk
snarr við Skotlands harra.

On the wolf's mouthful bright blades grew red
at a place called Torfnes;
young, the ruler caused that;
it fell upon a Monday.
Sang there slender swords,
south of the Ekkjall, as
the princeling, swift into conflict,
fought with Scotland's lord.

10. *Þorfinnr, towering in the van, slays Irishmen; he captures enemy warriors and burns*

Hátt bar Hjalta dróttinn
hjalm at geira jalmi
— ógnstœrir rauð Írum
odd — í ferðar broddi.
Minn dróttinn naut máttar
mildr und brezkum skildi;
hendi Hlǫðvis frændi
hermenn ok tók brenna.

High bore the liege of Shetlanders
his helmet in the tumult of spears
— the sweller of battle-dread reddened
his sword-point on Irishmen — in the van of his troop.
My bounteous liege wielded his strength
beneath a British shield;
Hlǫðvir's kinsman captured
warriors and began burning.

11. *The Scots' settlements are burned; Þorfinnr punishes them thrice in a summer.*

Týndusk ból, þá's brendu
— bráskat þat dœgr háski;
stǫkk í reyr en roknu
rauðr eldr — Skota veldi.
Morðkennir galt mǫnnum
mein; á sumri einu
fengu þeir við þengil
þrimr sinnum hlut minna.

Dwellings perished as they put to flame
— peril never ceased that day;
red fire leapt in the smoking
thatch — the realm of the Scots.
The battle-master paid men back their
malice; in a single summer
they got from the prince
three times over the poorer deal.

(?) Refrain: praise

12. *Þorfinnr is everywhere victorious; the skald offers praise*

Harri fekk í hverri
Hjaltlands þrumu branda
— greppr vill grams dýrð yppa —
gagn, sá's hæstr vas bragna.

Shetland's lord in every
thunderstorm of swords won victory
— the skald would extol the ruler's worth —
he who was highest of heroes.

Raiding expeditions

13. *The skald joins in an attack on Vatnsfjǫrðr; slaughter is made on a Friday morning*

Veit'k, þar's Vatnsfjǫrðr heitir,
— vas'k í miklum haska —
míns — við mannkyns reyni —
merki dróttins verka.
Þjóð bar skjótt af skeiðum
skjaldborg fría morgin;
gǫrla sá'k, at grindi
grár ulfr of ná sǫrum.

I know that, in the place called Vatnsfjǫrðr,
— I was in great peril
with the trier of men — there are tokens
of my lord's exploits.
The crew carried swiftly from the ships
the shield-wall on Friday morning;
well I saw how the grey wolf
stretched his jaws over the gashed corpse.

14. *Þorfinnr defeats Irish, 'British' and Scots; fire burns*

Ýmisst vann *sá* unn*ar*,
— írsk fell drótt — þá's sótti,
Bald*r*, eða brezkar aldir
(bra*nn* eldr) Skota veldi.

Diverse triumphs that Baldr of the sword won
— the Irish troop fell — as he attacked
the British people and
— fire blazed — the realm of the Scots.

Attack on England

15. *The skald praises Þorfinnr's seamanship*

Nemi drótt, hvé sæ sótti
snarlyndr konungr jarla;
eigi þraut við ægi
ofvægjan gram bægja.

Let liegemen mark how he made out to sea,
the quick-mettled king among jarls;
the invincible lord never ceased
to strive against the ocean.

16. *Þorfinnr attacks the English with a huge force*

Enn vas sú's Engla minnir
egghríð, né mun síðan
hǫr við helming meira
hringdrífr kom*a* þingat.

Then came the edge-blizzard which
the English remember, and never since then
with larger force will a lofty
ring-strewer come there.

Bitu sverð — en þar þurði —	Swords, slender-wrought, bit
þunngǫr — fyr Mǫn sunnan	— and there, south of Man, rushed forth
Rǫgnvalds kind — und randir	the heir of Rǫgnvaldr the Old —
ramlig folk — ens gamla.	the mighty troops beneath their targes.

17. *Þorfinnr advances his standards; his men rout the enemy; buildings are burned*

Stǫng bar jarl at Engla	The jarl bore his standard onto the
ættgrund, en rauð stundu	native soil of the English, and straightway
— vé bað vísi knýja —	— the leader called for banners to advance —
verðung ara tungu.	his liegemen reddened the eagle's tongue.
Hyrr óx, hallir þurru,	Flame grew, halls shrank;
herdrótt rak þar flótta;	the war-band drove men to flight there;
eim hratt, en laust ljóma,	the foe of branches flung out smoke, and
limdolgr, náar himni.	hurled light against the sky.

18. *Horns are sounded; Þorfinnr and his men make slaughter*

Margr vas millum borga	Many between the defences
— mildingr þrǫng at hildi —	— the bounteous one stormed into battle —
horna blǫ́str, þar's hristisk	were the horn-blasts, where waved the
hugsterks jǫfurs merki.	banner of the stout-hearted hero.
Vætr brá, 's vígljóst þótti,	Not a trace of fear, once it seemed light enough for battle,
vargsteypis her greypum,	seized the thief-feller's grim troop
— skulfu jǫ́rn, en ulfar —	— iron blades quivered and wolves
uggs, morgin — hræ tuggu.	chewed carrion — by morning.

Battle against Rǫgnvaldr Brúsason

19. *The jarls clash tragically at Rauðabjǫrg*

Óskepnan varð uppi	A harsh, monstrous thing came to pass
endr, þá's mǫrgum kendi	at that time, as mighty strife taught
hǫ́ligt róg at hníga,	many a man to fall
hǫrð, þar's jarlar bǫrðusk.	where the jarls fought.
Nær réðusk ástmenn órir,	My dear friends almost destroyed each other
eldhríð es varð síðan	as the sword-blizzard came about then
— ǫld fekk mein en milda	— the gracious troop took many
mǫrg — fyr Rauðabjǫrgum.	a gash — off Rauðabjǫrg.

20. *The skald witnesses the slaughter of comrades in the Pentland Firth*

Hvárntveggja sá'k hǫggva	Both my wealth-givers I watched
hirð á Péttlandsfirði	hack down their own retainers

— ór þrifusk mein at meiri —
mínn auðgjafa sína.
Sær blezk, en dreif dreyri
døkkr á saumfǫr kløkkva;
skaut á skjaldrim sveita;
skokkr vas blóði stokkinn.

— my pain grew the more —
in the Pentland Firth.
The sea churned, and blood dashed
dark on the pliant nail-row;
gore spurted on the shield-rail;
decking was spattered with blood.

Praise; prayers

21. *Extent of Þorfinnr's dominions*

Hringstríði varð hlýða
herr frá Þursaskerjum
— rétt segi'k þjóð, hvé þótti
Þorfinnr — til Dyflinnar.

Forced to heed the ring-harmer
were folk from Þursasker
— I tell men truly how
Þorfinnr was regarded — as far as Dublin.

22. *Þorfinnr will remain unsurpassed in the Orkneys until the end of the world; prayer*

Bjǫrt verðr sól at svartri,
søkkr fold í mar døkkvan,
brestr erfiði Austra,
allr glymr sær á fjǫllum,
áðr at Eyjum fríð*ri*
— inndróttar — Þorfinni
— þeim hjalpi goð geymi —
gœðingr m*yn*i fœðask.

The bright sun to swart will turn,
earth will sink in the dark ocean,
Austri's toil will be rent,
all the sea will roar over the mountains,
before in the Isles a finer
chieftain than Þorfinnr
— God help that guardian of his
retinue — will be born.

23. *The skald prays for Þorfinnr's soul*

Ættbœti firr ítran
allríks — en bið'k líkna
trúra tyggja dýrum —
Torf-Einars goð meinum.

The splendid ennobler of sovereign
Torf-Einarr's kin — and I pray
true mercies for the precious prince —
God keep far from harms.

Haraldsdrápa

War over Denmark

1. *Haraldr attacks Fjón; settlements are burned*

Rauð, en rýrt varð síðan
— rann eldr of sjǫt manna —

The sovereign reddened
— flame ran over dwellings of men —

frána egg á Fjóni,
Fjónbyggva lið, tyggi.

his bright blade on Fjón,
and then was diminished the Fjón-men's troop.

2. *Haraldr joins battle at the Niz estuary; he sails to Halland*

Hjalmǫru lét heyra,
hizi's rauð fyr Nizi,
tyggi, tyrfings eggjar
tvær, áðr mannfall væri.
Naðrs borð skriðu norðan
nýs at allvalds fýsi;
hlaut til Hallands skjóta
hrafnþarfr konungr stafni.

Helmet-bearers he made hear
that there before the Niz he reddened,
the sovereign, the sword's two edges
before men fell.
The new serpent's bulwarks slid
south at the all-ruler's desire;
to speed his prow to Halland was
the lot of the king, lavish to ravens.

3. *Haraldr disables Danish ships; he shoots spears; the shield-wall is broken*

Hrauð, sá's hvergi flýði,
heiðmærr Dana skeiðir
glaðr und golli roðnum,
geirjalm, konungr hjalmi.
Skjaldborg raufsk, en skúfar
— skaut hoddglǫtuðr oddum
bragna brynjur gǫgnum,
buðlungr — of ná sungu.

He cleared, who nowhere fled spear-clangour,
bright-renowned, the Danes' galleys,
glad under gold-reddened
helmet, the king.
The shield-wall shattered, and swords
— the hoard-destroyer shot spear-heads
through warriors' mailcoats,
the monarch — sang out over corpses.

4. *Sveinn [Ulfsson] is forced to flee his disabled ship*

Gekkat Sveinn af snekkju
saklaust enn forhrausti
— malmr kom harðr við hjalma —
(hugi minn es þat) sinni.
Farskostr hlaut at fljóta
fljótmælts vinar Jóta,
áðr an ǫðlingr flýði,
auðr, frá verðung dauðri.

Sveinn did not leave his vessel
without cause, outstanding in valour;
— steel struck hard on helmets —
that is my thought.
Fated to float was the choice bark
of the swift-spoken friend of Jutes
unmanned, before the noble one
fled from his dead liegemen.

Punitive raids on Upplǫnd

5. *Burning of settlements; hanging of rebels*

Gengr í ætt, þat's yngvi
Upplendinga brendi
— þjóð galt ræsis reiði —
rǫnn — þess's fremstr vas manna.

It befits his kin that the prince
put to flame the Uplanders' dwellings;
the people paid for the wrath of the ruler
who was foremost of men.

Vildut ǫflgar aldir,
áðr vas stýrt til váða,
— grams dolgum fekksk galgi —
gagnprýðanda hlýða.

Mighty men were unwilling,
before their course turned to ruin,
— the gallows were the lot of the lord's foes —
to heed the glorious victor.

6. *Haraldr deals harshly with the Raumar; the Heinir are subdued by fire.*

Eymðit ráð við Rauma
reiðr Eydana meiðir;
heit dvínuðu Heina;
hyrr gerði þá kyrra.

He did not soften his treatment of the Raumar,
the wrathful harmer of Isle-Danes;
the threats of the Heinir fell away;
fire made them quiet.

Invasion of England (1): Battle by the Ouse

7. *Haraldr makes great slaughter of the English by the Ouse [at Fulford]*

Þung rauð jǫrn á Englum
eirlaust — né kømr meira —
vísi vel nær Úsu
— valfall of her snjallan.

Weighty iron blades he reddened on Englishmen
ruthlessly, — and never will come —
the leader, hard by the Ouse
— greater slaughter upon a bold host.

8. *Standards are advanced and missiles hurled; thousands are slain*

Fell at fundi stillis
— framm óðu vé — móða
(ámt fló grjót) á gauta
glóðheitr ofan sveiti.
Þjóð hykk þaðra nǫðu
þúsundum togfúsa
— spjót flugu — líf at láta
— laus í gumna hausum.

Down flowed, at the ruler's conflict,
— standards stormed forth — upon wearied
men (dark stones flew)
ember-hot blood.
I think that there troops
quick on the draw by thousands
— spears flew — came to lose their lives
— free at men's skulls.

9. *Haraldr triumphs; the English earls flee to safety*

Gagn fekk gjǫfvinr Sygna
— gekk hildr at mun — vildra,
hinn's á hæl fyr mǫnnum
hreinskjaldaðr fór aldri.
Dunðu jarlar undan
— eir fekka lið þeira —
(mannkyn hefr at minnum
morgin þann) til borgar.

Victory he gained, the gift-friend
of prized Sygnir, — the battle went to his wish —
who in the face of men
bright-shielded never took to his heels.
The earls thundered away
— no mercy their troop received —
(the race of men holds in memory
that morning) to the stronghold.

Invasion of England (2): Battle [at Stamford Bridge]

10. *Haraldr orders troops ashore; an army from southern England attacks*

Uppgǫngu bauð yngvi	The prince ordered the advance ashore,
ítr með helming lítinn,	splendid, with a small force,
sá's á sinni ævi	he who in his lifetime
sásk aldrigi háska.	never felt fear of danger.
Enn of England sunnan	But northwards through England
ǫflugr herr at berjask	a mighty army marched
fór við fylki dýran;	to fight the excellent sovereign;
fundusk þeir af stundu.	they engaged straightway.

11. *Haraldr, fearless, wields his sword*

Hafðit brjóst, né bifðisk	No mean mettle — and the king's
bǫðsnart konungs hjarta	battle-swift heart did not tremble
í hjalmþrimu, hilmir	in the helmet-din — had the prince
hlítstyggr fyr sér lítit,	in himself, shunning trivial deeds,
þar's til þengils hersa	where, watching the lord of nobles,
þat sá herr, at skatna	the army saw that
blóðugr hjǫrr ens barra	the bloody sword of the zealous
beit dǫglinga hneitis.	subduer of princes bit men.

12. *Haraldr's pride brings his death in battle*

Olli ofrausn stillis	The ruler's excess of pride caused this,
orma látrs *því*'s máttit	that the foe of the reptiles' lair could not,
stáls í strǫngu éli	in the stern blizzard of steel,
stríðir elli bíða,	live to see old age,
sá's aldrigi aldins	that stainer of the claws of the
ótams lituðr hramma	troll-wife's old, untamed steed
viggs í vápna glyggvi	who never in the wind-storm of
varðrúnar sik sparði.	weapons spared himself.

13. *Haraldr's men join him in death*

Eigi varð ens œgja	Not unadorned was the
auðligr konungs dauði;	death of the fearsome king;
hlífðut hlenna sœfi	they did not protect the slayer of robbers,
hoddum roðnir oddar.	the spear-points, reddened with treasure.
Heldr køru meir ens milda	They chose, the liegemen of the gracious
mildings an grið vildi	liege, much rather than wishing quarter,
umb folksnaran fylki	around the battle-keen captain
falla liðsmenn allir.	to fall, all of them.

Praise, lament and prayer

14. *Renown of Haraldr, who sailed south from the Nið*

Vítt fór vǫlsungs heiti;	Wide went the prince's great name;
varð marglofaðr harða,	praised most highly was he
sá's skaut ór Níð nýtla	who skilfully launched from the Nið
norðan herskips borði.	southwards the warship's plank.

15. *The skald cannot conceive of Haraldr's valour being equalled; his death a loss*

Myrkt's, hverr meira orkar,	It is dark to me, for the skald
mér, alls greppr né sérat,	cannot see it, who will achieve more,
— harðr's í heimi orðinn	— the world has lost the stern
hrafngrennir — þrek jǫfnum.	raven-feeder — equal feats of strength.
Ert gat óslætt hjarta	He was endowed with the boldest,
— eljunfims — und himni	keenest heart under heaven;
mest — hefr mildingr kost*at*	the liege has put to the test the
minni hvers grams vinn*a*.	lesser deeds of every mettlesome lord.

16. *Haraldr's unequalled power and glory; his place in heaven*

Haraldr vissi sik hverjum	Haraldr knew himself, stern-spirited,
harðgeðr und Miðgarði	mightier than any lord
— dǫglingr réð til dauða	— the monarch commanded till death
dýrð slíkri — gram ríkra.	such glory — under Miðgarðr.
Hefr afreka e*n* øfra	The holy land on high
— ættstýrǫndum dýrri	— no rarer prince than that ruler of men,
hnígrat hilmir frægri —	none more renowned, will sink
heilǫg fold — til moldar.	to the soil — has the hero.

17. *The skald's prayers repay Haraldr's gift*

Bœnir hef'k fyr beini	I raise up prayers for the dealer of
bragna falls við snjallan	warriors' deaths to the wise
Girkja vǫrð ok Garða;	guardian of Greeks and of Garðar;
gjǫf launa'k svá jǫfri.	So I repay the prince for his gift.

Fragments

Strophes occasioned by the strife between the jarls of Orkney (c. 1044)

1. *The skald is loath to oppose [Rǫgnvaldr,] the sọn of Brúsi; he forsees an anguished choice if the jarls fight*

Drengr's í gegn at ganga
— gótt's fylgja vel dróttni;
ǫld leyní'k því aldri —
ófúss syni Brúsa.
Oss's, ef jarlar þessir
ógnbráðir til ráðask,
— hǫrð mun vinraun verða —
vandligr kostr fyr hǫndum.

This warrior is not keen to go
— good it is to support one's lord well;
I shall never conceal that from men —
against the son of Brúsi.
I have, if these jarls,
battle-hasty, attack one another
— harsh will be the ordeal of friendship —
a hard choice on my hands.

2. *The skald grieves at the jarls' conflict; the ruler exposes his ships to the wintry ocean*

Ek em, síz ýtar hnekkðu
jarla sætt, 's ek vætti,
— jǫfn fengusk hræ hrǫfnum —
hegju tr*auð*r at segja.
Sleit fyr eyjar útan
allvaldr bl*ǫu* tjaldi;
hafði hreggsvǫl dúfa
hrími f*ezk* umb líma.

I am loath, since men thwarted
the jarls' truce, as I foresaw,
— from both sides alike flesh was found for ravens —
to speak of events.
He wore to shreds out beyond the islands,
the all-ruler, dark awnings;
the snow-cold billow had
fastened itself in frost about the mast.

3. *The lord would have prevailed had not warriors betrayed him*

Gramr myndi sá gǫmlu
gunnbráðr und sik láði
— hann fekk miklu minna
mannspj*a*ll — koma ǫllu,
ef ílendra Endils
ættstafr hafa knætti
— vélti herr of Hjalta —
hjalm-Þrótta lið — drótti*n*.

That lord, battle-hasty, would have
brought all of the ancient land
— he had much the less
loss of men — under his sway,
if he, the staff of Endill's strain,
could have had the support
— the troop betrayed the Shetlanders' liege —
of the helmet-Óðinns, re-granted their land.

(?) From a poem for Knútr (d. 1035)

4. *Danes wear gold arm-rings and thank 'him' for one*

Bekks lá eldr ok axla ulfliðs Dǫnum miðli; ek sá armhrauð þakka eitt Skǫnunga hǫnum.	Fire of the stream was set between the wrist and shoulders of the Danes; I saw men of Skáney thank him for an arm-ring.

(?) From the *Blágagladrápa* for Haraldr (c. 1046)

5. *The prince sails far out and fights sea-battles*

Siklinga venr snekkjur sælútar konr úti; hann litar herskip innan — hrafns góð es þat — blóði.	The scion of princes trains longships to plunge in the sea far out; he stains warships within — that is the raven's gain — with blood.

From a memorial poem for Hermundr Illugason (d. 1055)

6. *Prayer for Hermundr*

Hjalp, dýrr konungr, dýrum, dags grundar, Hermundi.	Save, excellent king of day's land, the excellent Hermundr.

(?) From a memorial poem for Gellir Þorkelsson (d. 1073)

7. *Michael and God weigh men's deeds*

Mikjáll vegr þat's misgǫrt þykkir, mannvitsfróðr, ok allt et góða; tyggi skiptir síðan seggjum sólar hjalms á dœmistóli.	Michael weighs what seems wrongly done, ripe with wisdom, and all that is good; then the sovereign of the sun's helmet separates out men at his judgement-seat.

Unidentified fragments

8. *The wolf enjoys carrion from a sea-battle*

Svalg áttbogi ylgjar ógóðr — en varð blóði grœðir grœnn at rauðum — grandauknum ná — blandinn.	The evil scion of the she-wolf swallowed — and, mingled with blood, the green surge turned to red — the sand-swollen corpse.

9.

Kreisti knútu lostna klifs bein fjǫrusteini	The bone of the cliff pressed hard on the joint-bone, battered by beach-shingle.

10.

Sumar hvern frekum erni	Every summer to the greedy eagle

11.

Foldar fiðr	Plumage of the earth

Diplomatic Text and Commentary

Rǫgnvaldsdrápa

Verse One

Sources

Ólsh(Sep) p. 581: 2(69r), 4(64v), 61(126v), 321(260), 325V(82r), 325VII(39r), Bb(200r), Th(157r).
Orkns ch. 21, p. 54: 325III(1r), 332(34), 702(73), Fl(523), 48m(347r).

Context

After the battle of Stiklastaðir (Stiklestad), Rǫgnvaldr Brúsason journeys eastwards and stays, together with Haraldr Sigurðarson, at the court of King Jarizleifr (Jaroslav) in Garðaríki (N. W. Russia).
In *Ólsh(Sep)* the verse is simply prefaced by a loose paraphrase, *Þes getr Arnor iarla scalld. at Ravgnvalldr Brvsa son var lengi landvarnamaðr i Garþariki oc atti þar oRostor margar*:
Orkns contains a fuller account of Rǫgnvaldr's activities, then *Rdr* 1 is introduced, *Svá segir Arnórr jarlaskáld, at Rǫgnvaldr átti í Hólmgarði* [vv. ll. *í Garðaríki, í Gǫrðum*] *tíu fólkorrustur*:

Diplomatic and edited text

Deilldiz af sva alldin	Deildisk af svá't aldin
el g*ra*fn*in*ga þelar	él grafninga þélar
gavndlar nioðr í gavrþv*m*	gǫndlar Njǫrðr í Gǫrðum
gvNbraþr .x. háþi.	gunnbráðr tíu háði.

Prose order and translation

Deildisk af svá't gunnbráðr gǫndlar Njǫrðr háði tíu aldin él grafninga þélar í Gǫrðum.
It so fell out, that the war-hasty Njǫrðr of battle [warrior, Rǫgnvaldr] brought about ten ancient snow-storms of the graven shields' rasp [sword→battles] in Garðar.

Apparatus

(1) sva] *sva* at 4, 325V, 325VII, Bb, 332, 702, Fl, þviat 61, sem 321, 325III, *seri* Th **alldin]** alld*ri* 61, 325V, Bb, Th, alldun 325VII, alld*ir* 702, Fl (48m as 2) **(2) el]** els 61, iel 325V, ęl Bb ***grafninga*]** *gar*finga (or *gar*fniga) 325V, *gr*amninga 325VII, Bb, 332, 48m, grafningia 325III **þelar]** þelaz 321, þęlar Bb, hvela 702 **(3) gavndlar]** guNlar 61, Th, guNaR 325V, 325III, 332, 702, Fl, gǫ̇nlar Bb **nioðr (or moðr)]** niørdr 4, 61, 325V, 325VII, Bb (or mordr), Th, 332, Fl, ar 321, vorðr 325III, 702 **gavrþv*m*]** górdu Fl **(4) gvNbraþr]** gim*m*- 702 -brad Bb **.x.]** tíu 61, 321, 325V, 325VII, Th, 325III, Fl.

Commentary

1/1 *Deilldiz af* 'it fell out, happened'.

(a) *Af* is here more likely to be an adverb than a preposition, since it bears strong stress and alliteration. The phrasal verb *deilask af* is rare, but is attested in *Sturlunga saga*, where the meaning is 'be dealt out, carried on': *Kǫlluðu þeir at lengi mundi vǫrnin deilaz af úti* 'They said that the defence would be carried on for a long time out there' (I 191). In the present context, where there is no explicit subject, the meaning could well be 'it fell out, happened' (cf. the verb *skipta*, which also means both 'divide, deal' and 'happen').

(b) Finnur Jónsson in *Skjald* B and Finnbogi Guðmundsson in *Orkns* 1965, 54n. regard *af* as a preposition and construe *deildisk af aldri svá't gǫndlar Njǫrðr* ... 'it happened thus in [that period of the jarl's] life that the warrior ...'. But *aldri* has less strong MS support than *aldin*, and *af* ... *aldri* would be interrupted by *svá't*, which introduces the next clause, and such fragmentation is uncharacteristic of Arnórr. E. A. Kock (*NN* §§809 and 2710A) construes *af* as an adverb, but does not account satisfactorily for *aldri*, apparently favouring solution (d) below.

1/1 *sva at* (v. l.) 'so ... that'. The adopted reading links *deildisk af* 'it happened' with the succeeding lines of explanation.

1/1 *alldin* 'ancient'.

(a) This reading, which has by far the strongest MS authority, is taken to be acc. pl. neut., qualifying the battles expressed by *él grafninga þélar* '(snow-)storms of the graven shields' rasp'. Bjarni Aðalbjarnarson reads it thus, and translates, 'in the ancient manner' (*að fornum hætti*, *Hkr* 1941–51, II, 440n.). The battles could alternatively be 'old' in the sense of being far in the past, cf. *forn* in expressions such as *forn rǫk* 'ancient [long-past] events', *Lok* 25. A third possibility is that *aldin* refers to the 'hoary', grey flurries of weapons in battle. Arnórr applies the adj. *aldinn* to a wolf in *Hdr* 12, and in *Háv* 62 and *Ht* 67 it describes the sea (*marr*), and these usages could reflect the association of age with a grey, hoary appearance. If *aldin* does have the sense 'old' or 'hoary, grey' in *Rdr* 1 the image is somewhat bold, for I have found no other poetic context in which battle is described thus. However, the remaining possibilities for analysis of the line are still less satisfactory:

(b) V. l. *aldri*, if the shorter form of *aldrigi* 'never', would produce the nonsensical statement that the hero never fought ten battles in Garðar.

(c) It has been suggested that *aldri* is an adverbial dat. sing. from *aldr* 'age, lifetime', meaning 'once' (Vogt 1934, 15 and n. 3); but there is no evidence for this meaning, and it seems inconceivable that so common a word as *aldri* should have been used in so unexpected a sense.

(d) *At aldri* could be construed together, but the phrase appears in the lexicons only in idioms such as *ungr / hniginn at aldri* 'young / stricken in years'.

(e) V. l. *aldir* 'men' does not fit into the sense or the syntax of the helming.

1/2 *el grafninga þelar* 'snow-storms of the graven shields' rasp'. The 'rasp' (*þél*) 'of graven shields' is the sword and the '(snow-)storm' (*él*) of the sword is battle. *Grafningr* is recorded with the sense '(graven) shield' only in Arnórr's poetry; it occurs otherwise as a *heiti* for 'snake'.

1/3 *gavndlar niørdr* (v. l.) 'Njǫrðr of battle [Rǫgnvaldr]'. A kenning for 'warrior', which also occurs in a verse by Arnórr's older contemporary Þórðr Særeksson (Þ Sær 2, 2). The valkyrie name Gǫndul also occurs as an appellative meaning 'battle', as in the 12th-century *Rst* 32 *gǫndlar fýst* (emended from *gondla fystr*) 'eager for battle'. It is probably best taken as 'battle' here, since 'Njǫrðr of the valkyrie' would be unsatisfactory.

1/3 *í gavrþvm* 'in Garðar' or 'Garðaríki (N. W. Russia)'. For the location of this, as of other places and peoples mentioned in the text, see Maps 1 and 2.

Verse Two

Sources

SnE p. 164: R(72), T(40v), U(70), W(82).

Context

The helming belongs to a group of quotations which exemplify periphrastic terms for kings and jarls, in this case *Heita konr*. It is prefaced by the words, *En q(vað) sva Arnoʀ iRavgnvaldzdrapv*:

Diplomatic and edited text

Reð heita konr hlioti	Réð Heita konr hleyti
h*er*þarf v*ið* mic giorva	herþarfr við mik gerva;
styrk let oss of orkat	styrk lét oss of orkat
iarls megð af þ*vi* fregðar.	jarls mægð af því frægðar.

Prose order and translation

Herþarfr Heita konr réð gerva hleyti við mik. Styrk mægð jarls lét of orkat oss frægðar af því.
Beneficent to hosts, Heiti's scion [Rǫgnvaldr] made a marriage-alliance with me. The strong brother-bond / kinship-in-law with the jarl brought me renown because of that.

Apparatus

(1) hlioti] hlǒti T, hleyti U, hlætí W **(2) -þarf]** -þarfr others **(3) styrk]** stoʀr U **oss]** ǫll W **of]** v*m* U **(4) megð]** meg U **af]** at U.

Commentary

2/1 *heita konr* 'Heiti's scion [Rǫgnvaldr]'. Heiti occurs in kennings and in *Þul* III 1 and IV a 3 as the name of a legendary sea-king; but in the present context it may refer more specifically to a legendary ancestor of the hero, for Heiti is named in *Orkns* ch. 3 (p. 7) as great-great-great-grandfather of Rǫgnvaldr Mœrajarl, first jarl of Orkney.

2/1 ***hleyti*** **(v. l.)** ‘marriage-alliance, kinship-in-law’ is synonymous with *mægð* in line 4, and gives perfect sense. *Hljóti*, 3rd sing. / pl. subj. of verb *hljóta* ‘get, be allotted’, could make no sense in the context.

2/2 ***herþarfr*** **(v. l.)** ‘beneficent [lit. needful, useful] to hosts’. The nom. sing. masc. form is required with *Heita konr*.

2/3 ***of***. The expletive particle, for which no translation is possible or necessary. A study by Fidjestøl (1989) substantially confirms Kuhn’s view (1929) that the particle *of/um* is used with declining frequency during the main centuries of skaldic composition. Arnórr’s restrained use of the device is typical of the eleventh century.

Verse Three

Sources

SnE p. 114: R(51), T(29r), U(57), W(56), 757(5r).

Context

The couplet is one of a sequence quoted to illustrate kennings for ‘sky’.

Diplomatic and edited text

Saðr still*ir* hialpþv sniollv*m*	Sannr stillir, hjalp snjǫllum,
soltialda ravgnvaldi.	sóltjalda, Rǫgnvaldi.

Prose order and translation

Sannr stillir sóltjalda, hjalp snjǫllum Rǫgnvaldi.
True ruler of the sun’s awnings [clouds/sky→God], help the prudent Rǫgnvaldr.

Apparatus

(1) hialpþv] hialp T, W.

Hrynhenda

Verse One

Sources

Third GrT pp. 88 and 22: 748(11v), W(105)

Context

The couplet is cited in Óláfr hvítaskáld's *Málskrúðsfræði* to illustrate paragoge, the lengthening of a word by the addition of a letter or syllable. After the quotation Óláfr points to *knarra* as an example of such addition in the interests of metre (*til þæss at kveðanndi halldiz*).

Diplomatic and edited text

Klivfa let ec i kavpfavr dvfv	Kljúfa lét'k í kaupfǫr dúfu
knarra min*n* v*ið* borðin stinno.	knarra minn við borð en stinnu.

Prose order and translation

Lét'k knarra minn kljúfa dúfu við en stinnu borð í kaupfǫr.
I made my bark cleave the billow with its [lit. the] firm strakes on a trading voyage.

Apparatus

(1) Klivfa] Klifa W **kavpfavr]** kofvr W **dvfv]** drifv W.

Commentary

The couplet. The lines share the metre and seafaring theme of *Hryn* 2 which, on the evidence of Óláfr hvítaskáld (see Context to *Hryn* 2), belongs to the exordium of the poem. The two couplets answer well to the detail of the saga narratives about Arnórr's recitation before Magnús and Haraldr (see pp. 44–45). The assignment of the two couplets to this poem is further discussed in Cawley 1926–27 and Edwards 1979, 40–41.

1/1 *dvfv* 'billow'. For brief comment on this and other appellations for 'wave', see pp. 74–75.

1/2 *minn* 'my'. That the possessive pronoun here takes the form with short vowel is shown by the *aðalhending* with *stinnu* (cf. *þinn: minna Hryn* 13/4, *minn: innan Hryn* 16/6 and *minn: sinni Hdr* 4/4). In *Þdr* 20/4, on the other hand, *mínn* is indicated by the *aðalhending* on *sína*.

1/2 *við borðin stinno* 'with its firm strakes'.

(a) *Við* could be oppositional 'against' or instrumental 'by (means of)', as in *húðin ... skorpnuð við eld* 'the hide ... shrivelled by (exposure to) fire', *Njáls saga* ch. 132, p. 342. In either case the phrase would be adverbial, modifying *kljúfa*, hence 'cleave the billow with / against its firm strakes'. Analysed thus, the couplet gives a fine picture of the ship's motion through the waves.

(b) Finnur Jónsson in *Skjald* B took the *við* ... phrase to qualify *knarra*, hence 'bark / ship with firm strakes'.

Verse Two

Sources

Third GrT pp. 82 and 19: 748(11r), W(104).

Context

The lines are used to illustrate *macrologia*, which Óláfr hvítaskáld defines as a long sentence which contains matter irrelevant to the skald's subject. Óláfr adds that the figure is common at the beginning of poems. Arnórr's couplet is introduced, *Sæm arnoR qvað i Magnvs drapu*, and followed by the explanation that Arnórr here tells of his own difficult journeys, which is not relevant to the praise of the king.

Diplomatic and edited text

Sæinkvn v*arð* þa æ*r* hlæbarð hanka	Seinkun varð, þá's hlébarðs hanka
hnika ár hin liota bara.	hnika*ði* ǫ́r en ljóta bára.

Prose order and translation

Seinkun varð, þá's en ljóta bára hnika*ði* hanka hlébarðs ǫ́r.
There was drag, as the foul breaker drove against the cleat-bear's [ship's] oar.

Apparatus

(1) *varð*] *verð*r W **-barð] -barðz W **(2) hnika]** hnika or hinka W.

Commentary

The couplet.

(a) The analysis shown in the prose order above and in the translation is syntactically the most straightforward (and was adopted by Kock, *NN* §810). The couplet could be construed in two other ways, both of which are less satisfactory since they assume a complex intertwining of clauses which is uncharacteristic of *Hryn*.

(b) *Seinkun varð hanka hlébarðs ǫ́r, þá's en ljóta bára hnikaði* 'There was drag on the ship's [lit. cleat-bear's] oar, as the foul breaker tossed'. Here *ǫ́r* is a dat. of respect or disadvantage.

(c) *Seinkun hanka hlébarðs varð, þá's en ljóta bára hnikaði ǫ́r* 'There was drag on the ship, as the foul breaker drove against the oar'. *Hanka hlébarðs* 'ship' is here taken as an objective gen. governed by *seinkun* 'drag, delay'.[1]

2/1 *hlæbarðz* (v. l.) *hanka* 'cleat-bear [ship]'. Only the gen. sing. *-barðs* is compatible with the syntax of the couplet.

The *hanki* 'cleat' is a loop or other device which holds the cordage for the sails in a given position.

Hanka hlébarðr is clearly a kenning for 'ship' akin to many others which comprise an animal name as base word and a seafaring word as determinant, but the particular animal designated by *hlébarðr* (also a giant name in *Hárb* 20) is not certain. (a) It occurs as a name for 'bear' in *Þul* IV cc 1, in Grett 1, 3 and elsewhere, and 'ship' kennings with base word meaning 'bear' are well attested (Meissner 1921, 218).

(b) *Hlébarðr* is a *heiti* for 'wolf' in *Þul* IV ee 1, and 'wolf' is also attested in kennings for 'ship', although rather less frequently than 'bear' (Meissner 1921, 220).

(c) *Hlébarðr* is held to be an adoption, altered by folk etymology, of M. Lat. *leopardus* (*IEW* p. 1026; de Vries, s. v.), and it is conceivable that Arnórr meant 'leopard' here (cf. *bǫ́ru léón* 'lion of

[1] This arrangement is adopted by Björn M. Ólsen, *Third GrT* pp. 192–93 (reads *verðr, hnikar*), and by Finnur Jónsson in *Skjald* B. It is rejected by Kock, *NN* §810.

the wave [ship]' in a verse attributed to Sveinn tjúguskegg), but he does not in general show a taste for such exotic references.

2/2 *hnikaði* (em.) 'drove against'. MS *hnika* (infin. or 3rd pl. pres.) does not fit into the syntax of the couplet, and the best solution is to emend to the past sing. form.[2]

That *hnika* belonged to the first weak, or *-a* stem, conjugation is inferred from modern usage (e. g. Blöndal, s. v.), and from the Óðinn *heiti* Hnikuðr (*Þul* IV jj 1 and *Grí* 48), variant to the commoner Hnikarr.

The verb is not recorded elsewhere in ON, and yet its meaning can be established. In Mod. Icel. it can either be intransitive, meaning 'move, sway', or else it can govern a dat. object and mean 'move'. In Blöndal's two examples the object is something heavy, which suggests that *hnikaði* in Arnórr's line could mean 'drive, thrust against'. The related ON verb *hnekkja* 'throw back, thwart' supports this.

2/2 *ár* 'oar'. (Normalised) *ǫ́r* forms a very natural phrasal unit with *hanka hlébarðs* 'oar of the cleat-bear [of the ship]', cf. *élmars typpi* 'mast-heads of the storm-steed [of the ship]' in *Hryn* 10. The phrase is taken as dat. sing. object of *hnika[ði]* 'drove against', which gives excellent sense in the context, since delay or drag (*seinkun*) in the ship's advance would result from the counter-thrust of the sea against the oar. (For an alternative interpretation, see Sveinbjörn Egilsson 1860, s. v. *hlæbarðr*.)

Verse Three

Sources

Msk p. 116, Flat III 322: Msk(5v), Fl(787)
Hars(H-Hr) p. 196: H(33r), Hr(24r)
Third GrT pp. 77 and 17–18 (lines 3–4 only): 748(10v), W_1(103)
Fourth GrT p. 135 (lines 3–4 only): W_2(115)

[2] So Finnur Jónsson in *Skjald* B. For a metrical objection to the alternative emendation, to *hnikar*, see Konráð Gíslason, 1895–97, II, 66–67.

Context

In *Msk-Flat* and *Hars(H-Hr)*, the strophe is quoted within the account of Arnórr's audience with Magnús and Haraldr of Norway (outlined on pp. 44–45).
Third GrT: Lines 3-4 are cited to exemplify change of number as a form of solecism, and are followed by an explanation that plural is here used in place of singular.[3]
Fourth GrT: The writer points to Arnórr's use of *yðru* as illustrating *lepos* — the honorific use of the plural to compliment a man in authority. After the quotation he explains that it is not proper to use the plural for a common man, but rather a solecism.

Diplomatic and edited text

Magn*us* hlyððu til mattigs oþar
mangi ueit ec f*re*mra an*n*an
yppa raþo*m*c yðro cappi
iota g*ra*mr iq*v*ę̨þi flioto
høcr rettr er tv hỏrþa dro*tti*n*n*
hveʀ g*ra*mr e*r* þer storo veʀi
meiri verþi þin en þ*ei*ra
þ*ri*fnvðr allr vndz himen*n* rifnar.

Magnús, hlýð til máttigs óðar;
manngi veit ek fremra annan;
yppa rǿðumk yðru kappi,
Jóta gramr, í kvæði fljótu.
Haukr réttr estu, Hǫrða dróttinn;
hverr gramr es þér stóru verri;
meiri verði þinn an þeira
þrifnuðr allr, unz himinn rifnar.

Prose order and translation

Magnús, hlýð til máttigs óðar. Ek veit manngi annan fremra. Rǿðumk yppa yðru kappi, Jóta gramr, í fljótu kvæði. Réttr haukr estu, Hǫrða dróttinn. Hverr gramr es stóru verri þér. Allr þrifnuðr þinn verði meiri an þeira, unz himinn rifnar.
Magnús, hear a mighty poem. I know no other [is] more excelling. I mean to raise up your prowess, prince of Jutes, in a swift-running song. A just hawk you are, Hordalanders' lord. Every prince is far below you. May your whole success surpass [lit. be greater than] theirs, until the sky is riven.

[3] *Yðru*, referring to Magnús alone, is probably meant (cf. Context in *Fourth GrT*). Björn M. Ólsen (*Third GrT* pp. 186–87) suggested as one possibility that *rǿðumk* was meant, but the *-umk* form is quite orthodox in the 1st sing. of the middle voice.

Apparatus

(1) hlyððu] hlyttu Fl, hlyd H, Hr **(3) raþo*m*c]** raduzt Fl, raðv*m*z H, Hr, 748, W_1, raaðv*m* W_2 **(4) flioto]** flíota Fl **(5) høcr]** hauk*r* others **(6) storo]** storv*m* H, Hr **(7) þin]** þínn others **(8) þ*r*ifnvðr]** þ*r*íf naud*r* Fl **allr vndz]** adr Fl **himen*n*]** heímr Fl, himínín*n* H, Hr.

Commentary

3/1 *mattigs oþar* 'a mighty poem'. It appears that *máttigr*, applied to a poem, was rare enough to have had an appropriately powerful effect on the audience. Gert Kreutzer's survey of epithets used by skalds to describe their work includes only one other instance of a 'strong, mighty poem': Jór 5 *hróðr vann ... ramman* (1977, 239).

3/4 *iqvęþi flioto* 'in a swift-running song'. Kreutzer, remarking that Arnórr is the first skald to use the word *kvæði* (here and in *Hryn* 14), suggests that the older skalds' predilection for elevated diction led them to avoid *kvæði*, preferring the specifically poetic *bragr* and *óðr* (1977, 58–59).

Whether or not poetry in the *hrynhent* metre had a faster tempo than *dróttkvætt* poetry (Heusler 1925–29, I 304), its tendency to fall into a regular trochaic pulse makes Arnórr's use of the adj. *fljótr* peculiarly apt here. Kreutzer (1977, 206) seems to incline to the alternative interpretation of Arnórr's phrase: that it is to be linked with the comments of other (mainly later) skalds on their swiftness in composing, e. g. Egill's *Arbj* 1:

Emk hraðkvæðr	I am swift-spoken
hilmi at mæra.	in glorifying the ruler.

3/5 *høcr rettr er tv* 'a just hawk you are'. According to the extant records, Arnórr is the first skald to praise his patron through the metaphor of the hawk.[4] He re-uses the hawk image, now as a simile, in *Hryn* 16, and some years later Þjóðólfr calls the sons of Haraldr harðráði *haukar gǫrvir* 'accomplished hawks' (Þjóð A 4, 26). The image conveys the hero's boldness (cf. the same use of *haukr,*

[4] For a general discussion of the hawk in medieval Scandinavia, see Bernström 1962; also Frank 1978, 78.

haukligr 'hawk-like' and *hauklundr* 'hawk-spirited' in verse from the late 11th century onwards, notably in that quoted in *Hálfs saga ok Hálfsrekka*, vv. 51, 54 and 64, pp. 190, 191 and 193), and his sovereignty (cf. Guðrún's dream in *Vǫlsunga saga*, where a fine hawk which perches on her hand portends a king's son who will woo her, ch. 26, p. 44).

3/5 *hòrþa drottinn* 'Hordalanders' lord'. By synecdoche, 'King of Norway'. Fittingly for the opening of an encomium, Magnús's legitimate rule of Norway and Denmark is confirmed in this phrase and in *Jóta gramr* in the previous line. Magnús is again referred to as ruler of Hǫrðaland (Hordaland) in *Hǫrða vinr* (*Mdr* 1) and *hilmir Hǫrða* (*Mdr* 10 and 16); also as lord of the people of Mœrr (Møre) in *Mœra gramr* (*Hryn* 8) and of Sogn in *Sygna þengill* (*Mdr* 6). Haraldr Sigurðarson is *gjǫfvinr Sygna* in *Hdr* 9.

3/6 *storo* 'far, much'. *Stóru (verri)*, 'far (below you)', lit. '(worse) by much', is a dat. sing. neut. indicating degree of comparison, as in *eigi ... storu meiri uxi ok betri* 'not a much bigger or better ox' (*Sturlunga saga* I 119); cf. also expressions such as *litlu síðarr* 'a little later', *miklu meira* 'much more'.

3/8 *þrifnvðr allr vndz himenn rifnar* 'whole success; until the sky is riven'. *Unz himinn rifnar* is a variant of a formula also found on Swedish rune-stones, e. g. the Skarpåker stone (earlier 11th century), on which is cut the equivalent of the OIcel. *jǫrð skal rifna ok upphiminn* (Jansson 1977, 142–44).

Allr I construe with *þrifnuðr*. It could qualify *himinn*, hence 'whole sky', but the interruption of attributive adj. and noun by a conjunction would be exceptional in Arnórr's poetry.

Verse Four

Source

Magns(H-Hr) p. 23: Hr(3v)

Context

This is one of a sequence of strophes which describe Magnús's journey westwards and are linked by very brief prose comments. It is introduced, *Þess getr í Hrúnhendu,*[5] *at Magnús Ólafsson hèlt herskipum sínum austan or Garðaríki, fyrst í Eystrasalt ok svâ til Svíþjóðar: þar segir svâ*:

Diplomatic and edited text

Her skip vanto af h*ar*da stín*n*um
hlun*ne* geyst j salltid eyst*ra*
skiolldung*r* stet*t* a skoru*m* huelldan
skeid*ar* huf m*ed* gírzku skrudi
vafd*ir* litt en vend*ir* bífduzst
v*er*da h*ra*uck en nidr nam sauckua
geyst*iz* hlyr en h*r*istiz b*ar*a
h*r*imí stockín bun*ar* g*ri*mr.

Herskip vannt af harða stinnum
hlunni geyst í Salt et Eystra;
skjǫldungr, stétt á skǫrum hvéldan
skeiðar húf með girzku *rei*ði.
Vafðir lítt, en vendir bifðusk;
v*art*a hrǫkk, en niðr nam søkkva;
geystisk hlýr, en hrist*i* bára,
hrími stokkin, búnar grímur.

Prose order and translation

Vannt geyst herskip af harða stinnum hlunni í Salt et Eystra. Skjǫldungr, stétt á skeiðar húf, hvéldan skǫrum, með girzku *rei*ði. Vafðir lítt, en vendir bifðusk. V*art*a hrǫkk, en nam søkkva niðr. Hlýr geystisk, en bára, hrími stokkin, hrist*i* búnar grímur.

You made warships speed from the most firm launcher into the Eastern Salt. King, you boarded the ship's hull, curved by its jointed planks, [and] with Russian tackle. You wavered little, but masts shuddered. The prow jolted, and started to plunge. The bows surged on, and the billow, flecked with rime, shook the adorned figure-heads.

Commentary

4/2 hlunne 'launcher'. *Hlunnr* is the collective term applied to the rollers of hard wood by means of which ships were launched or dragged ashore (see Falk 1912, 28).

4/2 salltid eystra 'the Eastern Salt'. Apparently a poetic rendering of *Eystrasalt* or *et / hit eystra salt*, the Baltic. The details of Magnús's journey have been discussed by Johan Schreiner (1927–29).

[5] Since the text here is reproduced from *Magns(H-Hr)* in *Fms* VI, 1831, the length-marks in *Hrúnhenda* or *Hrýnhenda* (Contexts to *Hryn* 4, 5, 8, 13 and 15) are editorial.

4/3 *skiolldungr* 'king', lit. 'descendant of Skjǫldr' — a son of Óðinn and mythical ruler of Jutland (*SnE* pp. 6, 135 and 183–84). Arnórr uses the *heiti* five times, always in reference to Magnús. He may have intended the Danish associations of the word to flatter Magnús as the rightful ruler of Denmark, especially since the term was also much favoured by the skalds of Knútr inn ríki (Frank 1994, 194).

4/3 *huelldan* 'curved'. *Hvéldr* (or *hveldr*), here applied to *húfr* 'hull', is not otherwise known in ON. Blöndal records it for the modern language, although both his citations are from Sveinbjörn Egilsson's translations of Homer. In one of these the adj. is applied to ships: *sendi ... til hinna hveldu skipa*. *Hvéldr* is apparently related to *hvél* 'wheel', and although ON **hvéla* 'to shape like a wheel' is not recorded, cf. modern *kvela* (nynorsk) and, possibly, *kvelva* (Vest-Agder dialect) 'to arch' (Heggstad 1930, s. v. *hvéldr*; Torp 1963, s. v., on the other hand derives *kvelva* from ON *hvelfa*). The length of the vowel in *hvél / hvel* is discussed, with references, in the Supplement to Fritzner, s. v.

4/4 *huf* 'hull'. *Húfr* denotes specifically the third and fourth strakes from the keel, but can refer more generally to the central body of the ship as distinct from the bows and stern, as in the phrase *húfr ok halsar*.

4/4 *gírzku* 'Russian'. The adj. *girzkr* can mean 'Greek, Byzantine', but it also occurs as a doublet of *gerzkr* with the sense 'Russian, from Garðar', as, probably, in Arnórr's *Hryn* 9/8, where Hr reads *gírzkum* and Fl, *gerzskum* (see also Fritzner, s. v. *girzkr*). 'Russian' is clearly more appropriate here since Magnús is sailing from Garðar.

4/4 *reiði* (em.) 'tackle'. MS *skrúði* would add a supernumary member to the alliterative sequence on *sk-* and would fail to produce full rhyme with *skeiðar*. Emendation to the synonymous *reiði* seems justifiable especially since *Hryn* 9/1 affords a certain instance of the scribe of Hr (or its archetype) displacing the original rhyme-word by a synonym. The emendation was first proposed by Konráð Gíslason (1877, 54).

Reiði can refer either to the whole of a ship's equipment (as in the phrase *skip ok reiði*) or else specifically to the rigging (as in the phrase *segl / rá ok reiði* 'sail / sail-yard and rigging'). See Fritzner, s. v.

4/5 *vafdir litt* 'you wavered little'.

(a) The verb *vefja* commonly has the meaning 'fold, wrap' (material, etc.). When used, as here, of human subjects the sense is usually 'become embroiled' (in some difficult affair). From this it is not far to the sense 'hesitate, waver', and this is supported by *Ht* 64, *vafði lítt ... fram at sœkja* 'he little hesitated to launch an attack'. Under this interpretation the verse contrasts the immovable courage of Magnús with the turbulence of the sea, just as in *Þdr* 7b Þorfinnr is undaunted in the melée of the battle.

(b) The attractive suggestion that *vefja* 'wrap' here has the specific nautical sense 'take in sail, reef' is contextually plausible but not, to my knowledge, supported by usage elsewhere (Foote 1978, 63 and n. 26).

4/6 *varta* (em.) '?prow'. MS *v́da* could be expanded to normalised *verða* or *virða*, but the known senses of these do not fit the context. The syntax seems to demand a nom. sing. noun.

(a) *Varta* is the most widely accepted suggestion (first made in *CPB* II 592). *Varta* occurs in *Þul* IV z 8 (with v. l. *vortr)* among *heiti* for parts of a ship. It occupies the same metrical line there as *brandar* '(decorated) prows', and Hjalmar Falk held that *varta* too meant 'prow' (1912, 45). This conjecture yields good sense in *Hryn* 4, for 'prow' makes a highly appropriate subject to *hrǫkk, en niðr nam søkkva* 'jolted, and started to plunge', and it is perhaps supported by the occurrence of ON *varta* 'wart' and *geirvarta* 'nipple (of a man)', cf. the Mod. Icel. synonym *brjóstvarta.* It seems likely that a word meaning 'wart / nipple' should, because of its reference to a projection, develop the metaphorical sense 'prow'.[6] Compare *brjóst* 'prow' in Refr 4, 3 and other words which designate parts of the body and parts of a ship, e. g. *hals* 'neck / part of the forecastle' or *hlýr* 'cheek / bows'.

[6] The origin and meaning of *varta* in Þorbjǫrn svarti's sole extant verse and in the compound Gullvarta, the Norse name for the golden gate in Constantinople, are too uncertain to assist here: see Lidén 1928, 358–361. Brøgger and Shetelig (1950, 154) suggested that the nautical term *vorte* [*varta*] referred to a stout oak block that held the rudder upright against the gunwale.

(b) The suggestion that *verða* is the correct reading, meaning a plank covering used to protect (*verja*) the inside of a ship against breakers (made in *Fms* XII, 1837, 127) is attractive but I know of no record of the word in this sense.

4/7 *hristi* (em.) 'shook'. MS *hristiz bara* 'the billow shook / tossed' (intransitive) is an adequate reading, but it leaves *búnar grímur* 'adorned figure-heads' outside the syntax of the helming. The simplest solution is to emend to *hristi,* transitive 'shook', so that *bára* is the subject, and *búnar grímur* object, to the verb (as proposed by Konráð Gíslason, 1875–89, II 159).

The *-z* in MS *hristiz* may be an error influenced by the preceding reflexives, MS *bífduzst* and *geystiz*; or it may represent an attempt to make the syntax of the line complete, regardless of the syntax of the helming. This would be characteristic of the compiler of *H-Hr* (Louis-Jensen 1977, 152).

4/7 and 4/8 *bara* | *hrimí stockín* 'billow, flecked with rime'. The alternative construction, with *hrími stokkin* qualifying *varta,* is adopted in *Skjald* B but rejected by Kock, *NN* §811.

4/8 *grimr* 'figure-heads'. The normalised form *grímur* is established by both sense and metre.

Verse Five

Sources

Magns(Hkr) ch. 2, p. 8: K(495v), F(37r), J2(239v–240r), 39(12v), 47(3r)
Magns(H-Hr) p. 23: Hr(3v)
Ólsh(Sep) p. 615: 2(73r), 4(68v), 61(129v), 73(425), 325V(88r), 325VI(41r), 325VII(41r), Bb(205r), Th(160r).

Context

Magns(Hkr) and *Ólsh(Sep)*: Snorri prefaces the verse by a comment that Magnús and his force went overland to Helsingjaland. In *Ólsh(Sep)* the name of the *drápa* is given, and in unusual forms: *Sva segir ArnoR i hermandiNi* [vv. ll. *hryniandiNi, hryneande*]:

Magns(H-Hr): The strophe follows *Hryn* 4, separated only by a remark on the support Magnús won in Sweden, and by the introductory words, *Svá segir Arnór í Hrúnhendu:*

Diplomatic and edited text

Rav*ðar* barot rand*ir* siðan
r*imm*o yGr um sǫnsc*ar* bygð*ir*
e*igi* gaztu liðs cost lágan
l*an*dz folc sótti þ*er* til handa
avstan þ*ur*þut ulfa ferð*ar*
avldom kun*n*r með hvita scioldo
tungo rioðr til tir*ar* þinga
tekn*ir* m*enn* *oc* davRin recno.

Rauðar bǫ́ruð randir síðan,
rimmu Yggr, of sœnskar byggðir;
eigi gaztu liðskost lágan;
landsfolk sótti þér til handa.
Austan þurðuð, ulfa ferðar
ǫldum kunnr, með hvíta skjǫldu,
tungurjóðr, til tírar þinga
teknir menn, ok dǫrr en reknu.

Prose order and translation

Síðan bǫ́ruð rauðar randir, rimmu Yggr, of sœnskar byggðir. Eigi gaztu lágan liðskost. Landsfolk sótti til handa þér. Ulfa ferðar tungurjóðr, ǫldum kunnr, þurðuð austan, menn teknir til tírar þinga, með hvíta skjǫldu ok dǫrr en reknu.

Next you carried scarlet targes, battle-Óðinn, through Swedish settlements. No mean pick of troops you gained. The men of the land put themselves in your hands. Wolf-pack's tongue-reddener [warrior], renowned to peoples, you swept from the east, men chosen for glorious encounters, with white shields and chased spears.

Apparatus

(1) barot] baro J2, 47, 61, 73, 325V, 325VII, Bb, Th **siðan]** sidar 61 **(2) r*imm*o]** rymmu J2, RunnaR 73 **yGr]** ygr F, 4, 325VI, ygs Th **um]** so also F, 39, i others **sǫnsc*ar*]** sonsk*ar* J2, þrænsk*ar* 73 **(3) liðs cost]** lið- 4, 61, Th, lidskot Bb **(4) l*an*dz folc]** land- F, 2, 61, Bb, l*a*nd h*er* Hr, 73, 325VI **(5) þ*ur*þut]** þurðuz J2, þordut Hr, 61, 73, 325V, 325VII, þyrdvt Bb **ulfa]** umla Th **ferð*ar*]** sk*er*dir 61, ferd*ir* Bb **(6) avldom]** olldu 61 **með]** vid Hr, yf*ir* 61 **scioldo]** unclear 2 **(7) tungo]** tvGv 325V **til]** yf*ir* 61, med 73, 325VI **tir*ar*]** tirrar Bb **þinga]** vngr*ar* 61, þíngum 73, 325VI, unga 325VII, Th (8) ***oc*]** m*eð* 4, en 61 **recno]** rekn*na* 61.

Commentary

5/2 *rimmo yGr* 'battle-Óðinn, Óðinn of tumult'. A kenning for 'warrior', here Magnús.

Lines 5/3 and 5/4. Arnórr's reference to the Swedes' willing support of Magnús is illuminated by Sigv 9, 1–3, in which the skald praises Ástríðr, widow of Óláfr helgi, for generously helping her stepson Magnús to win Norway. She put his case to a great force of Swedes, assembled at Hangrar, near Sigtún, and (presumably) won them over.

5/5 *þurþut* 'you swept, rushed', from the past tense of *þyrja*. As the only verb in the *helmingr*, this must be construed as predicate to nom. pl. *teknir menn* (on which, see further below).

5/5 and 5/7 *ulfa ferðar ... tungo rioðr* 'tongue-reddener of the pack of wolves'. Warrior, who provides carrion for the beasts of the battlefield.

5/7 *til tirar þinga* 'for glorious encounters'. (a) Although similar in construction to a kenning, *tírar þing* is not a true kenning. *Þing* can stand alone in the sense 'battle' (as in Sigv 1, 11, the only sure example), and *tírar* 'of glory' has here an adjectival rather than substantival role (as also in *tírar fǫr* 'glorious journey', Tindr 1, 5).

(b) V. l. *tirrar* is suspect, since preserved only in the unreliable MS Bb, but it is an interesting reading, for it could be gen. sing. of a rare word for 'sword', an analogical variant of *tjǫrr*. *Tirr* occurs in all three MSS of *Krm* 3, *ok tir ruðum víða* 'and we reddened the sword far and wide', and *ǫltirr* '(?) magical sword' occurs among *sverða heiti* in *Þul* IV 1 2. (On *ǫltirr* see *IEW* p. 488; de Vries s. v.) 'Sword' is a very common element in battle kennings, including *hrings þing*, H ókr 1, 8.

5/8 *teknir menn* 'men chosen'. No recorded use of *taka / tekinn* alone suits the present context, but two meanings of *taka til* are possible if *teknir til tírar þinga* are construed together. (a) 'Choose, elect', completed either by the name of a position, e. g. 'king, mistress' *(konungs / frillu)*, by a more abstract term such as 'arbitration' *(gerðar)* or by an *at* ... clause (Fritzner, *taka til* sense (9)). This seems to give the best sense in the present context, although it is not specified by whom Magnús and company are 'chosen' — presumably God or an abstract destiny. This is Finnur Jónsson's interpretation in *Skjald* B. Kock accepts the sense 'chosen' for *teknir*, but does not construe it with *til tírar þinga*, which he takes rather with *þurðu* (*NN* §1133).

(b) *Taka e-n, e-s til e-s* can refer to reputation, as in *hann var til þess tekinn, at honum var verra til hjóna en ǫðrum mǫnnum* 'he had the reputation of being worse off for servants than others', *Grettis saga* ch. 30, p. 101, quoted in Fritzner, *taka til* sense (10). It is thus conceivable that *teknir til tírar þinga* means 'famed for glorious encounters'.

Verse Six

Note: In *Ólsh(Sep)* and *Magns(H-Hr) Hryn* 6a and 7 form a single strophe.

Sources

Magns(Hkr) ch. 2, pp. 8–9: K(496r), F(37r), J2(240r), 39(12v), 47(3v)
Magns(H-Hr) p. 24 (lines 1–4 only): Hr(3v)
Ólsh(Sep) p. 615 (lines 1–4 only): 2(73r), 4(68v), 61(129v), 73(425), 325V(88r), 325VI(41r), 325VII(41r), Bb(205r), Th(160r)
SnE(Arnamagn) II 498 (lines 1–4 only): W(168).

Context

In *Magns(Hkr)* and *Magns(H-Hr)* the verse is paraphrased, with the added comment that Magnús was welcomed by the Norwegians (this is elaborated in *H-Hr*), and then cited.
In *Ólsh(Sep)* it follows v. 5 with the simple link, *Oc eN sva*:
SnE: Snorri is citing kennings in which a man is referred to as provider of food for carrion-beasts, in this case *Yggjar mǫ́s fiðrirjóðr*.

Diplomatic and edited text

Austan comtu með allra hæstum	Austan komt með allra hæstum,
yGiar más i þrǫnda bygð*ir*	Yggjar mǫ́s, í þrœnzkar byggðir,
fiðri rioðr eN fiandm*enn* yðra	fiðrirjóðr, — en fjandmenn yðra
fálma q*va*þo ægis hialmi	falma kvǫ́ðu — œgishjalmi.
breiðaz vissu blágams fǫþ*ir*	Breiðask vissu, blágamms fœðir
benia cólgo yðr*ir* dólg*ar*	benja kolgu, yðrir dolgar

hrædd*ir* urðo fiorvi at forþa	— hræddir urðu fjǫrvi at forða
fiandm*enn* þin*ir* vesold sina.	fjandmenn þínir — vesǫld sína.

Prose order and translation

Yggjar mǿs fiðrirjóðr, komt austan í þrœnzkar byggðir með allra hæstum œgishjalmi, en kvǫ́ðu fjandmenn yðra falma.
Dolgar yðrir, benja kolgu blágamms fœðir, vissu vesǫld sína breiðask.
Fjandmenn þínir urðu hræddir at forða fjǫrvi.
Feather-reddener of Yggr's [Óðinn's] gull [raven→warrior], you came from the east into the Þrœndalǫg settlements with highest of all helm of terror, and your foe-men were said to falter. Your enemies, feeder of the swart vulture of wound-surf [warrior], knew that their wretchedness was growing. Your foemen were forced, fearful, to save their lives.

Apparatus

(1) allra hæstum] hæstv*m* tima 325V **hæstum]** hæstan*n* J2, 47, 2, 325VI, h*ra*ustv*m* Hr, hædstan 73, mestan W **(2) más]** márs F, 4, 73, W, mals 61, 325VI, Th, mal 325V, malms 325VII, Bb **þrǫnda]** þrænskar F, J2, 39, 47, 2, 4, 61, 73, 325V, 325VI, 325VII, Th, W, suænsk*ar* Hr, sęnskar Bb **bygð*ir*]** om. W **(3) rioðr]** mordr (or niordr) 61, mordr Th **yðra]** yðr*ar* J2, 47, yðrir 4 **(4) ægis]** ǫgis J2, 47, 2 **hialmi]** hialma Hr, W **(5) breiðaz]** breiðar 47 **vissu]** visu J2 **(6) benia]** bǫnia J2 **cólgo]** kolgór 47 **(7) at]** om. J2, 39, 47.

Commentary

6/2 *i þrænskar* (v. l.) *bygðir* 'to the Þrœndalǫg settlements'. My translation is equally valid for both readings, *Þrœnda*, lit. 'of the people of Þrœndalǫg (Trøndelag), and *þrœnzkar* 'of, belonging to Trøndelag'. The latter is supported by an overwhelming majority of MSS.

6/5 and 6/6 *blágams fǫþir* | *benia cólgo* 'feeder of the swart vulture of wound-surf [blood→raven→warrior]'. *Kolga* 'surf, wave', literally 'chill one', is according to Snorri a daughter of the sea-deities Rǫ́n and Ægir (*SnE* pp. 116 and 175).

Verse Seven

Note: In both sources 6a and 7 form a single strophe.

Sources

Ólsh(Sep) p. 615: 2(73r), 4(68v), 61(129v), 73(425), 325V(88r), 325VI(41r), 325VII(41r), Bb(205r), Th(160r)
Magns(H-Hr) p. 24: Hr(3v).

Context

As for 6a.

Diplomatic and edited text

unga*n* f*ra* ec þic eyþ*ir* þravngva	Ungan frá'k þik, eyðir, þrøngva,
ulfa g*ra*þar þ*eir*ra raþi	ulfa gráðar, þeira ráði;
scilld*ir* scǫck m*eð* scøþan þocka	skildir stǫkk með skœðan þokka
sceiþ*ar* branz f*yr* þér ór l*an*di.	skeiðar brands fyr þér ór landi.

Prose order and translation

Ulfa gráðar eyðir, frá'k þik ungan þrøngva þeira ráði. Skeiðar brands skildir stǫkk fyr þér með skœðan þokka ór landi.
Queller / destroyer of wolves' greed [carrion-provider, warrior], I have heard that you, when young, constrained their course. The shield-provider of the ship's prow [Sveinn Alfífuson] bolted before you, with baleful thought, from the land.

Apparatus

(1) unga*n*] Vnd*an*/v- 61, 325V, 325VII, Th, ung*r* Hr **þic]** þ*er* 325VII, *og* þíg Th, om. Hr **eyþ*ir*]** audlíngr Hr **(2) *gra*þar]** *gra*dr af 61, *gra*dr Hr **(3) scilld*ir*]** skiolldungr 61, 325V, 325VII, Th, Hr **scǫck]** þỏck 73, stod Th, stocc others.

Commentary

7/3 *scilldir* 'shield-provider'. (a) *Skildir* is an agent noun from *skilda* 'furnish with shields', which is attested in Þjóð A 3, 13 *skilda ... hǫmlur* 'fit the rowlocks with shields' and in Arnórr's *á við skildan* 'onto a shield-hung ship' (*Mdr* 19). The *skildir skeiðar brands* 'shield-provider of the ship's prow' is the usurper Sveinn Alfífuson, illegitimate son of Knútr inn ríki.

(b) V. l. *skjǫldungr* is unacceptable since it leaves *skeiðar brands* without function in the syntax.

7/3 *með scøþan þocka* 'with baleful thought'. This phrase may refer generally to Sveinn's hostility towards Magnús, who has caused his flight from Norway, or it may be a more specific allusion to his plan to launch an expedition of revenge against the treacherous Norwegians, reported in some saga accounts (*Fsk* pp. 193–94, *Magns(H-Hr)* p. 25, *Flat* III 263).

Verse Eight

Sources

Magns(H-Hr) p. 26: Hr(4r)
Flat III 264: Fl(761).

Context

Magnús takes Norway under his sway without bloodshed, welcomed by a people weary of Danish overlordship.
In *H-Hr* the verse is introduced, *Svâ segir Arnór í Hrúnhendu:*
In *Flat* it is attributed, together with *Mdr* 4, to 'Skule' (see further Ch. 2, section I).

Diplomatic and edited text

Eignaz namtu odal þcgna	Eignask namtu óðal þegna,
allan noreg gotna spialli	allan Nóreg, gotna spjalli;
m*an*gi rydr þíer milldingr an*n*ar	manngi ryðr þér mildingr annarr,
mæra g*ra*mr t*il* l*an*da ærv.	Mœra gramr, til landa œr*i*.

Prose order and translation

Gotna spjalli, namtu eignask óðal þegna, allan Nóreg. Manngi annarr mildingr, Mœra gramr, ryðr til landa œr*i* þér.
Counsellor of men, you came to win the estates of liegemen, all of Norway. No other monarch, King of the Mœrir, will clear himself lands when younger than you.

Apparatus

(1) odal] od*d og* Fl **(2) spialli]** spíalla Fl **(3) rydr]** e*r* ydr Fl **(4) mæra]** mæta Fl **ærv]** mæ*ri* Fl.

Commentary

8/4 *mæra gramr* 'King of the Mœrir, of the men of Mœrr (Møre)'. By synecdoche, 'king of the Norwegians'.

8/4 *œri* (em.) 'younger'. MSS *(til landa) ærv / mæri* do not make sense. Konráð Gíslason suggested emending *ærv* to *œri* 'younger', the ancient comparative to *ungr* (1877, 47–48). *Þér* in line 3 is probably a dat. of comparison, and *œri* would serve very well as the required comparative adj., hence '(no other monarch ...) younger than you', cf. Arnórr's other comments upon Magnús's youth, at length in *Mdr* 1 and 19 and elsewhere in the form of the epithet *(barn)ungr.* It is likely that the scribes of F1 and Hr (or their predecessors) would have been confused by an original *œri*, for it is believed to have been replaced by the analogical *yngri* in everyday usage by c. 1300 (see Jón Helgason 1928, 379–80). Indeed, Arnórr's is the last skaldic record of the form (here and in *Þdr* 5).

Verse Nine

Sources

Magns(H-Hr) p. 47: H(5v), Hr(6v)
Flat III 271: Fl(764).

Context

Hryn 9 and 10, concerning Magnús's voyage south, are quoted as a prelude to the legendary account of a feast in Denmark at which Hǫrða-Knútr entertained Magnús, only to be himself poisoned by a draught which Alfífa, mother of Sveinn, had intended for the Norwegian guest.
Snorri in *Hkr* omits reference to the poisoning. He does not quote *Hryn* 9 but sets *Hryn* 10 within an account of Magnús's voyage south to claim Denmark after the death of Hǫrða-Knútr in England.

Diplomatic and edited text

Síð*an* *var* *þat* er svðr m*eð* láðí
sikl*in*gr yttí flota míklv*m*
skiði *var* þa skr*ið*ar of avð*it*
skorðv re*n*di visv*n*dr norð*an*
safnaz bað til hv*er*rar homlv
hręðaz m*enn* v*ið* ætt*ar* klæðí
gívka þot*t*i gǫfvgt eiki
gǫ*r*ðzkv*m* hialmi peítv hialma.

Síðan vas þat's sunnr með láði
siklingr ýtti flota miklum;
skíði vas þá skriðar of auðit
skorðu; rendi Visundr norðan.
Samnask bað til hverrar hǫmlu
— hræðask menn við ættar klæði
Gjúka; þótti gǫfugt eiki
girzkum malmi — Peitu hjalma.

Prose order and translation

Síðan vas þat's siklingr ýtti miklum flota sunnr með láði. Þá vas skorðu skíði of auðit skriðar. Visundr rendi norðan. Bað Peitu hjalma samnask til hverrar hǫmlu. Menn hræðask við klæði Gjúka ættar. Eiki þótti gǫfugt girzkum malmi.
Later it happened that the sovereign launched a great fleet south along the coast. Then the ski of the ship's prop [ship] was granted motion. Visundr [Bison] charged from the north. He [Magnús] urged helmets from Poitou to rally at every rowlock. Men fear the garments of Gjúki's offspring [armour]. The oaken vessel seemed splendid with its Russian metal.

Apparatus

(1) *var* *þat* er] v*ann* þa Fl **láðí]** l*a*ndi Hr, Fl **(3) of]** om. Fl **(7) gívka]** giuku Fl **eiki]** ecke Fl **(8) gǫrðzkv*m*]** gírzku*m* Hr, g*er*zsku*m* Fl **hialmi]** malmí Hr, Fl **peítv]** petu Fl.

Commentary

9/4 *visvndr* 'Bison'. This was the name of a ship which, according to tradition, Óláfr helgi had built and which Magnús inherited (see Sigv 12, 3 and *Magns(Hkr)* ch. 19, p. 34). Þjóðólfr Arnórsson uses the same name to refer to Magnús's ship in his *Magnússflokkr* (Þjóð A 1, 4; c. 1045).

9/5 *safnaz* 'to rally'. The normalised form *samnask* is established by the *skothending* with *hǫmlu. Samna* also rhymes on *-m-* in a line by Arnórr's contemporary Bjarni Hallbjarnarson Gullbrárskáld: *emkak tamr at samna* (Bj H 3).

9/5 *homlv* ‘rowlock’. The term *hamla* refers strictly to a loop of leather or rope which holds the oar against the *hár*, the wooden support projecting from the upper strake of the gunwale.

9/6 *hręðaz* ‘fear’. This interesting use of the present tense is established by the rhyme *hræðask : klæði.*

9/6 and 9/7 *ættar klæðí* | *gívka* ‘the garments of Gjúki’s offspring [armour]’. Gjúki is the renowned king of the Burgundians. This kenning presumably alludes to Guðrún Gjúkadóttir’s heroic sons Hamðir and Sǫrli, for there are several ‘armour’ kennings containing their names, especially Hamðir’s. It might additionally refer to Gjúki’s sons Gunnarr, Hǫgni and Guttormr, but of these only Hǫgni, according to *LP* and Meissner (1921, p. 165), figures as the determinant in kennings for armour.

9/8 *gírzkum* (v. l.) *malmí* (v. l.) ‘Russian metal’. The MS form *g̊ðzkv̄* (i. e. *gǫrðzkvm*, cf. *dām̊k* beside *danmǫrk* elsewhere in H) is not otherwise attested, to my knowledge, and I assume it to be a graphic variant of *gerzkr/gerðskr*, cf. the variant forms *ger(ð)zki*, *gærzke* and *gørzci* for (Guðleikr) gerzki in MSS of *Ólsh(Sep)*, p. 120. Another, less likely, possibility is that it represents the dat. sing. masc. of an adj. **garzkr* ‘from Garðar’.

Girzkr could mean either ‘Russian, from Garðar’ or ‘Greek’, as explained in the Commentary to *Hryn* 4/4. The *girzkr malmr* which adorns the ship could be weapons which the warriors carry on board along with their armour, or iron plating such as protected the prow on some warships: Bǫlv 2 refers to *skeiðr brynjaðar* ‘armoured ships’, and see Shetelig and Falk 1937, 357. A further possibility is that *malmr*, as elsewhere in ON poetry, means ‘gold’, e. g. *skírr malmr*, lit. ‘bright metal’ in *Akv* 39 and *hǫfugr malmr*, lit. ‘heavy metal’, in Sigv 13, 16. It could hence refer to ornament on the prow, stern and / or mast-head.

In the main MS, *hialmi* is clearly a case of dittography from *hialma* later in the line.

9/8 *peítv hialma* ‘helmets from Poitou / Poitiers’. The phrase is probably used metonymically here to refer to Magnús’s helmeted warriors. I know of no parallel to this usage, although the personal names Hjalmr and Hjalmarr may have arisen from the notion that a man was the 'helmet' of his people. There is a precedent for the mention of a 'helmet from Poitou', for Sigvatr Þórðarson in his *Nesjarvísur* v. 14 (1016), says *peitneskum feltk ... hjalmi* (cf. *hjalmr enn valski* 'the French / foreign helmet', Sigv 13, 5). Arms from Poitou were apparently renowned, for *peita* came to be used in poetry as an appellative for 'spear'.

Verse Ten

Sources

Magns(Hkr) ch. 19, p. 34: K(506v–507r), F(39r), J2(247r), 39(15r), 47(6r)
Flat III 271: Fl(764)
Magns(H-Hr) pp. 47–48: H(5v), Hr(6v).

Context

Hkr: See Context to *Hryn* 9. The strophe is preceded by a short description of the ship Visundr: it has more than thirty benches and a gilded bison's head and tail at prow and stern.
Flat and *H-Hr*: See Context to *Hryn* 9. No comment separates the two strophes in *Flat*, but they are followed by, *Hier er nockut til visat vm ferdina hans*. In *H-Hr* a brief comment links the two: *Í þeirri ferð sigldi Magnús konúngr suðr til Danmerkr; svâ segir Arnór:*

Diplomatic and edited text

Lioto dreif a lypting utan	Ljótu dreif á lypting útan
lavðri bifþiz gullit ravða	lauðri — bifðisk goll et rauða;
fastligr hneigði furo geistri	fastligr hneigði fúru geystri
fyris garmr um skeið*ar* styre	fýris garmr — ok skeiðar stýri.
stirðum hellztu u*m* Stafangr norþ*an*	Stirðum helzt umb Stafangr norðan
stálum bifþuz fyri al*ar*	stǫlum — bifðusk fyrir álar;
upi gloðo elmars typpi	uppi glóðu élmars typpi
eldi glic i danaveldi.	eldi glík — í Danaveldi.

Prose order and translation

Ljótu lauðri dreif útan á lypting ok skeiðar stýri. Goll et rauða bifðisk. Fastligr fýris garmr hneigði geystri fúru. Helzt stirðum stǫlum norðan umb Stafangr í Danaveldi. Álar bifðusk fyrir. Élmars typpi glóðu uppi, eldi glík.

Foul surf surged in against the poop and the galley's helm. The red gold shuddered. Powerful, the fir-tree's hound [wind] pitched the rushing ship of fir. You steered sturdy prows from the north by Stavanger to the realm of the Danes / Denmark. Currents foamed in front. The storm-steed's [ship's] mast-heads glowed aloft, like fire.

Apparatus

(1) Lioto] Liotu*m* J2, Liot*ir* Hr **dreif]** v*ar*p Fl, H, Hr **(2) lavðri]** laudír Hr **bifþiz]** bifðoz 47, Hr, bífízt Fl **(3) -ligr]** -líga Fl, Hr **geistri]** geystri F, 39, Fl, H, Hr, glæstri J2, 47 **(4) fyris]** fyr*r*is Fl **garmr]** g*ra*mr 39, 47, ang*r* Fl, H, Hr **um]** oc J2, 47, Fl, H, Hr **styre]** styra Fl **(5) stirðum]** st*r*idu*m* Fl **hellztu]** hielldu Fl, hiellt H, Hr **u*m*]** om. F, Fl, f*yrir* H, Hr **(6) bifþuz]** bifðiz F, Fl **fyri al*ar*]** fyr*r*isalar Fl **fyri]** f*yrir* J2, fvri 39 **(7) -mars]** -mas Fl, Hr.

Commentary

10/2 *gullit ravða* 'the red gold'. The reference may be to gilding on the whole ship, or else — as Snorri seems to take it in the *Hkr* Context (above) — specifically to the prow and stern. *Skjald* B contains an unnecessary emendation here, dismissed by Kock in *NN* §813.

10/3 *furo* and **10/4 *fyris*** (normalised *fúru* and *fýris*), both 'fir / pine'. In line 4 the *aðalhending* with *stýri* strongly suggests that the vowel of *fýri* 'fir' is long.

(a) Bjarni Aðalbjarnarson suggested that *fýri* might be a poetic licence which provides the long first syllable necessary to the metre (*Hkr* 1941–51, III, 34n.)

(b) Konráð Gíslason, on the other hand, argued from MS spellings, etymology and ON word-formation that the words for 'fir', *fyri* and *fura*, had genuine variants with long vowels (1877, 45–47).

10/4 *fyris garmr* 'fir-tree's hound'. A kenning for 'wind'. V. l. *fýris angr* 'grief of fir' would make equally good sense in the context: cf. *almsorg* 'sorrow of the elm [wind]' E Sk 12, 16.

10/4 *oc* (v. l.) 'and'.

(a) V. l. *ok* gives good sense, linking *lypting* 'poop', the raised decking in the stern, with *skeiðar stýri* 'galley's helm', also in the stern, so that the two complete the clause *ljótu lauðri dreif á ...* 'foul surf surged against ...' *Ok skeiðar stýri* could be alternatively taken with *bifðisk goll et rauða* 'the red gold shuddered', but 'helm' and 'gold' are a rather ill-assorted pair.

(b) *Um skeiðar stýri* 'about the galley's helm' could grammatically be construed with *hneigði fúru geystri* | *fýris garmr* 'the fir-tree's hound [wind] pitched the rushing ship of fir'. The sentence would then contain two words for 'ship', which is awkward but not impossible.

(c) It is also not impossible that *skeiðar stýri* is acc. sing. of a 'seafarer' kenning referring to Magnús (so *Fms* XII, 1837, 131). 'Agent noun' kennings with *stýrir* as base word and 'ship' as determinant are recorded: see *LP* s. v. *stýrir*.

10/6 *bifþuz fyri alar* 'currents foamed in front'. *Álar* is most logically construed as subject to *bifðusk* 'shook, foamed'. MS *fyri* is here assumed to be the stressed adverb, normalised *fyrir*, and I translate 'in front [of the advancing ship]'. Kock (*NN* §814) suggested *(havet bävade) därvid* '(the sea trembled) at that'. The spellings *fyri* and *firi* are well attested in early MSS as alternatives to *fyrir* etc.

10/7 and 10/8 *upi gloðo elmars typpi* | *eldi glic* 'mast-heads of the storm-steed [ship] glowed aloft like fire'. Arnórr's punning use of *typpi* 'mast-heads, forelocks' is noted on p. 77.

A kenning by Sigvatr also embodies the conceit that gold on a mast-top gleams like fire: *húna hyrr* 'flame of the mast-tops [gold]' (Sigv 12, 16), and this may have inspired Arnórr's more fully developed simile. Reinskou pointed out that both skalds are referring to the ship Visundr, and suggested that gilding on the mast-head, since not mentioned in earlier poetry, may have been an innovation in Óláfr helgi's time (1922, 34–35). Hougen doubts whether the skalds' references to gold and gilded prows on ships out at sea are more than a poetic hyperbole (1974, 18–19).

Verse Eleven

Sources

Magns(Hkr) ch. 24, p. 39: K(509r–v), F(39v), J2(248r), 39(15v), 47(7r).

Context

Magnús leads a fleet against the rebellious Wends of Jómsborg: *Þess getr Arnórr jarlaskáld:*

Diplomatic and edited text

Heyra scaltu hve h*er*sciold barot	Heyra skalt, hvé herskjǫld bǫ́ruð,
hylmis kundr t*il* vinda grundar	hilmis kundr, til Venða grundar
hep*p*in*n* drottu af hlun*n*i slettum	— heppinn drótt af hlunni sléttum
hélug bǫrð i stefia meli	hélug bǫrð — í stefjaméli.
ald*ri* fra ec eɴ visi valdit	Aldri frá'k — en, vísi, valdið
vinda sorg at dǫglingr spendi	Venða sorg — at dǫglingr spenði
flavstum varð þa floð um ristit	(flaustum varð þá flóð of ristit)
fleiri scip t*il* oðals þ*eir*a.	fleiri skip til óðals þeira.

Prose order and translation

Hilmis kundr, skalt heyra í stefjaméli, hvé bǫ́ruð herskjǫld til Venða grundar. Drótt, heppinn, hélug bǫrð af sléttum hlunni. Aldri frá'k at dǫglingr spenði fleiri skip til óðals þeira, en, vísi, valdið Venða sorg. Þá varð flóð of ristit flaustum.

Ruler's kinsman, you shall hear in a refrain-section how you carried the war-shield to the land of the Wends. You dragged, well-starred, rime-spread prows from the smooth launcher. Never have I heard of a sovereign steering more ships against their patrimony, and, prince, you cause the Wends grief. Then was the flood cloven by ships.

Apparatus

(1) hve] hv*ar* F **(2) hylmis]** hilmís others **vinda]** vindl*an*dz F, 39, vinða 47 **(3) hep*p*in*n*]** heitin*n* J2, 47 **(4) hélug]** heilug J2(?), 47 **bǫrð]** borð J2, 39, 47 **(5) fra ec]** frac J2, 47 **visi]** vili J2, 47 **(6) vinda]** vinða F, 47 **spendi]** spenði F, 39 **(7) varð]** v*ar* others **um]** of others.

Commentary

11/2 *hylmis kundr* 'ruler's kinsman'. Magnús. *Hilmir* is presumably a specific reference to the renowned Óláfr helgi. Its literal meaning may be 'helmeted one' (*IEW* p. 243) or 'helmet-provider' (de Vries, s. v.).

11/4 *bǫrð* 'prows'. V. l. *borð* would make equally good sense in the context: 'you dragged rime-spread bulwarks from the smooth launcher'.

11/4 *i stefia meli* 'in a refrain-section'. On the part of the *stefjamél* in the structure of the *drápa*, see p. 31.

11/5 *eN* 'and'. Since MS *eN* is in a position of low stress I take it as the conjunction (normalised) *en* (so also Kock, who cites parallels in *NN* §815). The alternative possibility is that it is the adverb *enn* 'yet, still' and modifies *aldri frá'k*, hence 'never yet have I heard ...' (so *Skjald* B), or *vísi, valdit Venða sorg* 'prince, you still cause grief for the Wends'.

11/5 *valdit* 'you cause'. The use of the present tense verb alongside past tense forms might imply that Magnús was still undertaking or contemplating action against the Wends when Arnórr composed his *Hryn*, or else more generally that it is Magnús's habit or natural role to be making onslaughts on the Wends.

11/6 *vinda* (normalised *Venðr*). 'Wends'. Magnús's expedition against this pagan Slavic people was designed to curb their westward incursions on the coasts of N. Germany and Denmark. On the Wends, see Damgaard-Sørensen 1991.

The form of the name is difficult to establish. Early (non-Norse) evidence would point to an alternation of *e/i* as root vowel (see de Vries, s. v. *Vindr* 2). Arnórr's rhyme on *spendi* suggests *e* here, but in H ókr 7/2 the rhyme on *ginðu* suggests *i*. As for the consonant group, the fullest rhyme is obtained by reading *Venda* here, but other evidence suggests *-nð* as the correct form in a short-stemmed word at this date (see p. 105).

Verse Twelve

Sources

Magns(Hkr) ch. 24, pp. 39–40: K(509v), F(39v), J2(249r), 39(15v), 47(7r)

SnE p. 180 (lines 1–4 only): R(77), T(43r), 748II(8v), 757(7r).

Context

Hkr: The verse is paraphrased and then introduced, *Svá segir Arnórr jarlaskáld*:
SnE: Snorri is listing poetic names which can be applied equally to *keisari, konungr* or *jarl*. The helming is introduced, *Mildingr, sem Markvs q(vað)*:

Diplomatic and edited text

Scioldungr fortu um oþioð eldi
avðit *var* þa flotnum davða
hæstan kyndut hleNa þryst*ir*
hyriar lioma suðr a iomi
hv*er*gi þorði hall*ir* varða
heiþit folc i virki breiðo
buðlungr uNut b*or*gar m*onnum*
biǫrtum elldi stall hiǫrtu.

Skjǫldungr, fórt of óþjóð eldi;
auðit vas þá flotnum dauða;
hæstan kynduð, hlenna þrýstir,
hyrjar ljóma sunnr at Jómi.
Hvergi þorði hallir varða
heiðit folk í virki breiðu;
buðlungr, unnuð borgarmǫnnum
bjǫrtum eldi stalldræp hjǫrtu.

Prose order and translation

Skjǫldungr, fórt eldi of óþjóð. Þá vas flotnum auðit dauða. Hlenna þrýstir, kynduð hæstan hyrjar ljóma sunnr at Jómi. Heiðit folk þorði hvergi varða hallir í breiðu virki. Buðlungr, unnuð borgarmǫnnum stalldræp hjǫrtu bjǫrtum eldi.
King, you fared with flame through the evil tribe. Then were men fated with death. Crusher of thieves [just ruler], you kindled a towering blaze of fire south at Jóm. The heathen host dared not at all to defend halls in the broad stronghold. Royal one, you wrought in the townsmen terror-struck hearts, by means of bright flame.

Apparatus

(1) ***Scioldungr]*** Mildi*n*gr R, T, 748II, Milldin*n* ... 757 **fortu]** for R, T, 748II, ...ortu 757 **um]** of R, T, 757 **oþioð eldi]** þ... de 757 **(2)** ***var*]** varð R, T, 748II, 757 **davða]** da... 757 **(3) hæstan]** hesta 748II, illeg. 757 **þryst*ir*]** þreyt*ir* J2, þrysti 39 **(4) hyriar lioma]** ...oma 757 **a]** at others **iomi]** romí 748II **(8) stall hiǫrtu]** stall dræp híorto F, J2, 47, stall drap (?)hiartaz 39.

Commentary

12/1 *Scioldungr* 'King', lit.' descendant of Skjǫldr'. It is interesting that the opening word, and even the ascription, of *Hryn* 12 differs in the two prose works which preserve it, when both are the work of Snorri. I take *skjǫldungr* to be the original reading, *mildingr* the secondary one, since Snorri (or an early scribe of his *Edda*) could well have been led into error by the similar line *mildingr fór of munka veldi* in v. 12 of Markús Skeggjason's *Hrynhenda* (see further p. 26).

12/4 *at* (v. l.) *iomi* 'at Jóm'. V. l. *at*, being the agreement of all MSS except K, and the reading of H and Hr in *Mdr* 8/3 *at iomi,* is likely to be the skald's original. Jóm is present-day Wollin set on an island at the mouth of the Oder.[7]

12/7 and 12/8 *uɴut borgar monnum ... stall dræp* (v. l.) *hiǫrtu* 'you wrought in the townsmen terror-struck hearts'. V. l. *stalldræp hjǫrtu* is certainly correct, for the K reading, *stall hjǫrtu,* is metrically deficient. *Vinna e-m stalldræpt hjarta* is probably a secondary variant of the phrase *hjarta drepr stall* 'the heart is stopped / struck [with terror]' which Arnórr uses in *Þdr* 7 (see Commentary to lines 5 and 8). Halldór Halldórsson suggests that the adj. *stalldræpr* was formed by Arnórr himself (1963, 41 and 62). It otherwise only occurs in verse 15b of the *Háttalykill*, composed a century later.

Verse Thirteen

Sources

Magns(H-Hr) p. 68: H(9r), Hr(9r)
Flat III 281: Fl(769).

Context

H-Hr: The defeated Wends flee as far as the Skotborg river (modern Kongeå) where, caught up by Magnús's men, they surge into the

[7] O. Kunkel and K. A. Wilde carried out excavations at Jóm beginning in 1934; their findings are conveniently summarised by N. F. Blake in *Jómsvíkinga saga* 1962, ix–xi. W. Filipowiak found evidence of fire which he dated to the 1040s and identified with Magnús's attack on the town (Andersen 1977, 163).

water. So many are slain that their bodies make a causeway: *Svâ segir í Hrýnhendu:*
Flat: The strophe follows *Mdr* 10, prefaced *Ogh enn segir so:*

Diplomatic and edited text

Skíǫlldv*n*gr líetzt v*ið* skíra valldít	Skjǫldungr, lézt við skíra valdit
skotb*or*g*ar* á vínða sorgv*m*	Skotborgarǫ́ Venða sorgum;
yngv*i* v*ar* sa frægr er feíngvt	yngvi, vas sá frægr, es fenguð,
fǫrnvðr þ*inn* v*ið* helmi*n*g mín*n*a	fǫrnuðr þinn, við helming minna.
vare la þ*ar* valkǫstr hæʀ*r*i	Vári, lá þar valkǫstr hæri,
v*ar* þ*er* sígr skapaðr g*ra*ms hi*n*s dig*ra*	— vas þér sigr skapaðr grams ens digra —
vi*r*ðv*m* kvn*n* en víða rvn*n*in*n*	virðum kunn*r*, an víða runnin
v*ar*ga æt*t* of klifa mæt*t*i.	varga ætt of klífa mætti.

Prose order and translation

Skjǫldungr, lézt valdit Venða sorgum við skíra Skotborgarǫ́. Yngvi, sá fǫrnuðr þinn, es fenguð við minna helming, vas frægr. Vári virðum kunn*r*, valkǫstr lá þar hæri an varga ætt, víða runnin, mætti of klífa. Sigr ens digra grams vas skapaðr þér.
King, you caused griefs for the Wends by the gleaming Skotborg river. Sovereign, that, your success, which you won with a smaller troop, was famed. Defender, renowned to men, a corpse-pile lay there higher than the wolves' clan, run from far and wide, could climb over. Victory of the stout lord was granted you.

Apparatus

(1) líetzt] líet Hr, letz Fl **valldít]** vallde Fl **(2) vínða]** vínda Hr, Fl **(4) fǫrnvðr]** faurnud Hr, f*or* naud*r* Fl **(5) vare]** vaxi Hr, vor*ru* Fl **(6) skapaðr]** skapt*r* Hr **(7) rvn*n*in*n*]** -ín Hr, Fl **(8) æt*t* of]** ætt ef Hr, ættu*m* Fl.

Commentary

13/5 *vare* '(?) defender'. The reading *vare* is partially secured by the versification, for *v-* is required by the alliterative pattern and *-r-* by the internal rhyme. The vowel is almost certain to be long, since of all Arnórr's *hrynhent* lines only *Hryn* 2/2 fails to begin with a long syllable, and *hnika* there is doubtless corrupt, so that if no emendation is made the word is *vári*.

(a) *Vári* may be related to the verb *verja* and hence have the sense 'defender' (so de Vries, s. v. *vári* 1). It appears in *Húsdr* 2, where it is probably to be construed with *ragna* 'of the gods' or *ragna rein-* 'gods' land' to form an appellation for Heimdallr, who figures elsewhere as guardian of the gods (e. g. *vǫrðr goða* in *Grí* 13 and *Lok* 48). In *Hryn* 13 *vári* 'defender' would be an apostrophe addressed to Magnús and would be qualified by *virðum kunn[r]* 'renowned to men'. In meaning it would be similar to other *heiti* for 'prince' such as *skyli* 'defender' and *vísi* 'leader'. This appears to me the most satisfactory interpretation of *vári*, but there are alternatives, of which the following are the most plausible.

(b) Konráð Gíslason suggested that the original text had a word meaning 'son' or 'descendant' which would be defined by the genitive *grams ens digra* hence 'son of the stout lord [of Óláfr]' (1889, 352n.), and Björn M. Ólsen took up this suggestion, proposing that *vári* 'relative', etymologically linked with *várar* fem. pl. 'faith, compact', was the word in question; cf. also Vǫ́r, goddess of truces (1903, 108–109). Finnur Jónsson, in *Skjald* B, postulated *verja* as the word meaning 'son'.

(c) Kock proposed emending to *verja*, hence *verja valkǫstr* 'corpse-heap of men' (*NN* §816). This expression, however, would be tautologous and it has no parallel in ON, except for the still more unlikely construction proposed by Kock for *Mdr* 11 (see Commentary to *Mdr* 11/4).

13/6 *sígr ... grams hins digra* 'victory of the stout lord'. This phrase may allude to the legend that Óláfr helgi (also inn digri) helped his son Magnús to victory at the battle of Hlýrskógsheiðr (Lyrskovsheden). The legend is variously elaborated in the saga accounts, but recurring motifs are Óláfr helgi's appearance to Magnús and the booming sound which the Norwegians recognise as the bell Glǫð at Niðaróss (Nidaros, Trondheim), site of Óláfr's shrine. According to *Flat*, Magnús spurred on his men with the words, *Ver skǫ̂lum sigr faa þuiat hinn helgi Olafr konungr fer med oss* (III 279). Compare also the words of Einarr Skúlason who, composing a century after the event, says that Óláfr 'gave his bold heir victory' (*sigr gaf sínum ... frǫmum arfa*, E Sk 6, 30).

If interpretation (b) of 13/4 *vare* (above) were adopted, *sigr* and *grams ens digra* could not be construed together and interpreted thus.

13/7 *virðvm kunnr* (em.) 'renowned to men'. The reading *kunn* could only qualify *varga ætt* 'clan of wolves'. It seems unlikely that wolves should be described as 'renowned to men', especially when the synonymous *ǫldum kunnr* and *þjóðum kunnr* are applied to the hero in *Hryn* 5 and 15.

Verse Fourteen

Sources

Magns(Hkr) ch. 35, p. 64: K(519r), F(41v), J2(256r), 39(18r), 47(9v)
Knýtls ch. 22, p. 131 (lines 5–8 only): 20d(16v), 873(16v), 1005(3v)
Magns(H-Hr) p. 91: H(13r), Hr(11r).

Context

Hkr and *H-Hr*: Magnús winters peacefully in Denmark after his victory off Helganes (Helgenæs) and the flight of Sveinn Ulfsson (see Commentary to *Hryn* 15/6), and two verses are quoted to summarise his achievements, first O kík 1, 1 and then *Hryn* 14.
Knýtls: Magnús, it is stated, fought four battles in Denmark against Sveinn Ulfsson — at 'Erri' (v. l. 'Eyre'), off Áróss (Århus), at Hǫfn (Copenhagen) and on Fjón (Fyn), and there were further, lesser, engagements: *En þó segir Arnórr jarlaskáld í Magnússdrápu:*

Diplomatic and edited text

Hefn*ir* fengut yrkis efni	Hefnir, fenguð yrkisefni,
olafs g*er*vi ec slict at malom	Áleifs, gervi'k slíkt at mǫlum;
hlack*ar* lætr þu hrælavg drecka	Hlakkar lætr þú hrælǫg drekka
havka nu m*un* q*væþit* avkaz	hauka; nú mun kvæðit aukask.
fior*ar* hef*ir* þu randa ryr*ir*	Fjórar hefr þú, randa rýrir
reyr*ar* setrs a einom vetri	reyrar setrs, á einum vetri
allvaldr ertu ofvægr kallaðr	— allvaldr, estu ofvægr kallaðr —
ǫrva hrið*ir* frǫcn um g*er*var.	ǫrva hríðir frœkn of gǫrvar.

Prose order and translation

Áleifs hefnir, fenguð yrkisefni. Gervi'k slíkt at mǫlum. Þú lætr Hlakkar hauka drekka hrælǫg. Nú mun kvæðit aukask. Rýrir randa reyrar setrs, þú hefr frœkn of gǫrvar fjórar ǫrva hríðir á einum vetri. Allvaldr, estu kallaðr ofvægr.

Óláfr's avenger, you furnished matter for verse. I fashion such [deeds] into words. You allow Hlǫkk's [a valkyrie's] hawks [ravens] to quaff the corpse-sea [blood]. Now will the poem swell. Hewer of the shield-reed's home [sword→shield→warrior], you have, daring, performed four arrow-blizzards [battles] in one season. All-ruler, you are called invincible.

Apparatus

(5) þu] om. J2, 47 **randa ryr*ir*]** rim*m*ur reyrar 1005 **(6) setrs]** setr H, Hr **(7) ofvægr]** ofueg 20d **(8) ǫrva hriðir]** aurferd hirder 1005 **frǫcn um]** frønk um 873, frægn af 1005, frækin*n* H, Hr **um]** of F, J2, 39, ok 47 **ge*r*var]** gioruan 1005.

Commentary

14/2 *malom* 'words'. Gert Kreutzer cites this context as a particularly clear case of *mǫ́l* being used specifically to refer to the poetry, as opposed to the *yrkisefni* 'matter for verse, for composition' (1977, 86). My translation preserves the broader, more basic sense of *mǫ́l*, 'words, speech'.

14/3 and 14/4 *hlackar ... havka* 'Hlǫkk's hawks'. A kenning for 'ravens' or possibly for 'eagles', the other traditional birds of the battlefield. Hlǫkk, which is both a proper name for a valkyrie, and an appellative for 'valkyrie' and 'battle', is related to *hlakka* 'shriek' (de Vries, s. v.) and hence etymologically means 'noisy one'.

14/5 and 14/8 *fiorar ... ǫrva hriðir* 'four arrow-blizzards'. The 'four battles' fought in a single season (lit. winter) are probably those of Jóm, Ré (Rügen), Áróss and Hlýrskógsheiðr, all fought in 1043, and the verse seems to have been understood so by Snorri (Bjarni Aðalbjarnarson, *Hkr* 1941–51, III, 64n.). The author of *Knýtls*, as the context to the verse there suggests, thought otherwise. That the victory at Hlýrskógsheiðr followed the sacking of Jóm is probable (so Icelandic Annals for 1043, all versions except one: pp. 17, 108, 317 and 469, with p. 58 as the exception. Schreiner 1930–33, 39 favoured dating Hlýrskógsheiðr before Jóm).

14/5 and 14/6 *randa ryrir | reyrar setrs* 'hewer of the shield-reed's home'. *Randa reyr* 'reed of shields' is a sword, the sword's *setr* 'home, resting-place', a shield, and the shield's *rýrir* 'hewer, diminisher', a warrior.

Verse Fifteen

Sources

Magns(H-Hr) p. 85: H(12r), Hr(11r)
Flat III 284: Fl(770)
Knýtls ch. 22, p. 132: 20d(16v), 873(16v–17r).

Context

It is related that Sveinn flees from his disabled ships at Helganes, then Arnórr's strophe is quoted with the words, *Svâ sem segir í Hrýnhendu (H-Hr)*; *Ogh þessar orrostu getr þat skalld [Arnor] er so segir* (*Flat*); *Svá segir Arnórr í Magnússdrápu* (*Knýtls*).

Diplomatic and edited text

Diplomatic	Edited
Keppín*n* vantv þatz æ mvn vppí	Keppinn vannt, þat's æ mun uppi,
yg*g*íar veðr meða*n* hei*m*rin*n* byggíz	Yggjar veðr, meðan heimrinn byggvisk;
valgam*m*r skok j vapnarímv	valgammr skók í vápna rimmu
viðr helga nes bloðvgt fiðri	viðr Helganes blóðugt fiðri.
yng*vi* fektv ǫll m*eð* h*r*ingv*m*	Yngvi fekktu ǫll með hringum,
j*ar*l vissi sik folld*ar* missa	— jarl vissi sik foldar missa —
þioðv*m* kvnr en þv tokt siða*n*	þjóðum kunnr, (en þú tókt síðan)
þ*ei*ra flavst v*ið* sig*ri* meíra.	þeira flaust (við sigri meira).

Prose order and translation

Vannt keppinn Yggjar veðr, þat's mun æ uppi meðan heimrinn byggvisk. Valgammr skók blóðugt fiðri í vápna rimmu viðr Helganes. Þjóðum kunnr yngvi, fekktu ǫll þeira flaust með hringum. Jarl vissi sik missa foldar; en þú tókt síðan við meira sigri.
Thrustful, you fought Yggr's [Óðinn's] wind-storm [battle], which will ever be extolled while the world is peopled. The corpse-vulture [raven / eagle] ruffled his bloody plumage in the weapon-roar [battle] at Helganes. Sovereign renowned to men, you seized all their galleys — every one. The viceroy [Sveinn Ulfsson] felt his loss of land / knew he had lost land; and then you gained a greater victory.

Apparatus

(1) Keppín*n*] Kep*p*ír m*adr* Hr **þatz æ]** þ*at* æ Hr, Fl, þat er ey 20d, 873 **(2) yggíar]** ygi*ar* Fl **(3) valgam*m*r]** v*ar*gur Fl **-rímv]** rím*m*u others **(7) þioð*vm* kvnr]** þiodkudr 20d, 873 **kvnr]** kyr*r* Fl **siða*n*]** sid*ar* Fl.

Commentary

15/2 *heimrinn* 'the world'. The scansion of the line, *Yggjar veðr meðan heimrinn byggvisk* (´ x ´ ‿x‿ ´ x ´ x), confirms *heimrinn* as the original reading. This is striking, as a very early example of a noun with suffixed article. It seems to have been avoided in early *dróttkvætt*, for the earliest secure example is from the 12th century: *jarlinn sjálfann* in Rǫgnvaldr kali's Lv 11 (Kuhn 1983, §35).[8] Whether there is any significance in the common Orcadian connections of Arnórr and Rǫgnvaldr is difficult to say.

15/5 *ǫll með hringvm* 'all ... every one / every single'. *Með / at hringum* is recorded elsewhere in verse and prose, although not very common. Arnórr in *Mdr* 14/4 re-uses the phrase in the same collocation (with *allr*) and in reference to the same event (Magnús's capture of Sveinn's ships at Helganes).

15/6 *jarl* 'viceroy'. Sveinn Ulfsson, son of the English Wulfsige (ON Ulfr Sprakaleggsson) and of Ástríðr, sister of Knútr inn ríki, hence known also as Sven Estridsson. Appointed Magnús's viceroy over Jutland, he broke his oaths of loyalty and attempted to establish himself as king (e. g. *Magns(Hkr)* ch. 25, pp. 40–41).

[8] A possible 10th-century example is *hallærit* in Eyv Lv 14. The suffixed article is attested in the three MSS of *Hkr* in which the verse occurs, but it is not required, and hence not proven, by the metre. Similarly, the article -(i)*n* in Arnórr's *Þdr* 19/1 *Óskepnan* is not established by the metre. On the suffixed article, see Noreen 1923, §§160 and 472 and Finnur Jónsson 1901, 79–81 and 1921, 315.

Verse Sixteen

Sources

Msk p. 117; Flat III 322: Msk(5v), Fl(787)
Hars(H-Hr) p. 196: H(33r), Hr(24r)
SnE (Arnamagn) II 498 (lines 1–4 only): W(168).

Context

Msk-Flat and *H-Hr*: The verse is embedded, like *Hryn* 3, in the story of Arnórr's recitation at the court of Magnús and Haraldr.
SnE: The first helming is preceded by a list of agent nouns and other terms which can be used in kennings for 'man', including *ótti* which is exemplified here.

Diplomatic and edited text

Otti kvn*n*vð elgio*m* hętta
øþi veþrs ascelfþan grøþi
fengins gullz eþa føþit ella
flestan alldr vnd d*ri*fno tialdi
lican beʀ þic hvosso*m* havki
hollvinr min*n* i lypti*n*g in*n*an
alld*ri* sc*ri*þr vnd fylki fręg*ra*
farlict eiki visv*n*dr snarla.

Ótti, kunnuð elgjum hætta
œðiveðrs á skelfðan grœði,
fengins golls, eða fœðið ella
flestan aldr und drifnu tjaldi.
Glíkan berr þik hvǫssum hauki,
hollvinr minn, í lypting innan
— aldri skríðr und fylki fríðra
farligt eiki — Visundr snarla.

Prose order and translation

Ótti fengins golls, kunnuð hætta elgjum œðiveðrs á skelfðan grœði, eða fœðið ella flestan aldr und drifnu tjaldi. Visundr berr þik snarla glíkan hvǫssum hauki, hollvinr minn, innan í lypting. Aldri skríðr farligt eiki und fríðra fylki.
Terror of seized gold [generous ruler], you expertly [lit. know how to] risk elks of the raging gale [ships] on the tossing swell, or else you pass the most part of your life under spray-drenched awnings. Visundr [Bison] carries you, like a keen hawk, my true friend, inside the poop. Never shall glide a goodly oak [ship] with finer prince aboard.

Apparatus

(2) a] v*m* W **scelfþan]** skelf*an* Fl, skelf*ar* Hr **(4) flestan]** fræmztan W **d*r*ifno]** d*r*ifu Fl **(7) frę*gra*]** f*r*i*ð*ra H, Hr **(8) far-]** fag*r*- Fl **eiki visv*n*dr]** eikiu su*n*d Fl, eiki vishu*n*dr Hr.

Commentary

16/1 and 16/3 *Otti ... fengins gullz* 'Terror of seized gold [generous man, ruler]'. The *fengit* gold could have been won as war-spoils or else inherited or received as taxation.

16/1 and 16/2 *elgiom ... øþi veþrs* 'elks of the raging gale [ships]'. The aesthetic effect of this fine kenning in its context was discussed on p. 72.

16/4 *drifno tialdi* 'spray-drenched awnings'. The phrase *drifin tjǫld* is known from *Harkv* 5 (c. 900).

16/5 *lican ... hvossom havki* 'like a keen hawk'. The hawk image is discussed in the Commentary to *Hryn* 3/5.

16/7 *friðra* (v. l.) 'finer'. That *friðra* rather than *frægra* is the original reading is established by the *aðalhending* with *skríðr*.

Verse Seventeen

Sources

Msk p. 117; Flat III 322: Msk(5v), Fl(787)
Hars(H-Hr) p. 197: H(33r), Hr(24r).

Context

As for *Hryn* 3 and 16. In *Msk-Flat* v. 17 follows v. 16 without interruption. In *H-Hr* it is introduced, *Ok enn kvað hann um siglíng Magnúsar konúngs:*

Diplomatic and edited text

Eig*i* letvþ iof*ra* bagi	Eigi létuð, jǫfra bági,
yþro nafni mankyn hafna	yðru nafni mannkyn hafna;

hvarki fly*r*þv hlen*n*a þreytir
hyr ne malm i broddi styriar
hlvn*n*a e*r* se*m* ravþvll ren*n*i
reiþar bvni*n*gr vpp iheiþe
hrosa ec þ*vi* er h*er*scip glęsir
hlen*n*a dolgr eþa vitar bren*n*i.

hvártki flýrðu, hlenna *rýr*ir,
hyr né malm í broddi styrjar.
Hlunna es, sem rǫðull renni,
reiðar búningr, upp í heiði,
hrósa'k því es herskip glæsir
hlenna dolgr — eða vitar brenni.

Prose order and translation

Jǫfra bági, létuð eigi mannkyn hafna yðru nafni. Hlenna *rýr*ir, þú flýr hvártki hyr né malm í styrjar broddi. Búningr hlunna reiðar es sem rǫðull renni upp í heiði eða vitar brenni. Hrósa'k því, es hlenna dolgr glæsir herskip.

Subduer of lords, you did not allow the race of men to neglect your name. Destroyer of thieves, you flee neither fire nor steel in the forefront of battle. The array of the chariot of launchers [ship] is as though the sun were racing up in the bright sky, or beacons flaring. I praise the way that the foe of thieves adorns [his] warships.

Apparatus

(1) bagi] bægí Fl **(2) man-]** $\overset{n}{\bar{\mathrm{m}}}$- Fl, man*n*- H **(4) hyr ne malm]** hyr*r* næmen*n* Fl **(5) *er*]** ess Fl **(8) vitar]** uíta Fl.

Commentary

17/2 *mankyn* 'race of men'. The translation preserves the full value of both elements, but the context would also admit of the sense 'men, people', as also would *Hdr* 9. Dietrich Hofmann suggested that the development of meaning from 'the human race' to '(a limited number of) people, men' in the ON word points to OE influence (1955, 102), and this seems possible, especially in view of the extreme rarity of *mannkyn* in the early poetry. It also occurs in *H Hj* 25 (of uncertain date) but otherwise not before *Líknarbraut* (probably composed after 1300, Holtsmark 1965, 553). Arnórr could have come into contact with English usage through his father Þórðr who had spent some time in England, or through contacts with English speakers during his own stay at Knútr's court (implied in *Skáldatal*, *SnE (Arnamagn)* III 258 and 267) or conceivably during his years in Orkney.[9]

17/3 *rýrir* (em.) 'destroyer'. The MS *þreytir* yields perfectly good sense: 'persecutor of thieves', but fails to provide the necessary *skothending*. Substitution of *rýrir* is therefore necessary in view of Arnórr's usual exactitude in this respect, and that of his contemporaries. It was proposed by Konráð Gíslason, 1877, 56.

17/7 *glęsir* 'adorns'. I construe the verb as 3rd sing., predicate to *hlenna dolgr* 'foe of thieves [ruler, Magnús]'. It could alternatively be 2nd sing., in which case *þú* is the understood subject and *hlenna dolgr* an apostrophe.

Verse Eighteen

Note: In *Msk-Flat* 18 and 19 form a single strophe.

Sources

Msk p. 117; Flat III 322: Msk(5v), Fl(787)
Hars(H-Hr) p. 197: H(33r), Hr(24r).

Context

As for *Hryn* 3, 16 and 17.

Diplomatic and edited text

Mavno*m* litzc e*r* milldi*n*gr ren*n*ir
meíta hliþ*ir* sęvar sciþi
vn*n*ar ia*m*t se*m* osa*m*t ren*ni*
engla fylki hi*m*na þengils.

Mǫnnum lízk, es mildingr rennir
Meita hlíðir sævar skíði,
unnir jafnt sem ósamt renni
engla fylki himna þengils.

[9] See Commentary to *Mdr* 5/1–2, *Hdr* 15/2 and *Frag* 3/5–8 for other points of diction that Hofmann considers as possible cases of OE influence. Some of his claimed examples I have not noted, either because they are poorly evidenced or because they concern usages already well established in ON before Arnórr's time; see Hofmann 1955, 102–104.

Prose order and translation

Mǫnnum lízk, es mildingr rennir sævar skíði Meita hlíðir, jafnt sem engla fylki himna þengils renni unnir ósamt.
It seems to men, as the ruler makes the ski of the ocean [ship] skim Meiti's [a legendary sea-king] slopes [sea], just as though the angel-host of the skies' prince [God] were skimming the waves with him.

Apparatus

(2) meíta] meída Fl **hliþ*ir*]** hlid*ar* Hr.

Commentary

18/1 and 18/2 *rennir* | *meíta hliþir sęvar sciþi* 'makes the ski of the ocean [ship] skim Meiti's slopes [sea]'. *Rennir*, from the weak verb *renna* 'to make run', is here taken as governing *skíði* as its direct object in the dat. sing. It could alternatively, without any great difference of meaning, be taken as absolute, hence '(the ruler) skims Meiti's slopes with the ski of the ocean'. The *nygørving* here is discussed on pp. 72–73.

Line 18/3. The line contains triple (vocalic) alliteration rather than the expected double, but there is no other reason to suspect textual corruption.

Verse Nineteen

Note: In *Msk-Flat* 18 and 19 form a single strophe.

Sources

Msk p.117; Flat III 322: Msk(5v), Fl(787)
Hars(H-Hr) p. 197: H(33r), Hr(24r).

Context

As for *Hryn* 3, 16, 17, and 18. In *Msk-Flat* there are no introductory words, since vv. 18 and 19 are treated as one strophe. In *H-Hr* a brief link is inserted: *Ok enn er þetta þarí:*

Diplomatic and edited text

Eyþendr f*re*gn ec at elsca þioþir	Eyðendr fregn'k at elska þjóðir
in*n*drott þin e*r* hofþ at min*n*om	— inndrótt þín es hǫfð at minnum —
grøþi lostins gvþi it nęsta	grœði lostins goði et næsta
geima vals i þesso*m* heími.	geima vals í þessum heimi.

Prose order and translation

Fregn'k, at þjóðir elska eyðendr grœði lostins geima vals et næsta goði í þessum heimi. Inndrótt þín es hǫfð at minnum.
I hear that men love him who clears the ocean's steed [ship→sea-warrior], lashed by the surge, next after God in this world. Your personal troop is held in memory.

Apparatus

(1) Eyþendr] Eydíndr Hr **f*re*gn]** f*ra* H, Hr **(2) in*n*drott]** en d*ro*tt Fl **at min*n*om]** míníu*m* Hr.

Commentary

19/1 *Eyþendr* 'him who clears', lit. 'clearers'. *Þjóðir* is the subject, and *eyðendr* object, to *elska*. *Eyðendr* is grammatically pl. and forms a kenning with *geima vals* 'steed of the ocean [ship]'. The sea-warrior disables his enemies' ships by clearing them of crew and equipment in battle. This is the only example in ON poetry of a kenning formed from *eyðandi* and a determinant meaning 'ship'.

The reference of the kenning is slightly difficult to determine. (a) The pl. is probably used with sing. meaning to refer to Magnús (so Finnur Jónsson, who translates *søkrigeren* in *Skjald* B). There are other examples of this phenomenon amongst kennings for 'man' built on pres. parts. Hofgarða-Refr (Refr 1, 1) refers to the donor of a shield as *fleygjendr alinleygjar* [v. l. *alm-*], lit. 'hurlers of the arm-flame [of gold]', hence 'generous men', and Arnórr's *ættstýrǫndum* (dat. pl.), lit. 'rulers of men', seems to refer to Haraldr alone in *Hdr* 16/6 (see Commentary). Compare also the Eddaic *Guðr* II 5, where Sigurðr is referred to as *eigendr*, lit. 'owners' of the horse Grani. In *Hryn* 19 the abrupt transition to the grammatically sing. *þín* in line 2 is not a difficulty: compare *fórt, kynduð (Hryn* 12); *fenguð, lætr þú (Hryn* 14).

(b) It has been suggested that *eyðendr geima vals* refers to the two kings Haraldr and Magnús (*CPB* II 188n.), but the sing. *þú* on line 2 and the focus on Magnús throughout the poem render this unlikely.

19/1 ***fregn ec*** 'I hear'. The past tense variant *frá'k* would give equally good sense.

19/4 ***geima vals*** 'ocean's steed'. Ship. *Valr*, also a name for the falcon, is frequently used in poetry to refer to a horse, especially in 'ship' kennings on the pattern 'horse of the sea' (see *LP* s. v. *valr* 1 and 2).

Verse Twenty

Sources

SnE p. 185: R(79), T(43v), U(74), 748(21v), 748II(9v), 757(6v).

Context

Snorri tells how the names of famous dynasties, including the Skjǫldungar (descended from Skjǫldr in Denmark) have come to be used in poetry as appellations for rulers. The couplet is introduced simply, *Sem Arnor q(vað)*, but in MS 748, *Sva qvað Markvss* (see further p. 26).

Diplomatic and edited text

Skioldungr mv*n* þ*er* aNaR ald*ri*	Skjǫldungr, mun þér annarr aldri
æþ*ri* gr*a*mr v*n*d solv fæþaz.	œðri gramr und sólu fœðask.

Prose order and translation

Skjǫldungr, annarr gramr œðri þér mun aldri fœðask und sólu.
King, another lord loftier than you will never be born under the sun.

Apparatus

Line (1)] Skí... 757 **(2) gr*a*mr]** m*aðr* 748 **fæþaz]** fè... 757.

Magnússdrápa

Verse One

Sources

Magns(Hkr) ch. 1, p. 3: K (494r), F(37r), J2(238v–239r), 39(12r), 47(2v–3r)
Flat III 262: Fl(760)
Fsk ch. 44, pp. 208–9: Fsk A(202)
Magns(H-Hr) pp. 21–22: Hr(3v)
Ólsh(Sep) p. 614: 2(73r), 4(68r–v), 61(129v), 73(425), 325V(87v), 325VI(41r), 325VII(41r), Bb(204v–205r), Th(160r).

Context

The various sources take the account of Magnús's journey west from N. Russia up to differing points before quoting *Mdr* 1. The summary account in *Fsk* is brought to a close by *Mdr* 1. The others are more leisurely and incorporate at least one other verse.

In *Magns(Hkr)* and *Ólsh(Sep)* the title of the poem is specified, *Þess getr Arnórr jarlaskáld í Magnússdrápu*, but elsewhere only the skald is named.

Diplomatic and edited text

Nu hycc rioðanda reiþo
róg avrs þ*vi*at veitc g*er*va
þegi seimbrotar segia
seGiom hneitis eGia
vara xi allra
ormsetrs hati vet*ra*
hravstr þa er h*er*scip glæsti
horða vinr or gorðum.

Nú hykk rjóðanda reiðu
rógǫrs, því't veit'k gǫrva,
— þegi seimbrotar — segja
seggjum hneitis eggja.
Vasat ellifu allra
ormsetrs hati vetra,
hraustr þá's herskip glæsti
Hǫrða vinr ór Gǫrðum.

Prose order and translation

Nú hykk segja seggjum reiðu rógǫrs rjóðanda hneitis eggja, því't veit'k gǫrva. Þegi seimbrotar. Ormsetrs hati vasat allra ellifu vetra, þa's Hǫrða vinr, hraustr, glæsti herskip ór Gǫrðum.
Now I mean to tell men of the career of the strife-quick reddener of the sword's edges [warrior], for I know it fully. Let gold-breakers be

silent. The hater of the reptile's home [gold→generous prince] was not fully eleven winters when [he], the friend of Hordalanders, dauntless, arrayed warships to leave Garðar.

Apparatus

(1) hycc] hyG F, Fl, 325VI, hyg 39, hygg ec A, hyc 2, Th, hygk Bb **rioðanda]** ríǫðanda 47, ríodande Fl, Rioðan 73 **reiþo]** reðo F, 39, 4, 73, 325V, 325VII, raða J2, 47, ręðu 61, tedu Th **(2) róg avrs]** roghs hyrs A **róg]** rǫg Hr, rang 61, Raugg Th **veitc]** so also 47, væict A, veit others ***gerva***] gnogar A, gervd Bb **(3) þegi]** þeygi 61, Th, om. 325VII **seimbrotar]** -briotar J2, 39, 73, Bb, -stad*ar* Fl, sæims stafar A, -staf*ir* Hr, -b*ro*ta 2, 325VI, -briotr 4, 61, 325V, Th, sæima (?)briota 325VII **segia]** segg*ia* 61 **(4) hneitis]** hneítís heítv*m* Th **eGia]** eGiar J2, Hr, 61, Th, eGíu 73 **Lines (5)–(6)]** om. Hr **(5) vara]** so also J2, 47, vor*ar* Th, varat others **xi]** so also 39, Th, ellifo others **allra]** alla A **(6) ormsetrs]** ormsetr J2, 47, orms set*r*s Fl, Th **hati]** bati A, hatrí Th **vet*ra*]** bet*ri* Th **(7) hravstr]** hraust Fl, aust*r* 61 **glæsti]** glæstu Fl, geystuz 61.

Commentary

1/1 *reiþo* 'career'. *Reiða* covers a wide semantic range. My rendering, like Bjarni Aðalbjarnarson's 'activity' (*sýsla, iðja*, *Hkr* 1941–51, III, 3), assumes that attention is here focussed on Magnús's deeds, but *reiða* can also refer to a man's material splendour, often manifested in generous entertainment or equipping of retainers.

1/3 *seimbrotar* 'gold-breakers'. (Generous) men. It is not known before whom this *drápa* was declaimed, but it seems likely that the *seimbrotar* were liegemen of the deceased Magnús.

1/4 *hneitis* 'sword'. On this *heiti* see pp. 75–76.

1/6 *ormsetrs hati* 'hater of the reptile's home [generous prince, Magnús]'. The traditional abode of a dragon or reptile is a gold-hoard.

Lines 1/7 and 1/8. These lines are identical to the second couplet of a verse which is attributed in Fríssbók, the only MS in which it survives, to Hallar-Steinn, but which has been taken as belonging to the opening of Hallfreðr's *Óláfsdrápa* (Hfr 2, 1, c. 996):

Tólf vas elds at aldri	Twelve winters in age was
ýsetrs hati vetra	the hater of fire of the bow-home [hand→gold]
hraustr þás herskip glæsti	when, dauntless, the friend of Hordalanders
Hǫrða vinr ór Gǫrðum.	arrayed warships to leave Garðar.

Arnórr knew another poem of Hallfreðr (see Commentary to *Þdr* 22), and one cannot rule out the possibility that *Mdr* 1 is composed in imitation of him. On the other hand, the scribe of one or other verse, prompted by the similarity of the lines *ormsetrs hati vetra* and *ýsetrs hati vetra*, may have unwittingly substituted *hraustr ... Gǫrðum* for its original couplet, which is now lost. If so, the likelihood is that *hraustr ... Gǫrðum* belongs to Arnórr's verse rather than the other, since (i) it is found in all the numerous MS texts of *Mdr* 1; (ii) the adj. *hraustr* 'dauntless, bold' is also applied to the hero in *Mdr* 2, where it stands at the corresponding point in the verse; and (iii) the doubtful attribution of *Tólf vas elds* ... makes the text of the Hallar-Steinn / Hallfreðr verse also suspect.[10]

1/8 *horða vinr* 'friend of Hordalanders'. King of Norway, Magnús. The periphrasis anticipates Magnús's acquisition of power at the end of his voyage (cf. note to *Hryn* 3/5).

Verse Two

Sources

Magns(Hkr) ch. 1, p. 4: K(494r), F(37r), J2(239r), 39(12r), 47(3r)
Flat III 263: Fl(761)
Magns(H-Hr) p. 22: Hr(3v)
Ólsh(Sep) p. 614: 2(73r), 4(68v), 61(129v), 73(425), 325V(87v–88r), 325VI(41r), 325VII(41r), Bb(205r), Th(160r)
SnE p. 175 (lines 5–8 only): R(75), T(42r), 748(19r), 748II(7v).

[10] Bjarne Fidjestøl sees the 'Hallfreðr' verse as a spurious importation from the tradition about Magnús to that of Óláfr Tryggvason (1982, 107). Jan de Vries, on the other hand, inclined to the view that the lines are Hallfreðr's and are imitated by Arnórr (1952, 165).

Context

Magns(Hkr), Flat, Magns(H-Hr) and *Ólsh(Sep)*: The strophe follows *Mdr* 1, separated only by a brief note (in all except *Flat*) that Magnús continued his journey in spring to Sweden, and by brief introductory words.
SnE: Snorri includes the second helming in a long sequence of skaldic quotations which illustrate *heiti* for 'sea', and introduces it *Sallt, sem Arnorr q(vað):*

Diplomatic and edited text

Þing bavð ut hiɴ ungi	Þing bauð út enn ungi
eGrioðandi þioðo	eggrjóðandi þjóðum;
fim bar hirð *til* havmlo	fim bar hirð til hǫmlu
h*er*væðr ara bræðis	hervæðr ara bræðis.
salt scar hv́fi helltum	Salt skar húfi héltum
hravstr þioðk*onung*r avstan	hraustr þjóðkonungr austan;
baro b*ri*mlogs ryri	bǫ́ru brimlogs rýri
brimveðr at Sigtunom.	brún veðr at Sigtúnum.

Prose order and translation

Enn ungi eggrjóðandi bauð þjóðum út þing. Fim hirð ara bræðis bar hervæðr til hǫmlu. Hraustr þjóðkonungr skar salt héltum húfi austan. Brún veðr bǫ́ru brimlogs rýri at Sigtúnum.
The young edge-reddener [warrior] summoned men to the muster. Lively, the troop of the eagles' / eagle's feeder [warrior] went in war-garb to the oar-loops. The dauntless high-king clove the salt with rime-spread hull from the east. Sharp gales bore the diminisher of surf-fire [gold→generous lord] towards Sigtún.

Apparatus

(1) Þing] Þings 61 **(2) -rioðandi]** -riðandi 39 **þioðo]** þíod*ar* Th, þioðo*m* others **(3) fim]** fim*m* F, fimt 61, Th **hirð]** her*r* 39, hrid 61, Th ***til* havmlo]** i hǫmlur F, Fl, Hr, 325VI, Bb ***til*]** i 39, at J2, 47 **(4) -væðr]** -veðr J2, 39, 325VI, Bb, -uedr*s* Fl, -uę̇ðs 4, -næðr 325V, ʀædr Th **ara]** aara 61 **bræðis]** bredía Fl, brædir Hr **(5) hv́fi]** humi 61 **helltum]** huellt*um* Hr, heilltv*m* 325V **(6) avstan]** flavstum 325VI **Lines (7)–(8)]** om. 748II **(7) b*ri*mlogs]** bei*n*- (or bei*m*-) Fl, -log 39, -laugs 325V, logns Bb **ryri]** hlyri Bb **(8) brim-]** so also Th, brv́n others **at]** af Fl.

Commentary

2/1 and 2/2 *Þing bavð ut ... þioðom* (v. l.) 'summoned men to the muster'. *Þjóðum* gives an unusual but comprehensible construction, which seems to be blended from two common patterns: (i) *bauð út ... þjóðum*, corresponding to *bjóða út liði / leiðangri / sveitum* 'to call up troops', and (ii) *bauð þing* corresponding to *bjóða e-t* 'command', as in *Hdr* 10 *uppgǫngu bauð yngvi* 'the prince ordered the advance ashore'.

2/8 *brv́n* (v. l.) *veðr* 'sharp gales'. The vowel of *brún* is established by the full rhyme with *-tún-*.

(a) *Brúnn* has been taken by some scholars as an adj. meaning 'sharp, prominent, direct', derived from *brún* f. 'sharp edge' and interchangeable with the *i*-mutated adj. *brýnn.*[11] *Brúnn* in Sigv 12, 14, which rhymes with *-tún-*, qualifies *hjǫrr* 'sword', so that it could well mean 'sharp',[12] and in two 13th-century verses, *Ht* 50 and Sturl 5, 20, it describes a weapon and again may mean 'sharp' (cited by Dal, 1938, 221). The assumption of such an adj. is further supported by the pairs of mutated and non-mutated synonyms which are a familiar feature of ON lexis (e. g. the fem. nouns *bón/bœn* 'prayer', *sjón/sýn* 'sight' or the compound adjs. in *-lægr* beside the simplex *lágr* 'low'). The postulated phrase *brún veðr* 'sharp gales' is also semantically plausible. *Brýnn* is applied to a wind (*byrr*) in *Rst* 15, and in the *First Grammatical Treatise: Styri maðr þarf byrenn brýnna enn* ... 'The helmsman needs the wind sharper than ...' (p. 222). Compare also H harð 4 *skreið brýnt* 'skimmed straight ahead', applied to a ship. A final point in favour of the present interpretation is that Þjóðólfr Arnórsson, describing the same voyage, speaks of a 'raging gale' (*ótt veðr*, Þjóð A 1, 2).

(b) *Brúnn* 'dark-brown, black' is used in skaldic verse to describe blood or, in *Ht* 3, a ship. There is no other case in the lexicons where the epithet qualifies 'wind' or 'weather', although it would be a possible description if foam or clouds were darkening the air.

[11] See *Fms* XII, 1837, 126; Konráð Gíslason 1866, 282–83; and Finnur Jónsson in *Skjald* B and *LP* (s. v.).

[12] So Bjarni Aðalbjarnarson, *Hkr* 1941–51, II, 381n. Finnur Jónsson, on the other hand, takes *brúnn* as part of the compound *rauðbrúnn* (in *Skjald* B).

(c) *Brimveðr* 'surf-gales' would give good sense, but it fails to provide a rhyme with *-tún-*, and is very much a minority reading. It is presumably a dittography of *brim(logs)* in line 7.

Verse Three

Source

Magns(H-Hr) pp. 22–23: Hr(3v).

Context

As for *Mdr* 1 and 2. The introductory words mark the new phase in Magnús's journey: *Gekk Magnús konúngr þar á land, ok bjóst at fara landveg norðr í Noreg; svâ segir Arnór:*

Diplomatic and edited text

Geck aa suíod suíþiod saucki	Gekk á *Svíþjóð* søkkvi
sueíns e*r* f*re*md van*n* eína	Sveins, es fremð vann eina;
fyst*iz* olafs aust*an*	fýstisk Áleifs austan
afk*art* son*ar* hi*ar*ta	afkart sonar hjarta.
not*t* beid *ok* dag d*r*ottíns	Nǫ́tt beið ok dag dróttins
dygg f*er*d jad*ar* byg*va*	dygg ferð Jaðarbyggva;
fyst bad g*ra*mr j geysto	fýst bað gra*m* í geystu
gif*r*s ved*r* si*er* hlífa.	gífrs veðr*i* sér hlífa.

Prose order and translation

Søkkvi Sveins, es vann fremð eina, gekk á *Svíþjóð*. Afkart hjarta Áleifs sonar fýstisk austan. Dygg ferð Jaðarbyggva beið dróttins nǫ́tt ok dag. Fýst í geystu gífrs veðr*i* bað gra*m* hlífa sér.

The queller of Sveinn, who wrought nothing but triumph, marched into Sweden. The prodigious heart of Óláfr's son was urging westwards / from the east. The worthy host of Jaðarr-men awaited their liege night and day. Urgently, in their troubled she-troll's gale [mind], they begged the prince protect them.

Commentary

3/1 *suíþiod* (em.) 'Sweden'. The MS *suíod suíþiod* is clearly a scribal slip.

3/1 and 3/2 *saucki* | *sueíns* (normalised *søkkvi Sveins*) 'queller of Sveinn'. A highly specific kenning for Magnús, which neatly anticipates the flight of Sveinn Alfífuson from Norway on the arrival of Magnús, reported in *Mdr* 4. Similarily, *Áleifs sonr* in *Mdr* 3/3 and 3/4 may presage Magnús's recovery of his father's realm in *Mdr* 4.

3/4 *afkart* 'prodigious'. The adj. occurs in three contexts — *Akv* 35 and 38 and *Am* 71 — in which the sense 'exceedingly, monstrously forceful' is probable (see Dronke 1969, 69), but otherwise only in the problematic *Plác* 27. That the vowel of *-kart* in *Mdr* 3 is short is suggested by the rhyme *afkart : hjarta*, and this is supported by *afkarr : fjarri* in *Plác* 27 and *launkarr : fjarri* in Bj hit 2, 5. The shortened vowel is presumably a secondary development: an original long vowel is implied by the suggested etymological link with *kárr* 'lock, curl of hair' (*IEW* pp. 308–309, de Vries s. v. *kárr*), and by the pronunciation of Mod. Icel. *afkár* and *varkár*. See further Commentary to *Mdr* 5/1 *afkárlig*.

3/7 and 3/8 *fyst bad gram* (em.) ... *sier hlífa* 'urgently, they begged the prince protect them'.

(a) *Fýst* is taken in my translation as the neut. form of the p. p. *fýstr*, lit. 'impelled, encouraged,' used adverbially. *Dygg ferð Jaðarbyggva* is construed as the implied subject of *bað* as well as of *beið*, and *gram* as the object of *bað*; *sér* refers back to *ferð*. The emendation of *gramr* to *gram* is justifiable on the grounds that the scribe of Hr frequently alters the text when puzzled by its syntax.

(b) Kock construed lines 7–8 similarly (*NN* §2020), but read *fýst* as nom. sing. fem. of *fýstr*, qualifying *ferð*, hence 'eager host'.

(c) Finnur Jónsson's solution, in *Skjald* B, was to construe: *gramr bað fýst ... hlífa sér* 'the prince bade [his own] zeal be his defence', but this entails semantic difficulties.

3/7 and 3/8 *j geysto* | *gifrs vedri* (em.) 'in their troubled she-troll's gale': *Gífrs veðr* 'she-troll's gale' is clearly a kenning for 'mind, thought'. Snorri says *hvginn skal sva keNa, at kalla vind trǫllqvenna* 'thought is referred to by calling it wind of trollwomen' (*SnE* p. 191). Kennings of this kind sometimes imply 'courageous spirit, valour', as in Sindr 8:

hinns yfrinn gat jǫfra	he among rulers who was endowed with outstanding
óskkvánar byr mána.	wind of the ogre's desired woman.

Veðri (MS *vedr*) is a small emendation necessary to metre and syntax. The dat. case is indicated by the preposition *í* and the adj. *geystu.*

Geystr, lit. 'made to rush, rushing, aroused', can have the sense 'powerful', not necessarily involving motion, as in *enn geystri grǿðr*, referring to the wolf's hunger in *Nj* 19. It can also mean 'disturbed' in a figurative sense, as in, *sva var folkit geyst at fatt eitt let sem heyrði þetta er konungr mælti* (*Sverris saga* ch. 82, p. 88).

Given the possible meanings of *geystr* and *gífrs veðr*, the phrase as a whole could refer (a) to the *gramr* 'prince' (Magnús) and mean 'in his raging, mighty spirit', or (b) to the *Jaðarbyggva ferð* 'host of Jaðarr-men / men of Jæren' and mean 'in their troubled thoughts'. It was suggested above that *ferð* is likely to be the implied subject of *bað* in line 7. *Í geystu gífrs veðri* then yields the best sense if it is construed with *ferð*, and this analysis is followed in my translation.

Verse Four

Sources

Fsk ch. 47, p. 210: Fsk B(96), A(204–205)
Flat III 264: Fl(761)
Magns(H-Hr) p. 26: Hr(4r).

Context

In *Fsk* the verse is paraphrased, with minor elaboration, and then introduced, *Um þetta orti Arnórr jarlaskáld:*
Flat has the eccentric, *sem Skule kuad* (see further p. 26).
In *H-Hr Mdr* 4 is cited after *Hryn* 8 with the comment, *Þess getr ok í Magnúsardrápu, at Sveinn konúngr flýði or Noregi, þegar Magnús kom í land; þar segir svâ:*

Diplomatic and edited text

Flyði fylkir reiði	Flýði fylkir reiði
framr þioð k*onong*s ram*m*a	framr þjóðkonungs ramma;
stok firir auðvin okkro*m*	stǫkk fyr auðvin okkrum
armsnællz hate gellir	armsvells hati, gellir.

liet at noregs niota	Létat Nóregs njóta
nytr þengill gram lengi	nýtr þengill gram lengi;
h*ann* rak svei*nn* af sinv*m*	hann rak Svein af sínum
sokndiarfr faðr arue.	sókndjarfr fǫðurarfi.

Prose order and translation

Framr fylkir flýði ramma reiði þjóðkonungs. Armsvells hati, gellir, stǫkk fyr auðvin okkrum. Nýtr þengill létat gram lengi njóta Nóregs. Hann rak sókndjarfr Svein af sínum fǫðurarfi.
The audacious leader [Sveinn Alfífuson] fled the mighty fury of the high-king [Magnús]. The hater of arm-ice [silver→(generous) ruler, Sveinn], the howler, bolted from our treasure-friend. The doughty prince did not let the lord long enjoy Norway. He drove, daring in attack, Sveinn from his father's legacy.

Apparatus

(1) Flyði] Fluðe A, Fyllde Fl **(2) k*onong*s]** k*o*nung Fl, k*onun*gr Hr **(3) firir]** f*ra* Hr **auðvin]** od*d*uín Fl, audr*um* Hr **(4) armsnællz]** -svælz A (= suellz Hr), arnsuelgr Fl **hate]** hare A **gellir]** h*er*ser Fl **(5) liet at]** leit*ad* Hr **noregs]** noreg Fl, nõr Hr **(6) gram]** gr*a*mr Hr **(7) h*ann*]** þ*at* Hr **svei*nn*]** svæin A (= sueín Hr), S. Fl **sinv*m*]** sínu Fl **(8) faðr]** fod*r* Fl, faudr Hr.

Commentary

4/1 and 4/2 *Flyði fylkir ... framr* 'the audacious leader [Sveinn Alfífuson] fled'. The alliteration highlights the ironic juxtaposition of the verb 'flee' with the epithet *framr*, literally and figuratively 'forward'.

4/3 *okkrom* 'our'. This dual form is secured by the *skothending* with *stǫkk*. It should strictly mean 'of myself [Arnórr] and one other', but there is no obvious 'other' with whom Arnórr would pair himself when speaking of Magnús as his 'treasure-friend' (*auðvinr*), unless it is Gellir (see below). *Okkur* and *okkar* are used in Mod. Icel. as pl. pronoun and pronominal adj., but I do not know of evidence for this in the old language, so that it seems that Arnórr was allowing himself a poetic licence in using the dual to refer either to himself alone or to himself and other admirers of Magnús.[13]

4/4 *armsvælz* (v. l.) *hate* 'hater of arm-ice [silver→(generous) ruler]'. Snorri says that silver is referred to in kennings as *snær e(ða) svell eþa hela, þvíat þat er hvítt* 'snow or ice or rime, because it is white' (*SnE* p. 143).

4/4 *gellir* 'howler'. This is a rare and problematic word.

(a) One would expect from the verbs *gella* and *gjalla* the meaning 'screecher, howler' for the agent noun *gellir*, and this indeed fits the recorded usage. It is a derogatory nickname and, in the *þulur*, a *heiti* for 'ox' and 'sword'. In Mod. Icel. *gellir* is an appellative meaning 'noisy, loud-voiced man' (*hávaðamaður*; so Blöndal, s. v.). Such a word could well suggest the empty bragging of a coward, and hence be an appropriate term for Sveinn, the enemy of the hero. If this is the meaning of *gellir* in line 4, it must stand in apposition to *armsvells hati*.

(b) Gellir is also a proper name, and, as remarked on p. 46, Arnórr reputedly composed in memory of Gellir Þorkelsson. If *gellir* here were taken as an address to this or another Gellir, the dual possessive pronoun in *auðvin okkrum*, line 3, would be explained — especially since Gellir is said to have visited Magnús Óláfsson's court and to have received lavish gifts from him (*Laxdœla saga* ch. 78, pp. 227–28). However, it would be curious if the encomiastic elegy for Magnús were addressed to another individual (especially in the light of *þegi seimbrotar, Mdr* 1).

(c) Kock, in *NN* §817, tentatively connects *gellir* with MHG *gelle* m.'contender, rival' and emends MS *hate* to gen. sing. *hata* so that line 4 *armsvells hata gellir* can be rendered 'the rival of the hater of arm-ice [rival of Magnús, Sveinn]'. But on several counts this is unconvincing. (i) There is no evidence for ON *gellir* in this sense. (ii) MHG *gelle* is a weak noun, to which ON **gelli*, not *gellir* would be cognate. (Kock, in answer to this difficulty, cited ON doublets such as *endi / endir* and *visi / visir*.) (iii) *Gelle* and its OHG counterpart are

[13] Helgi Guðmundsson's study of the pronominal dual (1962) contains no early occurrences of *okkr* which throw light on the present context.

rare in German.[14] (iv) The interpretation involves the slight emendation of MS *hate* to *hata*.

Verse Five

Sources

Magns(Hkr) ch. 18, pp. 32–33: K(506r), F(39r), J2(246v–247r), 39(15r), 47(6r)
Flat III 272: Fl(765)
Fsk ch. 48, p. 216: Fsk B(99), A(211)
Magns(H-Hr) p. 49: H(5v), Hr(7r).

Context

Hkr: Snorri tells of a message which Magnús sent to the Danes after Hǫrða-Knútr's death in England, reminding them of his claim to Denmark, and takes *Mdr* 5 as a reference to this.
Fsk: As in *Hkr*, Hǫrða-Knútr is said to have died in England. Magnús receives the news in Norway and vows publicly to possess Denmark: *Svá segir Arnórr jarlaskáld.* There is no mention of an embassy to the Danes.
In *Flat* and *H-Hr*, the verse follows the account, mentioned in the Context to *Hryn* 9, of the feast held for Magnús in Denmark at which Hǫrða-Knútr is poisoned. In the *H-Hr* version Magnús declaims his vow straightway, while in *Flat* it is spoken after his return to Norway.

Diplomatic and edited text

Afkárlig v*ar*þ jarla
orðgnótt su e*r* hlavt d*ro*ttin
fylgðe efnd þ*vi* e*r* ylgiar
angr tæl*ir* reð mæla
ok fram i gny g*ri*m*m*um
g*ra*fnings und kló rafni
fus letz falla ræsir
feigr eða danmorc eiga.

Afkarlig varð jarla
orðgnótt, sú's hlaut dróttinn;
fylgði efnð því's ylgjar
angrtælir réð mæla:
at framm í gný grimmum
grafnings und kló hrafni
fúss lézk falla ræsir
feigr eða Danmǫrk eiga.

[14] OHG *gello / ello* 'rival' only occurs in glosses, translating Lat. *æmulus* (von Steinmeyer 1968– , s. v. *ello*). MHG *gelle* is only recorded in one, difficult, context in Benecke 1854–60, s. v.

Prose order and translation

Jarla orðgnótt, sú's dróttinn hlaut, varð afkarlig. Efnð fylgði því's ylgjar angrtælir réð mæla: at ræsir lézk fúss falla feigr und kló hrafni framm í grimmum gný grafnings eða eiga Danmǫrk.
The lordly wealth of words, with which the liege was endowed, was prodigious. His deeds matched what [he], the beguiler of the she-wolf's dolour [carrion-provider, warrior], did say: that the prince said, glad, he would drop doomed under the raven's claw, ahead in the cruel clash of the graven shield, or else possess Denmark.

Apparatus

(1) **Afkárlig]** AAkaflíg Fl, Af kærleg B **va*r*þ]** var A **jarla]** jofra B, arla A, H, Hr (2) **e*r*]** om. 39 **hlavt]** hi*er* Fl **d*ro*ttin]** d*ro*ttne Fl, d*ro*ttiɴ others (3) **fylgðe]** fylde Fl **efnd]** eimd B, e*r*fd Hr **þ*vi*]** þi J2, su Fl **e*r*]** at Hr (4) **reð]** læt 39 (5) ***ok*]** at others **g*ri*m*m*um]** g*ri*m*m*an Fl (6) **g*ra*fnings]** grafning 39, grams B **und]** od*d* Fl **kló]** flo Hr **rafni]** jamne B (7) **letz]** líet H (8) **feigr]** feigð 39.

Commentary

5/1 ***Afkárlig*** 'prodigious'. The word is unique in recorded ON, although *afkáralegur* occurs in Mod. Icel. and *afkárr* in the old language (see Commentary to *Mdr* 3/4). It appears from the internal rhyme with *jarla*, and from the parallel rhyme of *afkart : hjarta* in *Mdr* 3/4, that the vowel is short here.

5/1 and 5/2 ***jarla* | *orðgnótt*** 'lordly [lit. lords'] wealth of words'.

(a) *Jarla* and *orðgnótt*, consecutive in the text, are here tentatively construed together. The gen. of *jarl* probably has the adjectival sense 'lordly, fit for an earl' in *Háv* 97, where Óðinn declares that to possess Billingr's daughter or wife (*mær*) would seem *jarls ynði*, lit. 'a jarl's delight'.[15] Arnórr's phrase differs in so far as the gen. pl. rather than gen. sing. is here used adjectivally.[16]

[15] Quoted in support of *jarla orðgnótt* in *NN* §818. Some of Kock's other supposed parallels are unconvincing.

[16] It is possible that *jǫfra kappi* in *Vell* 7 means 'with lordly, heroic valour' and so exemplifies an adjectival gen. pl., but the strophe is difficult and the interpretation of *jǫfra kappi* disputed. Davidson in her edition takes *jǫfra* as a reference to the sons

Dietrich Hofmann suggests that the generalised sense of *jarlar*, 'noblemen', is influenced by the cognate OE *eorlas* or OS *erlos* (1955, 104).

(b) *Jarla* could alternatively define *dróttinn* in line 2, hence 'lord of jarls'. It would be unusual for Arnórr to arrange the elements of a kenning thus, but not unparalleled. In *Þdr* 22, for instance, *inndróttar* ... *geymi* 'guardian of his retinue' is interrupted by *þeim hjalpi goð* and by *Þorfinni* which belongs to a different clause.

5/3 and 5/4 *ylgiar* | *angr tælir* 'beguiler of the she-wolf's dolour [warrior]'. This is the first recorded occurrence of the agent noun *tælir* (although Sigvatr uses *tælandi* in a kenning in Sigv 13, 14), and its only occurrence in a kenning for 'warrior'.

5/5 *at* (v. l.) 'that'.

(a) *At* '(namely) that', the reading of all MSS except for K, produces a grammatically complicated structure, in which the second helming is a subordinate clause which amplifies *því* in *því's ylgjar* | *angrtælir réð mæla* 'what the beguiler of the she-wolf's dolour did say'. This being so, *lézk* is redundant: one would have expected a clause meaning 'that he would ...' rather than one meaning 'that he said he would ...' It was doubtless this rather tangled construction which gave rise to the simpler variant *ok*. As elsewhere, the awkwardness of the original is preserved in my translation.

(b) If *ok* were the correct reading, the second helming would form a clause co-ordinate with the *fylgði* ... clause in the first helming. Lines 3–4 would be parenthetic.

5/5 *fram* 'ahead'.

(a) I construe the adverb with *í gný* ... *grafnings*, hence 'ahead in the battle, in the van'. Although the adverb is usually directional, a static sense is also attested in phrases such as *aptr ok fram* 'fore and aft'.

(b) Kock, in *NN* §819, assumes here a temporal sense 'further, in the future' (*vidare, allt framjent*), but his two other citations (Sigv 12, 13 and Þjóð A 4, 3) could equally well support interpretation (a),

of Eiríkr and does not construe it with *kappi* (1983, 247 and 252).

since, as in *Mdr* 5, *framm* is juxtaposed with a phrase meaning 'in battle / battle-array'.

(c) Bjarni Aðalbjarnarson construes *falla framm* together as 'fall on his face' (*falla á grúfu*, *Hkr* 1941–51, III, 33n.).

5/5 and 5/6 *gny ... grafnings* 'clash of the graven shield [battle]'. On *grafningr*, see Commentary to *Rdr* 1/2.

Verse Six

Sources

Magns(Hkr) ch. 19, pp. 34–35: K(507r), F(39r), J2(247v), 39(15r), 47(6r)
Flat III 273: Fl(765)
Magns(H-Hr) pp. 50–51: H(6r), Hr(7r).

Context

All three prose works include *Mdr* 6 and 7 in their accounts of how Magnús assumed rule over Denmark.
In *Hkr* and *H-Hr*, *Mdr* 6 appears early in the narrative, as Magnús sails to Jutland.
In *Flat* it finishes off the brief account. *Mdr* 6 follows 7, prefaced by *Hier getr og þess ath Magnus konungr for af Noregi til Jotlandz þa er han [Arnor] kvad visu þessa:*

Diplomatic and edited text

Segia m*un* ec hve Sygna	Segja mun'k, hvé Sygna
b*ar* þengil	snarfengjan bar þengil
hallr *oc* hrimi sollin*n*	hallr ok hrími sollinn
hleborðz visundr norþ*an*	hléborðs visundr norðan.
setti bioðr at breiðo	Setti bjóðr at breiðu
brynþ*in*gs fetil stinga	brynþings — fetilstinga
fus toc ǫld við ǫsi	fús tók ǫld við œsi —
jotlandi gramr branda.	Jótlandi, gramr, branda.

Prose order and translation

Mun'k segja, hvé hléborðs visundr, hallr ok sollinn hrími, bar snarfengjan Sygna þengil norðan. Bjóðr brynþings, gramr, setti branda at breiðu Jótlandi. Ǫld tók fús við œsi fetilstinga.

I will tell how the bison of the lee-side [ship], listing and encrusted with rime, carried the quick-acting lord of the Sygnir from the north. The convenor of the corselet-meet, the fierce prince, beached his prows on broad Jutland. Folk, eager, received the impeller of sword-belt stabbers [swords→warriors].

Apparatus

(1) ec] om. Hr **Sygna]** svigna 39 **(2) b*ar* þengil]** in K written continuously with line (1); in others preceded by: snarfengían F, J2, 39, Fl, H, snarfengiar 47, snarfeng*an* Hr **(3)** ***oc*]** v*ar* Fl, Hr, v*ar*ð H **(4) hle-]** hlæ- J2, 39, Hr **visundr]** visvnd Hr **(5) bioðr]** blid*r* Fl, H, Hr **breiðo]** braðu J2, beidu Hr **(6) brynþi*n*gs]** byrdíngs Fl **fetil stinga]** megín þínga Fl, megính*ri*nga H, Hr **(8) jot-]** hiot- Fl **branda]** b*ra*ndi Hr.

Commentary

6/1 and 6/2 ***Sygna ... þengil*** 'lord of the Sygnir, of the men of Sogn'. By synecdoche, 'king of Norway'.

6/4 ***hleborðz visundr*** 'bison of the lee-side [ship]'. As Þjóð A 1, 4 and *Hryn* 9 show, Visundr was the ship that Magnús sailed to Denmark. Arnórr has here pressed *visundr* into double service as proper name and kenning element.

6/5 and 6/6 ***bioðr ... brynþings*** 'convenor of the corselet-meet'.

(a) This 'warrior' kenning is well paralleled, e. g. by *brynþings boði, Qrv* IX 8 and 34. In the analysis I adopt, it is taken as subject to *setti ... branda* 'beached his prows'. *Fetilstinga ... œsi* 'impeller of sword-belt stabbers [swords→warrior]' is assumed to form another kenning, object to *fús tók ǫld við ...* 'eager, folk received ...', and *gramr* '(fierce) prince, sovereign' in line 8 is taken in apposition to *bjóðr brynþings*.[17]

(b) Under an alternative interpretation, v. l. *blidr* would be adopted, i. e. adj. *blíðr* 'blithe', qualifying *gramr* in line 8, and the

[17] This is the analysis adopted by Finnur Jónsson (*Skjald* B), by Kock (*NN* §1295), and by Bjarni Aðalbjarnarson (*Hkr* 1941–51, III, 35n.) who, however, favours reading *æsi* 'god' rather than *œsi* 'impeller' as the base word of the kenning.

vowel of MS *bryn-* would be long (the metrically preferable alternative). In this case *brýnþings fetilstinga ... œsi* is construed as a single kenning, hence *fús tók ǫld við œsi fetilstinga brýnþings* 'eager, folk received the impeller of the pressing meet of sword-belt-stabbers [swords→battle→warrior]'. *Fetilstinga þing* is fairly certainly attested in the 13th-century *Nj* 8, and the assumption that *brýn-* is a prefixed epithet meaning 'pressing, urgent' would find some support in kennings such as *snarþing* [emended from MSS *suerting/svitting*] *fetilstinga* 'keen meet of sword-belt stabbers' (Sn St 4, 3) and *rammþing Glamma* 'mighty assembly of Glammi' in Arnórr's *Mdr* 9. The line *brynþing fetilstinga* occurs in the problematic *lausavísa* 1 of Eyvindr skáldaspillir, and the interpretation of that verse would be greatly helped by the assumption that *bryn-* (all MSS) stands for *brýn-* 'pressing' rather than *bryn-* 'corselet'.[18] However, the contexts in which *brynþing* must mean 'corselet-meet' (including Mark 1, 9 and the Eddaic *Sigrdr* 5) are numerous enough to show that (a) above must be considered the safer alternative in the present context.

Verse Seven

Sources

Magns(H-Hr) p. 51: H(6r), Hr(7r)
Flat III 272: Fl(765).

Context

As for *Mdr* 6 (which precedes v. 7 in *H-Hr* but follows it in *Flat*).

Diplomatic and edited text

Naði sikl*in*gr sið*an*	Náði siklingr síðan
sníallr ok da*n*mǫrk all*ri*	snjallr ok Danmǫrk allri
mattr ox d*re*ingia d*rot*t*ins	— mǿttr óx drengja dróttins —
dyʀ*r* norvegí at styʀa	dýrr Nóregi at stýra.
ǫngr hef*ir* an*n*aʀ*r* þei*n*gill	Engr hefr annarr þengill
aðr s*va* nogv laðí	áðr svá gnógu láði
b*ra*zsk at b*ra*gni*n*gs þ*ro*ska	— bráskat bragnings þroski —
b*ar*nvngr vnd sik st*rv*ngít	barnungr und sik þrungit.

[18] It also occurs in Þjóð A 4, 12, but the analysis of this is disputed (compare *Skjald* B and *NN* §1079D).

Prose order and translation

Snjallr, dýrr siklingr náði síðan at stýra Nóregi ok allri Danmǫrk. Mǫ́ttr drengja dróttins óx. Engr annarr þengill hefr barnungr þrungit und sik áðr svá gnógu láði. Bragnings þroski bráskat.
The daring, excellent prince attained then to rule Norway and the whole of Denmark. The strength of the warriors' liege waxed. No other lord, has, whilst a stripling, thrust under his sway before such ample lands. The sovereign's manhood did not fail.

Apparatus

(3) ox] *og* Fl **(4) norvegí]** noṙ Hr, nor̄. Fl **(5) ǫngr]** eíng*r* Hr, vng*r* Fl **(7) b*r*azsk at]** braskat Fl **þ*ro*ska]** þ*ro*ski Hr (8) **vnd]** v*id* Hr **st*rv*ngít]** þru*n*gít Fl.

Commentary

7/7 *þroski* (v. l.) 'manhood'. (a) The nom. case here is supported by *bráskat ... háski* 'peril did not cease' in *Þdr* 11. (b) I know of no record of an impersonal construction, *bregðask e-t/e-u*, which would have to be assumed if *þroska* were retained.

7/8 *þrungit* (v. l.) 'thrust'. (a) H's reading *strungit* has the appearance of a p. p. from a strong class III verb, but there is no other trace of such a verb in ON. (b) *Þrungit*, on the other hand, is entirely credible. Compare, e. g., *Gldr* 6 *þrǫng ... und sik jǫrðu.*

Verse Eight

Sources

Magns(H-Hr) p. 55: H(6v), Hr(7v)
Flat III 275: Fl(766).

Context

The verse is preceded by a paraphrase and brief introductory tag.

Diplomatic and edited text

Van*n* þa er víndr vm mínn*ir*	Vann, þá's Venðr of minnir,
vapnh*r*ið k*onv*ngr siða*n*	vápnhríð konungr síðan;

sveið of ám at jomí	sveið ófǫm at Jómi
jll *vir*kía hræ stíllír	illvirkja hræ stillir.
bv́k dró b*ra*ðla steikta*n*	Búk dró bráðla steikðan
bloðvgr v*a*rg*r* af gloðv*m*	blóðugr vargr af glóðum;
ran*n* áá oski*r*ð en*n*í	rann á óskírð enni
allf*re*kr bani hall*ar*.	allfrekr bani hallar.

Prose order and translation

Konungr vann síðan vápnhríð, þa's Venðr of minnir. Stillir sveið ófǫm illvirkja hræ at Jómi. Blóðugr vargr dró búk, bráðla steikðan, af glóðum. Allfrekr hallar bani rann á óskírð enni.

The king worked then a weapon-blizzard, which Wends remember. The ruler singed not a few wrong-doers' corpses at Jóm. The bloody wolf dragged a body, swift-roasted, from the embers. The most ravenous death of the hall [fire] darted on unbaptised brows.

Apparatus

(1) víndr] víndur Hr **vm]** of Hr, Fl **(3) sveið]** suef*ns* Fl **of ám]** ofaḿ Hr, of*an* Fl **at]** af Fl **jomí]** jomní Fl **(4) stíllír]** stille Fl **(5) b*ra*ðla]** bralla Fl **(6) v*a*rg*r*]** varge Fl.

Commentary

8/2 ***síðan*** 'then'. In construing the adverb with *vann* rather than *minnir* I am in agreement with Kock (*NN* §820) rather than Finnur Jónsson (*Skjald* B).

8/3 ***jomí.*** V. l. *jomní* (dat. sing; nom. sing. form unknown) resembles the Latin form of the name *Iumne*, used by Adam of Bremen in the late 11th century (vv. ll. *Iumm(e)* etc.; *Gesta* p. 80). On Jóm, see Commentary to *Hryn* 9/4 and n.

Verse Nine

Sources

Magns(Hkr) ch. 29, p. 46: K(512v), F(40r), J2(251r), 39(16v), 47(8r)
Flat III 275: Fl(766)
Magns(H-Hr) p. 55: H_1(7r), Hr_1(7v)
Magns(H-Hr) p. 75: H_2(10v), Hr_2(10r).

Context

Hkr and *H-Hr* p. 75: It is said that the strophe refers to a battle between Magnús, the victor of Hlýrskógsheiðr, and Sveinn Ulfsson. They engage *fyrir Vestlandi á Ré (fyrir vestan Aren,* H, Hr). After the battle Sveinn flees to Skáney. Magnús returns to Jutland, where he winters with a large company, keeping a close watch over his ships. *H-Hr* p. 55 and *Flat*: The setting here is quite different — a chance encounter in which Magnús, returning to Denmark from Jóm (before the battle of Hlýrskógsheiðr), triumphs over a large Viking fleet *fyrir Ré á Vestlandi (fyrir Vestland,* Hr).

Diplomatic and edited text

Fv́s let a re ræs*ir*	Fúss lét á Ré ræsir
ra*m*m þing hátt gla*m*ma	rammþing háit Glamma;
valsca ravð f*yrir* viðo	valska rauð fyr víðu
vestlandi g*ra*mr branda.	Vestlandi gramr branda.

Prose order and translation

Ræsir lét fúss rammþing Glamma háit á Ré. Gramr rauð valska branda fyr víðu Vestlandi.
The ruler set, eager, the mighty encounter of Glammi [a legendary sea-king→battle] in motion at Ré. The ruler reddened Frankish blades off wide Vestland.

Apparatus

(1) re] ré F, 39, 47, ræ Fl, Hr_1 **ræs*ir*]** hræsir H_1 **(2) ra*m*m-]** rym- H_2, Hr_2 **þing]** -þings F **hátt]** haít F, 39, H_1, Hr_2 **gla*m*ma]** ga*m*ma F, 39, ga*m*la Fl, glymía H_2, Hr_2 **(3) valsca ravð]** v*ir*du*m* rautt Fl, H_1, v*ir*du*m* raud Hr_1 **ravð]** h*ra*vn*n* H_2, Hr_2 **viðo]** om. F, Ridu Fl **(4) vestlandi]** vinlande Fl, Hr_1, víndl*a*ndí H_1, velldi Hr_2.

Commentary

9/1 *re* 'Ré (Rügen)'. The phrase *á Ré* suggests that the fighting was on land. The tradition of a sea-battle (in *Flat* and *H-Hr* p. 55) may rest on a false assumption that *fyr ... Vestlandi* 'off Vestland' in ll. 3–4 refers to the fighting rather than the island Ré (see note on 9/4 below). On the other hand, the account of the occasion of the battle in these two sources (above) is, because of the location of Ré, more plausible than that of *Hkr* and *H-Hr* p. 75 (see Bjarni Aðalbjarnarson, *Hkr* 1941–51, III 46n.).

9/2 ***hátt*** (normalised *háit*) 'set in motion, raised'. *Háit* is the older, and *hátt* the younger, form of the neut. sing. p. p. from the verb *heyja*. The disyllabic *háit* is the usual form in skaldic verse (Finnur Jónsson 1901, 105), and is indicated here by the metre. The use of the verb with the 'battle' kenning *rammþing Glamma* plays upon the legal phrase *heyja þing*; there are precedents for this in the work of Sigvatr and others.

9/3 ***valsca*** 'Frankish, French', or perhaps more broadly 'southern, foreign'. V. l. *virðum* would also give good sense: 'the ruler reddened blades on men'.

9/4 ***vestlandi***. This is the only record in ON of the place-name Vestland. The preposition *fyr* 'off, before' is compatible with the surmise that Vestland is a coastal area, either on the island Ré (Rügen), as assumed in *LP*, or on the mainland opposite Ré (modern W. Pomerania), as assumed by Flo, 1902, 272 and Bjarni Aðalbjarnarson, index to *Hkr* 1941–51, III. If the epithet *víðu* 'broad' has any literal significance and if the battle was fought on land, Vestland must have been on the mainland (as marked on map 1).

Verse Ten

Sources

Magns(Hkr) ch. 28, pp. 43–44: K(511r–v), F(40r), J2(250r), 39(16r), 47(7v)
Flat III 281: Fl(769)
Fsk ch. 50, p. 223: B(104), A(222; lines 1–4 only)
Magns(H-Hr) p. 65: H(8v), Hr(8v)
Ólsh(Sep) p. 630: 2(74v–75r), 61(130v), 321(285), 325V(90v), 325VI(42v), Bb(206v–207r), Th(161v).

Context

In *Hkr, H-Hr* and *Ólsh(Sep)*, the verse is quoted near the beginning of the account of the battle of Hlýrskógsheiðr. After receiving heartening portents, Magnús casts off his byrnie and rushes into the attack.

In *Flat, Mdr* 10 is the first of three verses by Arnórr which are quoted at the end of the brief account of the battle; it has the same summary role in *Fsk.*

Diplomatic and edited text

Oð með avxi breiða
odǫsin fram ræs*ir*
varð um hilmi hǫrða
hiordynr eN varp brynio
þa e*r* um scapt eN scipti
scapvǫrðr him*ins* jorðu
hel klavf havsa favlva
hendr tvær jofurs spendo.

Óð með øxi breiða
ódæsinn framm ræsir
— varð umb hilmi Hǫrða
hjǫrdynr — ok varp brynju,
þá's umb skapt — en skipti
skapvǫrðr himins jǫrðu;
Hel klauf hausa fǫlva —
hendr tvær jǫfurr spendi.

Prose order and translation

Ódæsinn ræsir óð framm með breiða øxi ok varp brynju. Hjǫrdynr varð umb Hǫrða hilmi, þá's jǫfurr spendi tvær hendr umb skapt; en skapvǫrðr himins skipti jǫrðu. Hel klauf fǫlva hausa.

The strenuous ruler stormed forth with broad axe, and cast off his byrnie. A sword-clash arose around the Hordalanders' lord, as the hero clenched both hands round the shaft; and heaven's shaping guardian allotted earth. Hel clove pallid skulls.

Apparatus

(2) odǫsin] odælin*n* 47, odræsin*n* 325V, Th **fram]** f*ra* Th **(3) varð]** vírd Th **um]** of 2, 325V, vnd 61 **hǫrða]** h*or*da*n* 61 **(4) hiordynr]** hrædyr Fl, hiorðine B , híǫrdyn H, Hr, hiordvnr Bb **eN]** so also 39, er J2, 47, *ok* others **brynio]** bryniu*m* Fl, Hr **(5) þa]** þ*ar* J2, 47, 2, þ*at* 321, 325VI **er]** om. 325V **um]** of F, B, Fl, H, 325V, Bb **eN]** er Bb **scipti]** skeptí Fl, skept*ir* 61, Th **(6) -vǫrðr]** v*or*d 61 **him*ins*]** hi*m*is 325V **Line (7)]** om. 61 **klavf]** klaup 321 **(8) tvær]** tueimr 61, Th, tveim 325V **jofurs spendo]** iof*ur* spend*ar* Th, iofuR spendi others.

Commentary

10/2 *odǫsin* 'strenuous, unsluggish'. *Ódæsinn* is recorded only here, although *dæsinn* and *dásinn* each appears once in *LP*, and *dási* m. 'sluggish, inactive person' twice. The literal sense of *ódæsinn* is 'not out of breath, unwearied' (cf. *dæsa(sk)* 'groan, lose one's breath from exhaustion', p. p. *dæstr* 'exhausted').

10/4 *ok* (v. l.) 'and'. Both *en* 'and / but' and *ok* give excellent sense, but *ok* has the stronger MS support.

10/6 *scapvǫrðr himins* 'heaven's shaping guardian'. A kenning for 'God'. *Skap-* in the *hap. leg. skapvǫrðr* probably has a double meaning, both parts stemming from a central notion of 'creating': (i) Active 'creating, fashioning' as in Þjóð A 4, 15 *skinna skapdreki* 'shaping dragon of hides', a whimsical kenning for 'tanner', and (ii) passive 'natural, fated' as in the adjs. *skapligr* 'natural, suitable' and *skapdauði* 'fated to die'. The first, active sense is stressed in my translation.

10/7 *hel* 'Hel'. The axe Hel had, according to Snorri, been owned by Magnús's father Óláfr (*Magns(Hkr)* ch. 28, p. 43). Theodoricus, in his *Historia*, p. 49, also reports that Magnús wielded his father's axe (not there named) two-handed at Hlýrskógsheiðr, and that it was shattered in the battle but is partly preserved in the cathedral at Niðaróss. Arnórr's play on the name of the goddess of death and her realm is discussed on p. 74.

10/8 *iofuʀ* (v. l.) *spendi* (v. l.) 'the hero clenched'. K's *hendr tvær jǫfurs spendu (umb skapt)* 'the hero's two hands clenched (round the shaft)' gives just as good sense as *hendr tvær jǫfurr spendi ...* 'the hero clenched both hands ...', but *jǫfurr spendi* has much the stronger MS authority. *Skjald* B prints *jǫfurs spendu.*

Verse Eleven

Sources

Magns(H-Hr) p. 68: H(9r), Hr(9r)
Flat III 281: Fl(769).

Context

H-Hr: Magnús fells the fleeing Wends until the corpses are piled up like waves on either hand. *Þess getr Arnór:*

Flat: Mdr 11 follows *Mdr* 10 and *Hryn* 13, with the words, *Og enn kuad hann*:

Diplomatic and edited text

S*va* hloð sikli*n*gr háfan
snaR*r* af vlfabaRi
h*ro*sag hvgfvllz vísa
hrækavst fírar æfi
at aleggiar yg*g*ia
allnáttfǫrvt mattið
ǫlld la vítt þot*t* villdí
vífmar yf*ir* klífa.

Svá hlóð siklingr hǫ́van
snarr af ulfa barri
— hrósa'k hugfulls vísa —
hrækǫst — fir*a* ævi,
at áleggjar Yggja*r*
allnǫ́ttfǫrull máttit,
— ǫld lá vítt — þótt vildi,
vífs marr yfir klífa.

Prose order and translation

Snarr siklingr hlóð svá hǫ́van hrækǫst af ulfa barri — hrósa'k ævi hugfulls vísa fir*a* —, at allnǫ́ttfǫrull marr áleggjar Yggja*r* vífs máttit klífa yfir, þótt vildi. Ǫld lá vítt.
The swift-moving sovereign heaped up so high a corpse-mound of wolves' barley [carrion] — I praise the life of the mettlesome liege of men — that, ever prowling by night, the steed of the river-limb-Óðinn's spouse [wolf, see Commentary] could not scale it, though he longed to. Men were strewn widely.

Apparatus

(1) sikli*n*gr] siklíngs Fl **(2) af]** vr Fl **-baRi]** -baur*r*e Fl **(3) h*ro*sag]** h*ro*sig Hr **(4) fírar æfi]** fíra Ræfe Fl **(5) yggia]** hyg*g*i*ar* Fl **(6) -fǫrvt]** -faurull Hr **mattið]** mattud Hr, Fl **(7) þot*t* villdí]** en valldí Hr **(8) vífmar]** -maar Hr, vifs m*ar*k Fl.

Commentary

11/4 *fira* (em.) 'of men'. (a) MSS *fírar* 'men' could be an apostrophe to the skald's audience (so Sveinbjörn Egilsson, 1828–46, VI, 63), but such an apostrophe would be without parallel in Arnórr's poetry. (b) The simple emendation to gen. pl. *fira* yields *fira vísi* 'liege of men', a phrase with abundant parallels, and this is my preferred solution. Alternatively, *fira* could be taken with *siklingr* in line 1 (so *Skjald* B) or with *hrækǫst* (Kock, *NN* §821), although the latter would yield the impossibly tautologous expression *hrækǫst fira af ulfa barri*.

11/5 and 11/8 *aleggiar Yggjar* (em.) ... *vífmar* 'steed of the river-limb-Óðinn's spouse'. The 'river-limb' is rock, the Óðinn of rocky land the giant, his spouse the giantess and her steed the wolf.

Yggjar is probably the original reading underlying MSS *yggia/hyggiar*. The Óðinn *heiti* Yggr 'Terrible' is a satisfactory base word to a kenning for rock-giant, for although it is not precisely paralleled, other 'giant' kennings contain the names of gods: *fjallgautr* 'mountain-Gautr [-Óðinn]', *Húsdr* 6, and *grjót-Móði* 'stone-Móði [the son of Þórr]', Anon XII D 4.

11/6 *allnáttfaurull* (v. l.) 'ever prowling by night'. On this striking epithet applied to the wolf, see p. 77 and n. 13.

Verse Twelve

Sources

Magns(Hkr) ch. 33, pp. 56–57: K(516v), F(41r), J2(254r), 39(17v), 47(9r)
Flat III 285 (lines 1–4 only): Fl(770)
Fsk ch. 50, p. 224: Fsk B(105), A(223–24)
Magns(H-Hr) p. 83: H(12r), Hr(10v)
SnE p. 148 (lines 5–8 only): R(66), T(37r), U(63), W(76), 748(16v), 748II(5r).

Context

Hkr and *H-Hr*: *Mdr* 12 opens a sequence of quotations from Arnórr and Þjóðólfr Arnórsson, and follows a remark that the battle off Helganes began in the evening, and that at the outset Magnús had a smaller force but larger and better-manned ships.
Fsk: *Mdr* 12 is cited after the events have been summarily narrated up to the point where, after a night-long battle, Sveinn flees ashore.
Flat: The verse follows a description of Sveinn's flight to Sweden after the battle of Áróss, Magnús's capture of Sveinn's ships and treasure, and his reprisals on the men of Skáney.
SnE: Mdr 12b is quoted to show that *maðr er kendr til viþa* — that a kenning for 'man' (here *reggbúss*) can have 'tree' as its base word.

Diplomatic and edited text

Vitt hefi ec heyrt at heiti	Vítt hef'k heyrt at heiti
helga nes þ*ar* e*r* elgi	Helganes, þar's elgi
vágs hiɴ viða frǫgi	vágs enn víða frægi
vargteit*ir* ravð m*ar*ga	vargteitir hrauð marga.
rǫck*ur* ǫndurt bað rand*ir*	Røkr ǫndurt bað randir
reɢbus saman leɢia	reggbúss saman leggja;
rógs scyia helt rygíar	rógskýja helt rýgjar
regni havst nótt gegnum.	regni haustnǿtt gegnum.

Prose order and translation

Hef'k heyrt, at heiti vítt Helganes, þar's enn víða frægi vargteitir hrauð marga vágs elgi. Ǫndurt røkr bað reggbúss leggja saman randir. Rógskýja rýgjar regni helt gegnum haustnǿtt.

I have heard that it is called broad Helganes, where the widely famed wolf-cheerer [carrion-provider, warrior] stripped many elks of the wave [ships]. At the beginning of twilight the tree of the ship [man] called for shields to be set together. The rain of the ogress of strife-clouds [shields→axe→battle] kept up through the autumn night.

Apparatus

(1) Vitt] Hitt A **hefi ec]** hæfir B, hofum A **heyrt]** hoᵉyt B **heiti]** héti F, 47, Fl, H, Hr, hæyti A **(2) er]** om. A **(3) vágs]** vox Fl, vægs A **hiɴ]** ens Fl, m*enn* (or in*n*) B **(4) -teit*ir*]** teit*r* Hr **ravð]** hravð J2, 47, H, Hr **m*ar*ga]** m*argan* Fl, B **(5) rǫck*ur*]** reyckr F, rǫkr J2, 47, T, 748, røkr 39, rekr B, ræykr A (= reykr 748II), rǫckr H, R, W, reckr Hr, rek... U **ǫndurt]** andrt B, ondur A, ...dvrt U **bað]** vár U **rand*ir*]** om. H, randar 748II **(6) reɢ-]** regn- B, r... U **(7) rógs]** so also J2, B, A, rog others **scyia]** skyɢia J2, skyi*ara* Hr, sk...a U **helt]** líet Hr **rygíar]** rygia R, T, W, 748II **(8) regni]** regin (or regni) R, r...ni U, rogni W, regn 748II **gegnum]** í g*e*gnum 748II.

Commentary

12/1 *Vitt* 'broad'.

(a) I take *vítt* as an adj. qualifying *Helganes*. The epithet may be more than conventional. The peninsula is roughly rhomboidal, broadening out from a very narrow isthmus, so that it would appear *vítt* from both the mainland and the sea.

(b) *Vítt* could alternatively be an adverb 'widely, far and wide' modifying *hef'k heyrt* 'I have heard'.

12/6 *reGbus* 'tree of the ship [seafarer, man]'. Both *regg* and *búss* appear in *þulur* but otherwise *regg* 'ship' is only found in the kenning *reggs rækjandi* 'seafarer', Þorm 1, 15, and in *Ht* 34, and *búss* '(box-) tree' only in Steinunn 1.

12/7 *rygíar* 'of the ogress'.

(a) The reading may be taken, as by Bjarni Aðalbjarnarson, as *rýgjar*, gen. sing. of the fem. noun meaning 'mighty woman, troll-woman' (*Hkr* 1941–51, III, 56–57n., following Konráð Gíslason 1875–89, II, 518.) Like other words for 'ogress' in similar constructions (Meissner 1921, 148), *rýgjar* could here form a kenning for 'axe' with *rógskýja* 'of strife-clouds [shields]' as the defining word. The *regn* 'rain' of the axe is then battle.

(b) An alternative also proposed by Bjarni is that *rýgr*, again like other words for 'ogress' (e. g. *gnepja* and *vígglǫð*), might be an 'axe' *heiti* in itself. *Rýgjar róg* 'strife of the axe' would then be 'battle', *rýgjar rógský* 'clouds of battle' would be 'shields' and the *regn* of shields once more 'battle'.

(c) V. l. *rygia* could be construed as acc. pl. of *Rygjar* 'Rogalanders' (standing for Norwegians), which would be object to the clause *bað randir* | *reggbúss saman leggja*, hence 'the tree of the ship [seafarer, Magnús] called for the Rogalanders to set their shields together' (so *Skjald* B). Such an object is not, however, necessary to the syntax, since *bað randir ... saman leggja* makes good sense — 'called for shields to be set together' — and *Rygja* is very much the minority reading.[19] Of the two analyses using the majority reading *rygjar*, (a) is the more straightforward and has been adopted in my translation.

12/8 gegnum 'through'. *Gegnum* is established here by the *aðalhending* on *regni,* but the variant *gǫgnum* is established in *Mdr* 13 and *Þdr* 2 by *aðalhendingar* with *Hǫgna* and *Rǫgnvalds*, respectively. Both variants are attested in other skaldic rhymes from

[19] Kock (*NN* §822) reads *Rygja* and construes *rógskýja ... Rygja* | *regni* 'the Rogalanders' battle'.

the 11th century, e. g. *þegnar : gegnum* (Halli 4), and *Rǫgnvalds : gǫgnum* (Sigv 3, 12).

Verse Thirteen

Sources

Magns(H-Hr) p. 84: H(12r), Hr(10v)
Flat III 283: Fl(770).

Context

In both recensions the strophe is connected with the battle at Helganes. In *H-Hr* it is introduced, *Magnús konúngr skaut handskoti alla nóttina; þess getr Arnór.* The compiler of *Flat* summarises the battle in a single paragraph and then quotes *Mdr* 13.

Diplomatic and edited text

DavRr líet drei*n*gia haRi	Dǫrr lét drengja harri
d*ri*vgspakr af þrek flivga	drjúgspakr af þrek fljúga
glæddi elldr af oddv*m*	— glœddi eldr af oddum —
almi skept a hialma	almi skept á hjalma.
lietat hilm*ir* hneítí	Létat hilmir hneiti
hogna veðr j gognv*m*	Hǫgna veðr í gǫgnum
jarn flvgv þykt se*m* þyrn*ir*	— jǫ́rn flugu þykkt sem þyrnir —
þiel h*ar*ðara sparða*n*.	þél harðara sparðan.

Prose order and translation

Drjúgspakr drengja harri lét dǫrr, almi skept, fljúga af þrek á hjalma. Eldr glœddi af oddum. Hilmir létat hneiti, þél harðara, sparðan í gǫgnum Hǫgna veðr. Jǫ́rn flugu þykkt sem þyrnir.
Ever wise, the warrior's liege made spears, hafted with elm, fly with [all] his strength at helmets. Flame sparked from spear-heads. The lord did not allow his sword, firmer than a file, to be spared throughout the wind-storm of Hǫgni [battle]. Iron [missiles] flew thick as thorns.

Apparatus

(3) glæddi] glæde Fl **(4) skept]** skept*r* Hr, skeytt*r* Fl **(5) hilm*ir*]** hilme Fl **(6) hogna]** hugn*ar* Fl **gognv*m*]** gegv*m* Hr **(7) þykt]** þyck Fl **(8) h*ar*ðara]** ard adra Fl.

Commentary

13/2 *drivgspakr* 'ever wise'. The compound is not recorded elsewhere in ON, but there are other adjs. prefixed by the intensive *drjúg-*, such as *drjúghvass* 'ever keen, very keen'.

13/6 *hogna veðr* 'wind-storm of Hǫgni [battle]'. The name Hǫgni denotes three legendary figures in ON poetry: (i) Hǫgni Gjúkason, the Burgundian hero, brother of Gunnarr; (ii) the father of Sigrún in the Eddaic lays of Helgi Hundingsbani; (iii) the father of Hild, alluded to in Bragi's *Ragnarsdrápa* and elsewhere. Arnórr's reference to Gjúki's descendants in *Gjúka ættar klæði* in *Hryn* 9/6–7, albeit conventional, might suggest that it was Hǫgni Gjúkason whom Arnórr intended to figure as the epitome of heroism in *Hǫgna veðr*.[20]

Verse Fourteen

Sources

Magns(Hkr) ch. 33, p. 58: K(517r), J2(254v), 39(17v), 47(9r)
Flat III 284: Fl(770)
Fsk ch. 50, p. 224: Fsk B(105)
Magns(H-Hr) p. 85: H(12r), Hr(11r).

Context

Hkr, Fsk and *H-Hr*: The strophe appears in the account of the battle at Helganes. In *Hkr* it follows Þjóð A 1, 22, with an introduction; in *Fsk* it follows uninterruptedly from *Mdr* 12; in *H-Hr* it follows *Hryn* 15.
Flat: The verse succeeds *Mdr* 15 immediately. Both are cited in connection with the battle south of Áróss, not with that off Helganes.

Diplomatic and edited text

Sceiðr toc biarn*ar* broðor	Skeiðr tók Bjarnar bróður
ballr scanungum all*ar*	ballr Skǫnungum allar

[20] Finnur Jónsson in *Skjald* B prints *Hǫgna væðr* 'Hǫgni's garb [armour]', perhaps influenced by the clothing metaphor in Arnórr's *Gjúka ættar klæði, Hryn* 9; but this is not justifiable since in the orthography of Hr and Fl graphic *e* does not usually stand for normalised *æ*. The form *væðr* is rejected by Kock in *NN* §823.

þioð reri þ*eir*ar tið*ar*	— þjóð røri þeirar tíðar
þingat g*r*amr með h*r*ingo*m*.	þingat — gramr með hringum.

Prose order and translation

Gramr, ballr Skǫ́nungum, tók allar skeiðr Bjarnar bróður með hringum. Þjóð røri þingat þeirar tíðar.
The monarch, baleful to Scanians, seized all the longships of Bjǫrn's brother [Sveinn], every one. Men rowed up at the right moment.

Apparatus

(1) toc] tokt B **broðor]** broðr J2, Hr, brod*er* Fl, B **(2) ballr]** balldr 39, B, hallr Fl **scanungum]** kan*n* vngu*m* Fl, Skæningu*m* B **(3) reri]** reyri J2, H **þ*eir*ar]** þ*eir*ra Fl.

Commentary

14/1 *Sceiðr* 'Longships'. The monosyllabic f. pl. *skeiðr* is attested by the metre, as also in the contemporary verse Bǫlv 2. Both *skeiðr* and *skeiðar* are used by Sigvatr: in Sigv 1, 3; 2, 7 and 7, 2 the metre of the line implies a disyllable, while Sigv 3, 9 *undan skeiðr at sundi* implies a monosyllable.

14/1 *biarnar broðor* 'Bjǫrn's brother'. This is Sveinn Ulfsson. Bjǫrn is mentioned together with Sveinn in *Knýtls* ch. 5, p. 97; also ch. 26, p. 141, and *Msk* p. 223.

14/2 *ballr scanungum* 'baleful to Scanians'.[21] The idiom *ballr e-m* 'harsh, fearsome to someone' may be paralleled in *B dr* 1 *réðo ... hví væri Baldri ballir draumar*, if *ballir* is to be construed as a predicative adj. governing *Baldri*. I know of no more secure example of *ballr e-m,* but the assumption of the idiom in *Mdr* 14 is supported by the following: (i) *Ballr* is not etymologically related to the strong verb *bella* 'harm',[22] which governs a dat. object, but the phonetic and

[21] This interpretation is adopted by Bjarni Aðalbjarnarson (*Hkr* 1941–51, III, 58n.). Finnur Jónsson in *Skjald* B and Kock, *Skaldediktningen* I 159, on the other hand, emend to gen. pl. *Skǫ́nunga*, which they take with *gramr*.

[22] De Vries, s. v., links it only with the weak verb *bella* 'use, deal with' (often of unfair dealings); so also *IEW* pp. 627–28 and 629.

semantic similarity of *bella* and *ballr* might have led speakers to use the phrase *ballr e-m* by analogy with *bella e-m*. (ii) Another model for the construction *ballr e-m* would be the commmon *reiðr e-m* 'angry with someone', cf. *hættr e-m* as in *hættr Serkjum* 'dangerous to Saracens' (Þjóð A 3, 2). (iii) The phrase *ballr Skǫ́nungum* is compatible with the historical fact that the men of Skáney (Skåne) earned Magnús's hostility by supporting his enemy Sveinn.

14/3 *þeirar tiðar* 'at the right moment, at a fortunate moment'. So Bjarni Aðalbjarnarson, who renders *tíð* as *heillastund*(?) (*Hkr* 1941–51, III, 58n.). Although *tíð* normally has a neutral sense which can be qualified by *góð / ill*, the possibility that it can have a favourable sense is suggested by its antonym *ótíð* 'bad season, bad weather, inappropriate time' and by the adj. *tíðr* 'accustomed, popular, beloved'.

Verse Fifteen

Sources

Magns(H-Hr) pp. 85–86: H(12r), Hr(11r)
Flat III 284: Fl(770)

Context

H-Hr: Mdr 15 is cited after *Mdr* 14, with the words, *Þar fèll mikit lið af Sveins mönnum, en sumir hlupu fyrir borð ok týndust; svâ segir Árnór:*
Flat: As for *Mdr* 14, the context is the battle of Áróss.

Diplomatic and edited text

Svei*ns* m*anna* rekr svn*n*an	Sveins manna rekr sunnan
savndvg lik at st*ra*vndv*m*	sǫndug lík at strǫndum;
vítt s*er* ǫlld f*yrir* vta*n*	vítt sér ǫld fyr útan
jotl*an*d hv*ar* hræ fliota	Jótland, hvar hræ fljóta.
vitn*ir* d*re*gr or vatní	Vitnir dregr ór vatni
van*n* ol*af*ssonr ban*n*at	— vann Áleifs sonr bannat —
bvk slitr v*ar*gr j vikv*m*	(búk slítr vargr í víkum)
valkavst arafǫstv.	valkǫst — ara fǫstu.

Prose order and translation

Sǫndug lík Sveins manna rekr sunnan at strǫndum. Ǫld sér vítt fyr útan Jótland, hvar hræ fljóta. Vitnir dregr valkǫst ór vatni. Áleifs sonr vann bannat ara fǫstu. Vargr slítr búk í víkum.
Sandy corpses of Sveinn's men are cast from the south onto the shore [lit. shores]. Folk see far and wide off Jutland where bodies float. The wolf drags a heap of slain from the water. Óláfr's son made fasting forbidden for the eagle. The wolf tears a corpse in the creeks.

Apparatus

(1) svn*n*an] om. Fl **(2) st*ra*vndv*m*]** st*ra*vndv Hr **(3) fy*rir*]** t*il* Hr **(4) hv*ar*]** om. Hr **(8) -fǫstv]** fǫ̇stu*m* Fl.

Commentary

15/3 *vítt* 'far and wide'. I have construed *vítt* as an adverbial neut. sing. It could alternatively be an adj. qualifying *Jótland.*

Verse Sixteen

Sources

Magns(H-Hr) p. 87: H(12v), Hr(11r)
Flat III 283: Fl(770)
Fsk ch. 50, p. 225: Fsk B(105).

Context

H-Hr: Magnús pursues Sveinn and his surviving troops to Skáney. Þjóð A 4, 4 is cited, and then *Mdr* 16: *Þessa getr ok Arnór, at Magnús konúngr gekk af skipum sínum á Skáney ok herjaði:*
Fsk: The context is similar, although it is not suggested that Magnús was pursuing Sveinn. Fsk A lacks *Mdr* 16 and the introduction to *Mdr* 17, so that the sentences about the raid on Skáney are incongruously followed by *Mdr* 17, about the raid on Falstr (Falster).
Flat: The verse follows immediately on *Mdr* 13 and Þjóð A 1, 21.

Diplomatic and edited text

Vppgav*n*gv van*n* yng*vi*	Uppgǫngu vann yngvi
itr loga*n*di noga	arflógandi gnóga;

ger*ð*i hilm*ir* horða	gerði hilmir Hǫrða
hiǫrþey a skaneyív.	hjǫrþey á Skáneyju.

Prose order and translation

Arflógandi yngvi vann gnóga uppgǫngu. Hǫrða hilmir gerði hjǫrþey á Skáneyju.
The wealth-squandering sovereign launched a mighty enough assault ashore. The Hordalanders' prince caused a thawing wind of swords [battle] on Skáney.

Apparatus

(2) itr] tyr Fl, arf B **loga*n*di]** log Fl **(3) horða]** h*ar*da Hr, órda Fl **(4) a]** j Fl.

Commentary

16/1 and 16/2 *Vppgavngv* ... *noga* 'assault ashore, mighty enough'. It is unnecessary to emend *noga* to *nogan*, i. e. *gnógan*, and to construe it with *hjǫrþey* 'battle' (as Finnur Jónsson does in *Skjald* B and *LP* s. v. *gnógr*).

16/2 *arf* (v. l.) *logandi* 'wealth-squandering'. The weak class 1 verb *lóga* 'destroy, squander, part with (to someone else)' is well attested in prose, although *LP* only contains one entry for the uncompounded verb.

The pres. part. *lógandi* 'destroying, squandering' demands a suitable object.

(a) V. l. *arf-* best serves this purpose. *Arfr* 'inheritance' can well stand for '(hereditary) treasure', as in *arfr Niflunga*, referring to gold in *Akv* 27. Hence *arflógandi* can mean 'squandering his inherited treasure (by giving it lavishly)', cf. the kenning *hoddlógendr* 'squanderers of the treasure-hoard' (*Ísldr* 2). *Arflógandi* in *Mdr* 16 could either be a kenning, standing in apposition to *yngvi* 'sovereign' or, as I have assumed, an adjectival pres. part. The remaining two readings are unsatisfactory:

(b) *Ítr* 'splendid, fine' is common in poetry as a laudatory prefix in words such as *ítrmaðr* 'great man' and *ítrskapaðr* 'finely shaped', and examples of *ítur-* prefixed to adjs. in Mod. Icel. are given by Blöndal, s. v. But *ítrlógandi* 'splendidly squandering / destroying' would scarcely be praise in the absence of an explicit object such as 'treasure'. *Ítr* could well be a corruption due to the influence of *Hdr* 10, whose first line is almost identical with *Mdr* 16/1:

Uppgǫngu bauð yngvi	The prince ordered the advance
ítr með helming lítinn	ashore, splendid, with a small force.

(c) The reading of Fl, *tyr log* (for *tyrlogandi*?), is clearly corrupt.

(d) Emendation is unnecessary, *Skjald* B (and *LP*) and Kock *NN* §2520 notwithstanding.

Verse Seventeen

Sources

Magns(Hkr) ch. 34, p. 62: K(518v), F(41v), J2(255v), 39(18r), 47(9r–v)
Flat III 285: Fl(770)
Fsk ch. 50, p. 225 (lines 1–4 only): Fsk B(105), A(224)
Magns(H-Hr) p. 89: H(12v), Hr(11r)
SnE p. 148 (lines 5–8 only): R(66), T(37r), U(64), W(77), 748(16v), 748II(5r).

Context

In *Hkr, Fsk, Flat* and *H-Hr* it is mentioned that Magnús next turned south. (On Fsk A, see Context to *Mdr* 16.)
Hkr and *H-Hr* specify that he went to Falstr on a punitive expedition against Sveinn's supporters.
SnE: Mdr 17b is quoted in the same context as *Mdr* 12b. The kenning exemplified is *auðar þorn*.

Diplomatic and edited text

Svic reð *eigi* ecko	Svik réð eigi eklu
allvaldr davnom giallda	allvaldr Dǫnum gjalda;
let fullhugaðr falla	lét fullhugaðr falla
falstr byGv*a* liþ tiGi	Falstrbyggva lið tyggi.
hloð eɴ hála tǫðo	Hlóð — en hǫla tœðu
hirð m*enn* ara gren*n*i	hirðmenn ara grenni —
avð*ar* þorn f*yr* ǫrno	auðar þorn fyr ǫrnu
ungr valkavsto þunga.	ungr valkǫstu þunga.

Prose order and translation

Allvaldr réð eigi gjalda Dǫnum svik eklu. Fullhugaðr tyggi lét lið Falstrbyggva falla. Ungr auðar þorn hlóð þunga valkǫstu fyr ǫrnu; en hirðmenn tœðu ara grenni hǫ́la.
The all-ruler did not repay the Danes for their deceit scantly. High-mettled, the monarch made the troop of Falstr-men fall. The young thorn-tree of treasure [man, prince] raised up heavy heaps of slain for eagles; and retainers served the eagle-feeder [carrion-provider, warrior] excellently.

Apparatus

(**1**) **ecko]** af eklo F, ek(k)lo others (**2**) **all-]** al- J2, Fl, Hr (**4**) **falstr]** flast*r* Hr **tiGi]** tig*g*ía Fl (**5**) **hloð]** hl... U **eN]** e*r* J2, 47 **hála]** hæla H, hardla 748II **tǫðo]** tiaðo F, teðu J2, 47, R, T, W, taðo 39, tyþo U (**6**) **ara]** arn- R, a... W **gren*n*i]** græn*n*i 47, U (**7**) **avð*ar*]** avða H **ǫrno]** aur*r*nu*m* Hr, ǫrnv*m* W, auNu*m* 748II (**8**) **ungr]** v... U **valkavsto]** valkos...o U **þunga]** þungo T, ...vnga U.

Commentary

17/1 ***eklo*** **(v. l.)** 'scantly', lit. 'with dearth, lack'. This is the first record of the noun *ekla* in ON poetry, apart from the title *Vellekla* which may be as old as the (late 10th-century) poem. The only other occurrence in LP is *af eklu* 'sparingly' in the 13th-century *Hálfs* VII 2, but *sumblekla* '?lack of drink' appears as a v. l. in Eg Lv 2.

Verse Eighteen

Sources

Magns(Hkr) ch. 34, p. 63: K(518v–519r), F(41v), J2(255v–256r), 39(18r), 47(9v)
Flat III 285: Fl(770)
Fsk ch. 50, pp. 225–26: B(105, lines 1–4 only), A(224)
Magns(H-Hr): H(12v), Hr(11r).

Context

The prose link-passages merely paraphrase and briefly introduce the verse. *Flat* and *Fsk* follow the quotation with a remark that the verse refers to Magnús reaching twenty years of age: *Hier visar til ath þessi uetr fyllir annan tòg alldrs Magnus konungs og var hann hid næsta vor eptir tuitògr ath alldre* (*Flat* version, *Fsk* shorter):

Diplomatic and edited text

EN ravð frán a fíoni
folld sotti gram drott*ar*
rans gallt h*err* fra hanom
hringsercs litaðr m*er*ki
miNiz avld hveR an*n*aR
jafnþarfr blám hrafni
ert gat hilm*ir* hiarta
h*er*scyld*ir* tǫg fyldi.

Enn rauð frǫn á Fjóni
— fold sótti gramr dróttar;
ráns galt herr frá hǫnum —
hringserks lituðr merki.
Minnisk ǫld, hverr annan
jafnþarfr blǫum hrafni
— ert gat hilmir hjarta —
herskyldir tøg fyldi.

Prose order and translation

Enn rauð hringserks lituðr frǫn merki á Fjóni. Dróttar gramr sótti fold. Herr galt ráns frá hǫnum. Ǫld minnisk, hverr herskyldir fyldi annan tøg jafnþarfr blǫum hrafni. Hilmir gat ert hjarta.
Further, the painter of the mail-coat [warrior, who spills blood] reddened bright banners on Fjón. The retinue's lord attacked the land. The people paid [dearly] for their robbery of him. Let men recall which troop-commander has lived out his second decade equally generous to the swart raven. The sovereign got a spirited heart.

Apparatus

(1) EN] Ec J2, Næst Fl, B, A, H, Hr **ravð]** bar J2, 47 **frán]** fram J2, 47, Fl **(2) folld]** f*ra*m F **gram]** gramr others **(3) rans]** þ*ar* J2, 47 **fra]** firir B **(5) miNiz]** min*n*te Fl, mintiz B **hveR]** hu*er*t Fl **an*n*aR]** an*n*an J2, 47, Hr **(6) -þarfr]** þ*ra*fn Fl, þarf B **(7) ert]** so also 39, snart B, avrt others **(8) -scyld*ir*]** -skylldi Hr **tǫg]** toc J2, taug*r* Hr.

Commentary

18/2 *gramr* (v. l.) 'lord'. The nom. sing. is required by the syntax of the helming, as well as being indicated by the readings of all MSS except K.

18/3 *rans* 'robbery / robbing'. The precise reference of *rán* is not clear from the verse nor from the prose accounts. Probably the Danes' intention to deprive Magnús of rule (and hence of revenue) is meant.

18/5 *miNiz* 'let men recall'. Despite the obscurities of the helming, the words *hverr ... jafnþarfr ... hrafni ... herskyldir* 'which troop-commander, equally generous to the raven' clearly imply that Magnús's prowess is being compared — presumably favourably — with that of others. In such a comparison (*ǫld*) *minnisk* is likely to be a challenging subjunctive, 'let men see if they can recall ...' implying that no equal will be found, but on purely formal grounds it could be indicative, 'men recall / will recall ...'.

Lines 18/5, 18/6, and 18/8, especially 18/5 *annan* (v. l.) 'second'.

(a) The reading *anaR* has the stronger MS authority, and is favoured by Kock in his *Skaldediktningen*, I 160. If it were adopted, the construction would be *minnisk ǫld, hverr annarr herskyldir, jafnþarfr blǫ́um hrafni, fyldi tøg* 'let men recall, which other troop-commander has, equally generous to the swart raven, completed ten'. The 'ten' would presumably be ten battles, but since nothing in the context indicates this, the helming would make poor sense. Further, it seems unlikely that *annarr* was the original reading and was altered in the course of transmission to *annan*, for *hverr annarr* would belong together grammatically, whereas v. l. *hverr annan* could not, and *annan*, if correct, is separated from the noun it defines (*tøg*) by three metrical lines.

(b) The *lectio difficilior annan*, in the phrase *fyldi annan tøg* 'completed his second ten', is further supported by the words which follow *Mdr* in *Flat* and *Fsk* (quoted in Context above). These suggest that the compilers of these MSS knew a traditional explanation that the verse referred to Magnús reaching his twentieth year, although the text as it stands in the two MSS cannot yield that meaning since it has the variant *annarr* rather than *annan*.

The balance of evidence is, therefore, slightly in favour of v. l. *annan* (adopted also in *Skjald* B). *Fyldi ... annan ... tøg* could mean 'completed his twentieth (battle)', but, as already mentioned, 'battle' is not specified in the strophe. Alternatively, *fylla* could refer to a span of time, as in the idiom *fylla sína lífsdaga* 'complete the days of one's life'.

I therefore construe the verse — albeit tentatively — as shown in the prose order and translate, 'Let men recall which troop-commander has, equally generous to the swart raven, lived out his second decade'.[23] By means of this rhetorical challenge the skald claims Magnús to have been without equal, not because no other had reached twenty years, but because no other so young had been *jafnþarfr blǫ́um hrafni* — had served the raven so well, had made carrion of so many of his foes. The construction is comparable to *Mdr* 19:

Ungr skjǫldungr stígr aldri jafnmildr á við skildan.	Never will a young king so bounteous board a shield-hung bark.

Here Arnórr is not claiming that no other prince will board a ship, but rather that none who does so will be *jafnmildr* 'equally bounteous'.

18/7 *ert* 'spirited'.

(a) The spelling *ert* occurs again in the text of *Hdr* 5/5, in MSS Msk, H and Hr (with v. l. *aurtt*, normalised *ǫrt*, in Fl), but not in any of the very numerous citations listed under *ǫrr* in *LP*. The prose lexicons, too, completely lack any record of an adj. *err*, although the similar forms *ern* and *errinn* are known, both meaning 'brisk, bold'. *Err* could perhaps be an independent form which, like them, has a different etymology to *ǫrr* (see de Vries on these words), but which has escaped the lexicographers' notice because it has been 'normalised' to *ǫrr*.

(b) V. l. *avrt* is neut. sing. of the familiar adj. *ǫrr* 'ready, bold, generous', as in Þjóðólfr's *aðalhending ǫrr : dǫrrum* (Þjóð A 1, 21). The collocation with 'heart' is matched in Þorm 2, 23 *Ǫrt vas Áleifs hjarta*. *Ert* could simply be a graphic variant of this since *e/ø* and *ø/ǫ* are common doublets. *Err* occurs as a variant of *ørr* 'scar': Fritzner Supplement, s. v. *err*.

18/8 *herscyldir* 'troop-commander'. Hfr 3, 1 *hǫlða skyldir* (v. l. *hauka*), lit. 'obliger, constrainer of men', is the only close parallel, although similar ideas are embodied in kennings such as *herstillir*, lit. 'troop-controller' and *herflýtir* 'troop-hastener'.

[23] So *CPB* II 191, where the idiom is translated, 'fulfilled his second tale of ten years'; also Bjarni Aðalbjarnarson, *Hkr* 1941–51, III, 63n.

Verse Nineteen

Sources

SnE p. 113: R(51), T(28v), U(57), W(56), 757(4v).

Context

This is the first of many skaldic quotations which illustrate kennings for ‘sky’, here *Ymis hauss*.

Diplomatic and edited text

Vngr skioldv*ngr* stigr ald*ri*	Ungr skjǫldungr stígr aldri
iafnmildr a við skiald*ar*	jafnmildr á við skildan
þes v*ar* grams v*nd* gavmlv*m*	— þess vas grams — und gǫmlum
gnog ravsn ymis havsi.	— gnóg rausn — Ymis hausi.

Prose order and translation

Aldri und gǫmlum Ymis hausi stígr ungr skjǫldungr jafnmildr á skildan við. Rausn þess grams vas gnóg.
Never beneath the ancient skull of Ymir [giant→sky] will a young king so bounteous board a shield-hung bark. The glory of that lord was ample.

Apparatus

(1) Vngr] Ȯ́gr T, Engr U **stigr**] stig T, sitr U **(2) skiald*ar***] scildar T, skilldan U **(3) þes**] illeg. 757 ***var***] varþ U, e*r* 757.

Commentary

The helming. This verse is an important point in the case for regarding *Mdr* as a memorial poem (see p. 29).

19/2 *skilldan* (v. l.) ‘shield-hung’.

(a) This reading, although only in MS U, is supported by the similar *scildar* in T. It is acc. sing. masc. p. p. from *skilda* ‘to array with shields’, and it qualifies *við* ‘(timber) ship’ (so Ólsen 1909, 293–94).

(b) *Skjaldar* ‘of the shield’ does not make sense in the context, nor does it supply the necessary *aðalhending* with *mildr*.

19/3 and 19/4 ***vnd gavmlvm ... ymis havsi*** 'beneath the ancient ... skull of Ymir'. On the mythical reference in this kenning for 'sky', see p. 74.

Þorfinnsdrápa

Verse One

Sources

SnE p. 88: R(40), T(23r), U(51), W(45), 757(3v).

Context

This, the first skaldic quotation in Snorri's *Skáldskaparmál*, illustrates the skalds' use of mythological *heiti* and kennings: *Sva sem segir ArnoR iarlaskald, at Oþinn heiti Allfavðr:*

Diplomatic and edited text

Nv hyc sliðr hvg*ar* segia	Nú hykk slíðrhugaðs segja
sið lett*ir* m*er* striþa	— síð léttir mér stríða —
þytr all favðvr ytv*m*	(þýtr Alfǫður) ýtum
iarls kostv b*ri*m hrosta.	jarls kostu (brim hrosta).

Prose order and translation

Nú hykk segja ýtum kostu slíðrhugaðs jarls. Síð léttir mér stríða. Hrosta brim Alfǫður þýtr.

Now I mean to tell men of the excellence of the fell-hearted jarl. Not soon will my anguish lighten. The mash-surf of the All-father [Óðinn's ale→poetry] roars.

Apparatus

(1) hyc] hyck U, W, om. 757 **hvg*ar*]** hugaz T, W (= hugaþs U), om. 757 **(2) sið lett*ir*]** siþlætr U **striþa]** striþv*m* U **(3) þytr]** þrytr 757 **all]** al- U, 757 **favðvr]** faudr T, favþrs U, foðr W **(4) kostv]** kosta U, kost W.

Commentary

1/1 and 1/4 *sliðr hvgaz/hugaþs* (v. l.) ... *iarls* 'fell-hearted jarl's'.

(a) *Slíðrhugaðr* is attested in a verse attributed to King Óláfr Haraldsson (Ól helg 3), and there are plentiful parallels to the compound, including *grimmhugaðr* and *harðhugaðr*.

(b) *Slíðrhugar jarls* 'of the jarl of savage heart' is a less likely construction, for the adjectival genitive is not common in ON,[24] and the other compound nouns in *-hugr* recorded by *LP* all have a noun, not adj., as the first element: *dróttinhugr* 'loyalty to a lord', *fjandhugr* 'enmity' etc. The *-ar* ending in MS *sliðr hvgar* may well be due to a misreading of *-az* in an antecedent MS.

1/3 and 1/4 *all favðvr ... brim hrosta* 'All-father's mash-surf'. Óðinn's drink, poetry. *Hrosti* 'mash' is the malt and liquid used in brewing. The myth of the mead of poetry, and kennings alluding to it, are discussed in Frank 1981 and Davidson 1983, 418–47.

Verse Two

Sources

Orkns ch. 20, p. 52: 325III(1r), 332(32), 702(77), 48m(346v).

Context

The verse is quoted to corroborate a statement that Þorfinnr kept his retainers and other magnates (*ríkismenn*) in food and drink all through the winter, unlike other rulers who usually show such bounty to their retainers only at Yule.

Diplomatic and edited text

Orms felle drakc allan	Orms felli drakk allan
alkostigr fan hrosta	alkostigr fen hrosta
ravsn drygðe þa ræsir	— rausn drýgði þá ræsir —
Ravgnvallz niðr i gỏgnv*m*.	Rǫgnvalds niðr í gǫgnum.

[24] A few examples of the gen. used to describe states of mind or attributes of people or things are given by Nygaard, 1905, §127 anm. 1.

Prose order and translation

Rǫgnvalds niðr, alkostigr, drakk hrosta fen allan orms felli í gǫgnum. Ræsir drýgði þá rausn.
The scion of Rǫgnvaldr, surpassing, drank the swamp of malt [ale] through all the serpent's slayer [winter]. The ruler exercised bounty then.

Apparatus

(1) drakc] *-c* unclear 325 **(2) fan]** fen others **(3) drygðe]** dugði 332, 48m **ræsir]** ręsis 332, 48m.

Commentary

2/1 *Orms felle* 'serpent's slayer'. Winter, which by its coldness almost kills snakes (many species hibernate). Such kennings are rare but not unknown: cf. (from the 12th century) *orms tregi* 'serpent's grief', Á ket, and Egill's 'summer' kenning *dalmiskunn fiska* 'mercy of valley-fish [snakes]', Eg Lv 6.

2/2 *fen* (v. l.) 'swamp'. The kenning *hrosta fen* 'swamp of mash [ale]' also appears in Egill's *St* 19 (with MS *fanst* emended to *fens*). There seems to be a playful echo here of *(Alfǫður) hrosta brim* '(Óðinn's) mash-surf [poetry]' in *Þdr* 1.

2/3 *ravsn drygðe ... ræsir* 'the ruler exercised bounty' or 'practised splendid hospitality'. That *rausn* 'magnificence' here refers specifically to Þorfinnr's lavish hospitality is suggested by the Context.

V. l. *rausn dugði ... ræsis* 'the ruler's bounty availed / was fitting' would also make good sense, praising Þorfinnr (the *ræsir*) by means of understatement. *Duga* is recorded in absolute use with an abstract subject, e. g. in *ef þitt œði dugir* 'if your wit is sufficient', *Vafþr* 20 and 22.

2/4 *Ravgnvallz niðr* 'scion, descendant of Rǫgnvaldr'. Þorfinnr. This Rǫgnvaldr is Þorfinnr's ancestor, Rǫgnvaldr inn ríki Eysteinsson, jarl of Mœrr in Norway, who, according to tradition, received Shetland and Orkney from Haraldr hárfagri in compensation for his son's death in battle (e. g. *Haralds saga hárfagra* ch. 22, *Hkr* I 122).

Verse Three

Sources

Msk p. 290: Msk(20v)
Fsk ch. 79, p. 300: Fsk B(150), A(324–25)
Ólskyrra (H-Hr) p. 439: H(79r), Hr(55r).

Context

After comments on the peaceful rule of Óláfr kyrri, son of Haraldr Sigurðarson, there is a detailed excursus on the ancient manner of seating men at drinking sessions in Scandinavian royal halls. It is reported that a revered counsellor would be placed in *et úœðra ǫndugi* 'the lower high-seat' opposite the ruler, and would receive toasts from him: *oc þotti þat vera mest virþing at sitia fyr konvngs adryccio. oc til þess at þetta se eigi logit þa segir ArnoR sva i(arla) skalld* (*Msk* version, which hence does nothing to contradict the impression that the verse is about Óláfr kyrri; the introduction in *Fsk* ends: *segir Arnórr jarlaskáld hversu hann sat með Þorfinni jarli*). After the quotation the compiler of *H-Hr* adds, *Hèr hrósar Arnórr því, at hann sat í úæðra öndvegi fyrir ádrykkju Þorfinns jarls, þá er hann var með honum í Orkneyum.*

Diplomatic and edited text

Het ec þa er hv*er*n vetr satv*m*	Hét'k, þá's hvern vetr sǫtum
h*ra*fns v*er*þgiafa iafnan	hrafns verðgjafa, jafnan
lið dracc g*ra*mr agoþar	— líð drakk gramr — á góðar,
gagnvart scipa sagn*ir*.	gagnvert, skipa sagnir.

Prose order and translation

Hét'k jafnan á góðar skipa sagnir, þá's sǫtum hvern vetr gagnvert hrafns verðgjafa. Gramr drakk líð.
I called always to the stalwart ships' companies, as I sat each winter facing the raven's feast-giver [warrior]. The lord drank ale.

Apparatus

(1) þa er] þeghar A **(2) -giafa]** -gefa Hr **(3) goþar]** gegnar B, goðþar A **(4) -vart]** -vært B,A (= v*er*t H, Hr).

Commentary

3/1, 3/3 and 3/4 *Het ec ... agoþar ... scipa sagnir* 'I called to the stalwart ships' companies'. *Hét'k* can make no sense here unless construed with *á*,[25] and *á* can scarcely govern anything but *góðar skipa sagnir*, since it is unstressed and immediately precedes *góðar*.[26] *Heita á e-n* is a well known idiom meaning 'to call on someone [god, saint or living human] for help' or, in battle contexts, 'to urge on, exhort', as in *hét á Háleygi, Hák* 3. In the present context Arnórr could have been calling on the company to hear his poetry, to fight loyally in future battles, or to join in toasts.

3/1, 3/2 and 3/4 *þa er hvern vetr satvm | hrafns verþgiafa ... gagnvart* 'as each winter I sat facing the raven's feast-giver [warrior]'. I take *sǫ́tum gagnvert hrafns verðgjafa* together, thus assuming a patterning of clause elements in the helming which is matched in two helmings of Sigvatr quoted by Kock in *NN* §826. *Sǫ́tum* is pl. in form but (especially in view of the prose Context) probably refers to the skald alone, just as *hét'k* does. For the alternation of sing. and pl. in the 1st person compare, e. g., *Drv* (XI) 11, *hlautk, þvít heima sǫ́tum* ... The honour accorded to court skalds, and their placing in the 'second high seat', is mentioned in *Egils saga* ch. 8: *Af ǫllum hirðmǫnnum virði konungr [Haraldr hárfagri] mest skáld sín; þeir skipuðu annat ǫndvegi* (p. 19).

3/2 *iafnan* 'always'.

(a) I take *jafnan* to modify *hét'k ... á góðar ... skipa sagnir*, thus stressing that it was a habit with Arnórr to address the assembled company.

(b) It could alternatively modify *líð drakk gramr* 'the lord drank ale', but this would detract from the terseness of the intercalated clause.

(c) It is less likely to modify the subordinate clause *þá's* ... since it would duplicate the meaning of *hvern vetr* 'each winter'.

[25] Finnur Jónsson, in *Skjald* B, takes *hét'k* together with *hrafns verðgjafa* and translates *tiltalte (drak til)* 'addressed (drank to)'; but *heita e-n* is not recorded with such a meaning.

[26] This is the solution adopted by the editors of *Fms* XII, 1837, 170, who render *hét'k* as *ávarpaði*, and by Kock, *NN* §826.

Verse Four

Sources

SnE p. 163: R(71–72), T(40v), U(70), W(82).

Context

The helming illustrates the statement that jarls and royal retainers can be referred to as the intimates or bench-mates of a king (*konvngs rvnar eþa malar e(þa) sessar*).

Diplomatic and edited text

B*era* sin en mic min*ir*	Bera sýn of mik mínir
morð keɴdz taka enda	morðkends taka enda
þess ofþengils sessa	þess of þengils sessa
þv*n*g mein syn*ir* vng*ir*.	þung mein synir ungir.

Prose order and translation

Mínir ungir synir taka bera sýn, þung mein of mik of enda þess morðkends þengils sessa.
My young sons begin to bear manifest, heavy sorrows for me at the death of the battle-skilled bench-mate of the monarch.

Apparatus

(1) sin en] syn v*m* U **(2) morð]** mærþ U **keɴdz]** kendr U, kend W **(3) þess of]** þ*essv*m U.

Commentary

The helming. In this helming, isolated from its poetic context and elusive in syntax, it is not easy to grasp the relation of the 'heavy sorrows' (*þung mein*) to the skald (*en / um mik*) and to Þorfinnr (*of þengils / ofþengils sessa*), nor to establish the meanings of *taka* and *enda*. All the analyses presented here have severe drawbacks, and one must suspect corruption in the text. Section (a) gives a rationale of the prose order above, while (b) and (c) set out what appear to me the most satisfactory alternatives.

(a) *Taka* is construed with infin. *bera*, hence 'begin to bear' (cf. the inceptive *taka mæla* in *Gríp* 16). *Mínir ... synir ungir* 'my young sons' is the subject, and *þung mein* 'heavy sorrows' the object, to *bera* (cf. *bera angr, Líkn* 10 and *bera stríð*, Kolb 2, 5, both 'suffer anguish / remorse').

MS *sin en mic* (line 1) does not make sense, however the helming is construed, so that the reading *syn vm mik*, i. e. *syn of mik*, has been adopted. *Sýn* 'manifest, visible' qualifies *mein* (cf. *sýnn skaði* 'manifest harm', referring to an abstract harm in *Hsv* 52), and *of mik* is assumed to mean 'for me, on my account', cf. *of / um sik* in expressions such as *sýsla / hyggja of sik* 'trouble about oneself'.[27] Thus *mínir ungir synir taka bera þung, sýn mein of mik* is interpreted, 'my young sons begin to bear heavy, manifest sorrows for my sake'.[28]

Of in line 3 is construed as a causal preposition,[29] governing *enda þess þengils sessa*, hence 'at / because of the death of the bench-mate of the monarch'. *Endi* 'death' is recorded, e. g., in the phrase *gera sínn enda* 'die', *Islendzk Æventyri*, I 72. *Morðkends* 'battle-skilled' or 'battle-renowned' could qualify *þengils* 'monarch', but since Þorfinnr, not the unnamed monarch, is the hero of the encomium, I construe it rather with *þengils sessa* 'bench-mate of the monarch [Þorfinnr]'. *Þengill* could refer to Óláfr helgi or to Magnús góði, both of whom Þorfinnr was obliged to placate (according to *Orkns* ch. 18, p. 38, and ch. 30, pp. 75–77). *Of enda þess morðkends þengils sessa* is understood as an elaboration of *mein*, hence 'sorrows at the death of the battle-skilled bench-mate of the monarch'.

(b) The main objection to analysis (a) is that it presupposes an extremely complex word order in the helming. In particular, the placing of the finite verb *taka*, far from the beginning of the clause, is uncharacteristic of Arnórr (and probably of skalds in general), as is that of *of* (line 3) if *þung mein of enda ...* 'heavy sorrows at the death ...' are taken together. The following analysis obviates these difficulties, but involves the assumption of some usages which are not

[27] So Konráð Gíslason 1877, 56, and *Skjald* B.

[28] Kock's interpretations of *taka* and *sýn* (*NN* §827) are unsupported by recorded usage.

[29] *Of* can hardly be the intensive prefix to the word *þengils* since *þengils* alliterates and must be fully stressed; nor can it be an expletive particle, since *þengill* does not belong to any of the categories of noun that usually follow the particle (Kuhn 1929, 26–31).

precisely paralleled in ON. The prose order and translation under this analysis would be:-

Þung, sýn mein bera of mik;	Heavy, manifest sorrows loom over me;
mínir ungir synir taka enda	my young sons learn of the death
þessum morðkends þengils sessa.	of that bench-mate of the battle-skilled monarch.

Bera of mik is here construed as predicate to *þung mein*, hence 'heavy sorrows loom over me'. This use of *bera of / yfir* is attested by Blöndal in a quotation from 1908 in which an observer states that he saw a black speck or cloud *bera yfir Látrafjöllin* (p. 71, col. a).

Taka is assumed to have the sense 'hear, learn, receive news of'. This receives some support from idioms such as *hann tók því vel* where *því* refers to news or a greeting; cf. also the partially synonymous *nema*, whose meaning shades into 'take in, understand' or 'listen to' (as in Arnórr's *nemi drótt, hvé ... Þdr* 15).

V. l. *þessum* is taken with *(enda ...) þengils sessa* as a dat. indicating possession or respect, hence 'death of that bench-mate of the monarch'. Since *sessa* is assumed to be dat. sing., *morðkends* 'battle-skilled' must qualify *þengils*.

(c) I am indebted to Professor Peter Foote for the following suggestion. The verse is construed (with prose order on right):

Bera sinn [or sín] — en mik minnir;	Ungir synir bera sinn [hlut / kost]
morðkends taka*t* enda	*or* sín [þung mein], en mik minnir;
þessum þengils sessa	þung mein taka*t* enda þessum
þung mein — synir ungir.	sessa morðkends þengils.

'Young sons endure their lot (*or* their heavy ills), but I remember; heavy ills do not begin to end for this bench-mate of the slaughter-renowned prince.'

This analysis is idiomatically more convincing than (a), but there are difficulties: the enigmatic *sinn / sín-*, the reading of *mínir* (all four MSS) as *minnir*,[30] especially when *mínir ... synir ungir* forms such a natural unit, the slight emendation to *takat*, and the use of the U

[30] *Minner* is, coincidentally, the reading of GKS 2368 4o, a MS of *Laufás-Edda*, whose readings for this helming are otherwise the same as those of W; see *SnE* (Faulkes 1979) p. 363.

variant *þessum* (also used in analysis (b)) which is likely to be a secondary reading.

The three analyses outlined here thus offer advantages balanced by drawbacks. It seems unlikely that any one solution will finally resolve the problems of the helming.

Verse Five

Sources

Orkns ch. 20, p. 43: 332(20), 702(74), Fl(521), (48m:343r)
Ólsh(Hkr) ch. 96, p. 160 (lines 5–8 only): K(319r–v), 325XI2e(2r)
Ólsh(Sep) p. 232 (lines 5–8 only): 2(29r), 4(21r), 61(96v), 68(28r), 73(147), 75a(21r), 325V(32r), Th(116v), Bb(157v)
SnE(Arnamagn) II 540 (lines 1–2 only): 757(6v).

Context

In the sagas the verse follows a sketch of Þorfinnr's appearance and character, and a statement that at the age of five he received Katanes (Caithness, v. l. *Katanes ok Suðrland*) and the title *jarl* from his grandfather Melkómr, King of the Scots.
In *SnE* the first two lines are quoted in a chapter of *hǫfðingja heiti*, to illustrate the use of *hilmir*.

Diplomatic and edited text

Hilm*ir* ravð i hialma
hreGi skelkings eGi*ar*
for aðr xv veri
fetrioðr hugins vet*ra*
goR letz grund at veria
gun*n* frǫkn oc til sǫkia
ǫri Einars hlyra
ǫngr m*aðr* und skyran*n*i.

Hilmir rauð í hjalma
hreggi skelkings eggjar;
fór, áðr fimmtán væri,
fetrjóðr hugins, vetra.
Gǫrr lézk grund at verja,
geðfrœkn, ok til sœkja
œri Einars hlýra
engr mannr und skýranni.

Prose order and translation

Hilmir rauð skelkings eggjar í hjalma hreggi. Fetrjóðr hugins fór, áðr væri fimmtán vetra. Engr mannr und skýranni œri Einars hlýra lézk gǫrr at verja grund, geðfrœkn, ok sœkja til.
The ruler reddened the sword's edges in the storm of helmets. The foot-reddener of Huginn / the raven [warrior] set forth before he was

fifteen winters. No man under the cloud-hall [sky] younger than Einarr's brother has declared himself ready to guard his realm, mind-bold, and to mount attacks.

Apparatus

(2) hreGi] hræg*g*... 757 **skelkings]** skelkiungs 702, skilfíngs Fl, skelkvins 48m, ...kelk...s 757 **(3) xv]** fimtan 702, Fl **(4) fet-]** fiót 702 **(5) goR]** geíR Bb **letz]** leiz 702, let 61, 75a, Bb **(6) gun*n*]** ged others **(7) ǫri]** errín*n* Fl (48m as 332), ór Bb **Einars]** an*n*ars 75a **hlyra]** hlyri Fl (48m as 332), 61, 73 **(8) ǫngr]** œingr Fl (= engr K, 4, 75a, 325XI), vn*n*gr Th **und]** j Fl, vn 325V (48m as 332).

Commentary

5/2 *skelkings* 'the sword's'.

(a) The form *skelkingr* is only recorded in *Þdr* 5 and *Þul* IV l 7 (as v. l. to *skelkvingr*), although *skelkuin* also occurs as a v. l. in Hfr 5, 5. A derivation from *skelkr* 'fear' has been suggested (de Vries, s. v.). It seems likely that in *Þdr* 5 *skelk-*, attested in a majority of MSS, is the original reading, and was replaced by the more familiar word *skilfingr* at some stage in transmission.

(b) V. l. *skilfingr* only occurs as a 'sword' *heiti* in the 13th-century *Kuml* 1 (in the line *hreggi skilfings eggjar*) and in a *þula* (*Þul* IV l 7), but it is also recorded in *Grí* 54 and *Þul* IV jj 8 as an Óðinn *heiti,* and in various contexts as a term for 'prince' (see *LP*, s. v.).

5/3 *for* 'set forth'. Björn M. Ólsen (1909, 289) suggested emending to *fár* 'few', since he found *fór* meaningless in the absence of a phrase indicating direction, but the absolute use of *fara* is attested in a military context in Sigv 11, 9: *ferk, ef þó skulum berjask,* 'I shall go, if we have to fight after all'.

5/4 *fetrioðr hugins* 'foot-reddener of Huginn / the raven'. Warrior, here Þorfinnr. Huginn, lit. 'Thought', one of Óðinn's two raven scouts (*Grí* 20, *SnE* pp. 42–43), here stands for 'raven' in general.

5/6 *ged* (v. l.) *frǫkn* 'mind-bold'. Both readings, *geð-* and *gunn-*, are well paralleled by synonymous compounds (e. g. *gunnbráðr / gunndjarfr; geðrakkr / geðhraustr*). *Geðfrækn* has the authority of all MSS except 332.

5/7 Einars hlyra 'Einarr's brother'. The kenning fleetingly recalls the young Þorfinnr's territorial wrangling with his half-brother Einarr rangmuðr 'Wry-mouth', who finally died in 1020 at the hands of Þorfinnr's henchman Þorkell (Icelandic Annals pp. 16, 57, 106, 316 and 468).

Verse Six

Sources

Orkns ch. 20, p. 46: 332(23), Fl(521), (48m:344r–v).

Context

Þorfinnr, threatened with a two-pronged attack from Karl Hundason and the Scots, sails north across the Péttlandsfjǫrðr (Pentland Firth). He reaches Dýrnes (Deerness), just south of Sandvík (Sandwick), but there Karl catches him up before his reinforcements arrive, and Þorfinnr chooses to fight rather than abandon his ships and goods. *Þdr* 6 is preceded by a remark that the battle was hard and long, and by the words, *Orrostu þessar getr Arnórr í Þorfinnsdrápu* (332 version; Fl reads, *Suo segir Arnorr jarlaskalld*):

Diplomatic and edited text

Endr hyG ec Karli kendu	Endr hykk Karli kendu
kyndo*m* jofur brynio	kyndóm jǫfur brynju
land vara lofðungs kund*ar*	— land vasa lofðungs kundar
lavst f*yrir* dyrnes avstan	laust — fyr Dýrnes austan.
fim*m* sneckiom reð fram*m*i	Fimm snekkjum réð frammi
fluGstyGr v*ið* hug dyGan*n*	flugstyggr við hug dyggvan
ravsn*ar* m*aðr* at ræsis	rausnarmannr at ræsis,
reiðr xi skeiðom.	reiðr, ellifu skeiðum.

Prose order and translation

Hykk jǫfur endr kendu Karli brynju kyndóm fyr austan Dýrnes. Land lofðungs kundar vasa laust. Flugstyggr rausnarmannr réð reiðr fimm snekkjum við dyggvan hug frammi at ellifu skeiðum ræsis.
I believe the hero once taught Karl the mail-coat's monstrous verdict [battle] east off Dýrnes (Deerness). The land of the ruler's son was not for the taking. The flight-shunning man of splendour [Þorfinnr]

steered, angered, five long-ships with doughty heart forth against the eleven galleys of the lord [Karl].

Apparatus

(1) Endr] Andr Fl (48m as 332) **hyG ec]** hyck Fl (48m as 332) **Karli]** ꝁl. Fl (48m as 332) **(2) kyndo*m*]** kyndu*m* Fl (48m as 332) **jofur]** lofut Fl (48m as 332) **(3) kund*ar*]** kíndar Fl (48m as 332) **(5) reð]** hellt Fl **(6) *við* ... dyGan*n*]** af ... dygg*um* Fl (48m as 332) **(8) xi]** ellifu Fl.

Commentary

6/1 *Karli*. I have assumed this to be the proper name Karl, not the appellative 'old man, churl'.[31] Although there is no evidence in Celtic sources for a king with such a name, 'Karl Hundason, Skotakonungr' figures prominently in *Orkns.* ch. 20. There have been many attempts to identify Karl. Taylor (1937) suggested that he could have been a mormaer of Ross, Sutherland or of both, who annexed Argyll at the death of the ruler whom *Orkns* names Melkómr, in 1029. Crawford favours the rather appealing possibility that Karl Hundason was the Scandinavians' name for MacBeth (1987, 71–72), while Donaldson equates him with Duncan (1988, 2), and Thomson takes him as a Mormaer of Moray (1987, 47–49). Hundi occurs, incidentally, as the name of a freedman of Scots family in *Laxdœla saga* ch. 6, p. 10.

6/2 *kyndom ... brynio* 'monstrous verdict of the mail-coat'. An unusual battle-kenning, in which the judicial metaphor conveys the grim finality of war; cf. *folkvandar dómr* 'verdict of the battle-rod [sword]' (V Gl 2), *brynþing* 'mail-coat assembly' (several occurrences, including *Mdr* 6), and *brynmót* 'mail-coat meet' (Sturl 5, 20). *Kyn-* 'marvellous(ly)' is usually prefixed to adjs., but *kynmálasamr* (*Qrv* VII 12), probably 'full of wondrous talk', shows that it can immediately precede a noun.

6/2 *jofur* 'hero, lord'. Þorfinnr. V. l. *lofut* in Fl makes no sense here.

[31] Munch (1852–63, I ii 854n.) suggested that *karl* in *Þdr* 6 was the appellative, and that it was later misunderstood as a proper name and the patronymic Hundason added.

6/3 lofðungs kundar 'ruler's son, descendant'. Þorfinnr. The *lofðungr* 'ruler', lit. 'praiseworthy one' (or 'descendant of Lofði', *SnE* p. 183) is Sigurðr digri Hlǫðvisson, if *kundr* is taken in its narrowest sense of 'son'. V. l. *kindar*, near-synonymous with *kundar*, is also a good reading.

Verse Seven

Sources

Orkns ch. 20, p. 47: 332(23), 702(74), Fl(521), (48m:344v).

Context

As for v. 6, which v. 7 follows directly.

Diplomatic and edited text

At lavgðo skip scatn*ar*	At lǫgðu skip skatnar
skilit fell heʀ a þilior	skilit; fell herr á þiljur;
svamo jarn i amo	svǫ́mu jǫ́rn í ǫ́mu
oþ havrð Scota bloði	óðhǫrð Skota blóði.
stall drapa streng*ir* gullo	Stall drapa — strengir gullu;
stal beit en*n* ran*n* sveiti	stál beit, en rann sveiti;
broddr flo bifþuz odd*ar*	broddr fló; bifðusk oddar
biartir þengils hiarta.	bjartir — þengils hjarta.

Prose order and translation

Skatnar lǫgðu skilit skip at. Herr fell á þiljur. Óðhǫrð jǫ́rn svǫ́mu í ǫ́mu blóði Skota. Þengils hjarta drapa stall. Strengir gullu, stál beit, en sveiti rann. Broddr fló. Bjartir oddar bifðusk.
Men steered ships decisively to the attack. Troops slumped to the decking. Rage-hard iron blades swam in the dark blood of Scots. The ruler's heart was not struck with terror. Bow-strings shrilled, steel bit, and gore flowed. Spear-head flew. Shining sword-points quivered.

Apparatus

(2) skilit] skilid 702 **(3) amo]** aumu Fl (48m as 332) **(4) havrð]** bord Fl (48m as 332) **(5) drapa]** d*re*pa Fl (48m as 332).

Commentary

7/1 *scatnar* 'men'. Since the remainder of the helming shows the shedding of Scottish blood it seems probable that the *skatnar* who steer ships into the attack (*at lǫgðu*) are the men of Orkney and that the troops who fall (*fell*) are the Scots.

7/2 *skilit* 'decisively'. The form could be nom. / acc. sing. neut. of the p. p. from *skilja* 'separate, discern', or it could represent *skilið*, the corresponding pl. form, since *d* and *t* are often equivalent graphs in unstressed syllables (so Björn M. Ólsen, 1909, 294). *Skilid* in 702 is also ambiguous, since in the orthography of that MS it could represent either *-it* or *-ið*.

(a) *Skilit* could be an adverbial use of the neut. sing. p. p. of *skilja*. This usually has the sense 'clearly, distinctly' and occurs in phrases involving 'distinct' hearing or telling, e. g. Hfr 3, 11 *skilit frá ek*. The adj. *skilinn*, however, can be applied to actions as well as words, e. g. *sniallr ok skilinn í øllv framferði* 'doughty and decisive in all action' (*Maríu saga* p. 326). This provides support for the rendering 'men steered ships decisively / unhesitatingly to the attack' which I have adopted (so also Finnur Jónsson in *Skjald* B and Finnbogi Guðmundsson, *Orkns* 1965, 47n.).

(b) *Skilið*, if applied to pl. *skip*, would mean 'separate', i. e. not linked together. But the writer of *Orkns* certainly did not understand the words thus, for he states that both leaders tied their fleets together (ch. 20, p. 46).

7/3 *amo* 'dark'. From the evidence of *LP* it appears that Arnórr was the first skald to use the epithet *ámr*, here and in *Hdr* 8/3.[32]

7/5 and 7/8 *stall drapa ... þengils hiarta* 'no terror struck the ruler's heart'. *Drapa* is past sing. of *drepa* 'strike' with the suffixed negative *-a*. This is the first secure example of the idiom *hjarta drepr stall* 'one loses heart, is afraid', although v. 10 of Eilífr Goðrúnarson's *Þórsdrápa* (c. 1000) contains a probable instance of it. Halldór Halldórsson concludes that the idiom is best explained as 'the heart

[32] Gen. pl. *ámra* appears in *Hafgerðingadrápa* (*Hafg* 1) but, as mentioned on p. 79, the dating of the fragment (traditionally before 1000) has been called into question.

stops beating', with *drepa stall* meaning 'stop, make halt' (1965, 38–64). A variant occurs in *Hryn* 12/7–8 (see Commentary).

The *þengill* in *Þdr* 7 is presumably the dauntless Þorfinnr.

Verse Eight

Sources

Orkns ch. 20, p. 48: 332(24–25), Fl(521), (48m:344v).

Context

The men of Orkney overrun Karl's flag-ship before it can be rowed free. Karl, with the few survivors on his ship, leaps onto another and flees, with Þorfinnr in pursuit.

Diplomatic and edited text

Þrima var þvigit scemri	Þrima vas þvígit skemmri;
þat v*ar* skiott at spiotu*m*	þat vas skjótt, at spjótum
mǫtr v*ið* min*n*a neyti	mætr við minna neyti
min*n* drottin*n* rak flotta	minn dróttinn rak flótta.
gol aþ*r* gr*a*ms m*enn* foli	Gall, áðr grams menn fellu,
guɴ mar um her saru*m*	gunnmǫ́r of her sǫ́rum;
h*ann* va sigr f*yrir* sun*n*an*n*	hann vá sigr fyr sunnan
sandvik ruðo branda.	Sandvík; ruðu branda.

Prose order and translation

Þrima vas þvígit skemmri. Þat vas skjótt, at minn mætr dróttinn rak flótta spjótum við minna neyti. Gunnmǫ́r gall of sǫ́rum her, áðr grams menn fellu. Hann vá sigr fyr sunnan Sandvík. Ruðu branda.
The battle was none the briefer for that. It happened swiftly that my precious liege put them to flight with spears and a smaller company. The battle-gull [raven / eagle] screamed above the wounded war-band, before the lord's men fell. He won victory south of Sandvík. They reddened swords.

Apparatus

(1) Þrima] Þruma Fl (48m as 332) **þvigit]** þeyge Fl (48m as 332) **(2) at]** m*ed* Fl (48m as 332) **(5) gol]** gall Fl (48m as 332) **foli]** fellu Fl, fǫli 48m **(6) um]** und Fl (48m as 332).

Commentary

Lines 8/1 to 8/4. The helming is difficult, for no interpretation adequately explains the contradiction between *þrima vas þvígit skemmri* 'the battle was none the briefer for that' and *þat vas skjótt...* 'it happened swiftly...' It is possible that *því(git skemmri)* originally referred to some action of Þorfinnr's enemies which was described in a previous verse, now lost.

8/2 and 8/4 *þat var skiott at ... minn drottinn rak flotta* 'it happened swiftly that ... my liege put them to flight'.

(a) The sequence *þat ... at* suggests that *at ... minn dróttinn ...* is best construed as a subordinate clause explaining *þat vas skjótt.*

(b) *Með*, v. l. to *at* in Fl, may well be the scribe's emendation, springing from his puzzled observation that *at* does not govern the immediately following *spjótum.* It is, however, adopted in *Skjald* B and in *Orkns* 1965, 48.

8/2 *spiotum* 'with spears'. (a) This phrase I construe with the clause *at ... flótta* in which it is embedded. (b) The alternative is to take it with *þrima vas þvígit skemmri* (so Björn M. Ólsen 1909, 296). This analysis has the disadvantage of assuming an extremely difficult word order, in which *spjótum* separates *at* from the clause it introduces, and, although it might explain *þvígit skemmri* ('the battle was none the briefer with spears', i. e. 'for all the number of spears'), it does not explain how, after a long battle, Þorfinnr 'swiftly' routed his enemies.

8/5 *gall* (v. l.) 'screamed'; ***fellu* (v. l.)** 'fell'. *Foli* in 332 is, as Ólafur Halldórsson points out (1964, 148), a mis-spelling of *fǫli*, i. e. *fœli*, past subj. sing. of *fela* 'hide, entrust, bury'. This is established by *fǫli* in 48m. But there is no suitable object to *fela* 'hide' in the helming (Ólsen's suggestion being eccentric, 1909, 296–97), so that the reading must be rejected in favour of v. l. *fellu.* V. l. *gall* 'screamed' not *gól* 'sang' must accordingly be chosen in order to complete the *skothending*. This is the best solution, but not a perfect one, since it would be difficult to account for the presumed corruption of *fellu* to *fœli.*

8/5 *grams menn* 'lord's men' and **8/6 *her sarum*** 'wounded war-band'. In view of the skald's usual practice of emphasising the enemy's losses, these phrases are best taken as references to Scots, while the victorious *hann* of line 7 is undoubtedly Þorfinnr.

8/8 *ruðo branda* 'they reddened swords'. (a) Ólafur Halldórsson finds the subjectless 3rd pl. verb *ruðu* suspect and emends to *ruðum* 'we reddened' (1964, 149–50, followed by Finnbogi Guðmundsson, *Orkns* 1965, 48). His objection, however, is not an overriding one, since *brendu*, if the correct reading in *Þdr* 11/1, likewise lacks an explicit subject, and the emendation to *ruðum* is not altogether convincing in the absence of evidence that Arnórr was present at this battle.

(b) *Ruðu* has an explicit subject if *áðr grams menn fellu ... ruðu branda* are read together as a single sentence, 'before the lord's men fell, they reddened their swords'.[33] But it is rare for a subordinate clause beginning with *áðr* to precede its main clause.

(c) I therefore favour taking *ruðu branda* 'they reddened swords' as a clause complete in itself (so also Kock, *NN* §829). The understood subject must be Þorfinnr and his men (the 'smaller company', *minna neyti*, of line 3).

Verse Nine

Sources

Orkns ch. 20, p. 50: 332(28), 702(74–75), Fl(522).

Context

In the land battle at Torfnes, Þorfinnr and his men attack, and Karl's Irish division is thrown into disarray. Karl then advances his standard against Þorfinnr in a grim struggle. He eventually flees — *en sumir menn segja, at hann hafi fallit. En Arnórr segir svá* (332 version; Fl similar):

Diplomatic and edited text

Vlfs tuGu ravð eGi*ar*	Ulfs tuggu rauð eggjar,
eitt þ*ar* er Torfnes heit*ir*	eitt þar's Torfnes heitir,

[33] Finnur Jónsson construes the verse thus in *Skjald* B, marking off *grams menn* by commas so that it is subject to *ruðu*.

ungr olli þi þengill
þ*at* var manadag fran*ar*
sungu þ*ar* t*il* þinga
þun*n* f*yrir* eccial sun*nann*
sverð er siklingr barðiz
snaR v*ið* skotl*anz* haRa.

— ungr olli því þengill —
(þat vas mánadag) fránar.
Sungu þar, til þinga,
þunn fyr Ekkjal sunnan,
sverð, es siklingr barðisk
snarr við Skotlands harra.

Prose order and translation

Fránar eggjar rauð ulfs tuggu, þar's eitt heitir Torfnes. Ungr þengill olli því. Þat vas mánadag. Þunn sverð sungu þar fyr sunnan Ekkjal, es siklingr snarr til þinga barðisk við harra Skotlands.
Bright blades grew red on the wolf's mouthful [carrion] at a place called Torfnes. Young, the ruler caused that. It was a Monday. Slender swords sang there south of the Ekkjall, as the princeling, swift into conflict, fought with Scotland's lord.

Apparatus

(1) tuGu] tugga 702 **ravð]** rę̨d 702 **(3) þi]** þui 702, Fl.

Commentary

9/1 *Vlfs tuGu* 'On the wolf's mouthful'. This kenning for '(bloody) corpse' is matched by *Munins tugga* 'raven's mouthful', which occurs in three skaldic contexts. *Tugga*, lit. 'chew, chewed mouthful' is not recorded in ON prose, but is known in Mod. Icel.

(a) Unless *eggjar* is pl. subj. to the sing. verb *rauð*, with *ulfs tuggu* as acc. sing. obj., *tuggu* must be dat. sing. and the use of *rauð* impersonal, hence 'bright blades were reddened on the wolf's mouthful'. There could alternatively be an understood pronoun: '[He] reddened bright blades ...'.

(b) V. l. *tugga* would be nom. sing., subject to *rauð* in (prose order) *ulfs tugga rauð fránar eggjar* 'carrion reddened bright blades'.

9/2 *Torfnes*, modern Tarbatness. The Norse name Torfnes, lit. 'Peat Headland', must represent a false etymology of the Gaelic *tairbeart* 'isthmus', common in place-names. There is — and presumably was — no peat at Tarbatness (Munch 1852–63, I ii 856, n. 1).

9/5 *til þinga* 'into conflict'.

(a) If *þing* is understood as 'conflict, battle' (see Commentary to *Hryn* 5/7), *snarr til þinga* forms a pattern of phrase often used by the skalds, as in *snarr til snerru* 'swift into battle' (*Ísldr* 19, 12th century), or *fúss til snerru* (E viðs 2, early 11th century). In view of these parallels, and in view of the warlike character of the strophe, I take *snarr til þinga* together as 'swift into conflict, ready for battle', applied to *siklingr* 'princeling' (so *Skjald* B).

(b) An alternative, favoured by Kock (*NN* §830), is to take *sungu þar til þinga þunn ... sverð* together as a bold image, 'slender swords sang there (?) in anticipation of conflict'.

(c) If *þing* were understood not as 'conflict' but as 'goods, booty' one could construe *siklingr barðisk til þinga við Skotlands harra* 'the princeling fought for goods / booty against Scotland's lord'.

9/6 *eccial.* The river Oykell, which flows into the Dornoch Firth. Ekkjall here refers especially to the Firth itself.

Verse Ten

Sources

Orkns ch. 20, p. 50: 332(28–29), 702(75), Fl(522), (48m:346r).

Context

Exactly as for v. 9, which v. 10 follows directly.

Diplomatic and edited text

Hatt bar hialta drottin*n*	Hátt bar Hjalta dróttinn
hialm at gei*ra* jalmi	hjalm at geira jalmi
ognstǫrir ravð irom	— ógnstœrir rauð Írum
odd i ferð*ar* broddi	odd — í ferðar broddi.
min*n* drottin*n* navt matt*ar*	Minn dróttinn naut máttar
mildr und brezku*m* skildi	mildr und brezkum skildi;
hendi Hlavðvis frendi	hendi Hlǫðvis frændi
h*er* m*enn* oc tok bren*n*a.	hermenn ok tók brenna.

Prose order and translation

Hjalta dróttinn bar hátt hjalm í ferðar broddi at geira jalmi. Ógnstœrir rauð Írum odd. Minn mildr dróttinn naut máttar und brezkum skildi. Hlǫðvis frændi hendi hermenn ok tók brenna.
The Shetlanders' liege bore high his helmet in the van of his troop in the tumult of spears. The sweller of battle-dread [warrior] reddened his point on Irishmen. My bounteous liege wielded his strength beneath a British shield. Hlǫðvir's kinsman captured warriors and began burning.

Apparatus

(2) jalmi] salmi Fl (48m as 332) **(5) navt]** hlaut Fl (48m as 332) **(7) -vis]** -vers 702, Fl (48m as 332) **(8) m*enn*]** man*n* Fl **oc]** en*n* 702, Fl **tok bren*n*a]** tokst sen*n*a 702.

Commentary

10/1 *hialta drottinn* 'liege of Shetlanders'. Here Þorfinnr, as also *Hjaltlands harri* 'Shetland's lord' in *Þdr* 12; but in *Frag* 3 I believe *Hjalta dróttinn* refers to Rǫgnvaldr Brúsason.

10/3 *irom* 'on Irishmen'. *Orkns* ch. 20, p. 49, perhaps extrapolating from this verse, states that Karl's ranks included supporters from Ireland.

10/6 *und brezkum skildi* 'beneath a British shield'. Perhaps the shield was a war-trophy captured in a raid on the *Bretar* or perhaps 'British' shields were prized as being particularly fine. On the meaning of *brezkr*, see Commentary to *Þdr* 14/3.

10/7 *Hlavðvis frendi* 'Hlǫðvir's kinsman'. Þorfinnr. Hlǫðvir Þorfinnsson was paternal grandfather of Þorfinnr. His career, to judge from *Orkns* ch. 11, p. 24, was unmemorable.

10/8 *oc tok brenna* 'and began burning'.

(a) The clause follows *hendi Hlǫðvis frændi hermenn*, so that *hermenn* may be the understood object of *brenna*, hence 'Þorfinnr captured [the surviving] warriors and burned [the slain]', although burning seems usually to be reserved for evil-doers, heathens and insurrectionists (cf. the reference to the burning of the Wendish dead in *Mdr* 8, also Fidjestøl 1982, 206). *Brenna* could alternatively refer to the burning of dwellings, and hence anticipate *Þdr* 11, though according to *Orkns* the burning did not immediately follow the battle (see Context to *Þdr* 11).

(b) V. l. *enn tokst senna* could mean 'yet again battle began' (cf. *tókst morð af því* in Sigv 8), for *senna* 'bickering' occurs as base word in 'battle' kennings such as *sverða senna* (Korm *Lv* 25 and *Ht* 6), and there is a possible parallel to *senna* alone meaning 'battle' in Þorm 1, 14 (so *Skjald* B; Kock, *NN* §698, disagrees). But since the fighting has already been fully described in *Þdr* 9 and 10 and the taking of prisoners mentioned, a statement that battle began would be inappropriate.

Verse Eleven

Sources

Orkns ch. 20, p. 51: 325III(1r), 332(31), 702(75), Fl(522), (*LR* p. 19, 48m:346v).

Context

Þorfinnr pursues the fleeing Scots and subdues the populace as far south as Fife. He then releases part of his troops, upon which the Scots plan to rise against him. Þorfinnr, furious, marches against them but they flee before battle is joined. The jarl resolves to burn all the district, requiting the Scots for their enmity and treachery, and his men carry this out ruthlessly. Men are slain, while the women and old folk escape to the woods, and others are captured; *Svá segir Arnórr jarlaskáld:*

Diplomatic and edited text

Tyndvz ból þa er brendo	Týndusk ból, þá's brendu
braðskat þ*at* dægr haski	— bráskat þat dœgr háski;
stavck i ræyr en ròknv	stǫkk í reyr en roknu
ravð elldr skota velldi	rauðr eldr — Skota veldi.
morðken*n*ir gallt mavn*nom*	Morðkennir galt mǫnnum
mæin a svmri eino	mein; á sumri einu
fengo þeir við þeingil	fengu þeir við þengil
þrim sin*n*vm lvt mina.	þrimr sinnum hlut minna.

Prose order and translation

Ból týndusk, þá's brendu Skota veldi. Rauðr eldr stǫkk í en roknu reyr. Þat dœgr bráskat háski. Morðkennir galt monnum mein. Á einu sumri fengu þeir þrimr sinnum minna hlut við þengil.
Dwellings perished, as they put to flame the Scots' realm. Red fire leapt in the smoking thatch. That day peril never ceased. The battle-master paid men back their malice. In a single summer they got three times over the poorer deal from the prince.

Apparatus

(1) þa] þar 702(?), *LR* **brendo]** brendi 332, 702, Fl, *LR* **Line (2)]** Brädur elldur Skotta velldi *LR* **braðskat]** braskat 332, 702, 48m, brazst atḥ Fl **(3) ræyr]** reyk 702 **en rǫknv]** en ŕokno 332, Fl, en*n* rǫkna 702 **(4) ravð]** ravðr 332, 702, Fl **(7) við]** u*m* Fl (48m as 325) **(8) þrim]** þremr Fl **mina]** min*n*a 332, 702, Fl.

Commentary

11/1 *brendo* 'they put to flame'.

(a) The pl. reading of the main MS is supported by the prose Context (above), in which it is the jarl's men who carry out the burning of the district.

(b) On internal evidence alone, v. l. *brendi* 'he [Þorfinnr] put to flame' would be equally acceptable.

11/2 *braskat* (v. l.) ... *haski* 'peril never ceased that day'.

(a) *Braðskat* does not belong to any known verb.

(b) V. l. *bráskat* ... *háski*, on the other hand, makes good sense, and provides the full rhyme which is required in an even line. Arnórr also uses *háski* in rhyme in *Hdr* 10/4 *sásk aldrigi háska*; but in *Þdr* 13/2 *haska* rhymes on *vas'k*, so that the suggestion of Konráð Gíslason must be considered, that vowel shortening produced a variant form *haski*. There is to my knowledge no other trace of this, but there is evidence, collected by him, of shortening before consonant groups in other words (1866, 242–305; the material relevant to the rhyme *vask : haski* is summarised by the same author, 1877, 49–50).

Line 2 in *LR* appears to be a product of confusion with line 4.

11/4 *ravðr* (v. l.) *elldr* 'red fire'. The ungrammatical *rauð* of the main MS appears to be a scribal slip.

11/5 *morðkennir* 'battle-master'. Þorfinnr (cf. adj. *morðkendr* 'battle-skilled' in *Þdr* 4). The often-used *kennir* means 'trier, tester, knower, experiencer' or perhaps, as Björn M. Ólsen suggested, 'he who makes another feel something' (1909, 292).

11/8 *þrim sinnvm* 'three times over', 'on three occasions'. The first two defeats of the Scots were at Dýrnes and Torfnes. The third presumably consisted in Þorfinnr's punitive attack on the Scots after the battle of Torfnes (see Context above).

The normalised *þrimr* is the form of the dat. of the numeral recorded in the oldest Icelandic MSS and appropriate to Arnórr's time. The later *þrim* developed by analogy with other dats. in *-m*,[34] and v. l. *þremr* is due to lowering of original *i* before a nasal (Seip 1955, 153).

Verse Twelve

Sources

SnE p. 180: R(77), T(42v–43r), 748II(8v), 757(7r).

Context

Þdr 12 appears among verses which illustrate terms proper to emperor, king and jarl alike. It is prefaced, *HaRi e(ða) heRa, sem q(vað) ArnoR:*

Diplomatic and edited text

HaRi feck ihv*er*ri	Harri fekk í hverri
hialtl*an*dz þrvmv branda	Hjaltlands þrumu branda
greppr vill g*ra*ms dyRð yppa	— greppr vill grams dýrð yppa —
gagn sa er nęstr er b*ra*gna.	gagn, sá's hæstr vas bragna.

[34] Noreen 1923, §277 anm. 5. *Þrim* appears twice in Larsson 1891, s. v. *þrír*, but the remaining eleven entries are of *þrimr*.

Prose order and translation

Harri Hjaltlands, sá's vas hæstr bragna, fekk gagn í hverri branda þrumu. Greppr vill yppa dýrð grams.
The lord of Shetland, he who was highest of heroes, won victory in every thunderclap of swords [battle]. The skald would extol the worth of the ruler.

Apparatus

(1) HaRi feck] H... ek 757 **(2) hialt–]** híat– 757 **branda]** b*ra*... 757 **Line (3)]** illeg. 757 **(4) nęstr]** hæstr 748II, illeg. 757 **er (2nd)]** var 757(?) **b*ra*gna]** ...gna 757.

Commentary

12/4 *hæstr* (v. l.) 'highest, loftiest'. *Hæstr* gives excellent sense in *sá's hæstr vas bragna* 'he who was highest of heroes' (literally or figuratively); *næstr* 'nearest, next' is never applied without further qualification to human subjects.

12/4 *var* (v. l.) 'was'. The present tense reading *er* in 'he who is highest of heroes' is ill matched with the past *fekk* in line 1, and inappropriate to a memorial poem.

Verse Thirteen

Sources

Orkns ch. 22, p. 58: 702(78), Fl(524), (*LR* p. 90).

Context

A great and bloody battle is fought at Vatnsfjǫrðr. It begins early in the day and ends in victory for the jarls; *Þess getr Arnnorr jarllaskalld* (version of Fl):[35]

[35] The relevant part of the text in 332 ends with the words, *orrustu þessar getr* just before *Þdr* 13 would have appeared.

Diplomatic and edited text

Veit eg þar *er* vatsfiordr heiter
varsk i miklu*m* häska
mins v*it* man*n*kyns reyní
m*er*kin dRottins verka
þiod bar skiott af skeid*um*
skialldb*or*g fria mórgin
g*er*la sá ek at g*ri*ndi
g*ra*r vlfr af ná sárum.

Veit'k, þar's Vatnsfjǫrðr heitir,
— vas'k í miklum haska —
míns — við mannkyns reyni —
merki dróttins verka.
Þjóð bar skjótt af skeiðum
skjaldborg fría morgin;
gǫrla sá'k, at gríndi
grár ulfr of ná sǫrum.

Prose order and translation

Veit'k merki verka dróttins míns, þar's heitir Vatnsfjǫrðr. Vas'k í miklum haska við mannkyns reyni. Þjóð bar skjótt skjaldborg af skeiðum fría morgin. Sá'k gǫrla, at grár ulfr gríndi *of* sǫrum ná.
I know there are tokens of the exploits of my lord, where it is called Vatnsfjǫrðr. I was in great peril with the trier of men. The crew carried swiftly the shield-wall from the ships on Friday morning. I saw clearly, how the grey wolf stretched his jaws over the gashed corpse.

Apparatus

(2) varsk] uásk Fl **(4) m*er*kin]** m*er*ki Fl **(6) fria mórgin]** fíra morgu*m* Fl **(7) sá]** fra Fl (*LR* as 702) **g*ri*ndi]** gínde Fl (*LR* as 702) **(8) af ná sárum]** um gna sara*n*n Fl, ad nä saarum *LR*.

Commentary

13/1 *vatsfiordr*. The most convincing location for Vatnsfjǫrðr, because of the equivalence of the two names, is Loch Vatten, an arm of the sea branching off Loch Bracadale on the west coast of Skye (so, e. g., Anderson 1873, 27, n. 2). The land thereabouts is relatively fertile, and would have made a profitable target for plundering and cattle-raiding. An alternative is Waterford in Ireland (Crawford 1987, pp. 74 and 233, n. 74).

13/2 *varsk ... häska* 'I was; peril'. The *aðalhending vask/vas'k : haska* is noted in the Commentary to *Þdr* 11/2.

13/3 *mannkyns reyní* 'trier of men', hence 'ruler'. The kenning probably denotes Þorfinnr and means specifically 'he who tries men's strength [in battle]', as does *hersa máttar reynir*, Mark 1, 30. However, it is conceivable that Arnórr also intended the kenning (and perhaps *míns dróttins* in lines 3 and 4) to refer to God, thus implying that God was supporting himself and Þorfinnr. All other recorded kennings meaning 'trier of men' (*hǫlða reynir*, Mark 1, 2 among them) refer to God.

13/7 *grindi* 'stretched his jaws'.

(a) The verb *grína* is barely attested in ON. It occurs in the narrative about Ragnarr loðbrók in the *Oddverja Annáll* s. a. 815 (in the late 16th-century AM 417 4o, *Icelandic Annals* p. 455). Ragnarr is credited with the words (in normalised spelling):

grína mundi grísir	the young pigs would show their teeth
ef galta bǫl vissu	if they knew of the boar's injuries.

In the versions of the couplet which appear in *Ragnars saga*, however, the verb is not *grína* but the more familiar *gnyðja* 'grunt' (p. 159, cf. pp. 158 and 161; also *Skjald* II A 238).

Magnús Ólafsson, in *LR*, translates *Þdr* 13/7 *gǫrla sá'k at gríndi* with *vidi ... ridere*; and Blöndal records *grína* with the senses 'grin', 'squeal / grunt' and 'stare'. De Vries regards *grína* as a strong verb, and the OHG cognate *grīnan* supports this, but *gríndi* in *Þdr* 13 is also supported by the fact that the verb is weak in Mod. Icel.

(b) V. l. *gínde* is past sing. of the verb *gina/gína* 'gape, yawn', the weak counterpart to strong *gína*. The verb is predicated in several other contexts to a word meaning 'wolf' and accompanied, as in *Þdr* 13, by words meaning 'over the corpse, carrion', e. g. E Sk 6, 29 *vargar... of hræ ginðu*. V. l. *gíndi* is thus wholly acceptable, but I have retained *gríndi* in my text since it is the reading of the main MS and the *lectio difficilior*.

The line lacks the expected *skothending*, but no obvious emendation suggests itself.

13/8 *um* (v. l., normalised *of*) *ná sárum* 'over the gashed corpse'. The reading *af* in 702 could be explained as a corruption either of an original *at*, preserved in *LR* in the spelling *ad*, or of an original *of*, preserved in MS Fl in its later form *um*. The phrase *of ná sǫrum* is supported by *of hræ (ginðu)* in E Sk 6, 29, quoted above.

Verse Fourteen

Source

Orkns ch. 22, p. 59: Fl(524).

Context

After the battle of Vatnsfjǫrðr eight years pass during which Þorfinnr uncomplainingly allows Rǫgnvaldr Brúsason to hold two thirds of the isles. Their summers are spent harrying, sometimes together and sometimes independently, *Sem Arnórr segir:*

Diplomatic and edited text

Ymizst ua*nn* sa e*r* un*ne*	Ýmisst vann *sá* unn*ar*
isk fell drott þa e*r* sot*t*i	— írsk fell drótt — þá's sótti,
balldrs edr bretzskar alld*ir*	Bald*r*, eða brezkar aldir
bra elldr skota uelldi.	(bra*nn* eldr) Skota veldi.

Prose order and translation

Sá unn*ar* Bald*r* vann ýmisst, þá's sótti brezkar aldir eða Skota veldi. Írsk drótt fell. Eldr bra*nn*.
That Baldr of the sword [warrior, Þorfinnr] won diverse [triumphs], as he attacked the British people and the realm of the Scots. The Irish troop fell. Fire blazed.

Commentary

The helming. The text as it stands in Flat is clearly corrupt. The chief problems are that the verbs *unni* and *brá* both require objects but do not both have them, and that *Baldrs* in isolation makes no sense. Since the problems are so closely interrelated I present two analyses complete — both possible but not entirely satisfactory; my own preference is for (a).[36]

[36] The helming is also cited by the writer of 21. 6. 7. (Advocates' Library, Edinburgh), a mid 18th-century copy of *Laufás-Edda*, to illustrate the kenning *þjóðeldr* 'gold'. Its readings here, as elsewhere, do not inspire great confidence, but are worth quoting since (as pointed out in *SnE* (Faulkes 1979) p. 131) they offer alternatives to the sole medieval text:

(a) *Skota veldi* 'the realm of the Scots' could grammatically be construed as object to any one of the verbs *unni* 'loved', *sótti* 'attacked' or *brá* 'changed, moved quickly' but *þá's sótti ... Skota veldi* clearly gives the best meaning. A statement that Þorfinnr 'loved (*unni*) Scotland' would be either untrue or crudely ironic, and a statement that 'fire changed' (*eldr brá*) Scotland would make little sense, unless *brá* were assumed to have the extended meaning 'changed the appearance of, ravaged'.[37] *Brá eldr* is also metrically suspect, since a syllable ending in a long vowel here stands before a word which begins with a vowel, so that on two counts emendation to the intransitive *brann eldr* 'fire blazed' is expedient. An original *brann* could have been 'corrected' to *brá* by someone who mistakenly read the line *brann eldr Skota veldi* as a syntactic unit and found the intransitive *brann* incompatible with the object *Skota veldi*.

The problems of the remaining subject-less verb *unni* and the isolated *Baldrs* are perhaps best solved by Finnur Jónsson's emendation of MS *sa er unne ... balldrs* to *sá unnar ... Baldr* (*Skjald* B and 1934, 45). This would be an acceptable kenning for 'warrior'. *Unnr* m. 'sword' is a rare word, which de Vries (s. v.) connects with *vinna* 'do, perform' or 'win'. It is attested in a verse by Helgi trausti Óláfsson (10th century), in the phrase *unnar ítrtungur* 'bright tongues of the sword', i. e. 'sword-blades', and possibly in *Harð* 18 (14th century). *Baldr* figures as the base word of several kennings for 'warrior / man' with determinant 'sword / spear', and Arnórr's poetry contains examples of 'warrior' kennings based on other gods' names (Yggr and Njǫrðr).

The co-ordinated noun phrase *eða brezkar aldir* 'and the British people' I construe as object, with *Skota veldi*, of *sótti* (so Finnur Jónsson, 1934, 45). That the conjunction *eða* (MS *edr*) precedes *brezkar aldir*, the first of the co-ordinated phrases, is not a difficulty: cf. the placing of *ok Danmǫrk allri* in *Mdr* 7. *Brezkar aldir* could alternatively be subject, with *írsk drótt*, of *fell* (so *Skjald* B; the meaning of *brezkr* is discussed below).

Ymist van*n* ott ä sumrum,
ÿrsk fiell drött alsötte, [or al sötte]
Baldr eda brattkar alldre,
Biodellz skeÿta vellde.

[37] So Finnur Jónsson in *LP* s. v. *bregða*, and Kock *NN* §831, who translates 'laid waste' (*ödde*). Kock assumes *sótti* to be intransitive.

(b) Under the second analysis the MS text is preserved but *unni* is assumed (I think unjustifiably) to have the implied object 'battle', so that *sá's unni ... þá's sótti* means 'the one who bestowed / loved [battle] when he attacked' (so Finnbogi Guðmundsson, *Orkns* 1965, 59n.). *Brá* in *brá eldr Skota veldi* is taken in the sense 'destroyed'. Two interpretations of MS *balldrs* are compatible with this analysis. (i) Finnbogi Guðmundsson construes it with *eða brezkar aldir* and offers the ingenious (though unsubstantiated) conjecture that *Baldrs aldir* refers to the Norse-Gaelic settlers of western Scotland — 'Baldr's' because Baldr was the most Christ-like figure in Norse paganism and would thus symbolise the mixed religion of these people. (ii) *Baldrs eldr* could be an (otherwise unparalleled) variant on the kenning formula 'Óðinn's flame' meaning 'sword'. Hence *Baldrs ... eldr brá Skota veldi* could be construed as a wittily concise reference to ravaging with fire (*eldr*) and the sword (*Baldrs eldr*).

14/2 ***isk*** (normalised *írsk*) 'Irish'. The MS spelling may reflect the scribe's pronunciation of the word: cf. MS spellings such as *þoskr* for *þorskr* 'cod' or *fystr* for *fyrstr* (Noreen 1923, §272, 3).

14/3 ***bretzskar*** 'British'. ON *brezkr*, *Bretar* and *Bretland* occur with reference to Celtic peoples, especially those of Wales and Strathclyde. It is difficult to arbitrate between these two main possibilities in this verse. The flanking references to *Skota veldi* and *írsk drótt* might favour Strathclyde, but on the other hand cf., e. g., *Msk* pp. 318 and 321, where *Bretland* clearly refers to Wales, since Anglesey lies off it and is said to constitute one third of it. An alternative possibility is that *brezkr* is used loosely to mean 'English' here, since we know from *Þdr* 16–18 that Þorfinnr attacked the English; another possible skaldic instance of this is v. 5 of *Liðsmannaflokkr* where, in a description of fighting by the Thames, it is said that the sword rings out *á brezkum brynjum*.[38]

[38] See Poole 1987, 292–98, for a convenient review of the usage of *Bretar / brezkr* in ON sources. Poole inclines to think that Arnórr is referring to the 'Britons' of Strathclyde here; he puts a good case for taking the *Liðsmannaflokkr* reference as being to the Welsh. (I am indebted to Dr Judith Jesch for reminding me of this reference.)

Verse Fifteen

Sources

SnE p. 161: R_1(71), T_1(39v), W(81)
SnE p. 174: R_2(75), T_2(41v), U(69), 748(19r), 748II(7r).

Context

(i) Discussing poetic terms for rulers, Snorri mentions first the *keisari*, then kings who rule *þjóðlǫnd*, then 'those men who are called jarls (*iarlar*) or tributary kings (*skattkonvngar*), and they are designated by the same terms as a king, except that those who are tributary kings cannot be called kings of nations (*þioðkonvngar*) — *ok sva q(vað) ArnoR i(arla)skald of ÞorfiN iarl:*
(ii) *Þdr* 15 appears again as the first of many skaldic citations which illustrate *heiti* for 'sea', here *ægir*. It is introduced, *Sem Arnor q(vað) ok fyR var ritat:*

Diplomatic and edited text

Nemi drott hve sia sotti	Nemi drótt, hvé sæ sótti
snarly*n*dr k*onvng*r i*ar*la	snarlyndr konungr jarla;
e*igi* þravt v*ið* ǽgi	eigi þraut við ægi
of vægia*n* *gra*m bægia.	ofvægjan gram bægja.

Prose order and translation

Drótt nemi, hvé snarlyndr konungr jarla sótti sæ. Eigi þraut ofvægjan gram bægja við ægi.
Let liegemen mark how the quick-mettled king among jarls made out to sea. The invincible lord never ceased to strive against the ocean.

Apparatus

(1) hve sia] vina U, sæ R_2 **Lines (1) to (4) sotti ... bægia]** s. s. k. j. 748II **sotti]** sveiti R_2 **Lines (3) to (4)]** om. U **(4) of vægia*n*]** ovægiN R_2, T_2, 748 ***gra*m]** *fra*m R_2 **bægia]** beia T_1, T_2.

Commentary

15/2 ***konvngr iarla*** 'king among jarls'.

(a) The words *konungr jarla*, consecutive within the metrical line, are best construed as a single figurative phrase meaning 'king among jarls', cf. *konungr sprunda* 'king among women', Oddi 2 (mid 12th century), and *konungr vífa*, referring to Mary in v. 5 of the 14th-century *Maríudrápa*.

(b) An alternative analysis is to take *drótt ... jarla* 'jarl's retinue' as a unit, leaving *konungr* as a designation for Þorfinnr. The words which precede the quotation in *SnE*, to the effect that jarls can be 'designated by the same terms as a king', might suggest that Snorri construed the verse thus. But, as Konráð Gíslason suggested (1877, 59), Snorri probably cited the verse because it contains the word *gramr*, which is indeed applicable to jarls as well as kings, not because of the word *konungr*. The *heiti* exemplified by the other skaldic citations in this section of *SnE* are of a similar kind to *gramr*, e. g. *fylkir* and *mildingr*. Moreover, there is little or no evidence that skalds used the word *konungr* of men who were not kings, for *kongar* in *Gd* 52 (14th century) may well be used, with deliberate exaggeration, in its full sense of 'kings'.[39]

15/3 ***ǽgi*** 'ocean'. Possibly a reference to the sea-god as well as the sea, against whom Þorfinnr *bægir* 'contends, strives'.

15/4 ***of vægian*** 'invincible', lit. 'out-weighing, over-powerful'. V. l. *óvæginn* 'unyielding' would also give excellent sense.

Verse Sixteen

Sources

Orkns ch. 24, p. 61: 702(75), Fl(528)
SnE p. 164 (lines 5–8 only): R(72), T(40v), U(70), W(82).

[39] *Kongar* is glossed *fyrstelige personer (kardinalerne?)* in *LP*.

Context

Orkns: Þorfinnr launches an assault on England, supported by Rǫgnvaldr Brúsason and troops from Orkney, Caithness and elsewhere in Scotland, Ireland and the Hebrides. Hǫrða-Knútr is away in Denmark, and when the defending English chieftains confront the jarls they suffer defeat in a grim battle. The jarls then plunder, kill and burn widely.
SnE: The second helming occurs in the same context as *Rdr* 2 and *Þdr* 4, and is quoted to illustrate the kenning *Rǫgnvalds kind*. *Rdr* 2 is quoted with the words, *EN q(vað) sva ArnoR iRavgnvaldzdrapv*, and then *Þdr* 16 with, *Ok eN kvað hann of ÞorfiN iarl:*

Diplomatic and edited text

En*n* *var* su e*r* Engla min*n*ir	Enn vas sú's Engla minnir
egghrid ne mu*n* sidan	egghríð, né mun síðan
här vid helming meira	hǫ́r við helming meira
h*ri*ng mi komid hingad	hringdrífr kom*a* þingat.
bitu sv*e*rd en*n* þar þorde	Bitu sverð — en þar þurði —
þun*nger* f*yrir* Mani svn*n*an	þunngǫr — fyr Mǫn sunnan
Rǫ̂gnvallds kind vnd rand*ir*	Rǫgnvalds kind — und randir
Ramlig folk hins gamla.	ramlig folk — ens gamla.

Prose order and translation

Enn vas egghríð sú's Engla minnir, né mun síðan hǫ́r hringdrífr kom*a* þingat við helming meira. Þunngǫr sverð bitu ramlig folk und randir, en þar fyr sunnan Mǫn þurði kind Rǫgnvalds ens gamla.
Then came the blade-/edge-blizzard which the English remember, and never since then will a lofty ring-strewer [(generous) ruler] come there with a larger force. Slender-wrought swords bit the mighty troops beneath their targes, and there, south of Man, rushed forth the heir of Rǫgnvaldr the Old.

Apparatus

(1) En*n*] Eín Fl **(3) här]** hatt Fl **(4) mi]** d*ri*fr Fl **komid]** komit Fl **hingad]** þi*n*gat Fl **(5) þorde]** þurde Fl, U, þvrþ*ir* R, þurdo T, W **(6) f*yrir*]** yvir U **Mani]** maun others **(7) vnd]** en U **(8) -lig]** -ligt Fl, U.

Commentary

16/2 and 16/4 *ne mun sidan ... koma* (em.) 'and since then no [ring-strewer] will come'. MSS *komid/-it* is syntactically unsatisfactory and could well be due to a misreading. Emendation to *koma* was favoured by Kock (*NN* §832) and Finnbogi Guðmundsson, *Orkns* 1965, 61.

16/4 *hring drifr* (v. l.) 'ring-strewer'. The reading of the main MS, *hring mi*, makes no sense.

16/4 *þingat* (v. l.) 'there'.

(a) *Né mun síðan komit hingat* is interpreted as 'it will not henceforth be made known to us' (... *til vor fregnad*) in Magnús Ólafsson's gloss to the verse in 702, but I have found no evidence for the use of *koma* in the sense 'be made known, reported'.

(b) The v. l. *þingat* 'thither, there', i. e. 'to England' or 'south of Man', on the other hand, gives excellent sense.

Lines 16/5 to 16/8. The syntax of the helming is not obvious. Both *ramlig(t) folk* 'mighty troops/troop' and *(Rǫgnvalds) kind (ens gamla)* 'the heir (of Rǫgnvaldr the Old)' are grammatically ambiguous: each could be nom., subject of *þurðu/þurði* 'rushed', or acc., object of *bitu sverð* 'swords bit'.[40]

It appears that the scribes of MSS T and W, and probably of U and Fl, took 'mighty troop' as the subject of 'rushed', since the two MSS (T and W) which read pl. *þurðu* also have pl. *ramlig folk*, while the two (U and Fl) which read sing. *þurði* also have sing. *ramligt folk*. But the corollary, if this analysis were adopted (as it is in *Skjald* B), would be that the swords pierced Þorfinnr — an unlikely admission within a panegyric and unmatched in the remainder of *Þdr*.

16/5 *þurde* (v. l.) 'rushed'.

(a) *Þurði* and *þurðu*, from *þyrja* 'rush', are both good readings, but *þurði* must be selected if Þorfinnr (*Rǫgnvalds kind*) is the subject.

[40] Finnbogi Guðmundsson (*Orkns* 1965, 61n.) suggests that *kind* is dat., hence presumably *bitu sverð kind Rǫgnvalds* 'swords bit for Rǫgnvaldr's heir'; but it seems inconceivable that the skald, had he wished to state this, should have used phrasing of which the most obvious meaning was that his hero was wounded.

(b) *Þorde* 'dared' could make sense since an absolute use is recorded (normally in the idiom *þora fyrir e-m* in the lexicons, although the slips held by the Arnamagnæan Dictionary have several examples outside this idiom); but the MS evidence is against it.

16/6 *þunnger* 'slender-wrought'. The adj. is unique in recorded ON, but *þunngjör/-ger* is recorded for the modern language by Blöndal, as are *fínger(ður)* and *smáger(ður)*, and cf. ON *þunnsleginn* (Fritzner Supp).

16/6 *maun* (v. l.) 'Man'. The (dat. sing.) *Mani* has no parallel in ON, Mǫn being the usual form. It either represents a misreading or is influenced by the Celtic forms of the name (Manu and variants, Hogan 1910, 536).

16/7 and 16/8 *Rǫ́gnvallds kind ... hins gamla* 'the heir / descendant of Rǫgnvaldr the Old'. Rǫgnvaldr is called *inn ríki ok inn ráðsvinni* in *Orkns* ch. 3, p. 7, never *inn gamli*. Perhaps Arnórr or others dubbed him with this nickname in order to distinguish him from Rǫgnvaldr Brúsason. On this Rǫgnvaldr, see Commentary to *Þdr* 2/4.

Verse Seventeen

Sources

Orkns ch. 24, p. 61: 702(76), Fl(525), (*LR* p. 28).

Context

As for *Þdr* 16, since v. 17 follows it directly.

Diplomatic and edited text

Stóng bar jall at engla	Stǫng bar jarl at Engla
ættgru*n*d en*n* hravd stu*n*du	ættgrund, en rauð stundu
ve bad vísi knya	— vé bað vísi knýja —
vórdung ara tungu	verðung ara tungu.
hyʀ ox hallir þurru	Hyrr óx, hallir þurru,
h*eimdro*tt rak þar flotta	herdrótt rak þar flótta;
eim hratt en*n* laust lioma	eim hratt, en laust ljóma,
limdolgur nær himne.	limdolgr, náar himni.

Prose order and translation

Jarl bar stǫng at ættgrund Engla, en verðung rauð stundu tungu ara. Vísi bað knýja vé. Hyrr óx; hallir þurru; herdrótt rak þar flótta. Limdolgr hratt eim, en laust ljóma náar himni.
The jarl bore his standard onto the native soil of the English, and his liegemen reddened straightway the tongue of the eagle. The leader called for banners to advance. Flame grew; halls shrank; the war-band drove [men] to flight there. The foe of branches [fire] flung out smoke, and hurled light against the sky.

Apparatus

(1) at] a Fl **(2) hravd stu*n*du]** Raud stundu*m* Fl **(4) vǫ́rdung]** uerþung Fl **(5) hallir]** hale*r* Fl **(6) h*eim*-]** h*er*- Fl **þar]** om. Fl **(7) eim]** œímr Fl (*LR* as 702) **(8) -dolgur]** -dolgs Fl (*LR* as 702) **nær]** nær*r* Fl.

Commentary

The strophe. The motifs which make up this verse are examined in ch. IV, III B.

17/2 *stundu* 'straightway'.

(a) *Stundu* usually appears in the phrase *af stundu*, as in *Hdr* 10 *fundusk þeir af stundu* 'they engaged straightway', but *stundu*, although not otherwise recorded, could be a shortened variant of the phrase (so Finnbogi Guðmundsson, *Orkns* 1965, 62n.), since the skalds' handling of prepositional phrases is often freer than that of prose writers.[41] The rendering 'straightway' in *Þdr* 17 is supported by the word *þegar* in *Orkns*: *en þegar at jarlar kómu við England, tóku þeir at herja* (ch. 24, p. 61).

(b) V. l. *stundum* 'at times' does not give good sense.

17/6 *herdrott* (v. l.) 'war-band'. (a) The *herdrótt* which puts men to flight is presumably the same body of men as the *verðung* 'retinue' in line 4 — Þorfinnr's men. The word is also recorded in Sturl 5, 11 and is reminiscent of near-synonymous compounds such as *herfolk, herfloti* and *herlið*.

[41] Nygaard (1905, §118, b) has examples of bare datives which in prose would be accompanied by the preposition *á*.

(b) *Heimdrótt* is a *hap. leg.* In the context of *Þdr* 17 the 'native troop' would be the defending army, the English. But the evidence of *Þdr* 17–18 is that they were routed.

17/7 *eim hratt* 'flung out smoke'. This I take as predicate to *limdolgr* 'fire' (line 8). V. l. *eimr hratt* 'smoke belched forth' would also be grammatically acceptable, since the absolute use of *hrinda* is recorded, e. g. in *hratt stundum fyrir, en stundum dró frá* 'sometimes drifted in front [of the moon] and sometimes moved away' (*Grettis saga* ch. 35, p. 121, of cloud).

17/7 and 17/8 *laust lioma* | *limdolgur* 'the foe of branches [fire] hurled light'. I construe *limdolgr* as an active subject to *laust* as well as to *hratt*, although it would also be reasonable to take *en laust ljóma ... náar himni* 'and light was cast up against the sky' as a separate, impersonal construction.

On the resemblances between these lines and *Vǫluspá*, see ch. IV, III B.

17/8 *limdolgur nær himne* 'foe of branches; against the sky'. A disyllabic form of the preposition 'near' is required by the metre here and in other skaldic lines. The form **náar* was inferred from the Gmc. evidence by Sievers (1889, 133–34, followed by others, including Finnbogi Guðmundsson, *Orkns* 1965, 62).

Verse Eighteen

Source

Orkns ch. 24, p. 62: 702(76).

Context

The strophe follows *Þdr* 16 and 17 directly.

Diplomatic and edited text

Marg*ur* v*ar* millu*m* borga	Margr vas millum borga
milldingr þróng at hilldi	— mildingr þrǫng at hildi —
hornablastr þ*ar* e*r* hristiz	horna blǿstr, þar's hristisk
hugsterks jof*ur*s merki	hugsterks jǫfurs merḳi.

vátr brá e*r* vigliost þotti	Vætr brá, 's vígljóst þótti,
vargsteypis h*er* greypu*m*	vargsteypis her greypum,
skulfu jarn en*n* vlfar	— skulfu jǫrn, en ulfar —
vggs morgu*n* hræ tuggu.	uggs, morgin — hræ tuggu.

Prose order and translation

Margr horna blǫ́str vas millum borga, þar's merki hugsterks jǫfurs hristisk. Mildingr þrǫng at hildi. Vætr uggs brá greypum her vargsteypis, 's þótti vígljóst morgin. Jǫ́rn skulfu, en ulfar tuggu hræ. Many were the horn-blasts between the defences, where the banner of the stout-hearted hero waved. The bounteous one stormed into battle. Not a trace of fear seized the grim troop of the thief-feller, once it seemed light enough for battle in the morning. Iron blades quivered, and wolves chewed carrion.

Commentary

18/5 *vætr* (em.) 'not a trace, nothing'. The emendation, first proposed by Gudbrand Vigfusson (1887–94, I, 43, n. 12), is necessary since *vátr* 'wet' could make no sense in the helming.

18/8 *morgun* (normalised *morgin*) 'in the morning, by morning'.

(a) *Morgin* is here tentatively read as an adverbial acc. of time,[42] cf. *fría morgin* 'on Friday morning' in *Þdr* 13, and *margan morgin* '(on) many a morning', Sigv 5, 1. From the semantic point of view it is best construed with *'s vígljóst þótti* 'once it seemed light enough for battle', though the division of line 8 into parts of three clauses conflicts with Arnórr's usual practice; but it could belong with any or all of the four clauses in the helming.

(b) A compound *morginhræ* 'morning carrion' could alternatively be assumed, whimsically reminiscent of *morgunverðr* / *-matr* 'breakfast'. Þorbjǫrn þyna, in his sole extant *lausavísa* (c. 955), spoke of the carrion-greedy raven demanding its *morginbrǫ́ð*. Cf. also Arnórr's macabre application of the culinary *bráðla steikðan* to corpses in *Mdr* 8.

(c) Kock's suggestion that *uggs morginn* is a unitary phrase meaning 'morning of terror', a constrasting expression to

[42] So Finnbogi Guðmundsson in *Orkns* 1965, 62n.; he uses the alternative, probably more modern, spelling *morgun*.

feginsmorginn 'morning of joy', recorded in E Sk 1, 2, removes the difficulty of assuming a three-part line (*NN* §833). It also accords with the most natural metrical interpretation of the line, as an E type, ´ ` x ´ ´ x. The comparison is, however, hardly persuasive, for while *fegin(s)* is based on an adj. and very commonly figures in compound expressions, *uggs* is a noun and is not otherwise recorded in this rôle.

(d) Finnur Jónsson, in *Skjald* B, emends *morgun* to *-inn* and *vigliost* in line 5 to *-ljóss* in order to obtain *es morginn þótti vígljóss* 'when the morning seemed light enough for fighting'. But the problem of the partitioning of line 8, mentioned under alternative (a), arises again and the emendation is not strictly necessary.

Verse Nineteen

Sources

Orkns ch. 32, p. 83 and ch. 56[43]: Fl_1(529), Fl_2(538).

Context

(i) *Þdr* 19 and *Þdr* 22 are first quoted at the end of ch. 32, a summary chapter on the life and death of Þorfinnr. They are introduced, *Þessar vísur váru kveðnar um orrostu þeira Rǫgnvalds jarls Brúsasonar ok Þorfinns jarls.*

(ii) The two verses occur again, together with Arnórr's *Frag* 2 and v. 8 of Bjarni Hallbjarnarson Gullbrárskáld's *Kalfsflokkr*, at the end of ch. 56, which concerns Páll, son of Þorfinnr. The verses have no connection with the preceding prose, and there are no introductory words to explain their inclusion at this point.

Diplomatic and edited text

Oskepna*n* uard up*p*i
endr þa e*r* mórgu*m* kende
haligt Rog at hniga
hord þar er jallar bórduzst
næ*rr* reduzst astm*enn* or*ir*
elld h*ri*d en uard sidan
olld fek mæín hín millda
morg fir*ir* rauda biorgu*m*.

Óskepnan varð uppi
endr, þá's mǫrgum kendi
hǫ́ligt róg at hníga,
hǫrð, þar's jarlar bǫrðusk.
Nær réðusk ástmenn órir,
eldhríð es varð síðan
— ǫld fekk mein en milda
mǫrg — fyr Rauðabjǫrgum.

[43] The verse is not printed at its second appearance in *Orkns* (p. 122).

Prose order and translation

Endr varð hǫrð óskepnan uppi, þá's hǫ́ligt róg kendi mǫrgum at hníga þar's jarlar bǫrðusk. Ástmenn órir réðusk nær, es eldhríð varð síðan fyr Rauðabjǫrgum. Ǫld en milda fekk mǫrg mein.
At that time a harsh, monstrous thing came to pass, as mighty strife taught many a man to fall where the jarls fought. My dear friends almost destroyed each other, as the sword-blizzard came about then off Rauðabjǫrg. The gracious troop took many a gash.

Apparatus

(3) Rog] rȯg Fl_2 **(5) nær*r*]** nær Fl_2 **(6) en]** er Fl_2 **(7) olld]** aull Fl_2.

Commentary

19/5 *reduzst* 'destroyed each other'.

(a) *Ráða* occurs with the meaning 'betray' or 'seal another's fate', often specifically by killing or causing death, as in G Súrs 21, *segja ... Þórketil ráðinn* 'report that Þórketill has been killed', and *ráða e-n* can mean 'to plot someone's death' (Fritzner s. v., sense (7)). The juxtaposition of *ráða* in this sense with *nær* 'almost' is matched in Þjóð A 1, 19, where it is said of Sveinn Ulfsson as Magnús threatens battle against him:

Nefa Knúts vas þá nýtum nær sem ráðinn væri.	Then it was for the excellent nephew of Knútr almost as though he were destroyed.

Therefore it seems likely, though far from certain, that *Nær réðusk ástmenn órir* in *Þdr* 19 means 'My dear friends almost destroyed one another'.

(b) The alternative translation 'attacked' is suggested by the context. *Ráðask* is not, to my knowledge, found elsewhere meaning 'attack one another', but such idioms as *ráða(sk) á* and *ráða til e-s* have this sense. Further, since *ráðask* often implies motion, as in *ráðask þangat / í burt*, *ráðask nær* in *Þdr* 19 could well mean 'move close(r) to each other', hence by litotes 'attack each other'.

(c) If the reading *en* in l. 6 were adopted, lines 5 and 6 could represent chronologically distinct stages in the battle: 'My dear friends approached each other [off Rauðabjǫrg], and then battle came about'.

19/5 *astmenn orir* 'my dear friends', lit. 'our / my beloved men'. Arnórr's patrons Þorfinnr and Rǫgnvaldr.

19/6 *elld hrid* 'sword-blizzard [battle]'. *Eldr*, like *logi*, usually means 'fire', but is also listed among the *heiti* for 'sword' in *Þul* IV l 8; cf. *elda runnr* 'tree of swords [warrior]' in *Ód* 11 (12th century). It would be a strange coincidence if, as Finnur Jónsson assumes in *Skjald* B, original *oddr* 'point' had been corrupted to *eldr* both in *Ód* 11 and in *Þdr* 19.[44] Cf. also, perhaps, the difficult Þ hreð 7 (14th century), where the words *elds þruma* 'thunder of the ? sword' appear to form a kenning for 'battle'.

19/6 *er* (v. l., normalised *es*) 'as'.

(a) The reading *eldhríð es varð síðan* 'as the sword-blizzard came about then' is satisfactory.

(b) The position of *en* 'and' in the middle of the clause *eldhríð ... síðan* renders it suspect, for in all other contexts where Arnórr uses *en*, it is the first word in the clause.

19/7 *olld* 'troop, men'. The 'gracious / peaceable troop' (*ǫld en milda*) who 'took many a gash' could be Rǫgnvaldr's own men, or the moderate men of both sides who had no wish for strife.

19/8 *morg* 'many'. Formally nom. sing. fem. or nom. / acc. pl. neut., *mǫrg* could qualify either (a) *ǫld en milda*, hence 'many gracious men' (so *Skjald* B and *Orkns* 1965, 83); or (b) *mein*, hence 'many gashes'. There is no objective criterion that will determine the choice here. I have taken *mǫrg mein* together.

19/8 *rauda biorgum*, lit. 'red (iron) ore rocks'. Probably Roberry (see Map 2). This is compatible with the Rauðabjǫrg of the verse and the saga both in its geographical situation and in its phonetic form, especially if one assumes, as A. B. Taylor does, that Roberry derives from Rauðabergi, locative sing. of Rauðaberg, a by-form of Rauðabjǫrg (1931, 43–44; Taylor discusses the alternative locations).

[44] Emendation to *odd-* in *Þdr* 19 was originally proposed by Gudbrand Vigfusson, 1887–94, I 59, n. 4.

Verse Twenty

Sources

Orkns ch. 26, pp. 68–69: Fl(526), 702(79).

Context

Þorfinnr, hard pressed in the battle off Rauðabjǫrg, retires for a short time and then rejoins the fighting, now with the support of Kalfr Árnason and his six crews. He brings up his ship against Rǫgnvaldr's in a fierce struggle.

Diplomatic and edited text

Huorn*n* tueg*g*ia sa ek hog*g*ua
h*ir*d a petlandz f*ir*de
uor þ*ri*fuzst mei*n* ath meiri
mín aud giafua sína
siar*r* bler*r* en dræif dreyre
dóckr a sau*m*fór klocka
skaut a skialldri*m* suœíta
skockr uar blode stockín*n*.

Hvárntveggja sá'k hǫggva
hirð á Péttlandsfirði
— ór þrifusk mein at meiri —
mínn auðgjafa sína.
Sær blezk, en dreif dreyri
døkkr á saumfǫr kløkkva;
skaut á skjaldrim sveita;
skokkr vas blóði stokkinn.

Prose order and translation

Sá'k hvárntveggja mínn auðgjafa hǫggva sína hirð á Péttlandsfirði. Ór mein þrifusk at meiri. Sær blezk, en døkkr dreyri dreif á kløkkva saumfǫr. Sveita skaut á skjaldrim. Skokkr vas stokkinn blóði.
I watched both my wealth-givers hack down their own retainers in the Pentland Firth. My pain grew the more. The sea churned, and dark blood dashed on the pliant nail-row. Gore spurted on the shield-rail. Decking was spattered with blood.

Apparatus

(1) Huorn*n* tueggia] Huortueggi 702 **ek]** om. 702 **hoggua]** hógna (or hógua) 702 **(2) pet-]** fet- 702 **(3) uor]** mi*er* 702 **(4) giafua]** -giafi 702 **(5) bler*r*]** blezt 702 **(6) sau*m*fór]** rvmspór 702 **klocka]** klocku (or -ri) 702 **(7) skialldri*m* suœíta]** skiolldin hvíta 702 **(8) skockr]** skokk 702 **stockín*n*]** stokkin 702.

Commentary

The strophe. Uncharacteristically, 702 contains many nonsensical readings while Fl has a superior text. Fl is therefore adopted as the main MS.

20/1, 20/2 and 20/4 *Huornn tueggia sa ek hoggua | hird ... mín aud giafua sína* 'Both my wealth-givers I watched hack down their own retainers'.

(a) The readings of 702 are syntactically coherent and give good sense in the context: 'each of my wealth-givers watched his retainers being hacked down'.

(b) The version in Fl, however, in which the skald figures as witness to the action, is especially convincing (and is adopted in *Skjald* B), for Arnórr speaks of his own feelings in line 3 and is known to have been present at the battle.

20/2 *petlandz firde*. This is the first record of the name Péttlandsfjǫrðr in ON. The Pentland Firth is named after the Picts, the early inhabitants of the mainland on its south side.

20/5 *blezt* (v. l.) 'churned'. MS *blerr* is not a known verbal form; but v. l. *blezt* would be 3rd sing. past of *blandask* 'mix' and would give good sense. The usual construction is *blandask e-u* or *blandask við e-t*, so that in the present context one must assume either that *blóði* 'with blood' is implied, or that *blezk* simply means 'blended with itself, churned'.

20/6 *a saumfǫ̊r klocka* 'on the pliant nail-row'.

(a) *Saumfǫr*, lit. 'stitch-row', the row of nails along each strake, is recorded in ON prose although not elsewhere in poetry, and it occurs in Mod. Icel.[45] It is *kløkkr* 'pliant' in the sense that it gives with the motion of the ship in heavy seas; cf. Hfr 3, 14 *blóð kom á þrǫm þíðan* 'blood hit the pliant [lit. thawed] gunwale', and *Sverris saga* ch. 81, p. 87, where it is said that the ship Mariusúð *varð ...*

[45] On the word *saumfǫr*, particularly in relation to the ship-name Naglfar (in *Vsp* 50), see Lie 1954, 158–59. I see no justification for Lie's assumption (p. 159 and n. 7) that *saumfǫr* in *Þdr* 20 is a *pars-pro-toto* expression for 'ship'.

kløkk mjǫk in heavy seas. *Kløkkr* also has associations with weeping, and hence intensifies the already fateful atmosphere of the verse.

(b) The meaning of v. l. *rvmspǫr* is obscure. *Rúm* n. is a compartment of a ship, the space given to each pair of oars, but there is no known word *spǫr* which would be compatible with this.

20/7 ***skialldrim*** 'shield-rail'. The *skjaldrim* was either the topmost strake of a vessel or a specially fitted ledge on the outside of the gunwale on which the shields were hung for decoration.

20/8 ***skockr*** 'decking'. As a nautical term, *skokkr* is confined to skaldic poetry, and in none of the six contexts in which it occurs is its precise reference clear. But, partly on the basis of etymology and partly by inference from the use of *skokk* in Swedish dialect, it has been established that *skokkr* is virtually synonymous with *þiljur*, designating the loose decking planks on the bottom of the ship (see Lindquist 1928 and Ljunggren 1939, 26–28).

Verse Twenty One

Sources

Ólsh (Hkr) ch. 103, p. 174: K(330v).
Ólsh (Sep) p. 255: 2(32r), 4(24r), 73(157–58), 75a(23v), 325V(33v), 325VI(19v), 325VII(17r), Fl_1(405), Bb(160v), Th(119r)
Orkns ch. 32, p. 81: Fl_2(529).

Context

The verse is preceded by a comment on Þorfinnr's pre-eminence, which ends, *Hann eignaðisk Hjaltland ok Orkneyjar, Suðreyjar, hann hafði ok mikit ríki á Skotlandi ok Írlandi. Á þat kvað Arnórr jarlaskáld* (*Hkr* version; *Orkns* reads, *Hann eignaðisk níu jarldóma á Skotlandi ok allar Suðreyjar ok mikit ríki á Írlandi. Svá segir Arnórr jarlaskáld*):

Diplomatic and edited text

Hringstriþi varð hlyða
h*er*r f*ra* þ*ur*sa sc*er*iom
rét*t* segi ec þioð hv*e*R þotti
Þ*or*fiNz til dyfliNar.

Hringstríði varð hlýða
herr frá Þursaskerjum
— rétt segi'k þjóð, hvé þótti
Þorfinnr — til Dyflinnar.

Prose order and translation

Herr varð hlýða hringstríði frá Þursaskerjum til Dyflinnar. Segi'k þjóð rétt, hvé Þorfinnr þótti.
Folk were forced to heed the ring-harmer [(generous) ruler] from Þursasker to Dublin. I tell men truly how Þorfinnr was regarded.

Apparatus

(1) Hringstriþi] Hrafnsfœde Fl_2 **-striþi]** -stríðr 73, Th **varð]** v*ar* 2, 75a, 325V **hlyða]** hlyðin*n* 2, 73, 75a, 325V **(2) fra]** fy*rir* 2, 75a **þ*ur*sa]** þyssa 325VII, þíassa Th **(3) rét*t*]** rettr 4 **segi ec]** segi 2, 325V, segir þ*er* 73, segit þer 75a **þioð]** om. 75a **hv*e*R]** hue 73, 75a, 325V, VI, VII, Fl_1, Fl_2 **þotti]** þótti þótti 75a **(4) Þ*or*fiNz]** þorfinr 325V, Bb (or -z), Fl_1 Th, þorf⸗ 325VI, þf Fl_2.

Commentary

21/2 *þursa sceriom*, lit. 'Giants' skerries'. Dublin (*til Dyflinnar*) presumably marks the south-western extremity of Þorfinnr's sphere of influence, so that one would expect Þursasker to be its north-eastern limit, just as it is the eastern boundary of Scandinavian Scotland in *Hákonar saga Hákonarsonar*, ch. 265, p. 149 (MS *þussa-sker*). Finnbogi Guðmundsson's identification of Þursasker with The Skerries, a group of islets in the extreme east of the Shetlands, is therefore plausible.[46]

21/3 and 21/4 *hue* (v. l.) *þotti þorfinr* (v. l.) 'how Þorfinnr was regarded'. The variant readings *hvé/hverr* and *Þorfinns/Þorfinnr* yield four possible ways in which the lines can be interpreted. Whichever readings are adopted, the result is a subordinate clause dependent on *rétt segi'k þjóð* ... 'I tell men truly ...'

(a) *Hvé þótti Þorfinnr*, lit. 'what kind of man Þorfinnr seemed / how Þ. was regarded', is found in MSS 325V, Fl and probably also 325VI (abbreviated *þorf⸗*). I have adopted this reading, following *Orkns* 1965, 81, although it is only marginally superior to (b) and (c) below.

[46] *Orkns* 1965, 81–82, nn. Quite close by are fishing grounds which Crawford (1987, 75, following Jakobsen) notes had the traditional name 'de Tussek', possibly a reminiscence of Þursa-/Þussasker.

(b) *Hverr þótti Þorfinns* is the reading of K (the main MS) and two others. If the meaning were 'who was considered Þorfinnr's subject' it would accord particularly well with the remainder of the helming, but I am hesitant to assume that the gen. *Þorfinns* can mean 'subject of Þorfinnr'.

(c) *Hverr þótti Þorfinnr*, lit. 'who Þorfinnr was considered to be'. That *hverr* can mean 'what ... like, how great' in such a context is clear from the sentence, *Hęvir mer helldr at hugleiða hver ec em nv. en minnaz áþat hvilíc ec var fire stundo* in *Alexanders saga*, p. 88. But the construction *hverr ... Þorfinnr* in *Þdr* 21 only occurs in MSS Bb and Th, which are among the textually poorest of the relevant MSS. The reading is nevertheless adopted in both *Skjald* B and *Skaldediktningen*.

(d) The remaining reading, *hvé þótti Þorfinns* (in three MSS), makes no sense.

21/4 *til dyfliNar* 'to, as far as Dublin'. That Þorfinnr fought the Irish (*Þdr* 10 and 14) seems likely enough, but that he subdued them in any permanent sense seems a dubious hyperbole, given the complete absence of his name from Irish sources.

Verse Twenty Two

Sources

Orkns ch. 32, p. 83, and ch. 56[47]: Fl_1(529), Fl_2(538)
SnE p. 113 (lines 1–4 only): R(51), T(28v), U(57), W(56), 757(4v–5r).

Context

Orkns (i) The verse is quoted in ch. 32 together with *Þdr* 19 (see Context). The introductory note that the verses were composed about the battle between Rǫgnvaldr and Þorfinnr is in fact only appropriate to *Þdr* 19.
Orkns (ii) *Þdr* 22 is, like *Þdr* 19, *Frag* 2 and Bj H 8, appended without comment and quite incongruously to ch. 56.

[47] The verse is not printed at its second appearance in *Orkns*, p. 122.

SnE: The first helming is cited to exemplify a kenning for 'sky', in this case *erfiði Austra.*

Diplomatic and edited text (lines 1–4 of text from MS R, lines 5–8 from Fl$_1$)

Biort v*er*þr sol at svart*ri*	Bjǫrt verðr sól at svartri,
savk*kr* fold i mar davckva*n*	søkkr fold í mar døkkvan,
brestr erfiþi avstra	brestr erfiði Austra,
allr glymr siar afiollv*m*	allr glymr sær á fjǫllum,
adr at eyi*um* f*r*id*um*	áðr at Eyjum fríð*ri*
ín*n* drot*t*ar þ*or*f.	— inndróttar — Þorfinni
þ*eim* healpe gud geyme	— þeim hjalpi goð geymi —
gædi*n*gar u*el* tædu.	gœðingr my*ni* fœðask.

Prose order and translation

Bjǫrt sól verðr at svartri; fold søkkr í døkkvan mar; erfiði Austra brestr; allr sær glymr á fjǫllum, áðr gœðingr fríð*ri* Þorfinni my*ni* fœðask at Eyjum. Goð hjalpi þeim geymi inndróttar.

The bright sun will turn to black; earth will sink in the dark ocean; Austri's toil [sky] will be rent; all the sea will roar over the mountains, before a chieftain finer than Þorfinnr will be born in the Isles. God help that guardian of his retinue.

Apparatus

(1) Biort v*er*þr] Brest v*ar*d T **svart*ri*]** sortna Fl$_1$ **(2) fold]** ...lld W **mar]** lóg Fl$_1$ **(3) avstra]** hít eystra Fl$_1$, Fl$_2$ **(4) glymr]** brunar Fl$_1$, Fl$_2$ **a]** vnd U, m*ed* Fl$_1$, Fl$_2$ **(6) drot*t*ar]** drótt Fl$_2$ **þ*or*f.]** þ*or*finn*i* Fl$_2$ **(7) healpe gud]** hialp gud *og* Fl$_2$ **Line (8)]** gædíngr min*ní* fædaz Fl$_2$.

Commentary

The strophe. There are clear and probably deliberate echoes of Hallfreðr's *erfidrápa* for Óláfr Tryggvason, vv. 25, 26 and 29. Particularly striking are the (otherwise unparalleled) 'sky' kennings *niðbyrðr Norðra* 'burden of Norðri's [a dwarf's] kin' and *erfiði Austra* 'burden of Austri [a dwarf]', and the parallel construction of Hfr 3, 29 and *Þdr* 22. In each, helming (a) contains apocalyptic imagery and (b) contains a declaration that the world will be destroyed before a ruler to equal (or surpass) the skald's hero will be born, together with a prayer for the hero's soul. The wording *áðr ... gœðingr myni fæðask*

(v. l. in *Þdr* 22/8) is identical. Lines 1 and 2 also bear a striking resemblance to *Vsp* 57:

Sól tér sortna,	The sun begins to blacken,
sígr [v. l. søkkr][48] fold í mar	earth sinks into the ocean,

and to *Vsp* 41, *svǫrt verða sólskin* (v. l. to *svart var þá sólskin*).

22/1 *at svartri* 'to black, swart'. The v. l. *sortna* makes some sense in the first line *bjǫrt verðr sól at sortna* 'the bright sun will (?have to) turn black'; but it appears in only one MS (Fl_1), and may be a corruption influenced by *Vsp* 57, *sól tér sortna*.

A number of other readings in the first helming are rejected since peculiar to Fl.

22/3 This line has gained fame in the title of an article by Kuhn (1969) in which it figures as a classic example of an 11th-century metrical innovation, by which the first *hending* falls on a verb which unusually precedes the first alliterating syllable (pp. 87–88 above).

22/3 *erfiþi avstra* 'Austri's toil [sky]'. A kenning making concise reference to the myth that the sky is held up by four dwarves, Austri, Vestri, Norðri and Suðri (*SnE* p. 15).

22/5 *fríðri* (em.) 'finer'. The second helming does not make sense as it stands in either of its two appearances in MS Fl. Emendation of *fríðum* to *fríðri* is among the minor alterations necessary.[49] The supposed corruption could easily have taken place under influence of the following *eyjum*.

The implication that Þorfinnr was 'fine, handsome' may, as suggested in ch. IV, be a poetic fiction, and it could have sprung from Arnórr's desire not only to eulogise Þorfinnr but also to avoid reproducing the obvious *skothending áðr : góðu* which Hallfreðr had used in the corresponding place. *Fríðr* does occur as a description of moral rather than physical qualities, as when *einn forfríðr faðir*

[48] Reading of *SnE* MSS R, T, W and 756.

[49] It was first proposed by Gudbrand Vigfusson, 1887–94, I 59, n. 9, and has been adopted by subsequent editors.

renders *sanctus vir* in the *Heilagra manna sögur*, II 521, but the usage is rare.

22/6 and 22/7 *ínn drottar ... geyme* 'guardian of his retinue'. This is a well chosen kenning for Þorfinnr in view of his goodness to his men (which is praised in *Þdr* 2).

22/8 *gædingr* (v. l.) *myni* (em.) *fædaz* (v. l.) 'chieftain will be born'.

(a) The reading of Fl_1, '(?)chieftains served well' (from *tæja* 'help, serve') does not fit the sense of the strophe.

(b) That of Fl_2, on the other hand, gives excellent sense with the minor alteration of *minni* to *myni*, hence '(the world will end before) a chieftain (finer than Þorfinnr) will be born'.

Verse Twenty Three

Sources

SnE p. 164: R(72), T(40v), U(71), W(82).

Context

The helming is cited because of the kenning *ættbœtir Torf-Einars* in the same context as *Rdr* 2, *Þdr* 4 and *Þdr* 16b.

Diplomatic and edited text

Ætt bæti fiðr itra*n*	Ættbœti firr ítran
allriks en ec bið likna	allríks — en bið'k líkna
trvra tiggia dyrv*m*	trúra tyggja dýrum —
torfein*ars* gvð meinv*m*.	Torf-Einars goð meinum.

Prose order and translation

Goð, firr ítran ættbœti allríks Torf-Einars meinum; en bið'k dýrum tyggja trúra líkna.

God, keep the splendid ennobler of sovereign Torf-Einarr's kin far from harms; and I pray for the precious prince true mercies.

Apparatus

(1) Ætt] At T, Et W **fiðr]** fiʀ U **(2) likna]** liknar U **(3) trvra]** t*r*vrar U **tiggia]** ti...a U.

Commentary

23/1, 23/2 and 23/4 *Ætt bæti ... allriks ... torfeinars* 'ennobler of sovereign Torf-Einarr's kin', lit. 'betterer of the family of all-powerful Torf-Einarr'. Þorfinnr. Einarr, Rǫgnvaldr Mœrajarl's youngest son, enjoyed a long and successful rule in the Orkneys c. 900. His nickname 'Turf-' or 'Peat-' is explained, albeit dubiously, in *Orkns* ch. 7, p. 11: *Hann fann fyrstr manna at skera torf ór jǫrðu til eldviðar á Torfnesi á Skotlandi* (cf. note on Torfnes, *Þdr* 9/2, and Crawford 1987, 153 on peat-cutting).

Ættbœtir is a *hap. leg.*, although *ættarbœtir* occurs in prose.

23/1 *fiʀ* (v. l.) 'keep far from'.

(a) The verb *firra* 'keep far from, save, defend from', of which *firr* is the imperative, governs the acc. of the person and dat. of the thing, and hence is ideally compatible with the grammar and meaning of the remaining words in the context.

(b) R's reading *fiðr* 'finds' produces a highly unlikely sentence.

23/2 *ec bið* (normalised *bið'k*) 'I pray'. The metre of the line suggests that the pronoun *ek* should be postposited and contracted (so *Skjald* B and *Skaldediktningen*) as in almost every occurrence in Arnórr's poetry (the emphatic *Ek em* and *ek vætti* in *Frag* 2 and *ek sá* in *Frag* 4 are exceptional).

Haraldsdrápa

Verse One

Sources

Hars(Hkr) ch. 52, p. 133: K(553v), F(48r), J2(278r), 39(26v), 47(19v). Hars(H-Hr) p. 294: H(52r), Hr(38r).

Context

Haraldr Sigurðarson and his lieutenant Kalfr Árnason are harrying in Denmark. Anchored off Fjón (Fyn), the king sends Kalfr ashore on a disastrous expedition in which he and other Norwegians are slain. When Haraldr discovers this he takes terrible revenge by plundering and killing: *Svá segir Arnórr*:

Diplomatic and edited text

Ravð eɴ ryrt varð siþ*an*	Rauð, en rýrt varð síðan
raɴ elldr um siot m*anna*	— rann eldr of sjǫt manna —
frána eɢ a fioni	frána egg á Fjóni,
fiónbyɢia liþ tyɢi.	Fjónbyggva lið, tyggi.

Prose order and translation

Tyggi rauð frána egg á Fjóni, en Fjónbyggva lið varð síðan rýrt. Eldr rann of sjǫt manna.
The sovereign [or leader, Haraldr] reddened his bright blade on Fjón, and the Fjón-men's troop was then diminished. Flame ran over dwellings of men.

Apparatus

(1) varð] van*n* H, Hr **(2) um]** of F, 47 **m*anna*]** om. Hr **(4) -byɢia]** -byɢva F, 47, Hr **tyɢi]** tíɢi others.

Verse Two

Sources

Msk p. 211; Flat III 363: Msk(13r), Fl(805)
Hars(H-Hr) p. 318: H(56v), Hr(41r).

Context

In *Msk-Flat*'s account of the battle at the Niz (Nissan) estuary, the Norwegians have cleared the enemy ships and Sveinn Ulfsson (Sven Estridsson) has fled ashore. Þjóð A 3, 16 and Arnórr's *Hdr* 2, 3 and 4 are added as an appendix, without any indication of the exact stage in the battle to which they refer.
In *H-Hr*, *Hdr* 2 is integrated into the narrative at a slightly earlier stage, after the statement that in the latter part of the night the Danish ranks scattered in flight, because Haraldr had boarded Sveinn's ship, rushing forward and hacking to both sides.

Diplomatic and edited text

Hialm aro letz þu heyra	Hjalmǫru lét heyra,
hiz er ravtt fyr nizi	hizi's rauð fyr Nizi,

tiggi tyrfins eGiar
tvę́R aþr manfall veri
naþrs borþ scriþv nordan
nys at allvalldz fysi
hlavt til hallandz sciota
hrafnþarfr k*onvngr* stafni.

tyggi, tyrfings eggjar
tvær, áðr mannfall væri.
Naðrs borð skriðu norðan
nýs at allvalds fýsi;
hlaut til Hallands skjóta
hrafnþarfr konungr stafni.

Prose order and translation

Tyggi lét hjalmǫ́ru heyra, 's rauð tyrfings eggjar tvær hizi fyr Nizi, áðr mannfall væri. Borð nýs naðrs skriðu norðan at fýsi allvalds; hrafnþarfr konungr hlaut skjóta stafni til Hallands.
The sovereign [Haraldr] made helmet-bearers [warriors] hear that he reddened the sword's two edges, there by the Niz, before men fell. The bulwarks of the new serpent [ship] slid from the north at the desire of the all-ruler [Haraldr]. Lavish to ravens, the king got to speed his prow to Halland.

Apparatus

(1) letz þu] let Fl, liezt Hr **heyra]** heyía Fl **(2) hiz]** hitz others **ravtt]** Raud others **nizi]** nidzí Fl **(3) tiggi]** tyrfe Hr **tyrfins]** tyrfíngs others **(4) manfall]** $\overset{\text{n}}{\bar{\text{m}}}$- Fl, man*n*- H, Hr **(5) naþrs borþ]** nadr bords Fl **borþ]** bordi Hr **(6) at]** aa Hr **all-]** al- Hr **(7) hallandz]** hall landz Fl **sciota]** skuta Hr **(8) stafni]** sta*n*fi Fl.

Commentary

Lines 2/1 to 2/4. The verb *heyra* 'hear', on the evidence of the lexicons, is always transitive,[50] and the only possible object to *heyra* here is the clause *es rauð ... tyrfings eggjar tvær* 'that he reddened the sword's two edges'. The *hjalmærir* 'helmet-bearers', lit. 'envoys of the helmet', who hear the sword could be Haraldr's own men (compare the watching comrades in *Hdr* 11); but the sense of the helming is more pointed and more coherent if one assumes that the enemy warriors are meant: they hear the whirr as the king swings his sword to redden it in their own blood, whereupon they fall dead (*áðr mannfall væri*). An alternative suggestion (for which I am indebted to

[50] *LP*'s sole example of the 'absolute' use of *heyra*, in *Am* 66, is not valid since there is an understood object — the sound of Gunnarr's harping.

P. J. Frankis) would be that the *hjalmærir* are a wider body of people who hear news of the hero's deeds in battle.

2/1 *let* (v. l.) 'made'. The 2nd sing. form *letz þu* in the main MS is incongruous in the context of a memorial poem, and of the 3rd sing. verbs in the strophe.

2/2 *hiz er* (normalised *hizi's*) 'that there'. The monosyllabic MS spellings *hiz/hitz*, nowhere else recorded, may reflect a scribal attempt to rid the opening of the line, perhaps written *hizi er*, of the superfluous syllable. The syllable is better removed by *bragarmál* (see p. 104), here elision of *e* in *er/es*.

2/3 *tyrfins* (normalised *tyrfings*) 'the sword's'. Tyrfingr is the enchanted sword of the legends preserved in *Heiðreks saga*, apparently so renowned that Arnórr could use it to mean 'sword' in general. *Tyrfingr* occurs in a verse from the saga (*Herv* III 6), and as a 'sword' *heiti* in *Þul* IV 1 7, but nowhere else with this meaning. The etymology of the word is obscure, but it has been connected with *tyrvi*, a resinous wood (Falk 1914, 62; de Vries s. v.), with *torf* 'turf' (*IEW* pp. 489–90) and with a Gothic tribal name (Falk 1914, 62).

2/5 and 2/6 *naþrs ... nys* 'of the new serpent'. The phrase is particularly apt here, since, according to *Hars(Hkr)* ch. 59, p. 141 and *Hars(H-Hr)* p. 308, the winter before the encounter at the Niz, King Haraldr had a dragon-prowed ship built according to the dimensions of Óláfr Tryggvason's ship Ormr inn langi 'the Long Serpent'. In Þjóð A 3, 13, which also concerns the battle at the Niz, Haraldr's ship is again referred to as *naðr*.

2/8 *hrafnþarfr* 'lavish to [lit. useful to, supplying the needs of] ravens'. The adj., a compressed equivalent of Arnórr's phrase *(jafn)þarfr hrafni* (*Mdr* 19), is a *hap. leg.* In meaning it is comparable to *vargholl*r 'gracious to wolves', used in Þjóð A 3, 12 and elsewhere.

Verse Three

Sources

Msk p. 212; Flat III 363: Msk(13r), Fl(805)
Hars(H-Hr) p. 318: H(56v), Hr(41r).

Context

In *Msk-Flat* the verse follows immediately upon *Hdr* 2.
In *H-Hr* the brief statement is interjected, that Sveinn's ship was so thoroughly cleared that all its crew were dead but for those who had leapt into the sea or onto smaller ships.

Diplomatic and edited text

Hravd sa er hv*er*gi flyþi	Hrauð, sá's hvergi flýði,
heid mę́iʀ danasceidir	heiðmærr Dana skeiðir
glaþr vnd und gvlli roþno*m*	glaðr und golli roðnum,
geir ialm k*onvngr* hialmi	geirjalm, konungr hjalmi.
scaldborg ravþz en scufar	Skjaldborg raufsk, en skúfar
scavtt hoddglavtuþr oddo*m*	— skaut hoddglǫtuðr oddum
bragna brynior gavgno*m*	bragna brynjur gǫgnum,
buþlvngr of na songo.	buðlungr — of ná sungu.

Prose order and translation

Heiðmærr konungr, sá's hvergi flýði geirjalm, hrauð glaðr und golli roðnum hjalmi skeiðir Dana. Skjaldborg raufsk, en skúfar sungu of ná. Hoddglǫtuðr, buðlungr, skaut oddum gǫgnum brynjur bragna.
The bright-renowned king, who nowhere fled spear-clangour, cleared, glad under gold-reddened helmet, the galleys of the Danes. The shield-wall shattered, and swords sang out over corpses. The hoard-destroyer [generous prince, Haraldr], the monarch shot spear-heads through the mailcoats of warriors.

Apparatus

(2) mę́iʀ] milldr Fl, -mær H, Hr **-sceidir]** skeídar Fl **(3) vnd und]** m*ed* Fl, vnd H, Hr **gvlli]** glle Hr **(4) hialmi]** híalm Fl, híalma Hr **(5) scald-]** skiall- Fl, skialld- H, Hr **ravþz]** ʀauzt Fl, ravfz H, Hr **scufar]** skufa Fl **(6) scavtt]** skaut others **hoddglavtuþr]** haud*d* glautu*nd*r Fl, hodd h*ra*udud*r* Hr **oddo*m*]** broddv*m* H, Hr **(7) brynior]** bryn*ir* Fl **(8) buþlvngr]** budlu*n*g Fl.

Commentary

3/2 *heid mær* (v. l., normalised *mærr*) 'bright-renowned'. MS *mę́iʀ* must be a corruption of *-mę́ʀ* (*-mærr*), while *mildr* 'mild, generous', the reading of Fl alone, is likely to be a secondary variant. (Variation between *mærr* and *mildr* also occurs in the text of *Hdr* 13/5.)

Heið- in *heiðmærr* has two possible senses. (a) 'Brightly, gloriously', cf. *heiðr* m. 'honour, glory', *heið* f. 'brightness of the sky' or adj. *heiðr* 'clear, bright, radiant'. The adj. can be used figuratively, as in *heiðr orðrómr* (*Ht* 48) which, with its collocation of 'bright' with 'reputation, renown', supports my suggested translation 'bright-renowned' for *heiðmærr*. (b) 'For, with gifts, rewards', cf. *heið* f. 'gift, reward, pay' as in *heiðmaðr*, *heiðþegi*, of men in a ruler's pay. Hence *heiðmærr* could alternatively — or even simultaneously — mean 'renowned for bounty'.

3/5 *scufar* 'swords'. *Skúfr*, in the sense 'sword', otherwise only occurs in *Þul* IV l 2 (MSS *stvfr* and *skofr*), where the entry could well derive from Arnórr's verse. *Skúfr* may originally have meant 'sword with a tassel at the hilt', since the same form is recorded in prose with the sense 'tassel, tuft' (Falk 1914, 60; *IEW* p. 821).

3/8 *buþlvngr* 'monarch'. (a) I assume this nom. sing. form to stand in apposition to *hoddglǫtuðr* 'hoard-destroyer', as subject to the verb *skaut* 'shot'. (b) V. l. *buðlung* does not make sense in the context. (c) Finnur Jónsson in *Skjald* B emended to gen. sing. *buðlungs*, which he took with *skjaldborg*, hence 'the prince's shield-wall'; Kock (*NN* §838) preferred *skúfar buðlungs* 'the prince's swords'.

Verse Four

Sources

Hars(Hkr) ch. 63, pp. 150–51: K(561v), F(49r), J2(283v–284r), 39(27r), 47(21v)
Hars(H-Hr) p. 319: H(56v), Hr(41r)
Msk p. 212; Flat III 363–64: Msk(13r), Fl(805).

Context

Hkr: The Norwegians board Sveinn's ship and clear it so thoroughly that only those who leap overboard survive, *Svá segir Arnórr jarlaskáld:*
H-Hr and *Msk-Flat*: The strophe follows *Hdr* 3, preceded by a sentence that calls attention to Arnórr's opinion that Sveinn Ulfsson only fled when his situation was desperate.

Diplomatic and edited text

Geckat Svein*n* af sneckio
saclavst iɴ forravsti
malmr com harðr v*ið* hialma
hugi miɴ v*ar* *þat* sin*n*i
farscostr lavt at fliota
fliotmæltz vin*ar* jóta
aðr eɴ ǫðlingr flyði
avðr fra v*er*þung davðri.

Gekkat Sveinn af snekkju
saklaust enn forhrausti
— malmr kom harðr við hjalma —
(hugi minn es þat) sinni.
Farskostr hlaut at fljóta
fljótmælts vinar Jóta,
áðr an ǫðlingr flýði,
auðr, frá verðung dauðri.

Prose order and translation

Enn forhrausti Sveinn gekkat saklaust af snekkju sinni. Hugi minn es þat. Malmr kom harðr við hjalma. Farskostr fljótmælts vinar Jóta hlaut at fljóta auðr, áðr an ǫðlingr flýði frá dauðri verðung.
Sveinn, outstanding in valour, did not go without cause from his vessel. That is my thought. Steel struck hard on helmets. The choice bark / ship of the swift-spoken friend of Jutes [Sveinn] was fated to float unmanned, before the noble one fled from his dead liegemen.

Apparatus

(1) af] om. Hr, ath Fl **sneckio]** sin*ne* 47, sni*n*kiu Fl(?) **(2) -lavst]** -laus 47 **for-]** ty- 47 **(3)** ***við*]** áá Fl **(4) hugi]** hug*r* Hr, Fl ***var*]** so also J2, er others **(5) farscostr]** f*a*rkost*r* Hr, Fl, farskott´ 47 **lavt]** hlaut Fl, H, Hr **at]** om. Fl **fliota]** flestu Hr **(6) fliotmæltz]** fliót*t* mætz F, 39, fliot mætz 47, fliotmaltz H, Hr, fiol níotz Fl **(7) aðr eɴ]** adr en adr en Hr **(8) avðr]** audz Fl **fra]** om. 47 **davðri]** daud*er* Hr.

Commentary

4/2 ***forravsti*** 'outstanding in valour'. Compounds with intensive *for-* are not particularly common, although *forsnjallr* and *forljótr* are recorded in poetry, and *forfagr*, *forhagr* etc. in prose. V. l. *týhraustr* 'divinely, wondrously valiant' is peculiar to MS 47, as are several readings in this strophe. It occurs in *SnE*, p. 32: *Þat er orðtak, at sa er tyhravstr, er vm fram er aðra menn ok ecki setz fyrir* 'It is a saying that a man who is superior to others and never hesitates is Tyr-valiant'. Cf. also *týmargr* etc.

4/4 *er* (v. l.) 'is', normalised *es*. The past tense in *hugi minn vas þat* 'that was my thought' would only have any point if the skald had been present at the events he commemorates, and there is no evidence to suggest that he was.

4/6 *fliotmæltz* 'swift-spoken'. *Fljótmæltr vinr Jóta* appears to be a very apt designation for Sveinn Ulfsson, if the saga accounts are at all trustworthy. According to them, Sveinn's eloquence proved troublesome both to Magnús Óláfsson and to Haraldr, as when his persuasive speech at the Vébjǫrg (Viborg) assembly won over the Jutlanders from their loyalty to Magnús (e. g. *Flat* III 274).

Verse Five

Sources

Ólsh(Hkr) ch. 121, p. 208: K(357v), 325XI 2f(2r)
Ólsh(Sep) p. 316: 2(38v), 4(31v), 61(102v), 68(37r), 73(208), 75a(26v), 75b(3v), 325V(40r), 325VI(26v), 325VII(21v), Bb(168v), Fl(434), Th(126r).

Context

The verse is quoted in a context totally unrelated to Haraldr Sigurðarson: an account of how Óláfr Haraldsson subdued and Christianised the farmers of Valdres. Their land is burned and plundered, and hostages are taken.

(i) The introductory words in some MSS allow of the interpretation that the strophe is only about Óláfr: *Þess getr arnoʀ iarla skalld ...* MSS 61, 68; 75b, 325VII, 325XI, Bb and Th add, *at Ólafr konungr hafðe brent upplond.*

(ii) Others refer to Óláfr but specify that the verse comes from a poem about Haraldr: *Þess getr Arnórr jarlaskáld, er Óláfr konungr hafði brennt á Upplǫndum, þá er hann orti um Harald, bróður hans* (K version):

Diplomatic and edited text

Gengr i ætt þ*at* e*r* yngvi	Gengr í ætt, þat's yngvi
uplendinga breɴdi	Upplendinga brendi
þioð gallt r[æ]sis reiði	— þjóð galt ræsis reiði —
ravɴ þ*ess* e*r* fremstr e*r* m*anna*	rǫnn — þess's fremstr vas manna.
villdut avflgar alld*ir*	Vildut ǫflgar aldir,
aðr v*ar* styrt t*il* váða	áðr vas stýrt til váða,
grams dólgum fek*k*z galgi	— grams dolgum fekksk galgi —
gagnpryðanda lyða.	gagnprýðanda hlýða.

Prose order and translation

Gengr í ætt, þat's yngvi brendi rǫnn Upplendinga. Þjóð galt reiði ræsis, þess's fremstr vas manna. Ǫflgar aldir vildut hlýða gagnprýðanda, áðr vas stýrt til váða. Galgi fekksk dolgum grams.
It befits his kin that the prince put to flame the dwellings of the Uplanders. The people paid for the wrath of the ruler who was foremost of men. Mighty men were unwilling to heed the glorious victor, before their course turned to ruin. The gallows were the lot of the lord's foes.

Apparatus

(1) i ætt] at 61, riett 75b(?), 325XI, Bb, Fl, i att Th **þ*at*]** þar 2, 75a, 325V, Fl **yngvi]** yngri 325VI **(3) r[æ]sis]** æ supplied from others, lacuna K **(4) ravɴ]** so also 68, 325VI, rann others **þ*ess*]** so also 68, Th, sa others **fremstr]** fremzt 73, fyrstvr Bb **e*r* (2nd)]** var 2, 4, 68, 73, 75a, 75b, 325V, 325VII, Bb, Fl, Th **(5) villdut]** willdu/v- 73, 75a, Fl **avflgar]** auflg*ra* 61, avflg*ra*r 68, aulfgar 325VI, ofgar Fl **alld*ir*]** alldar 2, 68, allda 61, alldrí 73 **(6) styrt]** stef*n*t Th **(7) fek*k*z galgi]** feck galga Th **(8) gagnpryðanda]** gagl- 73, 75a, -pryðinda 2, pryþan 325V, -prydande Fl.

Commentary

5/1 ***Gengr i ætt*** 'It befits his kin, runs in the family'. The interest of the idiom, which is not precisely paralleled in ON, is that it is capable of two interpretations. Under one the strophe contains an implied comparison between Óláfr helgi (in whose saga it is quoted) and

Haraldr, but under the other it concerns only one, unnamed prince. The question was fully explored by Konráð Gíslason (1879, esp. 158–59), and much of the following discussion is indebted to his.

(a) That *ætt* here has its common meaning 'kin, family', and that *gengr í ætt* means 'it befits his kin' is suggested by the adj. *ættgengr* 'characteristic of the family' and by Mod. Icel. *ganga í ætt* 'to run in the family'. If this interpretation is correct, the subject to *gengr í ætt* is the clause *þat's yngvi brendi Upplendinga rǫnn* and the overall sense, 'the prince [*yngvi*, Haraldr] takes after his half-brother Óláfr in that he burned the dwellings of the Uplanders'. Context (ii) above shows that at least some compilers or scribes understood the strophe thus, and this is the solution favoured by Konráð Gíslason.

(b) *Ganga* can have the figurative sense 'it is current' (of a report or story), as in *geingr þersi saga ... mest af Suerri konungi* (*Flat* II 533), and *í ætt* can mean 'from generation to generation' as in *Ht* 89, *þat spyrr framm í ǫtt* 'it is told down the generations, is famed'. *Hdr* 5/1–2 could hence be rendered, 'It is related from generation to generation, how the prince burned the Uplanders' dwellings'. This would of itself be an acceptable interpretation, but it fails to explain how the strophe came to be associated with Óláfr helgi. It can hardly come from a *drápa* about Óláfr, for Arnórr was less than twenty when Óláfr died, and there is no hint in the extant sources that he composed about him.

5/2 uplendinga 'Uplanders'. These are the people of the provinces that stretch inland to the north of the Oslo fjord — Raumaríki, Hringaríki, Haðaland and Heiðmǫrk (respectively modern Romerike, Ringerike, Hadeland and Hedemark). The prose sources differ in their explanation of Haraldr's raid on Upplǫnd, claiming either that the people there had given allegiance and revenues to Hákon jarl Ívarsson, or that they had insisted on retaining privileges granted them by Óláfr Haraldsson for their service at the battle of Nesjar (c. 1015). There is reason to think the second explanation the more credible of the two.[51] In either case the men of Upplǫnd may have been expressing a more general resistance to royal domination over the region (see Andersen 1977, 151–52).

[51] See Bull 1927, 40–44, and following him Bjarni Aðalbjarnarson, *Hkr* 1941–51, II xvii; also Schreiner 1928.

5/4 *þess er* 'who'. Both *þess's* and v. l. *sá's* (MSS *þess er*, *sa er*) give excellent sense. *Þess's* would be dependent on a gen. word (*ræsis*) within an intercalated sentence, while *sá's* would modify the subject of the main sentence (*yngvi*), so that *þess's* may be regarded as the *lectio difficilior*. Since *þess* is also the reading of K, the main MS, it seems more likely to be the skald's original.

5/4 *var* (v. l.) 'was'. The present tense verb in *'s fremstr es* [MS *er*] *manna* 'who is foremost of men' can scarcely have been applied to a deceased hero and must be an error, perhaps influenced by the preceding relative particle *er* or by *gengr* in line 1.

5/5 *avflgar alldir* 'mighty men' and **5/7 *grams dólgum*** 'lord's foes'. The rebellious men of Upplǫnd.

5/8 *gagnpryðanda* 'glorious victor', lit. 'him who makes victory splendid': Haraldr.

Verse Six

Sources

SnE p. 178: R(76), T(42v), U(80), 748(19v), 748II(8r), 757(6r).

Context

Snorri quotes the helming to exemplify the use of *hyrr* as a poetic appellation for 'fire'.

Diplomatic and edited text

Ǫmþit rað v*ið* ravma	Eymðit ráð við Rauma
reiðr eydana meiþ*ir*	reiðr Eydana meiðir;
heit dvinvþv hveina	heit dvínuðu Heina;
hyʀ ger*þ*i þa kyʀa.	hyrr gerði þá kyrra.

Prose order and translation

Reiðr Eydana meiðir eymðit ráð við Rauma. Heit Heina dvínuðu. Hyrr gerði þá kyrra.
The wrathful harmer of Isle-Danes did not soften his treatment of the Raumar. The threats of the Heinir fell away. Fire made them quiet.

Apparatus

Line 1] illeg. 757 **Ǫmþit]** Ǿmdit T, Eymþit U, Æymdit 748, Eímdí 748II **(2) reiðr]** reiþir U **eydana meiþ*ir*]** eyda... d*ir* 757 **(3) dvinvþv]** dyniodo T, dvínvdum 757 **hveina]** heina U, 748, 757, huna 748II **Line 4]** h... þa k... 757 **hyʀ]** h*er*r U.

Commentary

6/1 ***Ǫmþit*** 'He did not soften, make feeble' (so Konráð Gíslason, 1879, 195–97). *Eymðit*, the reading of MSS U and 748, may also be represented by *Ǫmþit* in R, the main MS, since (normalised) *ey* is among the values of the symbol *ǫ* in R, though rare (see *SnE(Arnamagn.)* III xvi–xvii).

According to *LP*, this is the only poetic context in which *eyma* (a derivative of adj. *aumr* 'wretched, piteous, poor') occurs, but the same sense is recorded in prose (*Fornaldar sögur nordrlanda* III 221–22). With Arnórr's ironically understated comment on the king's vengeance here, compare the first couplet of *Mdr* 17.

6/3 ***heina*** **(v. l.)** 'Heinir, men of Heiðmǫrk'. The reading *hveina* must be an error influenced by the preceding *dvinvþv*, and v. l. *huna* 'Huns' makes no sense.

Verse Seven

Sources

Msk p. 269; Flat III 391: Msk (18v), Fl(817)
Hars(H-Hr) p. 407: H(74r), Hr(52v).

Context

In *Msk-Flat*, Arnórr's *Hdr* 7, 8 and 9 are cited as supplementary authorities after the saga account of the battle by the Ouse. The sentence, *Þess getr oc Aruoʀ* [sic] *hverso mikil oc aget þesi orrosta varþ* precedes *Hdr* 7.
H-Hr: The slaughter of the English is still in progress. Once Valþjófr jarl has fled, Haraldr and his men encircle Mǫrukári's division from the rear — *Fèllu þá hundröðum enskir menn; svâ segir Arnórr* (so H; Hr reads ... *Steinn*):

Diplomatic and edited text

Þvng ravð iarn*n* a englo*m*	Þung rauð jǫrn á Englum
eirlavst ne cø*mr* meira	eirlaust — né kømr meira —
vis ivel nę́r vso	vísi vel nær Úsu
valfall v*m* her sniallan.	— valfall of her snjallan.

Prose order and translation

Vísi rauð þung jǫrn eirlaust á Englum vel nær Úsu, né kømr meira valfall of snjallan her.
The leader reddened weighty iron [blades] ruthlessly on Englishmen hard by the Ouse, and never will come greater slaughter upon a bold host.

Apparatus

(3) vis ivel] visi vel others.

Commentary

The helming. On the battle by the Ouse, see Schofield 1966, esp. 692.

7/3 *vel nę́r vso* 'hard by the Ouse'.

(a) The words, consecutive in the text, are here construed together. I know of no other record of *vel nær e-u,* but the syntactic pattern of adverb and prepositional phrase is attested, e.g. in *(a morgin) miog i þenna tima dags* '(tomorrow) at this very time of day', *Stjórn* p. 372. Also in favour of the postulated idiom is the existence of the compound *allnær*, which occurs in the phrase *allnær Úsu*, in a verse (Steinn 3, 2) describing the same battle as *Hdr* 7. Just as *vel mikill* and *vel góðr* correspond to *allmikill* and *allgóðr*, so *vel nær* could correspond to *allnær*. OE in fact provides examples of such an idiom, including *we ... wel neah stodan þam bearwum* 'we stood very close to the woods' (*Letter of Alexander,* p. 43). *Vel nær Úsu*, if correctly rendered 'hard by the Ouse, very close to the Ouse', matches the saga accounts, according to which Haraldr and his men were ranged on the river bank itself (e. g. *Msk* p. 268).

(b) *Vel* could alternatively modify *rauð* 'reddened' (Kock, *NN* §806), or *meira valfall* 'greater slaughter' (Finnur Jónsson, *Skjald* B and 1934, 45–46); but in both cases the word order would be disjointed and the meaning uncharacteristically tepid.

Verse Eight

Sources

Msk p. 270; Flat III 391: Msk(18v), Fl(817)
Hars(H-Hr) p. 409: H(74r), Hr(53r).

Context

In *Msk-Flat* the strophe follows *Hdr* 7, separated from it only by the words, *Oc enn q(vað) hann*:
In *H-Hr* it is preceded by a short account, in prose and verse, of the slaughter of the English who were cut off from escape by the stream and the marshy ground.

Diplomatic and edited text

Fell at fvndi stillis	Fell at fundi stillis
f*ra*m oþo ve moþa	— framm óðu vé — móða
amt flo griot a gavta	(ámt fló grjót) á gauta
gloþheitr ofan sveiti	glóðheitr ofan sveiti.
þioð hycc þaðra naþo	Þjóð hykk þaðra nǫ́ðu
þusv*n*du*m* togfvsa	þúsundum togfúsa
spiot flvgv lif at lata	— spjót flugu — líf at láta
lavs i gv*m*na havso*m*.	— laus í gumna hausum.

Prose order and translation

Glóðheitr sveiti fell at fundi stillis ofan á móða gauta. Ámt grjót fló. Vé óðu framm. Hykk togfúsa þjóð nǫ́ðu þaðra at láta líf þúsundum. Spjót flugu laus í gumna hausum.
Ember-hot blood flowed at the ruler's / controller's conflict down upon wearied men. Dark stones flew. Standards stormed forth. I think that troops quick on the draw came to lose their lives by thousands there. Spears flew free at men's skulls.

Apparatus

(1) fvndi] fu*n*du Hr **(3) amt]** ott Fl, an*n*t Hr **(4) -heitr]** -heit Fl **(5) hycc]** hygt Fl **naþo]** nada Fl **(6) þusv*n*du*m*]** þushu*n*du*m* Hr **togfvsa]** taug- Fl, tók- H, t̊- Hr **(7) lif]** laus Hr **lata]** lati Fl.

Commentary

8/2 and 8/3 *moþa ... a gavta* 'upon wearied men'. I take *móða* as acc. pl. masc. adj. qualifying *gauta* 'men'. The word is sometimes used specifically of battle-weariness, e. g. Þjóð A 4, 6 *hjaldrs móðr* (v. l.) 'exhausted by battle', or *eggmóðr* 'blade-weary', applied in *Grí* 53 and *Hamð* 30 to *valr* 'the slain'.

Gauta has been considered a point of difficulty in the strophe (see, e. g., Finnur Jónsson 1934, 46–47). The recorded meanings of *gautr*, pl. *gautar*, are threefold: (a) *Gautar* is an ethnic name referring to the Gauts, the people of Väster- and Östergötland, S. Sweden. (b) *Gautr* is a name for Óðinn (cf. Gauti and Gautatýr), and as such it can function as a base word in kennings for 'man / warrior'. (c) I take *gautar* as the rare *heiti* for 'men',[52] which is probably an extension of sense (a) 'Gauts', just as *got(n)ar* 'men' is an extension of *Gotar* 'Goths'. It appears in the verse printed in *Skjald* as Anon (XIII) B 33: *spjót drifu grǫ́n á gauta* 'grey spears pelted the men'; and *gauta spjalli* 'confidant of men' appears as a v. l. to *gumna spjalli* in Stúfr 4, a verse contemporary with *Hdr* (c. 1067).

I construe *á móða gauta* 'upon wearied men' with *fell ofan sveiti* 'blood flowed down', cf. Hást 3:

blóð fell varmt á virða,[53]	blood fell warm on men,
valdǫgg.	the dew of carnage.

It could alternatively (or simultaneously) be read with *ámt fló grjót* 'dark stones flew'.

8/3 *amt* 'dark'. The adj. is sing., qualifying the collective *grjót* 'stones', cf. *gránt grjót* 'grey stones' in E Sk 6, 35.

[52] So also various editors, including those of *Fms* XII, 1837, 164, and Kock, *NN* §2523.

[53] MSS *vala / vira*. *Varmt* is v. l. to *vart*.

8/4 *gloþheitr* 'ember-hot'. The word occurs in *Lækningabók Íslenzk* p. 73, and cf. *glóðrauðr* 'ember-red', describing fire in Sturl 5, 5 and *brennheitr* 'burning hot', of bread in E Sk 6, 35. On its effect in context, see pp. 77–78.

8/6 *þusvndum* 'by thousands'. Arnórr is probably speaking poetically rather than factually here. The compiler of *H-Hr* certainly thought so, for he claims (in the Context to *Hdr* 7, above), *fèllu þá hundröðum enskir menn*; and the Irish monk Marianus, writing at Mainz at the end of the 11th century, numbers the English dead at over one thousand laymen and a hundred priests (*Chronicon*, p. 559).

8/6 *togfvsa* 'quick on the draw'. An acc. sing. fem. adj. qualifying *þjóð* 'men'. *Togfúss* is not attested elsewhere, nor is the simplex *tog* recorded in poetry, but in prose it usually means 'rope, line'. Here and in related words the basic notion is of 'pulling' (e. g. verb *toga*) or 'drawing' (e. g. verb *tjúga*, especially applied to the drawing of swords). The element *tog* also appears in the poetic compounds *at eggtogi* (*Hfl* 14)[54] and *at / á sverðtogi* (*Ht* 54 and *Hálfs* VIII 4), in which the sense is 'at the drawing of the sword', i. e. 'in battle'. There are examples of compound adjs. in *-fúss* whose first element denotes 'battle', e. g. *bǫðfúss*, *sóknfúss* and *vígfúss*. *Togfúss* can therefore be translated with some confidence as 'quick on the draw' or 'eager for battle'. If this is correct, the phrase 'troops quick on the draw', applied to the defeated enemy, further develops the delicate irony already effected by the contrast between *nǫ́ðu* 'succeeded, managed to' and the ignominious *líf at láta* 'to lose their lives'. Guðbrandur Vigfússon nevertheless found *togfúsa* unsatisfying and believed it to be a scribal substitution for a phrase meaning 'dike by the Ouse' (*CPB* II 185).

Vv. ll. *taug-* and *tók-* may well be corruptions of *tog-*. The abbreviated *t̊ fusa* in MS Hr is also expanded to *tók-* by Finnur Jónsson in *Skjald* A, but probably represents an otherwise unknown *torfúsa* '(?)difficult-eager', i. e. '(?)not eager' (cf. abbreviated *n̊dan* for *nordan*). The reading *torfúsa* is adopted by Finnur Jónsson in *Skjald* B but rejected by Kock in *NN* §2523.

[54] The helming containing the phrase is numbered 14 in *Skjald* B but 18 in *Skjald* A.

Verse Nine

Sources

Msk p. 270; Flat III 391: Msk(18v), Fl(817)
Hars(H-Hr) p. 409: H(74r), Hr(53r)

Context

In *Msk-Flat* the strophe follows *Hdr* 7 and 8 directly.
In *H-Hr* it is prefaced by a few summary comments about the battle, including the statement that the jarl Valþjófr, with the English survivors, fled to the stronghold at York: *Svâ segir Arnórr*:

Diplomatic and edited text

Gagn*n* fecc giofvinr sygna	Gagn fekk gjǫfvinr Sygna
gecc hilldr at mvn villdra	— gekk hildr at mun — vildra,
hin*n* e*r* a hel fyr m*onnv*m	hinn's á hæl fyr mǫnnum
hreinscialldar for alld*ri*	hreinskjaldaðr fór aldri.
dyndo iarlar vndar	Dunðu jarlar undan
eir fecca liþ þ*eir*a	— eir fekka lið þeira —
man*n*kyn [hef*ir*] at minno*m*	(mannkyn hefr at minnum
morgon þan*n* til borgar.	morgin þann) til borgar.

Prose order and translation

Gjǫfvinr vildra Sygna fekk gagn, hinn's hreinskjaldaðr fór aldri á hæl fyr mǫnnum. Hildr gekk at mun. Jarlar dunðu undan til borgar. Lið þeira fekka eir. Mannkyn hefr þann morgin at minnum.
The gift-friend of prized Sygnir gained victory, he who, bright-shielded, never took to his heels in the face of men. The battle went to his wish. The earls thundered away to the stronghold. Their troop received no mercy. The race of men holds that morning in memory.

Apparatus

(1) giofvinr] giaf- others, -vín*n*r Hr **sygna]** sygg*n*ía Fl **(3) hel]** hæl others **(4) -scialldar]** -skialldad*r* Hr **(5) dyndo]** du*n*du Fl **vndar]** und*an* others **(7) man*n*-]** $\overset{n}{\bar{\mathrm{m}}}$ Fl **hef*ir*]** supplied from others, lacuna Msk **(8) morgon]** morgi*n* Hr.

Commentary

9/1 *giofvinr sygna* 'gift-friend of Sygnir, of the men of Sogn', hence 'King of the Norwegians'. V. l. *giafvinr* would be equally acceptable. Either variant is a *hap. leg.*

9/4 *hreinskialldadr* (v. l.) 'bright-shielded, bearing a bright shield'.

(a) Although a *hap. leg.*, *hreinskjaldaðr* resembles the phrase *hreinar randir* (*Ht* 8) and the adjectival p. ps *skjaldaðr* and *fagrskjaldaðr*, and makes excellent sense as an epithet qualifying *hinn*, i. e. Haraldr. This reading is adopted by Finnur Jónsson in *Skjald* B and Kock in *Skaldediktningen.*

(b) One cannot, however, reject the possibility that *hreinskjaldaðr* is a happy emendation by the scribe of Hr, and that *hreinskjaldar* is the original reading. It is the *lectio difficilior*, and has the stronger MS support, but it is difficult to place within the syntax of the helming. The possible constructions are *gagn hreinskjaldar* 'victory of the bright shield', *hildr hreinskjaldar* 'battle of the bright shield' and *fyr mǫnnum hreinskjaldar* 'before the men of the bright shield [?warriors]', but none of these expressions can be paralleled.

9/5 *iarlar* 'earls'. The English earls are named in the *Anglo-Saxon Chronicle* as Morcere and Eadwine (versions C, D and E, s. a. 1066), but in Norse sources as Mǫrukári and, erroneously, Valþjófr (on whom, see Scott 1953–58).

9/8 *til borgar* 'to the stronghold / city'. This is York (ON Jorvík). Fulford, the site of the battle, lies about two miles down-river.

Verse Ten

Sources

Msk p. 273; Flat III 393: Msk(19r), Fl(818)
Hars(H-Hr) pp. 413–14: H(75r), Hr(53v).

Context

Haraldr, realising an attack from the English is imminent, draws up his men in battle-order at *Stanfvrþo bryGio* (Stamford Bridge). In *Msk-Flat*, *Hdr* 10 is cited, with the introduction, *sem ArnoR s(egir)*, immediately after Haraldr's closing words of encouragement to his troops have been reported. The compiler of *H-Hr*, before quoting the verse, adds a remark on the immensity of the enemy's forces, both cavalry and foot.

Diplomatic and edited text

Vppgongv bavd yngvi
itr m*eð* helmi*n*g litin
sa e*r* asiN*n*i ęfi
sasc alld*re*gi hasca
en*n* v*m* england svN*n*an
avflvgr heR at beriasc
for við fylki dyran
fvNdvz þ*eir* af stvndo.

Uppgǫngu bauð yngvi
ítr með helming lítinn,
sá's á sinni ævi
sásk aldrigi háska.
Enn of England sunnan
ǫflugr herr at berjask
fór við fylki dýran;
fundusk þeir af stundu.

Prose order and translation

Ítr yngvi, sá's aldrigi á sinni ævi sásk háska, bauð uppgǫngu með lítinn helming. Ǫflugr herr fór enn sunnan of England at berjask við dýran fylki. Þeir fundusk af stundu.
The splendid prince, he who never in his life feared danger, ordered the advance ashore with a small force. But a mighty army marched from the south through England to fight the excellent sovereign. They engaged straightway.

Apparatus

(3) asiN*n*i ęfi] sin*ne* [aa] æfí Fl **(5) en*n*]** en Fl.

Commentary

The strophe. On the battle of Stamford Bridge, see Brooks 1956; on the unreliability of the saga accounts, Bjarni Aðalbjarnarson in *Hkr* 1941–51, III, xxxii–xxxiii.

10/5 *enn* 'But'. The translation represents a minor and seemingly necessary editorial sleight-of-hand. The alliteration and internal rhyme of the line favour reading a long syllable, which would be the stressed adverb *enn* 'still, further', rather than an unstressed short syllable *en* which would be the conjunction 'but'; but the latter seems more natural in context.

Verse Eleven

Sources

Hars(Hkr) ch. 92, pp. 189–90: K(582v), F(53r), J2(297v), 47(27v)
Fsk ch. 69, pp. 286–87: Fsk A (306–7)
Hars(H-Hr) p. 418: H(76r), Hr(54r)
Msk p. 277; Flat III 395: Msk(19v), Fl(819).

Context

Hkr and *H-Hr*: The Norwegians are deceived by the apparent flight of the English into breaking their shield-wall. Seeing what straits his men are in, Haraldr plunges into the thick of the fighting with such vigour that the English (in Snorri's version) are on the point of fleeing.
Fsk and *Msk-Flat*: The English cavalry, by sheer force of numbers, gain the upper hand so that the Norwegians break ranks. Again, the narrative centres on Haraldr's headlong attack, and Stúfr blindi's v. 8 is cited to illustrate. *Hdr* 11 then follows, introduced by the words, *En þetta kvað Arnórr jarlaskáld* (*Fsk*); *oc þetta segir ArnoR isino q(vęþi)* (*Msk-Flat*):

Diplomatic and edited text

Hafþi briost ne bifþiz
bavðsnart k*onvng*s hiarta
i hialmþ*ri*mo hylm*ir*
hlít styGr f*yr ser* litit
þ*ar*s t*il* þengils hersa
þat sa h*er*r at scatna
bloðugr hioR ens baRa
beit davglinga hneitis.

Hafðit brjóst, né bifðisk
bǫðsnart konungs hjarta
í hjalmþrimu, hilmir
hlítstyggr fyr sér lítit,
þar's til þengils hersa
þat sá herr, at skatna
blóðugr hjǫrr ens barra
beit dǫglinga hneitis.

Prose order and translation

Hlítstyggr hilmir hafðit lítit brjóst fyr sér, né bifðisk bǫðsnart hjarta konungs í hjalmþrimu, þar's herr sá þat til þengils hersa, at blóðugr hjǫrr ens barra dǫglinga hneitis beit skatna.
The prince, shunning trivial deeds, had no mean mettle in himself, and the battle-swift heart of the king did not tremble in the helmet-din, where the army, watching the lord of nobles, saw that the bloody sword of the zealous subduer of princes bit men.

Apparatus

(1) Hafþi] Hafðeð A, Hafþit H, Hr, Msk, Fl **bifþiz]** bifduz Hr **(2) -snart]** -svart A **(3) -þ*ri*mo]** þrumu A **hylm*ir*]** fylkir A, hilm*ir* others **(4) hlít]** lið- A **fyr *ser*]** ok þo Fl **(5) þ*ars*]** þas Fl ***til*]** þ*vi* at Hr, e*r* Fl **þengils]** þ*ar*far H, Hr, Msk, Fl **hersa]** h*er*iar F **(6) sa h*err* at]** siatn*ad*e Hr **herr]** m*enn* H, Msk, Fl **(7) baʀa]** bara Fl.

Commentary

11/1 and 11/4 *Hafþit* (v. l.) *briost ... fyr ser litit* 'no mean mettle had [the prince] in himself'. *Brjóst* can mean 'breast, chest', hence figuratively 'courage' (as in *hlífði brjóst ... hringdrífs frǫmu lífi* 'his courage protected ... the bold life of the ring-strewer', Sturl 2, 3) or 'defence, defender(s)' (as in *bysc til forysto. oc at vera briost fyr ollom Noregs mọnnom* 'offered himself as a leader and as a defence for all the Norwegians', *Msk* p. 308). *Fyr sér* can mean 'in front of him(self)', or 'in, of him(self)' as in the phrase *mikill / lítill fyrir sér.*

These alternative senses combine with the alternative readings *hafði* and *hafðit* to yield several possible interpretations of *Hdr* 11, the most satisfactory of which are:

(a) Reading *hafði*: 'He had little defence in front of him' (so *Hkr* 1941–51, III, 189 and 190n.). This would imply that Haraldr was in the forefront of the fighting.

(b) Reading *hafðit*: 'He had no small courage / defence in himself', with the suffix *-t* negating *lítit* (so Jón Thorkelsson, 1884, 41, and *Skjald* B). This analysis is followed in my translation.

11/4 *hlít styʀ* 'shunning trivial deeds'. This compound adj. only occurs in one other context, a helming by Steinþórr (?11th century), where it is applied to Óðinn, 'burden of Gunnlǫð's arms' (*Gunnlaðar arma farmr*). The kenning for Óðinn is embedded in one for poetry, so that the context throws no light on the meaning of *hlítstyggr*.

Styggr 'shy of, shunning' is recorded in compounds with first elements meaning 'delay' (*bilstyggr*), 'flight' (*flóttstyggr, flugstyggr*) or 'guile / harm' (*læstyggr, meinstyggr*). The meaning of *hlít-* is more elusive.

(a) *Hlít* f. 'sufficiency' and *hlíta við* 'to suffice, do' suggest the meaning 'shunning (mere) sufficiency, trivial deeds', i. e. 'energetic, zealous' for *hlítstyggr*, and this finds support in the adj. *óhlítuligr* 'not trivial', hence 'great', applied to the battle of Áróss in O kík 1, 1.

(b) The verb *hlíta*, governing the dat., can mean 'to rely on'. *Hlítstyggr* could therefore mean 'shunning reliance (on others)', hence 'relying solely on himself', as in the adj. *einhlítr*, which occurs with this meaning in both prose and verse.

I have adopted interpretation (a), but (b) is an attractive alternative. It may well be that Arnórr intended a double meaning here.

11/8 davglinga hneitis 'subduer [lit. striker / wounder] of princes'. Haraldr.

Verse Twelve

Sources

Msk p. 273; Flat III 393: Msk(19r), Fl(818)
Hars(H-Hr) p. 417: H(75v), Hr(53v).

Context

In *Msk-Flat Hdr* 12 is quoted immediately after *Hdr* 10.
In *Hars(H-Hr)* an interlude separates *Hdr* 10 and *Hdr* 12, in which the English king Haraldr Guðinason (Harold, son of Godwine) comes to Tósti (Tostig), his own brother but Haraldr Sigurðarson's ally, with a peace offer which is rejected. The saga reports the common opinion (*mál manna*) that Tósti's proposal to return to the ships when confronted by the enemy had been the best. The author adds that the Norwegian king's excessive zeal (*ofrkapp*) — his refusal to act with caution lest it should be construed as cowardice — led to disaster. The verse is cited to confirm this.

Diplomatic and edited text

Olli ofravsn stillis	Olli ofrausn stillis
ormalatrs þ*at* er mattit	orma látrs þ*ví*'s máttit
stals istrongo eli	stáls í strǫngu éli
striþir elli biþa	stríðir elli bíða,
sa er alld*re*gi alldins	sá's aldrigi aldins
ota*m*s litvþr hra*m*ma	ótams lituðr hramma
vigs ivapna glyGvi	viggs í vápna glyggvi
varþrvnar sic sparþi.	varðrúnar sik sparði.

Prose order and translation

Ofrausn stillis olli þ*vi* í strǫngu éli stáls, 's stríðir orma látrs máttit bíða elli, sá lituðr hramma aldins, ótams varðrúnar viggs 's aldrigi sparði sik í vápna glyggvi.
The ruler's [Haraldr's] excess of pride caused this in the stern blizzard of steel, that the foe of the reptiles' lair [gold→(generous) ruler, Haraldr] could not live to see old age, that stainer of the claws of the old, untamed troll-wife's steed [wolf→warrior] who never spared himself in the wind-storm of weapons.

Apparatus

(1) stillis] still*ir* Hr **(2) þ*at*]** om. Fl, þ*ar* Hr **mattit]** mattud Fl, mattið H, Hr **(6) litvþr]** vítudr Fl, b*ru*dr Hr(?) **(7) glyGvi]** gleyse Fl.

Commentary

12/1 *ofravsn* 'excess of pride', lit. 'over-magnificence'. The word poses the same question as *ofermōd*, lit. 'over-courage' in the OE *Battle of Maldon* line 89: does it denote a heroic flaw or a heroic virtue? I take *ofrausn* to have a pejorative sense here, as it has in Sigv 11, 11, where Sigvatr is reproaching Magnús Óláfsson for destroying the dwellings of his subjects:

ofrausn es þat jǫfri	it is an excessive show of force in
innanlands at vinna.	the king to fight in his own realm.

Also in other contexts (including Sturl 4, 11) *ofrausn* is deplored or has unhappy consequences (see Fritzner, s. v., for prose examples).

The *ofrausn* which is said in *Hdr* 12 to have caused Haraldr's death could be specifically his presumption in marching from the ships without armour, his decision to tackle the superior English host (as suggested by the Context to the verse in *H-Hr*) or his reckless zeal once the fighting was under way; or the reference could be, more generally, to Haraldr's overweening ambition in invading England: cf. Þjóðólfr's comment (Þjóð A 4, 27) that it was *þarflaust* 'needlessly' that Haraldr called up troops for the expedition westwards.

12/2 *því* (em.) 'this, that'. The emendation of MS *þat*, first proposed by Sveinbjörn Egilsson (1828–46, VI, 387n.), is undoubtedly necessary since *olli* and other parts of *valda* are nowhere else recorded governing acc. rather than dat. V. l. *þar* makes no better sense.

12/6, 12/7 and 12/8 *litvþr hramma* ... *viggs* (em.) ... *varþrvnar* 'stainer of the claws of the troll-wife's steed [wolf→warrior]'. *Viggs* is a slight and well-justified emendation. MS *vigs* '(?)of battle' would not make sense, nor would it provide an exact consonantal rhyme with *glygg-*. *Varðrún* occurs, according to *LP*, only in the present context and in *Þul* IV c 5, a list of *trollkvenna heiti*.

Verse Thirteen

Sources

Hars(Hkr) ch. 92, p. 191: K(583r), F(53r), J2(298r), 47(27v)
Fsk ch. 70, p. 288: Fsk A(308)
Hars(H-Hr) p. 420: H(76r), Hr(54r)
Msk p. 278; Flat III 396: Msk(19v), Fl(819).

Context

Once Haraldr Sigurðarson has fallen, the English Haraldr Guðinason offers peace to Tósti and the surviving Norwegians, but all shout out against it, *ok sǫgðu svá, at fyrr skyldi hverr falla um þveran annan en þeir gengi til griða við enska menn, œpðu þá heróp. Tókst þá orrosta í annat sinn. Svá segir Arnórr jarlaskáld*: (*Hkr* version; others similar).

Diplomatic and edited text

Eigi varð ins yGia
avðligr k*onung*s davði
hlifþut hleNa svǿfi
hoddum roðn*ir* oddar
helldr kuro meiR ens millda
mildings eN gri*þ* vildi
um folc sn*ar*an fylki
falla liðs m*enn* all*ir*.

Eigi varð ens œgja
auðligr konungs dauði;
hlífðut hlenna sœfi
hoddum roðnir oddar.
Heldr køru meir ens milda
mildings an grið vildi
umb folksnaran fylki
falla liðsmenn allir.

Prose order and translation

Eigi varð dauði ens œgja konungs auðligr. Hoddum roðnir oddar hlífðut hlenna sœfi. Allir liðsmenn ens milda mildings køru meir heldr falla umb folksnaran fylki an vildi grið.
The death of the fearsome king was not unadorned. Reddened with treasure, the spear-points did not protect the slayer of robbers. All the liegemen of the gracious liege chose much rather to fall beside the battle-swift captain than wishing quarter.

Apparatus

(1) yGia] ygía F, H, ǫgia J2 (=ęgia 47, æghea A, øgia Msk, ægía Fl), yga Hr **(3) hlifþut]** hlif þót*t* F, hlifðv H **hleɴa]** hlǫn*n*a J2, se*n*na H **svǿfi]** svæfí F, sǫfe J2, 47 (=sæfi A, H, Hr, Fl, søfi Msk) **(4) hoddum]** hǫddu*m* J2 **roðn*ir*]** reknir A, H, Hr, Msk, Fl **oddar]** broddar A, Hr, Msk, Fl, brodda*n* H **(5) meiʀ ens]** om. Hr **meiʀ]** m*en*n meiʀ*r* H, m*enn* Fl **millda]** mǫra J2 (=mæra 47, A) **(7) um]** of J2, 47.

Commentary

13/2 *avðligr* 'unadorned'. There are at least four possible interpretations of *auðligr* in *eigi varð ... auðligr konungs dauði*, of which (a) has been chosen since it rests on the only other occurrence of the word.

(a) *Auðligr* is recorded in Sturl 4, 15: *vasa auðligr floti* 'the fleet was not bare [not lacking in fine trappings]'. The adj. here may well be a doublet of the *i*-mutated *eyðiligr* which appears in Þ loft 2, 5:

vasa eyðilig	not empty [fruitless] was
ǫrbeiðis fǫr.	the arrow-bidder's expedition.

These two contexts would suggest that Arnórr's *auðligr* derives from the adj. *auðr* 'empty, void, desolate', cf. *auðn* f. and *eyði* n. 'waste, desert'. If this is so, the skald may be saying that the king's death was not without splendour, i. e. that it was dignified by the presence of gilded weapons and by the loyalty of Haraldr's war-band, both mentioned in the strophe. Alternatively, his meaning could be ironic: the king's death was not void, unproductive, for many died with him (so Flo 1902, 272).

(b) An alternative translation of lines 1–2, 'Not fated, unnatural was the death of the fearsome king', is adopted in *Skjald* B. It is based on the possibility that *auðligr* is related to adj. *auðinn* 'determined by fate', *auðr* m. and *auðna* f. 'destiny, fate, fortune' (cf. *skapligr* 'suitable, fit', related to *skap* 'condition' and *skǫp* 'fate'). The skald could perhaps be hinting that the king's death was due not to an inexorable destiny but to his own stubborn thirst for glory. Compare Commentary to *Hdr* 12/1 *ofravsn*, including the citation from Þjóðólfr.

(c) *Auð-* could be connected with *auðr* m. 'riches, prosperity' as in *auðigr* 'wealthy' and many compounds, including Arnórr's *auðgjafi* 'wealth-giver', *Þdr* 20. *Eigi auðligr*, hence, could mean 'not profitable' (so *Fms* XII, 1837, 166), perhaps referring to death curtailing a relationship of patronage. To describe a king's death in this way would be paralleled in *Gráf* 11:

réðat oss til auðar ... Haralds dauði.	Haraldr's death did not bring me prosperity.

(d) *Auð-* could mean 'easy / easily' as in *auðkendr* 'easily recognised' or *auðfenginn* 'easily obtained'. *Eigi auðligr* would mean in this case 'not easy', implying by understatement that Haraldr's death came about in a bitter or painful way (so Kock, *NN* §1136). Compare *Beowulf* 2586, where the OE cognate *ēaðe* is used in an ironic understatement about the hero's death, beginning, *Ne wæs þæt ēðe [ēaðe] sīð* ... 'It was no easy journey ...'.

13/3 *hlifþut* 'did not protect'.

(a) The meaning of *oddar hlífðut hlenna sæfi* could be straightforwardly, 'the [Norwegians'] spear-points did not protect the slayer of robbers [Haraldr]', i. e. the row of spears afforded no defence.

(b) On the other hand, *hlífðut* could well be an ironic understatement: the [enemy] points did not spare him — indeed, they were the death of him. The ironic use of *hlífa* is matched in *Finnboga saga*, p. 35, where the hero, being presented with his wrestling opponent, is told, *þarftu ekki at hlífast við, því at ekki skal hann hlífa þér* 'you need not spare yourself, for he will not spare you'.

13/3 svófi (normalised *sæfi*) 'slayer'. Coupled with *hlenna*, *sæfir* forms a kenning for a just prince, with the literal sense 'putter-to-sleep of criminals'.

Verse Fourteen

Sources

Msk p. 280, Flat III 397: Msk(19v), Fl(820)
Hars(H-Hr) p. 422: H(76v), Hr(54r).

Context

Hdr 14, 15 and 16 are quoted as an appendix to the account of the battle of Stamford Bridge, although they do not expressly describe the fighting. The introduction reads, *Arnórr jarlaskáld kvað um þessa orrustu, sem nú var frásagt, at Haraldr konúngr háði síðarst, ok lið hans, í erfidrápu þeirri, er hann orti um Harald konúng* (*H-Hr* version; *Msk-Flat* similar, though Fl has *Arni* for *Arnórr*):

Diplomatic and edited text

Vitt for vavlsvngs heiti	Vítt fór vǫlsungs heiti;
varþ marglofaðr harþa	varð marglofaðr harða,
sa er scavt or niþ nytla	sá's skaut ór Nið nýtla
norþan h*er*scips borþi.	norðan herskips borði.

Prose order and translation

Vǫlsungs heiti fór vítt. Varð harða marglofaðr sá's skaut nýtla herskips borði norðan ór Nið.
The prince's great name went far and wide. He was most highly praised, who launched skilfully the warship's plank from the north out of the Nið.

Apparatus

(1) heiti] hæt*ti* Hr **(3) or]** ǫr H **Line (4)]** nord*r* hafskida bordv*m* Fl.

Commentary

14/1 *vavlsvngs* 'prince's'. Here Haraldr. Vǫlsungr was the grandfather of Sigurðr, and the name, in the sing. or pl., is also used to designate his descendants, including Sigurðr himself in *Sigsk* 13.

Lines 14/3 and 14/4. Arnórr's reference to sailing from the river Nið (Nid) may be intended specifically to recall Haraldr's building and launching of a new warship there c. 1062, before the battle of the Niz, as celebrated in Þjóð A 4, 18–21.

14/2 *marglofaðr* 'highly praised, much praised'. A *hap. leg.*, but cf. *margfríðr*, *margríkr* etc.

14/3 *nytla* 'skilfully, doughtily'. This adverb is also unique, but the adj. *nýtligr* 'profitable' occurs in Ótt 2, 3, applied to *fǫr* 'journey'. The notion common to both is 'useful'.

Verse Fifteen

Sources

Msk p. 281, Flat III 397: Msk(19v), Fl(820)
Hars(H-Hr) pp. 422–23: H(76v), Hr(54v).

Context

As for *Hdr* 14.
In *Msk-Flat* v. 15 is separated from v. 14 only by the words, *Oc enn q(vað) hann.*
H-Hr has a more wordy introduction: *Arnórr kallar sèr úvíst, at nökkurr annarr konúngr undir heimssólu muni með slíkri hugprýði ok hreysti barizt hafa, sem Haraldr konúngr. Arnórr kvað*:

Diplomatic and edited text

Myrct er hv*err* meira orkar
m*er* allz greppr ne serat
harþr e*r* iheimi orþiN
h*ra*fngreN*n*ir þrec iofno*m*
ert gat vslett hiarta
elivnfi*ms* vnd hi*m*ni
mest hef*ir* milldi*n*gr costot
miNi h*ve*rs gr*a*ms vinnor.

Myrkt's, hverr meira orkar,
mér, alls greppr né sérat,
— harðr's í heimi orðinn
hrafngrennir — þrek jǫfnum.
Ert gat óslætt hjarta
— eljunfims — und himni
mest — hefr mildingr kost*at*
minni hvers grams vinn*a*.

Prose order and translation

Myrkt's mér, alls greppr né sérat, hverr orkar meira, jǫfnum þrek. Harðr hrafngrennir's orðinn í heimi. Gat mest ert, óslætt hjarta und himni. Mildingr hefr kost*at* minni vinn*a* hveṛs eljunfims grams.

It is dark to me, for the skald cannot see it, who will achieve more, equal feats of strength. The stern raven-feeder is lost to the world. He was endowed with the boldest, keenest heart under heaven. The liege has put to the test the lesser deeds of every mettlesome lord.

Apparatus

(2) serat] sæi ath Fl **(3)** ***er* iheimi]** vr heim Hr **heimi]** hemí Fl **(4) þrec iofno*m*]** þræls iaf*n*an Fl **(5) ert]** aurtt Fl **vslett]** oskelf*r* Fl, vsliótt H, Hr **(6) elivn-]** æsi*n*- Fl **vnd]** uid Fl **(7) costot]** kaustud Fl, kostvð H, Hr **(8) g*ra*ms vinnor]** g*ra*mr vin*n*r Hr.

Commentary

15/2 *ne* 'not'. *Né* as the negative particle (distinct from the conjunction 'nor, and not') is well attested in ON poetry composed in *ljóðaháttr* or based on Gothic or German heroic subject matter, but extremely rare in *dróttkvætt* composition before 1200. Hans Kuhn found only four sure examples there, and suggests English influence in the present context, as in Ótt 3, 11 (1936, 432–33). Dietrich Hofmann also suspects Anglo-Danish influence here (1955, 78 and 104–105).

15/3 *er iheimi orþiN* 'is lost to the world / the world has lost'.

(a) The verb *verða* can have the sense 'to lose someone by death', e. g. Hfr 3, 28, *hef'k orðinn goðfǫður* (see Dronke 1969, 121, note to *Atlamál* 21/4). *Harðr hrafngrennir es í heimi orðinn* could thus mean 'the stern raven-feeder is lost to / in the world', with the implication, 'the world has lost / mankind is bereft of the raven-feeder'.

(b) *Harðr's í heimi orðinn hrafngrennir,* if taken in its more straightforward sense, 'the raven-feeder has become stern in the world', would appear a strange statement to make of one already dead, but in view of the use of the perfect tense in lines 7–8 the possibility must remain open that the skald intended this sense.

15/4 *þrec iofnom* 'equal feats of strength'.

(a) I take the phrase as dative object to *orkar* 'achieves', standing in apposition to *meira*, so that *Myrkt's mér, hverr orkar meira,* [*hverr orkar*] *jǫfnum þrek* means 'It is dark to me who will achieve more, [who will even achieve] equal feats of strength.'

(b) The alternative, adopted in *Skjald* B, of construing *þrek jǫfnum* as an adverbial phrase, yields poor sense: 'who will achieve more with strength equal to his'.

15/5 *ert* 'bold'. On this form, see Commentary to *Mdr* 18/7.

15/6 *elivnfims* 'mettlesome', lit. 'enduring-agile'. The adj. qualifies *grams* 'lord' in line 8. It also occurs in the 12th-century *Rst* 33.

15/7 *mest*, lit. 'most'. (a) The adverb could well qualify *hefr ... kostat* (em.) in the second helming, hence 'the liege has tested to the utmost the lesser deeds of every mettlesome lord'. But the first sentence, 'he was endowed with a bold, keen heart under heaven' would then be (for Arnórr) uncharacteristically tepid praise, for in such statements he and others usually add a superlative to the phrase meaning 'under heaven / on earth'. The 'highest under heaven' motif is discussed by Fidjestøl, 1982, 190–93.

(b) I therefore construe the superlative *mest* with *ert, óslætt* in line 5, hence 'boldest, keenest'. This is a rare construction, but not unparalleled: cf. *Skí* 32, where *meirr leiðr* performs the function of the comparative form *leiðari*, and Nygaard 1905, §64.

Lines 15/7 and 15/8, especially *kostat* (em.) and *vinna* (em.).

(a) *Hefr mildingr kostut minni hvers grams vinnur* is grammatically unsatisfactory, since *hefr* should here govern a p. p. either in the neut. sing. (*kostat*) or in the fem. pl. (*kostaðar*) in agreement with the object *vinnur*. Moreover, the verb *kosta* 'try, tempt', except where impersonal, always governs a gen. object. These two factors lead one to adopt the minor emendations of *costot* to *costat* (normalised *kostat*) and of *vinnor* to gen. pl. *vinna*, and to translate 'the generous prince has put to the test the lesser deeds of every lord'.

(b) Finnur Jónsson's analysis in *Skjald* B is unacceptable since it involves two alterations of the text, assumes an otherwise unrecorded noun *kostuðr*, and splits line 7 into four segments.

(c) Kock's interpretation (*NN* §841), 'the prince has for the most part found every lord's deeds to be the less', is based on the unwarranted assumption that *kosta* can govern the acc. and can mean 'find, prove'.

Verse Sixteen

Sources

Msk p. 281; Flat III 397: Msk(19v), Fl(820)
Hars(H-Hr) p. 423: H(76v), Hr(54v).

Context

The verse is cited together with *Hdr* 14 and 15, and linked to v. 15 by the briefest of phrases: *Oc eN*:

Diplomatic and edited text

Haralldr vissi sic hv*eriom*	Haraldr vissi sik hverjum
harþgeþr vnd miðgarþi	harðgeðr und Miðgarði
davgli*ngr* reþ t*il* davþa	— dǫglingr réð til dauða
dyrð slic*ri* gra*m* rikra.	dýrð slíkri — gram ríkra.
hefir afreka ens of*ra*	Hefr afreka e*n* øfra
ettstyrv*n*do*m* dyri	— ættstýrǫndum dýrri
hnig*rat* hilm*ir* freg*ri*	hnígrat hilmir frægri —
heilog folld til molldar.	heilǫg fold — til moldar.

Prose order and translation

Harðgeðr Haraldr vissi sik ríkra hverjum gram und Miðgarði. Dǫglingr réð slíkri dýrð til dauða. Heilǫg fold e*n* øfra hefr afreka. Hilmir dýrri, frægri ættstýrǫndum hnígrat til moldar.
Stern-spirited, Haraldr knew himself mightier than any lord under Miðgarðr. The monarch commanded such glory till death. The holy land on high has the hero. No prince rarer, more renowned than that ruler of men, will sink to the soil.

Apparatus

(4) rikra] rik*ar* Hr **(5) ofra]** aurva Fl **(6) ettstyrv*n*do*m*]** ætt- Fl, att- H, Hr, -styrend*um* Fl, -styrǫndv*m* H **dyri]** dyr*um* Fl, dyʀ*ri* H, Hr **(7) hnig*rat*]** hi*n*gad Fl, hní (or huí) g*ra*tt Hr.

Commentary

16/2 *miðgarþi*, lit. 'the middle enclosure'. In Norse cosmography, the home of men, which lies between Ásgarðr, the realm of the gods, and Niflheim, the dark abode of Hel or the dead.

16/5 *afreka* 'hero, champion'. The noun is a *hap. leg.*, but its meaning can be deduced from similar words in ON: see p. 77.

16/5 and 16/8 *en* (em.) *ofra* ... *heilog folld* 'the holy land on high'. There is no masc. or neut. noun which MSS *ens ofra* could qualify.

(a) Kock takes *heilǫg fold ens øfra* to mean 'the holy land of the High One [God]' (*NN* §842), but there is no evidence for *enn øfri* meaning God, and it seems unlikely that a mere comparative would be used of him. A slight emendation therefore seems necessary.

(b) Finnur Jónsson in *Skjald* B emends to *et øfra*, which he takes with *heilǫg fold* in the sense 'up there' (*deroppe*). Adverbial *et øfra* most usually means 'by the inland route' and is accompanied by a verb of motion and some indication of destination, but 'up there, in the air' does find some support, albeit slight: see Fritzner s. v. *efri*, sense 1a.

(c) (*Heilǫg fold) en øfra*, although not recorded elsewhere, would be a natural expression for 'heaven', and it is the solution adopted in my translation. *Fold* occurs in kennings for 'heaven': *éls fold*, lit. 'blizzard's land' (*Pl* 26) and *skýfold* 'cloud-land' (*Mgr* 43). *En øfra* is to some extent supported by Hallfreðr's use of *ofar lǫndum* to mean 'in heaven' in a similar context (Hfr 3, 29):

Kœns hafi Kristr enn hreini	May the spotless Christ have the
konungs ǫnd ofar lǫndum.	wise king's soul, above the world.

16/6 *ettstyrvndom* 'ruler of men', lit. 'rulers of generations / rulers among their kin'. This dat. pl. form is difficult to place in the syntax of the helming, but since it could make no sense with the first clause it must belong with the second, *dýrri, frægri hilmir hnígrat til moldar* 'no rarer prince, none more renowned, will sink to the soil'.

(a) I take *ættstýrǫndum* to be a grammatical pl. used for sing., just as Arnórr himself uses pl. *geima vals eyðendr*, lit. 'clearers of the ocean's steed [of the ship]' to designate King Magnús in *Hryn* 19/1 (see Commentary). In the present context the pl. form affords no metrical advantage, so that the motivation could only be Arnórr's desire to flatter. *Ættstýrǫndum*, interpreted thus, fits very well as a dat. of comparison referring to Haraldr in the sentence 'no rarer prince than that ruler of men ...'

(b) *Ættstýrǫndum* could alternatively be construed, as by Kock, as a loosely used dat. meaning 'among rulers of men' (*NN* §842).

There is no trace of such a usage among Nygaard's entries for the dat. case (1905, §§100–120), but since the use of the dat. is more flexible in skaldic verse than in prose, this interpretation may be considered possible.

16/6 *dyri* 'rarer, more excellent' and **16/7 *fregri*** 'more renowned'. These comparative adjs. must be grammatically parallel, qualifying *hilmir* 'prince', the only masc. sing. noun in the helming.[55]

Verse Seventeen

Sources

SnE p. 159: R(70), T(39r), U(68), W(81), 748(18v).

Context

Snorri quotes *Hdr* 17 among helmings which illustrate kennings for Christ, and introduces it, *Grickia konvngr, sem ArnoR q(vað):*

Diplomatic and edited text

Bǫn*ir* hefi ec fir*ir* beini	Bœnir hef'k fyr beini
b*ra*gnafallz v*ið* sniallan	bragna falls við snjallan
gr*i*kia vǫrð *ok* garþa	Girkja vǫrð ok Garða;
giof lavnac sv*a* iofri.	gjǫf launa'k svá jǫfri.

Prose order and translation

Hef'k bœnir fyr beini bragna falls við snjallan vǫrð Girkja ok Garða. Svá launa'k jǫfri gjǫf.
I raise up prayers for the dealer of warriors' deaths to the wise guardian of Greeks and of Garðar. So I repay the prince for his gift.

Apparatus

(1) Bǫn*ir*] Bǽn W, bæn*ar* 748 **fir*ir*]** f*ra* 748, om. U **(2) -fallz]** fiallz U **v*ið*]** v*m* U **(3) gr*i*kia]** girkia T, W, 748, grickia U **(4) lavnac (or -at)]** launat T **sv*a*]** s...

[55] *Dýrri* cannot qualify *afreka*, as Finnur Jónsson assumes in *Skjald* B, since the acc. sing. masc. form would be *dýrra*.

Commentary

17/3 *grikia* (normalised *Girkja*) *vǫrð ok garþa* ‘guardian of Greeks and of Garðar [N. W. Russia]’. It has been suggested that this interesting kenning for ‘God’ alludes to the fact that Haraldr was long at odds with the papacy, and followed an ecclesiastical policy which in some respects resembled that of Byzantium and Russia (Johnsen 1969, 50). Whether or not this is so, the kenning is appropriate since it mentions the very sphere where the young Haraldr distinguished himself (1035–45/46; see Bagge 1990).

The normalised spelling *Girk-* is based on the evidence of skaldic rhymes, including the contemporary *virk : Girkjum* (Stúfr 2).

The juxtaposition of *Garða*, normally a territorial name, with *Girkja* might suggest that the skald is here applying it to the inhabitants of Garðaríki (so Kuhn 1971, 15), a usage that might have arisen by analogy with Svíaríki : Svíar, Raumaríki : Raumar etc.

17/4 *giof lavnac sva iofri* ‘so I repay the prince for his gift’. According to tradition, it was after receiving the gift of a gold-chased spear that Arnórr promised Haraldr that he would compose an *erfidrápa* for him if he outlived him (p. 45 above).

Fragments

Fragment One

Sources

Orkns ch. 26, pp. 66-67: 702(78), Fl(526)

Context

Part-way through the sea-battle off Rauðabjǫrg between the jarls Þorfinnr and Rǫgnvaldr, Arnórr is put ashore along with the dead and wounded: *Hann gekk á land ok kvað vísu*:

Diplomatic and edited text

Drengr e*r* i gegn at gänga	Drengr’s í gegn at ganga
gott er fylgia vel drottni	— gótt’s fylgja vel dróttni;
olld leyn ek þui alldri	ǫld leyní’k því aldri —
ofvs syne Brvsa	ófúss syni Brúsa.

oss er ef *jarlar* þe*ss*er	Oss's, ef jarlar þessir
ognbradir til rädast	ógnbráðir til ráðask,
hǫ́rd mun vínraun v*er*da	— hǫrð mun vinraun verða —
vandligr kostur f*yr* hondum.	vandligr kostr fyr hǫndum.

Prose order and translation

Drengr's ófúss at ganga í gegn syni Brúsa. Leyni'k aldri ǫld því. Gótt's fylgja vel dróttni. Oss's vandligr kostr fyr hǫndum, ef þessir ógnbráðir jarlar ráðask til. Hǫrð vinraun mun verða.
This warrior is not keen to go against the son of Brúsi. I shall never conceal that from men. It is good to support one's lord well. I have a hard choice on my hands, if these battle-hasty jarls attack one another. A harsh ordeal of friendship will come about.

Apparatus

(1) Drengr] Dreíng Fl **(2) fylgia vel]** at fylgía Fl **(3) olld]** elld Fl **leyn ek]** leyníg Fl.

Commentary

1/1 ***Drengr*** '(Young) warrior'. Arnórr, following a recognised skaldic convention, here uses *drengr* to refer to himself in the third person. The semantics of *drengr* and *þegn* are examined in Jesch 1993.

1/2 ***fylgia vel*** 'support well'. The reading of Fl, *gótt's at fylgja dróttni*, also makes good sense.

1/3 ***olld leyn ek þui alldri*** 'I shall never conceal that from men'. The line is identical with l. 7 of Sigvatr's Lv 25.

1/4 ***syne Brvsa*** 'son of Brúsi [Sigurðarson]'. Rǫgnvaldr jarl, nephew of Þorfinnr.

Fragment Two

Source

Orkns ch. 56, p. 122n.: Fl(538).

Context

The verse is cited at the same curiously unsuitable point as *Þdr* 19 and *Þdr* 22 (see Context to *Þdr* 19).

Diplomatic and edited text

Em ek sitz yt*ar* hnektu	*Ek em*, síz ýtar hnekkðu
iarlla sætt e*r* ek vættí	jarla sætt, 's ek vætti,
jofn fenguz hræ hrofnu*m*	— jǫfn fengusk hræ hrǫfnum —
hægíu trudr at sægia	hegju tr*au*ðr at segja.
sleít f*yrir* eyiar vtan	Sleit fyr eyjar útan
allvalldr blaa tialldí	allvaldr bl*ǫ́u* tjaldi;
hafdi hrægsuol dufa	hafði hreggsvǫl dúfa
hrími fast v*m* líma.	hrími f*ezk* umb líma.

Prose order and translation

Ek em tr*au*ðr at segja hegju, síz ýtar hnekkðu sætt jarla, 's ek vætti. Jǫfn hræ fengusk hrǫfnum. Allvaldr sleit bl*ǫ́u* tjaldi fyr útan eyjar. Hreggsvǫl dúfa hafði f*ezk* hrími umb líma.

I am loath to speak of events, since men thwarted the truce between the jarls, as I foresaw. From both sides alike flesh was found for ravens. The all-ruler wore to shreds dark awnings out beyond the islands. The snow-cold billow had fastened itself in frost about the mast.

Commentary

2/1 *Ek em* (em.) 'I am'. The expected internal rhyme with *hnek-* is lacking, for MS *Em ek* would here probably contract to *Em'k*, and even if *ek* were syllabic it would be the second, weaker member of the metrically resolved pair *em ek* and hence unsuitable for carrying the internal rhyme. Emendation to *ek em* therefore seems justified, especially since the verse texts in Fl are generally of poor quality.

2/1 *ytar* 'men'. It seems likely that the men who — directly or indirectly — destroyed the peace between the jarls were Kalfr Árnason and his Norwegian followers who, according to *Orkns* ch. 25, stirred up discontent in Þorfinnr over Rǫgnvaldr's controlling two-thirds of the Isles.

2/3 *jofn fenguz hræ hrofnum* 'from both sides alike flesh was found for ravens'. As Björn M. Ólsen pointed out (1909, 299), the sentence cannot mean that an equal number of men were slain on both sides at Rauðabjǫrg, since Arnórr states in *Frag* 3 that one jarl's losses were much smaller.

2/4 *trauðr* (em.) 'loath'. MS *trudr* (?*trúðr* 'juggler') can have no meaning in this context.

Lines 2/5 to 2/8. The helming is difficult to interpret, and its second couplet is almost certainly corrupt. Its content — detailed seafaring description — contrasts so sharply with that of the first helming that one might suspect that the two originally belonged to separate strophes.

2/5 and 2/6 *sleít ... tialldí* 'wore to shreds awnings'.

(a) *Slíta* 'tear, break' usually governs an acc. object, but it is also used in the sense 'wear out' with a dat. object denoting some kind of clothing or footwear. This seems the best explanation of *sleit blǫ́u tjaldi* in the enigmatic lines 5-6. The *allvaldr* (probably Þorfinnr) perhaps 'wore to shreds dark awnings' by using them out in stormy seas, rather than returning to harbour, which is where the ship's *tjald* would be most regularly used. Arnórr praises Magnús góði in *Hryn* 16 for spending his time either out at sea or *und drifnu tjaldi* 'under spray-drenched awnings'.

(b) An attractive alternative would be to take *slíta tjǫldum* as a phrase synonymous with *bregða tjǫldum* 'strike tents / take down awnings' and related idioms. Clearing a ship of its awnings would be a pregnant action — a necessary preliminary to battle. But I know of no evidence that *slíta tjǫldum / tjaldi* was used in this sense.

(c) Björn M. Ólsen (1909, 299) suggested that *sætt* 'truce, peace' in line 2 is carried over into the second helming and understood as object to *allvaldr sleit* 'the all-ruler tore' in line 5, but this seems improbable, especially since there is no trace of such a linkage between the two helmings in any other strophe by Arnórr.

2/5 *eyiar* 'islands'. It is impossible to know whether the word is to be read as the common noun or as the place-name equivalent to Orkneyjar, as apparently in *Þdr* 22.

2/6 *blǫu* (em.) 'dark'. The metre requires a disyllabic form and the following *tjaldi* points to dat. sing. neut. *blǫ́u* as the case required (Sievers 1878, 515; Konráð Gíslason 1875-89, II 266).

2/7 and 2/8 *hafdi hrægsuol dufa* | *hrími fezk* (em.) 'the snow-cold billow had fastened itself in frost ...'. The nom. *hreggsvǫl dúfa* 'snow-cold billow' is subj. to *hafði* which, since it has no obj., must be an auxiliary verb, forming a pluperfect tense with a p. p.

(a) There is no p. p. in the helming as it stands but the emendation to *fezk*, i. e. *fest-sk* from *festa*, which I have adopted produces one. Alternatives are:

(b) Björn M. Ólsen suggested emending *hrími* to *hrímat* 'encrusted with frost' (1909, 301; also Finnbogi Guðmundsson, *Orkns* 1965, 122n.). This is plausible, and the verb *hríma* is known in the modern language (Blöndal, s. v.), but the only trace of it in ON is in the p. p. s *úhrímaðr* and *úhrímðr*, which mean 'not encrusted with soot' (Fritzner, s. v.).

(c) Kock (*NN* §835) emends *líma* to *límat* 'encrusted' and reads:

Hafði hreggsvǫl dúfa	The snow-cold billow had
hrími fast um límat.	encrusted [it] thickly with frost.

An objection to this is that the object of *hafði* ... *límat* must be understood as a repetition, now acc. sing., of *blǫ́u tjaldi* 'dark awnings' in line 6. An advantage is that *sleit* ... *tjaldi* in the previous clause would be explained.

2/8 *vm líma* 'about the mast'.

(a) Björn M. Ólsen (1909, 300-301) suggested that *límí*, which like *vǫndr* means 'rod, switch', is also synonymous with *vǫndr* in referring to coloured decoration on a sail, or here on the ship's awnings. He reads *líma blǫ́u tjaldi* 'the decoration of the dark awnings' together as obj. to 'the wave had thickly encrusted with frost ...'. But this assumes *tjaldi* to be a possessive dat., which is otherwise very unusual when the possessor is an inanimate object.[56]

(b) It seems more likely that Arnórr used *límí* in the sense 'mast' (so also Finnbogi Guðmundsson, *Orkns* 1965, 122n.), just as *vǫndr* can mean 'mast' and indeed is used by Arnórr in this sense in *Hryn*

[56] The parallels cited by Ólsen, in Nygaard 1905, §100 anm. 3, are not close.

4. The semantic development from 'rod, twig, plant' to 'mast' is also exemplified by the word *laukr* 'leek, upright plant, mast'. *Hreggsvǫl dúfa hafði fezk hrími um líma* 'the snow-cold billow had fastened itself in frost about the mast' is, in my view, the most satisfactory analysis that can be obtained without recourse to more drastic emendation. For the picture of rime fastening on a surface, compare the OE *Seafarer* line 32, *hrīm hrūsan bond* 'hoar-frost fettered the earth', and for frozen waves compare *Beowulf* 1133–34, *winter ȳðe belēac* | *īsgebinde* 'winter locked up the waves in a bond of ice'.

Fragment Three

Source

Orkns ch. 26, p. 69: Fl(526)

Context

The verse appears shortly after *Þdr* 20. Rǫgnvaldr's ships are attacked and cleared by Kalfr Árnason and his men. Seeing that, the Norwegians sent by King Magnús to support Rǫgnvaldr flee, leaving very few craft with the jarl. This, the writer remarks before quoting the verse, was the turning point.

Diplomatic and edited text

<table>
<tr><td>Gramr munde sa gȯmlu
gunn bradr und síg lade
hann fek myklu mínna
mann spioll koma óllu
ef j lendra endils
ættstafr hafa knœttí
uellti herr um hiallta
hialm þrotta lid drotíns.</td><td>Gramr myndi sá gǫmlu
gunnbráðr und sik láði
— hann fekk miklu minna
mannspjall — koma ǫllu,
ef ílendra Endils
ættstafr hafa knætti
— vélti herr of Hjalta —
hjalm-Þrótta lið — dróttin.</td></tr>
</table>

Prose order and translation

Sá gunnbráðr gramr myndi koma ǫllu gǫmlu láði und sik — hann fekk miklu minna mannspj*a*ll — ef ættstafr Endils knætti hafa lið ílendra hjalm-Þrótta. Herr vélti of Hjalta drótti*n*.
That battle-hasty lord would have brought all of the ancient land under his sway — he had much the less loss of men — if he, the staff of Endill's strain, could have had the support of the helmet-Óðinns

[warriors], re-granted their land. The troop betrayed the Shetlanders' liege.

Commentary

3/1 *Gramr* 'lord', **3/5-6 *endils* | *ættstafr*** 'staff of Endill's strain' and **3/7-8 *hiallta ... dróttin* (em.)** 'Shetlanders' liege'. These three expressions for a ruler must all refer to the same man, and this must be Rǫgnvaldr Brúsason, unless the traditions about the battle of Rauðabjǫrg in *Orkns* ch. 26 are completely awry. According to the saga, Rǫgnvaldr almost prevails, but is eventually defeated because of the defection of his allies and, far from tightening his hold over Orcadian territory, is obliged to take refuge in Norway. These points, apart from the flight to Norway, are all matched in the verse.

Endill is a legendary sea-king, here standing for princes, or seafaring princes, in general.

The necessary emendation of MS *drotins* to *dróttin* was proposed by Björn M. Ólsen (1909, 297-98).

3/1 and 3/2 *gǫmlu ... lade* 'ancient ... land'. Presumably the reference is to Orkney and Shetland.

3/3 and 3/4 *mínna* | *mannspjall* (em.) 'the less loss of men'. *Minna* is acc. sing. neut., but MS *mann spioll* (*mannspjǫll*) acc. pl. neut. *Minna mannspjall* is perhaps a better emendation than *minni mannspjǫll*, for a scribe could well have altered *spjall* to *spjǫll* in order to secure what he considered a perfect rhyme with *ǫllu*, although a rhyme of *a* : *ǫ* would have been acceptable.

3/5 and 3/8 *j lendra ... hialm þrotta* 'helmet-Óðinns [warriors], re-granted their land'. The identity of the *ílendir* warriors who treacherously failed to support Rǫgnvaldr is disputed.

(a) Finnbogi Guðmundsson suggests that *ílendr* can refer to a man who has been outlawed but has regained his right to live in the land, and cites from *Egils saga* ch. 56, p. 156 in support of this (*Orkns* 1965, 70n. and xxxiv). If *ílendr* does have this sense in *Frag* 3, it describes exactly the position of Kalfr Árnason as described in *Orkns* chs 25-26: King Magnús promises him that he can repossess his estates in Norway, if he supports Rǫgnvaldr against his friend Þorfinnr. When the battle begins Kalfr at first holds aloof but eventually responds to the egging of Þorfinnr and enters the conflict on his side. This marks the turning point in the battle. The allusions in the present verse become entirely comprehensible if it is assumed that Kalfr and his men are meant. There are, however, other possibilities.

(b) The most usual meaning of *ílendr* is 'settled, resident in the land' (e. g. *Flat* II 24 and 374; *Fms* VI 254). Some scholars, presumably taking this as a starting-point, have interpreted *ílendr* as meaning 'native' (for which the usual term is *innlendr*) and hence have understood the *ílendir* warriors of *Frag* 3 to be islanders who betrayed Rǫgnvaldr.[57] But although the men of Orkney and Shetland were obliged to side either with Rǫgnvaldr or Þorfinnr at Rauðabjǫrg, there is no implication in Arnórr's poetry or in *Orkns* that they were treacherous.

(c) *Ílendr* can mean 'arrived in the land', as when Knútr, newly arrived in Denmark, is described thus in Sigv 10, 9. The Norwegian crews (a separate band from Kalfr and his men) whom King Magnús sent to support Rǫgnvaldr were *ílendir* in this sense; but although they eventually fled from the battle, they were scarcely guilty of treachery against Rǫgnvaldr.

Fragment Four

Source

SnE(Svb. Eg.) p. 234: 743(73)[58]

Context

The helming is cited in the *Laufás-Edda*, in a section headed *Í gulls heitum*. It illustrates the kenning *bekks eldr*.

[57] So Finnur Jónsson in *Skjald* B and Björn M. Ólsen, 1909, 298. Ólsen specifically mentions the Shetland islanders. Dietrich Hofmann (1955, 103) also interprets *ílendr* in the sense 'native', which he suggests may be influenced by OE *inlende*.

[58] The helming is also preserved in GKS 2368 4o (*Laufás-Edda*), printed in *SnE* (Faulkes 1979) p. 348, but the text is poorer.

Diplomatic and edited text

Beks lä elldr *og* axla	Bekks lá eldr ok axla
ulflids daun*um* midli	ulfliðs Dǫnum miðli;
eg sa armraud þ*ack*a	ek sá armhrauð þakka
eitt skanunga hanum.	eitt Skǫ́nunga hǫ́num.

Prose order and translation

Bekks eldr lá miðli ulfliðs ok axla Dǫnum. Ek sá Skǫ́nunga þakka hǫ́num eitt armhrauð.
Fire of the stream [gold] was set between the wrist and shoulders of the Danes. I saw men of Skáney thank him for an arm-ring.

Commentary

4/1 and 4/2 *og axla* | *ulflids* 'the wrist and the shoulders'. Pl. *axla* and sing. *ulfliðs* are a rather ill-assorted pair. Possibly *ulfliðs* was chosen in preference to *-liða* for metrical reasons.

4/2 *daunum* 'of the Danes'. *Dǫnum* appears to belong, as a possessive dat. (Nygaard 1905, §100 anm. 3), with *ulfliðs ok axla*, indicating those on whose arms gold was set. Who these Danes were cannot be known with certainty, but *Skáldatal* lists Arnórr among the poets who composed in honour of Knútr inn ríki, so that the helming may well praise Knútr's generosity to his retainers.[59]

4/3 *armraud* (normalised *armhrauð*) 'arm-ring'. The compound apparently belongs with *eitt*, and so must be neut., and the context suggests that it must mean 'arm-ring', cf. *armbaugr* in *Lok* 13. Finnur Jónsson emends to *armband (Skjald* B and 1934, 47). The MS spelling *raud* could, however, represent *-hrauð*, cf. ON *hrjóða* and OE *hrēodan* 'adorn', both recorded solely or mainly as p. p. s. Kock (*NN* §843) assumes *armhrauð* to be cognate with OE *earm(h)rēad* 'arm-ornament' which occurs in *Beowulf* 1194:

wunden gold,	gold forged into rings,
... earmhrēade twā.	two arm-ornaments.

[59] Finnur Jónsson (*Skjald* B and 1934, 47) proposes emendations, especially of *daun̄* to *grami*, which are too drastic to be acceptable.

The OE word is fem. and the postulated ON one neut., but the two genders commonly interchange, and the correspondence of phonetic form, of meaning and even of context (the giving of a princely gift) makes this an attractive solution.

4/4 ***skanunga*** 'men of Skáney'. This is best taken as acc. pl., object to *sá* 'saw' and subject to *þakka* 'thank'. Skáney (Skåne) was a Danish province in the 11th century, and the *Skǫnungar* are doubtless the *Danir* of line 2; but it remains obscure why several men should thank 'him' (*hǫ́num*) for the gift of a single arm-ring (*armhrauð ... eitt*).

Fragment Five

Sources

SnE p. 184: R(79), T(43v), U(74), 748(21r), 748II(9r), 757(6v).

Context

Snorri is discussing poetic terms for rulers, and cites Arnórr's verse to illustrate the use of *siklingr*.

Diplomatic and edited text

Sikl*in*ga venr sneckivr	Siklinga venr snekkjur
síalvtar konr vti	sælútar konr úti;
h*ann* litar h*er*skip iNa*n*	hann litar herskip innan
h*ra*fns goð er þ*at* bloþi.	— hrafns góð es þat — blóði.

Prose order and translation

Siklinga konr venr snekkjur sælútar úti. Hann litar herskip innan blóði. Þat es hrafns góð.
The scion of princes trains longships to plunge in the sea far out. He stains warships within with blood. That is the raven's gain.

Apparatus

(1) Sikl*in*ga] Siglinga U, Siklinka 748 **sneckivr]** sneckio U, s... 757 **(2) síalvtar konr]** styr*ir* lvtar gramr konr U, siolíot*ar* konr 748II, ...luta... 757 **(3) iNa*n*]** in... 757 **(4) h*ra*fns]** hrafn 757.

Commentary

5/1 and 5/2 *Siklinga ... konr* 'Scion of princes'. On the possibility that this could be Haraldr Sigurðarson harðráði, see p. 35.

5/1 and 5/2 *venr sneckivr* | *síalvtar ... vti* 'trains longships to plunge in the sea far out'. The adj. *sæ- / sjálútar*, a *hap. leg.* whose literal meaning is 'sea-bending', is here construed as being predicative. It could alternatively be attributive (so *Skjald* B).

Fragment Six

Source

SnE p. 114: R(51), T(28v), U(57), W(56), 757(5r).

Context

The couplet is one of five fragments by Arnórr which Snorri uses, among others, to illustrate kennings for 'sky / heaven'.

Diplomatic and edited text

Hialpþv dyʀ k*onvn*gr dyrv*m*	Hjalp, dýrr konungr, dýrum,
dags grvnd*ar* h*er*mv*n*di.	dags grundar, Hermundi.

Prose order and translation

Dýrr konungr dags grundar, hjalp dýrum Hermundi.
Excellent king of day's land (sky→God), save the excellent Hermundr.

Apparatus

(1) **Hialpþv]** hialp U.

Commentary

6/2 *hermvndi.* On the identity of Hermundr, see p. 46.

Fragment Seven

Sources

SnE p. 115: R(51), T(29r), U(57), W(56), 757(5r).

Context

The helming appears later in the same passage as *Frag* 6 above.

Diplomatic and edited text

Mikáll vegr þ*at* er misg*er*t þick*ir*
manvitz froðr *ok* allt it goþa
tiGgi skiptir siþ*an* seGiv*m*
solar hialms adæmi stoli.

Mikjáll vegr þat's misgǫrt þykkir,
mannvitsfróðr, ok allt et góða;
tyggi skiptir síðan seggjum
sólar hjalms á dœmistóli.

Prose order and translation

Mikjáll vegr, mannvitsfróðr, þat's þykkir misgǫrt ok allt et góða. Tyggi sólar hjalms skiptir síðan seggjum á dœmistóli.
Michael weighs, ripe with wisdom, what seems wrongly done, and all that is good. The sovereign of the sun's helmet [cloud/sky→God] then separates out men at his judgement-seat.

Apparatus

(1) Mikáll] Mikiall T, Mikill e*r* or Mikils e*r* W.

Commentary

The helming. On the Christian content of this striking half-strophe, see Edwards 1982-83, 40-41; on its background, see p. 35 above.

7/2 *manvitz froðr* 'ripe with wisdom'. The compound is unique, but cf. *manvitsfrægr* in the 13th-century *Níkdr* 2.

Fragment Eight

Sources

SnE p. 168: R(73), T(40v), U(78), 748(20r), 748II(6v), 757(6r).

Context

The helming is quoted, with the words, *Ylgr* (*ulfr*, 748II), *sem Arnorr q(vað)*, among skaldic fragments that illustrate *heiti* for 'wolf'.

Diplomatic and edited text

Svalg at*t*bogi ylgiar	Svalg áttbogi ylgjar
ogoðr en var bloþi	ógóðr — en varð blóði
græþ*ir* græɴ at ravþv*m*	grœðir grœnn at rauðum —
g*ra*ndavknv*m* na blandiɴ.	grandauknum ná — blandinn.

Prose order and translation

Ógóðr áttbogi ylgjar svalg grandauknum ná, en grœnn grœðir, blóði blandinn, varð at rauðum.
The evil scion of the she-wolf [wolf] swallowed the sand-swollen corpse, and the green surge, mingled with blood, turned to red.

Apparatus

Lines (1) to (4) -knvm] virtually illeg. 757 **(1) at*t*-]** at- T, 748II **(2) var]** v*a*rð 748 **(3) græþ*ir*]** gradug*r* 748II **at]** af 748II **(4) g*ra*ndavknvm]** brandvoxnv*m* U, g*ra*nauknu*m* 748II.

Commentary

8/2 and 8/3 *varð* (v. l.) ... *at ravþvm* 'turned to red': I have found no trace of *vesa at* with dat. adj. in the sense 'turn to, become', but *verða at*, represented in the minority reading *varð*, is attested in this usage, as in *Þdr* 22/1 *Bjǫrt verðr sól at svartri.*

8/4 *grandavknvm* 'sand-swollen'. The compound *grandaukinn*, which qualifies *nár* 'corpse', is unique, and its meaning elusive.

(a) *Grand* could mean 'sand' (so Kock, *NN* §2522), cf. ON *grand* 'grain' as in *ekki grand* 'not a grain, not a morsel', *grandi* n. 'strip of beach' and Nynorsk *grande* 'sand-bank, sand-bar'. *Grandaukinn* 'increased, swollen with *grand*' could then imply that the dead men had taken in sand and become bloated by it. Bodies are described as lying on sand in Sigv 2, 7, Þjóð A 1, 16 and Bǫlv 4. Þórðr Særeksson (Þ Sær 2, 4) says that the slain warriors lying in the shallows had sand in their mouths, and Arnórr himself pictures 'sandy corpses' being driven ashore in *Mdr* 15. The interpretation 'swollen with sand' is thus supported by other contexts, as well as being in harmony with Arnórr's taste for graphic and grotesque description. An alternative solution is possible:

(b) *Grand* commonly has the meaning 'harm, injury'. Compounded with *aukinn*, it could have the sense 'swollen with wounds' (cf. *bolginn nár* 'swollen corpse', *Jómsv* 31) or perhaps 'increased [in number] by injury / disaster'.

Fragment Nine

Source

SnE (Svb. Eg.) p. 238: 743(100)[60]

Context

The couplet occurs in the same brief work as *Frag* 4, the heading this time being *Steinn heitir*. The lines are introduced, *Klifs bein, sem Arnórr kvað*:

Diplomatic and edited text

Kreisti knutu lostna	Kreisti knútu lostna
klifsbein fiǫru steini	klifs bein fjǫrusteini

Prose order and translation

(?) Klifs bein kreisti knútu, lostna fjǫrusteini.
(?) The bone of the cliff [rock] pressed hard on the joint-bone, battered by beach-shingle.

Commentary

9/2 *klifsbein* 'bone of the cliff'. Probably, as Magnús Ólafsson takes it to be in *Laufás-Edda*, a kenning for stone or rock (cf. *foldar bein*, *Yt* 26, and *Hlǫðynjar bein*, Vǫlust 2, both 'bone of the earth').

[60] The text of MS GKS 2358 4o of *Laufás-Edda* differs only orthographically; it is printed in *SnE* (Faulkes 1979) p. 399.

Fragment Ten

Sources

Third GrT pp. 14 and 65: W(101), 748(9v), 757(2v).

Context

Arnórr's line occurs in the chapter *De Barbarismo* as an example of alteration of letters: *vm stafa skipti verðr barbarismus. sem aʀnorr qvað.* It is followed by the explanation that *hvern* replaces *hvert* in order to complete the internal rhyme, *til þess at kveðandi halldiz* (v. l. *hendingar halldiz i drottkveðvm hetti*).

Diplomatic and edited text

Svm*ar* hv*er*n frekv*m* erní	Sumar hvern frekum erni

Translation

Every summer to the greedy eagle.

Commentary

The line: see p. 36.

Svmar hvern 'Every summer'. The form *hvern* is established by the *aðalhending* with *erni*, and in its turn proves the masc. gender of *sumar(r)*. Elsewhere in ON the word 'summer' is clearly neut., or else the context does not show its gender, and Arnórr's is the best evidence for the original masc. gender (which survives in other Gmc. languages, and is occasionally attested in later Icelandic, see Blöndal s. v.).

frekvm erní 'to the greedy eagle'. This is probably the indirect object in a statement to the effect that the hero feeds, or gladdens, the eagle each summer (by making carrion out of his enemies).

Fragment Eleven

Source

SnE (Svb. Eg.) p. 234: 743(72).

Context

This most exiguous of fragments appears in the *Laufás-Edda*.[61] Apart from 'Arnórr j[arla]sk[áld]' which follows the two words, they are isolated from the main body of the text. They have been inserted — apparently as a later addition — under the heading, *Gras: gras skal kenna hár eðr hadd, ull, reifi, fiðr, fax jarðarinnar.*

Diplomatic text and translation

folldar fiðr	plumage of the earth [grass]

Commentary

The rarity of this kenning is noted on p. 69. It encapsulates a parallel between macrocosm and microcosm (grass grows on the earth like plumage on a bird) akin to the kinds of 'argument from design' which, according to the Prologue to *Snorra Edda*, led post-diluvian man to apprehend the possibility of a single omnipotent Ruler. (Snorri's thinking here resembles twelfth-century Platonism: see Clunies Ross 1987, 14 for summary and references).

[61] Its preservation in various MSS of *Laufás-Edda* is noted by Jón Helgason (1966, 179) and Faulkes (*SnE* (Faulkes 1979) pp. 272n. and 345n.

Appendix A
Tables showing Distribution of Arnórr's Verses in MSS

Notes

(i) * indicates a single helming, preserved in isolation, in Tables 1–5. In Tables 6–8 almost all quotations are of single helmings, so that these are unmarked, while ˣ indicates a single couplet.
(ii) 'a' or 'b' (e. g. 5a, 5b) indicates a helming which, although preserved alone in the MS in question, belongs to a strophe preserved complete in one or more other MS.
(iii) Bracketed numbers indicate that a verse is lacking from a text which otherwise corresponds with that of other MSS of the same recension.

Table 1: MSS of ÓLÁFS SAGA HELGA (SEP.)

	2, 325V, Bb, Th,	73 (Rdr 1, Mdr 10 copied from 325V)	75a	321 (copy of 75a)	325VI	61	68	4	75b	325VII	Flat (see also Tables 3 & 4)
Rdr	1*	1*		1*		1*		1*		1*	
Hryn	5,6a‿7*	5,6a‿7*			5,6a‿7*	5,6a‿7*		5,6a‿7*		5,6a‿7*	
Mdr	1,2,10	1,2,10		10	1,2,10	1,2,10		1,2		1,2	
Þdr	5b,21*	5b,21*	5b,21*	5b,21*	21*	5b,(21*)	5b,(21*)	5b,21*		(5b),21*	21*
Hdr	5	5	5	5	5	5	5	5	5	5	5

Table 2: MSS of HEIMSKRINGLA

	K	F	39	J2	47	325XI2e	325XI2f
Hryn (all in Magns)	5,6,10,11,12,14	5,6,10,11,12,14	5,6,10,11,12,14	5,6,10,11,12,14	5,6,10,11,12,14		
Mdr (all in Magns)	1,2,5,6,9*,10, 12,14*,17,18	1,2,5,6,9*,10,12, (14*),17,18	1,2,5,6,9*,10,12, 14*,17,18	1,2,5,6,9*,10,12, 14*,17,18	1,2,5,6,9*,10,12, 14*,17,18		
Þdr (both in Ólsh)	5b,21*					5b	
Hdr (v.5 in Ólsh, rest in Hars)	1*,4,5,11,13	1*,4,11,13	1*,4	1*,4,(5),11,13	1*,4,11,13		5

Table 3: MSS of MORKINSKINNA, FAGRSKINNA, HULDA-HROKKINSKINNA and FLATEYJARBÓK.

	Msk	Fsk A	Fsk B	H	Hr	Flat (see also Tables 1 & 4)
Hryn (3 and 16–19 in Hars, rest in Magns)	3,16,17,18*,19*			3,9,10,13,14,15,16, 17,18*,19	3,4,5,6a‿7*,8*,9, 10,13,14,15,16,17, 18*,19*	3,8*,9,10,13,15, 16,17,18*,19*
Mdr (in Magns)		1,4,5,10a,(10b), 12,(14*,16*), 17a,18a,(18b)	4,5,10,12,14*, 16*,17a,18	5,6,7,8,9*(twice), 10,11,12,13,14*,15, 16*,17,18	1,2,3,4,5,6,7,8, 9*(twice),10,11,12, 13,14*,15,16*,17, 18	1,2,4,5,6,7,8,9*, 10,11,12a,13,14*, 15,16*,17,18
Þdr (in Ólskyrra)	3*	3*	3*	3*	3*	
Hdr (in Hars)	2,3,4,7*,8,9,10,11, 12,13,14*,15,16	11;13		1*,2,3,4,7*,8,9,10, 11,12,13,14*,15,16	1*,2,3,4,7*,8,9,10, 11,12,13,14*,15,16	2,3,4,7*,8,9,10,11, 12,13,14*,15,16

Table 4: MSS of ORKNEYINGA SAGA

	325III	702	LR	332	48m	Flat (see also Tables 1 & 3)
Rdr	1*	1*		1*	(words from) 1*	1*
Þdr	2*,11	2*,5,7,9,10,11, 13,16,17,18,20	(words from) 11,13,17	2*,5,6,7,8,9,10,11	2*,(words from) 5,6,7,8,10,11	(2*),5,6,7,8,9,10, 11,13,14*,16,17, 19(twice),20,21*, 22(twice)
Frag		1				2,3

Table 5: MSS of KNÝTLINGA SAGA

	20d	873	1005
Hryn	14b,15	14b, 15	14b, (15)

Note: ^{x} indicates a single couplet; all other citations in Tables 6–8 are of helmings.

Table 6: MSS of SNORRA EDDA (SKÁLDSKAPARMÁL)

	R,T	U	W	748	748II	757
Rdr	2,3^{x}	2,3^{x}	2,3^{x}			3^{x}
Hryn	12a,20^{x}	20^{x}		20^{x}	12a,20^{x}	12a,20^{x}
Mdr	2b,12b,17b,19	12b,17b,19	12b,17b,19	2b,12b,17b	2b,12b,17b	19
Þdr	1,4,12,15(twice), 16b,22a,23	1,4,15 (om. 2nd time),16b,22a,23	1,4,15,16b,22a,23	15	12,15	1,5/1–2,12,22a
Hdr	6,17	6,17	17	6,17	6	6
Frags	5,6^{x},7,8	5,6^{x},7,8	6^{x},7	5,8	5,8	5,6^{x},7,8

Table 7: DERIVATIVES of SKÁLDSKAPARMÁL

(a) ORMS EDDU-BROT

MS W only: Hryn 6a and 16a

(b) LAUFÁS-EDDA

MS 743: Frags 4, 9[x], 11 (half-line)

Table 8: MSS of GRAMMATICAL TREATISES

(a) THIRD GRAMMATICAL TREATISE

	W	748	757
Hryn	1[x],2[x],3^{3-4}	1,2,3^{3-4}	
Frag	10 (one line)	10 (one line)	10 (one line)

(b) FOURTH GRAMMATICAL TREATISE

MS W only: Hryn 3^{3-4}

Note: [x] indicates a single couplet; all other citations in Tables 6–8 are of helmings.

Appendix B
Comparison of the Present Edition with that of Finnur Jónsson in *Skjaldedigtning* A

1. Substitution of MSS

(a) For verses from *Orkns*, MS 702 and not 762 is used in the present edition (see p. 18).
(b) For *Knýtls*, MS 1005 and not 41 is used (see p. 20 and n. 16).

2. Additions

(a) 321, a MS of *Ólsh(Sep)*, supplies a text of *Rdr* 1 and *Mdr* 10 where 75a is defective.
(b) 75b, a MS of *Ólsh(Sep)*, contains *Hdr* 5.
(c) The *Hkr* MS J2 contains *Hdr* 1 and 4.
(d) The *Orkns* MS 702 contains *Rdr* 1 and *Þdr* 2, 8 and 16 (it is used as the main MS for *Þdr* 16).
(e) Two further sources contain readings (mainly single words and phrases) from the verses in *Orkns*: the marginalia in AM 48 fol., and *Specimen Lexici Runici*.
(f) The *SnE* MS 757 contains two lines from *Þdr* 5.
(g) The *SnE* MS 743 contains a half-line by Arnórr which I designate *Frag* 11.

3. Omissions

(a) The texts of *Rdr* 1 and *Mdr* 10 in the *Ólsh(Sep)* MS 73 are omitted (see p. 7).
(b) MS 757, in its text of the *Third GrT*, does not contain *Hryn* 3, 3–4 as indicated in *Skjald*.

4. Change of main MS

In *Rdr* 1, the *Ólsh(Sep)* MS 2, not 61, has the better text and has been selected as the main MS. Further changes of priority are:

Verse(s)	Main MS	
Hryn 1 and 2	748	not W
Hryn 7	2	not 4
Mdr 4	Fsk B	not Hr
Þdr 19	Fl col. 529	not Fl col. 538
Þdr 20	Fl	not 702/762.

5. Change of recension

In the lists of works and MSS which precede the verses in *Skjald* A, MSS are sometimes assigned to an inappropriate group. For *Rdr* 1, for example, Finnur Jónsson includes MS Fl with MSS of *Ólsh(Sep)*, although its text corresponds more closely with that of *Orkns* MSS at that point. Similarly:

Verse(s)	MS	MS affiliation	
Mdr 1, 2 & 10	Fl	stands alone	not with Ólsh(Sep) MSS
Þdr 5	Fl	with Orkns MSS	not Ólsh(Sep)
Hryn 5 & 6	Hr	stands alone	not with Hkr MSS
Hdr 6	325XI 2f	with Hkr MSS	not Ólsh(Sep)

Throughout Part Two of this book Msk and Fl are, because of their close textual affinity in the relevant parts, treated as representatives of a separate recension, as are H and Hr. In *Skjald* A all four MSS are grouped together.

6. Change of sigla

(a) MS Hulda (AM 66 fol.) is designated H throughout, whereas it is designated variously H and 66 in *Skjald*.

(b) MS Morkinskinna is designated Msk, in parallel with Fsk (Fagrskinna), not Mk.
(c) The *SnE* MS designated '1eβ' in *Skjald* A is now (in this book, and generally) designated 748II.

7. Change of reading

My own reading of the MSS has produced a text and apparatus somewhat different from those printed in *Skjald*. The differences are too numerous to list individually, but mainly trivial, without implications for the interpretation of the text. Indeed, at least as far as Arnórr's output is concerned, tribute may be paid to the accuracy of Finnur Jónsson's reading, especially bearing in mind the prodigious volume of his scholarly output.

8. Changes in the editorial reconstruction of the poems

Note: The titles used are the same, except that the poem I designate *Haraldsdrápa* is headed 'Erfidrápa om kong Harald hårdråde' in *Skjald*, and my heading *Fragments* corresponds approximately to 'Vers af ubestemmelige digte, samt én lausavísa'. The numbers below all refer to verses, whether these are whole strophes, half strophes or smaller fragments.

Poem	**This edition**	**Skjald**
Rǫgnvaldsdrápa	1–3	1–3
Hrynhenda	1	2
	2	3
	3	1
	4–20	4–20
Magnússdrápa	1–12	1–12
	13	14
	14	13
	15–19	15–19

Þorfinnsdrápa	1	4
	2	2
	3	1
	4	3
	5–11	5–11
	12	18
	13	12
	14	14
	15	13
	16	15
	17	16
	18	17
	19	20
	20	21
	21	23
	22	24
	23	25
Haraldsdrápa	1–4	1–4
	5	7
	6	8
	7	9
	8	10
	9	11
	10	12
	11	14
	12	13
	13	15
	14	16
	15	17
	16	18
	17	19
Fragments	1	Frag 5
	2	Þdr 19
	3	Þdr 22
	4	Frag 3
	5	Frag 2
	6	Herm. Ill
	7	Frag 1

8	Hdr 5
9	Frag 4
10	Hdr 6
11	—

Appendix C
Careers of Arnórr's Heroes: Chronological and Bibliographical List

THE WRITTEN evidence for the events commemorated in Arnórr's poetry is often fragmentary and of doubtful reliability, and the following outline must be read as no more than a distillation of the more plausible of the traditional accounts. Dates, many of them approximate, are deduced from the sources named and / or obtained from the *Icelandic Annals*.

For all of the four main heroes, descriptions and more or less continuous biography can be found in the Norse-Icelandic kings' sagas, to which references are given at the beginning of each entry, while skaldic poetry and prose works in languages other than ON throw light on individual episodes. Full references to the works cited can be found in the Bibliography, section B. As throughout the book, references to all skaldic verse except Arnórr's are abbreviated according to the conventions of *LP*, and follow the ordering of *Skjald.*

Some further detail about specific events celebrated by Arnórr is given in the Contexts and Commentaries to individual verses in Part Two, and in Edwards 1979, ch. IV. Further information and bibliography on matters of Norwegian history is available in recent histories such as Andersen 1977 and Helle 1991, and on the historical and archaeological context of the Orkney earldom in Cruden 1958, Morris 1985 and Crawford 1987.

For the location of places named below, see Maps I (Scandinavia and the Baltic) and II (The British Isles).

I Magnús Óláfsson

Sources for Magnús's career as a whole: *Ágrip* chs 26 and 33–39; *Flat* III 252–88 and 306–34, *Fsk* chs 34 and 44–54; *Knýtls* chs 21–22, *Magns(H-Hr)* passim, *Magns(Hkr)* passim, and *Msk* pp. 3–14 and 87–141.

c.1025	Magnús born, son of King Óláfr Haraldsson of Norway (inn digri, later inn helgi) and his mistress Álfhildr.
1030	Defeat and death of Óláfr at Stiklastaðir (Stiklestad).
1030–35	Magnús fostered by King Jarizleifr (Jaroslav) in Holmgarðr (Novgorod).
1035	Collected by former enemies of Óláfr helgi; they journey to Norway, arriving in the Þrœndalǫg (Trøndelag); usurper Sveinn Alfífuson retreats to Denmark, purposing revenge. Arn *Hryn* 4–8 and *Mdr* 2–4, Bj H 6, Sigv 9,1–3 and 11,6, Þjóð A 1,1–3.
1035–c.1046	Rule in Norway. Bj H 7, Kolgr, Sigv *Bersǫglisvísur*, Þ flekk 1–2.
1036	Death of Sveinn Alfífuson in Denmark.
1042	On death of Anglo-Danish monarch Hǫrða-Knútr in England, Magnús sails a large fleet to Denmark; establishes laws and taxes, appoints deputies and returns to Norway. Arn *Hryn* 9–10 and *Mdr* 5–7, Þjóð A 1,4, Adam of Bremen, *Gesta* p. 135, Roskilde *Chronicon* I 377, Saxo, *Gesta* p. 300, Theodoricus, *Historia* pp. 45–46.
1043	In response to Wendish incursions on N. Germany and Denmark, Magnús attacks the Wends in their base of Jóm (Jumne, now Wollin). Arn *Hryn* 11–12 and *Mdr* 8, Adam of Bremen scholion 56(57), p. 137.
1043	Battle against vikings at Ré (Rügen). Arn *Mdr* 9.
1043	Victory against Wends on Hlýrskógsheiðr (Lyrskovsheden). Defeated Wends slain, after long pursuit, at Skotborg river (Kongeå). Arn *Hryn* 13 and *Mdr* 10–11, E Sk 6,28–30, O kík 1,1, Þ fagr 1, Þjóð A 1,6–7, Adam of Bremen p. 137, Saxo pp. 302–303, Theodoricus p. 49.
1043–44	War against Sveinn Ulfsson (Sven Estridsson) after he, as Magnús's Anglo-Danish viceroy in Denmark, had attempted to gain power for himself. Battle off Áróss (Århus), followed by harrying of Selund (Zealand) and Fjón (Fyn). Respite, Sveinn gathering more troops. Arn *Hryn* 14 (summary); Þjóð A 1,5 (Sveinn's oaths); O kík 1,1, Þjóð A 1,8–16 and 4,1

	(battle off Áróss); Þjóð A 1,17–20 and 4,1–3 (subsequent ravaging).
c.1045	Major victory against Sveinn Ulfsson off Helganes (Helgenæs), followed by harrying of Skáney (Skåne), Falstr (Falster) and Fjón. Arn *Hryn* 15 and *Mdr* 12–15, Þjóð A 1,21–23, Sven Aggesøn, *Historie* p. 88 (battle off Helganes); Arn *Mdr* 16–18, Þjóð A 1,24 and 4,4–8 (subsequent ravaging).
1046	Magnús dies, not in battle; possibly in Denmark. (Divergent traditions about final stages in war against Sveinn and about date and cause of Magnús's death; see p. 46, n. 8 on date.) O kík 1–2, Þjóð A 4,10, *Anglo-Saxon Chronicle* 'D', s. a. 1048 in error for 1047, Saxo p. 303, William of Malmesbury, *De Gestis* II 318.

II Haraldr Sigurðarson

Sources for Haraldr's career as a whole: *Ágrip* chs 30, 32 and 38–41; *Flat* III 288–400; *Fsk* chs 34 and 50–72; *Hars(H-Hr)* passim; *Hars(Hkr)* passim; *Knýtls* chs 22–25; *Msk* pp. 70–284.

c.1015	Born, son of Sigurðr sýr Halfdanarson and Ásta Guðbrandsdóttir (mother also of Óláfr Haraldsson helgi).
1030	Fights at Stiklastaðir, afterwards making his way to Miklagarðr (Constantinople).
1030–c.1045	Exploits in Byzantium and the Mediterranean with the Varangian guard. Bǫlv 1–6, H harð 1–7 and 15, Illugi 1–4, Stúfr 2–4, Valg 1–4, Þ Skegg, Þjóð A 2,1 and 3,1–7 and 4,13, Adam of Bremen pp. 153–54, Saxo pp. 305–6, Theodoricus p. 57.
c.1045	Return to Scandinavia. Briefly harries Denmark with Sveinn Ulfsson then re-aligns with half-nephew Magnús Óláfsson, receiving a half-share in the rule of Norway in exchange for gold and military support. Bǫlv 7, Valg 5–9, Þjóð A 3,9 and 4,9, Adam of Bremen p. 154, Theodoricus pp. 50–51 and 54–55.
c.1047–64	Intermittent war against Sveinn Ulfsson over Denmark, including raid on Fjón and, in 1062, major

	victory by the Niz (Nissan) estuary. Peace signed 1064. Arn *Hdr* 1 (Fjón); Bǫlv 7, Stúfr 5, Adam of Bremen p. 154 (on duration of the war); *ASC* 'D' s. a. 1049=1048 (Sveinn's appeal for English support); Arn *Hdr* 2–4, Steinn *Nizarvísur* and *Ulfsflokkr*, Stúfr 7, Þjóð A 3,12–17, 4,18–21 and 24, Saxo pp. 306–7 (battle by the Niz).
c.1065	Ravaging of Upplǫnd to punish the withholding of taxes (and possibly defection to Hákon jarl Ívarsson). Arn *Hdr* 5–6, Þjóð A 3,18–21.
1066	On death of Edward the Confessor, invasion of England in alliance with Tósti (Tostig, son of Godwine and brother of Harold). Victory at Fulford and surrender of nearby York, closely followed by battle at Stamford Bridge against Harold and an army marched from S. England. Defeat and death. Anon XI Drömme- og varselsvers 8–11, Ulfr, Þjóð A 4,27, Adam of Bremen scholion 83(84), p. 196, *ASC* 'D' and 'E' s. a. 1066, Saxo p. 308, William of Malmesbury I 281 (the expedition launched); Arn *Hdr* 7–9, *Haraldsstikki*, Steinn 3,2–4; *ASC* 'C' and 'D' s. a. 1066, Florence of Worcester, *Chronicon* I 226, Symeon of Durham, *Opera* II 180, Arn *Hdr* 10–13, H harð 18–19, Stúfr 8, Þjóð A 4,26–27, Adam of Bremen p. 196, *ASC* 'C', 'D' and 'E' s. a. 1066, Orderic Vitalis, *Ecclesiastical History* II 168, Symeon of Durham II 180–81, Theodoricus p. 57, *Vita Ædwardi Regis* p. 58, William of Malmesbury I 281 (battle of Stamford Bridge).

III Þorfinnr Sigurðarson

Sources for Þorfinnr's career as a whole: *Orkns* chs 13–32, *Ólsh(Sep)* pp. 230–55 and 638–39, and *Ólsh(Hkr)* chs 96–103 (largely representing one and the same literary tradition).

c.1009	Born, son of Sigurðr Hlǫðvisson inn digri and a daughter (name unrecorded) of 'Melkómr Skotakonungr'.

c.1020	Half-brother Einarr killed, probably because of territorial rivalry, by Þorkell, henchman of Þorfinnr.
c.1021	Half-brother Brúsi, by swearing allegiance to King Óláfr Haraldsson, gains an additional third share of Orcadian territory. Þorfinnr also swears allegiance. Ótt 2,9 (possible allusion). Later Þorfinnr takes the two-thirds share in exchange for organising defence.
c.1023–?	War against 'Karl Hundason' and the Scots, possibly over revenues of Caithness. Includes victories at sea off Dýrnes (Deerness), and on land at Torfnes (Tarbatness). Arn *Þdr* 6–11.
1030x1035	Brúsi dies. His son Rǫgnvaldr gains two-thirds share of territory by guaranteeing military support for Þorfinnr.
1036–44	Raiding expeditions (often in company with Rǫgnvaldr) to Vatnsfjǫrðr (Loch Vatten), mainland Scotland, England and possibly Wales. Arn *Þdr* 13–14 and 16–18.
c.1044	Friction between Þorfinnr and Rǫgnvaldr, perhaps inflamed by Kalfr Árnason, culminates in battle at Rauðabjǫrg (?Roberry). Kalfr, although bribed by King Magnús Óláfsson to support Rǫgnvaldr, intervenes on Þorfinnr's side. Arn *Þdr* 19–20 and *Frags* 1–3, Bj H 8.
c.1045	Rǫgnvaldr killed by Þorfinnr's liegeman Þorkell Ámundason.
c.1045–c.1065	Last years either more pious and peaceful or not adequately covered by sources. Possibly led viking attack on England in 1058. Adam of Bremen pp. 224 and 271 (appointment of bishop for Orkneys), *Annals of Tigernach* p. 399 (Orcadian attack on England).

IV Rǫgnvaldr Brúsason

Sources for whole career: *Orkns* chs 19, 21–22 and 24–30; *Ólsh(Sep)* pp. 253–54, 499, 580–81 and 638–39; *Ólsh(Hkr)* chs 100, 102 and 180; *Hars(Hkr)* ch. 1.

c.1011	Born, son of Brúsi Sigurðarson; mother unknown.
c.1021–35	Mostly abroad, firstly with King Óláfr Haraldsson, left by father as pledge of good faith. Fights at Stiklastaðir in 1030, then travels to Holmgarðr (Novgorod), where fights for Jarizleifr (Jaroslav). Arn *Rdr* 1, *Legendary Saga* chs 78 and 79.
1035	Journeys to Norway with young Magnús Óláfsson. Returns to Orkneys at news of father's death.
1036–c.1044	Joins Þorfinnr jarl Sigurðarson in raiding expeditions.
c.1044	Battle of Rauðabjǫrg (see above). Rǫgnvaldr flees to Norway.
c.1045	Returned, Rǫgnvaldr and Þorfinnr both attempt unsuccessfully to 'burn in' the other. Rǫgnvaldr escapes the fire but is killed by Þorfinnr's man Þorkell.

Bibliography, with Abbreviations

Note: Throughout the Bibliography, the form 'Copenhagen' is used for that city, however spelt in the work in question; 'Oslo' represents that city under its modern name or the former Christiania / Kristiania.

A. Manuscripts, Facsimiles and Editions

1. Abbreviations of manuscript collections and text series

AM: Den Arnamagnæanske Samling, Copenhagen
CCI: Corpus Codicorum Islandicorum Medii Ævi, Copenhagen
EIMF: Early Icelandic Manuscripts in Facsimile, Copenhagen
GKS: Den gamle kongelige samling, Copenhagen
Holm: Kungliga biblioteket, Stockholm
IF: Íslenzk Fornrit
Lbs: Handritasafn Landsbókasafns Íslands, Reykjavík
NKS: Den nye kongelige samling, Copenhagen.
STUAGNL: Samfund til Udgivelse af Gammel Nordisk Litteratur, Copenhagen
UB: Universitetsbiblioteket i Oslo.

2. Manuscripts, with facsimiles and editions

MSS are grouped according to content and ordered as in Chapter One. 'Printed' implies that the text of a MS is printed in its entirety, whether normalised or in its original orthography; 'used' implies that readings from a MS are incorporated into the critical apparatus of the edition(s) concerned.

The Separate Óláfs saga helga of Snorri Sturluson (Ólsh(Sep))

By far the most thorough discussion of the MSS is by O. A. Johnsen and Jón Helgason in their edition, *Saga Óláfs konungs hins helga*, Oslo 1941 (here denoted *Ólsh(Sep)*). They provide details of the genealogy, history and content of each MS, and in certain cases orthographic features are noted. The saga was previously edited in *Fornmanna sögur* (*Fms*) IV–V, Copenhagen, 1829–30, and by P. A. Munch and C. R. Unger, *Saga Ólafs konungs ens helga*, Oslo 1853.

2: Holm Perg. 4o nr 2. Facsimile: *Óláfs saga ens Helga: MS Perg 4to No. 2 in the Royal Library of Stockholm*, with introduction by Jón Helgason, CCI 15 (1942). Printed as main MS in *Ólsh(Sep)*. Described in *Ólsh(Sep)* pp. 879-90.
75a: AM 75a fol. Used in *Ólsh(Sep)*. Described in *Ólsh(Sep)* pp. 898-910.
321: AM 321 4o. Used in *Ólsh(Sep)*, where 75 defective. Described in *Ólsh(Sep)* pp. 916-21.
325V: AM 325V 4o. Used in *Ólsh(Sep)*. Described in *Ólsh(Sep)* pp. 922-28.
325VI: AM 325VI 4o. Used in *Ólsh(Sep)*. Described in *Ólsh(Sep)* pp. 928-34.
73: AM 73a fol. Described in *Ólsh(Sep)* pp. 979-80.
61: AM 61 fol. Facsimile: *The Great Sagas of Olaf Tryggvason and Olaf the Saint: AM 61 fol.*, ed. Ólafur Halldórsson, EIMF 14 (1982). Printed in *Fms* I-V (1825-30). Described in *Ólsh(Sep)* pp. 970-78.
68: AM 68 fol. Specimen facsimile: CCI 7 (1935) 43. Used in *Ólsh(Sep)*. Described in *Ólsh(Sep)* pp. 890-98.
4: Holm Perg. 4o nr 4. Used in *Ólsh(Sep)*. Described in *Ólsh(Sep)* pp. 941-52.
75b: AM 75b fol. Used in *Ólsh(Sep)*. Described in *Ólsh(Sep)* pp. 910-11.
325VII: AM 325VII 4o. Used in *Ólsh(Sep)*. Described in *Ólsh(Sep)* pp. 934-40.
Bb: Bergsbók, Holm Perg. fol. nr 1. Facsimile: *Bergsbók*, ed. Gustaf Lindblad, EIMF 5 (1963). Described in *Ólsh(Sep)* pp. 1005-25.
Flat: see below.
Th: Tómasskinna, GKS 1008 fol. Facsimile: *Thomasskinna*, ed. Agnete Loth, EIMF 6 (1964). Described in *Ólsh(Sep)* pp. 1034-42.

Heimskringla (Hkr)

The principal editions are by Finnur Jónsson (I-IV, vol. IV being notes to the verses, Copenhagen 1893-1901) and Bjarni Aðalbjarnarson

(I-III, ÍF 26-28, 1941-51). References below are to both editions, abbreviated FJ and BA. The introduction to BA III contains brief descriptions of the MSS and their history, but no information on graphic or orthographic features. FJ I includes some brief comment on these. The edition by Bergljót S. Kristjánsdóttir and others (I–III, vol. III being a most useful *Lykilbók*, Reykjavík, 1991) has a text in modernised spelling.

Kringla (vellum fragment containing no verses by Arnórr): Facsimile: *Kringla og Jöfraskinna i Fototypisk Gengivelse*, ed. Finnur Jónsson, STUAGNL 24, 1895.

K: AM (35), 36 and 63 fol. Printed in FJ and BA. Described in FJ I i-v; BA III lxxxiii-lxxxvi.

F: Codex Frisianus or Fríssbók, AM 45 fol. Facsimile: *Codex Frisianus*, with introduction by Halldór Hermannsson, CCI 4 (1932). Printed in *Codex Frisianus*, ed. C. R. Unger, Oslo 1871. Used in FJ and BA.

39: AM 39 fol. Used in FJ and BA. Described in FJ I xv-xviii; BA III lxxxvi-lxxxvii.

J1: AM 37 fol. (vellum fragment Jöfraskinna, containing no verses by Arnórr): Facsimile as for Kringla, above.

J2: AM 38 fol. Used in FJ and BA. Described in FJ I xxvi-xxvii; BA lxxxviii-lxxxix.

47: Eirspennill, AM 47 fol. Printed in *Eirspennill*, ed. Finnur Jónsson, Oslo 1913-16. Used in BA. Described in BA III xc.

325XI 2e: AM 325XI 4o, fragment 2e. Used in *Ólsh(Sep)*. Described in FJ I xxix-xxx and *Ólsh(Sep)* pp. 959-60.

325XI 2f: AM 325XI 4o, fragment 2f. Used in *Ólsh(Sep)*. Described in FJ I xxix-xxx and *Ólsh(Sep)* p. 955.

Morkinskinna, GKS 1009 fol. (Msk)

Facsimile: *Morkinskinna*, with introduction by Jón Helgason, CCI 6 (1934). Printed in *Morkinskinna*, ed. Finnur Jónsson, STUAGNL 53 (1928-32), and described there, pp. i-viii.

Fagrskinna (Fsk)

The classic editions are by Finnur Jónsson, STUAGNL 30 (1902-3) and Bjarni Einarsson, *Ágrip af Nóregskonunga sǫgum. Fagrskinna -*

Nóregs konunga tal, ÍF 29 (1984). These are abbreviated below as FJ*Fsk* and BE.

Fagrskinna (vellum fragment containing no verse by Arnórr). Facsimile: *Palæografisk Atlas*, ed. Kr. Kålund, Copenhagen 1905, nos. 23-24.

Fsk A: AM 303 4o. Used in FJ*Fsk* and BE, and printed as main text where Fsk B defective. Described in FJ*Fsk* p. ix.

Fsk B: UB 371 fol. Printed in FJ*Fsk* and BE. Described in FJ*Fsk* pp. v-vi and xv-xxvii (on orthography of the 'B' class).

Hulda-Hrokkinskinna (H-Hr)

The compilation is edited in *Fms* VI (1831). An edition of Hulda, with variant readings from Hrokkinskinna, is in preparation by Jonna Louis-Jensen for Editiones Arnamagnæanæ. A full investigation of the manuscripts and their textual relations is found in Louis-Jensen 1977 (see Bibliography B for full reference).

H: Hulda, AM 66 fol. Facsimile: *Hulda, Sagas of the Kings of Norway 1035-1177*, ed. Jonna Louis-Jensen, EIMF 8 (1968). Printed in *Fms* VI (1831). Briefly described in *Fms* VI, 1-2.

Hr: Hrokkinskinna, GKS 1010 fol. Used in *Fms* VI, and briefly described there, pp. 2-3.

Flateyjarbók, GKS 1005 fol. (Flat/Fl)

Finnur Jónsson 1927, 139-90 reviews the content and history of the codex (see Bibliography B). The only full edition is *Flateyjarbók* [ed. C. R. Unger and Guðbrandur Vigfússon], I-III, Oslo 1860-68. Brief notes on orthography are given in III xx-xxii, and the MS is more fully described in *Ólsh(Sep)* pp. 1026–34. Facsimile: *Flateyjarbók*, with introduction by Finnur Jónsson, CCI 1 (1930).

Orkneyinga saga (Orkns)

The most recent edition of the saga is by Finnbogi Guðmundsson in ÍF 34 (1965). It contains notes on the history and content of the MSS, but not on orthography. Sigurður Nordal's edition (STUAGNL 40, 1913-16), from which Finnbogi has drawn some of his material, does supply details of the orthography and abbreviations of the vellum MSS. The two editions are designated FG and SN below.

325III: AM 325IIIb 4o. Printed in SN and FG. Described in SN pp. xxxi-xxxiii; FG p. cix.

702: Isl. R. 702 4o (Universitetsbiblioteket, Uppsala). Brief extracts printed in SN and FG; otherwise used in critical apparatus to both. Described in SN pp. xxii-xxvii; FG pp. cx-cxi; also *Ólsh(Sep)* pp. 946-47.

LR: Specimen Lexici Runici. Published by Ole Worm, Copenhagen 1650. Used in SN and FG. Described in SN pp. xxvii-xxxi; FG pp. cxi-cxii; also Faulkes 1964, esp. 92-94 on the extracts from *Orkns* (see Bibliography B).

332: AM 332 4o. Printed in SN and FG, where 325III defective; otherwise used in critical apparatus. Described in SN p. xxxiv; FG p. cxxii (briefly); see also Ólafur Halldórsson 1964, esp. 131-32 (full reference in Bibliography B).

48m: Marginal notes to AM 48 fol. Used sporadically in FG. Described in FG p. cxxii; also Ólafur Halldórsson 1964, 132 and 145-50.

Fl(at): Flateyjarbók. For general works, see above. *Orkns* text printed in SN and FG where other MSS defective; otherwise used in critical apparatus.

Knýtlinga saga (Knýtls)

The standard editions are by C. af Petersens and E. Olson in *Sǫgur Danakonunga*, STUAGNL 46 (1919-25, abbreviated P-O below) and by Bjarni Guðnason in *Danakonunga sǫgur*, ÍF 35 (1982).

20d: AM 20d fol. Used in P-O and described pp. xv-xvi there.

873: NKS 873 4o. Used in P-O and described pp. xi-xii.

1005: AM 1005 4o. Used in both editions and described in P-O pp. xxii-xxiii.

Snorra Edda (SnE)

The accounts of the *SnE* MSS given in the Arnamagnæan edition (Copenhagen 1848-87, abbreviated *Arnamagn* below) have still not in general been superseded; they are summarised in Finnur Jónsson's edition of 1931 (FJ below), which is the only one to include a complete critical apparatus. Anthony Faulkes' edition, *Snorri Sturluson, Edda: Prologue and Gylfaginning* (Oxford 1982, reprinted London 1988), and *Snorri Sturluson, Edda: Háttatal* (Oxford 1991) is based on the R text, with selective use of variants from other MSS. A complementary edition of *Skáldskaparmál* is in press.

R: Codex Regius, GKS 2367 4o. Facsimile: *Codex Regius of the Younger Edda*, with introduction by Elias Wessén, CCI 14 (1940). Printed in *Arnamagn* I and FJ. Described in *Arnamagn* III ii–xlv; FJ pp. iv–v.

T: Codex Trajectinus, 1374 Cod. MS, Universitetsbibliotheek, Utrecht. Facsimile: *Codex Trajectinus: The Utrecht manuscript of the Prose Edda*, ed. Anthony Faulkes, EIMF 15, Copenhagen 1985; also specimen facsimile in *Palæografisk Atlas*, ed. Kr. Kålund, Ny Serie (Copenhagen 1907), no. 36. Printed in *De Codex Trajectinus van de Snorra Edda*, ed. W. van Eeden, Leiden 1913, and (in modernised spelling) in *Snorra Edda*, ed Árni Björnsson, Reykjavík 1975. Used in FJ. Described by van Eeden, pp. i–vi (on provenance and history); FJ pp. v–vii.

U: De la Gardie 11, Universitetsbiblioteket, Uppsala. Facsimile: *Snorre Sturlasons Edda, Uppsala-Handskriften DG 11*, ed. Anders Grape, Stockholm 1962; vol. II, containing introduction, transcript, palæographic commentary and word index, with G. Kallstenius and O. Thorell, Uppsala 1977. Printed in *Arnamagn* II 250–396. Used elsewhere in *Arnamagn* and in FJ.

W: Codex Wormianus, AM 242 fol. Facsimile: *Codex Wormianus*, with introduction by Sigurður Nordal, CCI 2 (1931). Printed in *Edda Snorra Sturlusonar, Codex Wormianus*, ed. Finnur Jónsson, Copenhagen 1924. The fragment known as 'Orms Eddu-Brot' is printed in *Arnamagn* III 495–500. Used in *Arnamagn* and FJ. Described in *Arnamagn* III xlv–lxi and FJ pp. vii–x.

743: AM 743 4o. Printed in *Edda Snorra Sturlusonar*, ed. Sveinbjörn Egilsson (Reykjavík 1848–49), pp. 232–39, and in *Two Versions of Snorra Edda from the 17th Century. I Edda Magnúsar Ólafssonar (Laufás Edda)*, ed. Anthony Faulkes, Stofnun Árna Magnússonar á Íslandi, Rit 13 (Reykjavík 1979).

748: AM 748 Ib 4o. Facsimile: *Fragments of the Elder and the Younger Edda*, with introduction by Elias Wessén, CCI 17 (1945). Printed in *Arnamagn* II 397–494. Used in *Arnamagn* and FJ. Described in *Arnamagn* III lxix–lxxii; FJ xiv–xvi.

748II: AM 748II 4o. Facsimile: as for 748. Printed in *Arnamagn* II 573–627. Used in *Arnamagn* and FJ. Described in *Arnamagn* III lxxii–lxxvi; FJ pp. xiii–xiv.

757: AM 757a 4o. Printed in *Arnamagn* II 501–72. Used in *Arnamagn* and FJ. Described in *Arnamagn* III lxxvi–lxxviii; FJ pp. xvi–xvii.

Third and Fourth Grammatical Treatises (Third GrT and Fourth GrT)

The three relevant MSS - W, which contains both treatises, and 748 and 757, which contain only *Third GrT* - have been noted above. They are discussed with particular reference to the treatises in Björn M. Ólsen's *Den tredje og fjærde grammatiske Afhandling*, STUAGNL 12, 1884, and page references are to that edition.

W: Printed by Ólsen; described pp. lii–liv.
748: Printed by Ólsen; described pp. xlvii–lii.
757: Used by Ólsen; described pp. lv–lviii.

B. Printed Works: Primary Sources and Secondary Literature

Notes: Abbreviations of frequently cited periodicals, series, lexicons and other volumes are incorporated.
Individual skaldic poems are not listed separately, but can be traced through the index of *Skjaldedigtning*.
Primary sources, except for Latin chronicles of known authorship, are listed with title first; dates given for these refer to the edition, not the original composition. Secondary literature, and editions cited for their introductory or editorial material rather than text, are listed with author or editor first.
Icelandic authors, except those with hereditary surnames, are entered under their first names. Accents and diacritics (e.g. á, ä or å) are ignored in the alphabetisation.

Adam of Bremen. *Gesta Hammaburgensis Ecclesiæ Pontificum.* 191 7. Ed. Bernhard Schmeidler, 3rd edition. Monumenta Germaniae Historica, Scriptores Rerum Germanicarum, 2. Hannover and Leipzig.
Aggesøn, Sven: see Sven Aggesøn

Ágrip af Nóregskonunga sǫgum. Fagrskinna - Nóregs konunga Tal. 1984. Ed. Bjarni Einarsson. ÍF 29.

Åkerblom, Axel. 1917. 'Bruket av historiskt presens i den tidigare isländska skaldediktningen'. *ANF* 33, 293–314.

Alexander Jóhannesson: see *IEW*.

Alexanders saga. 1925. Ed. Finnur Jónsson. Copenhagen.

Amory, Frederic. 1982. 'Towards a Grammatical Classification of Kennings as Compounds'. *ANF* 97, 67–80.

Amory, Frederic. 1988. 'Kennings, Referentiality, and Metaphors'. *ANF* 103, 87–101.

Andersen, Per Sveaas. 1977. *Samlingen av Norge og kristningen av landet*. Bergen etc.

Anderson, Joseph (ed.). 1873. *The Orkneyinga saga*, trans. Jon A. Hjaltalin and Gilbert Goudie, Edinburgh.

Anderson, S. R. 1973. '*U*-umlaut and Skaldic Verse'. In *A Festschrift for Morris Halle*. New York; 3–12.

ANF: *Arkiv för nordisk filologi*. Lund.

Anglia: *Anglia, Zeitschrift für englische Philologie*. Tübingen.

[*Anglo-Saxon Chronicle*:] 1892–99. *Two of the Saxon Chronicles Parallel*, ed. John Earle and Charles Plummer, I–II. Oxford.

Annals of Tigernach (Fourth Fragment). 1896. Ed. and trans. Whitley Stokes in *Revue Celtique* 17, 337–420.

ANO: *Aarbøger for nordisk Oldkyndighed og Historie*. Copenhagen.

APS: *Acta Philologica Scandinavica*. Copenhagen.

ASC: see *Anglo-Saxon Chronicle*.

ASPR: *The Anglo-Saxon Poetic Records* I–VI. 1931–53. Ed. George Philip Krapp and Elliott van Kirk Dobbie. New York.

BA: Bibliotheca Arnamagnæana. Copenhagen.

Bagge, Sverre. 1990. 'Harald Hardråde i Bysants'. In *Hellas og Norge. Kontakt, Komparasjon, Kontrast*. Ed. Øivind Anderson and Tomas Hägg. Bergen; 169–92.

Bandamanna saga. 1981. Ed. Hallvard Magerøy. London and Oslo.

Battle of Maldon, The: in *ASPR* VI, 1942, 7–16.

Beiträge: *Beiträge zur Geschichte der deutschen Sprache und Literatur*, ed. Hermann Paul and Wilhelm Braune, Halle.

Benecke, G. F., W. Müller and F. Zarncke. 1854–61. *Mittelhochdeutsches Wörterbuch*. Leipzig.

Beowulf: in *ASPR* IV, 1953, 3–98.

Bernström, J. 1962. 'Hökar'. *KLNM* 7, 294–300.

Bjarnar saga Hítdœlakappa. 1938. Ed. Sigurður Nordal and Guðni Jónsson in *Borgfirðinga sǫgur*, ÍF 3, 109–211.

Bjarni Aðalbjarnarson. 1936. *Om de norske kongers sagaer*. Skrifter utgitt av det Norske Videnskaps-Akademie i Oslo, II. Historisk-Filosofisk Klasse, 1936, no. 4 (published 1937).

Bjarni Aðalbjarnarson: see also *Heimskringla*.

Bjarni Einarsson. 1974. 'On the rôle of the verse in saga-literature'. *Mediaeval Scandinavia* 7, 118-25.

Bjarni Einarsson: see also *Ágrip* / *Fagrskinna*.

Bjarni Guðnason: see *Danakonunga sǫgur*.

Björn Halldórsson. 1814. *Lexicon Islandico-Latino-Danicum*. Copenhagen.

Blake, N. F. (transl. and ed.). 1962. *Jómsvíkinga saga / The Saga of the Jomsvikings*. London.

Blöndal: Sigfús Blöndal. 1920-24. *Islandsk-dansk Ordbog*. Reykjavík. Supplement, 1963, by Halldór Halldórsson and Jakob Benediktsson, Reykjavík.

Borgfirðinga sǫgur. 1938. Ed. Sigurður Nordal and Guðni Jónsson. ÍF 3.

Brodeur, A. G. 1952. 'The Meaning of Snorri's Categories'. *University of California Publications in Modern Philology* 36. Berkeley etc; 129-48.

Brøgger, A. W. and H. Shetelig. 1950. *Vikingeskipene*. Oslo.

Brooks, F. W. 1956. *The Battle of Stamford Bridge*. East Yorkshire Local History Series 6. York.

Bugge, Alexander. 1914. 'Arnor Jarlaskald og det første Kvad om Helge Hundingsbane'. *Edda* 1, 350-80.

Bull, Edvard. 1927. 'Håkon Ivarssons saga'. *Edda*, 33-44.

Cawley, F. S. 1926-27. 'A Note on Two Fragments of Arnórr Jarlaskáld'. *SS* 9, 13-17.

Celander, H. 1906. 'Om dateringen av judövergången ð > d i fornisländskan och fornnorskan'. *ANF* 22, 24-78.

Chase, Martin. 1985. '*Concatenatio* as a Structural Element in the Christian *Drápur*'. In *The Sixth International Saga Conference, 28. 7. - 2. 8. 1985, Workshop Papers*. Copenhagen; 115-29.

Clover, Carol J. 1978. 'Skaldic Sensibility'. *ANF* 93, 63-81.

Clunies Ross, Margaret. 1987. *Skáldskaparmál: Snorri Sturluson's* Ars Poetica *and Medieval Theories of Language*. Odense.

CPB: Gudbrand Vigfusson and F. York Powell (eds.). 1883. *Corpus Poeticum Boreale* I-II. Oxford. Reprinted New York 1965.

Crawford, Barbara E. 1987. *Scandinavian Scotland*. Leicester.

Cruden, Stewart. 1958. 'Earl Thorfinn the Mighty and the Brough of Birsay'. In *Þriðji Víkingafundur / Third Viking Congress, Reykjavík 1956*. Ed. Kristján Eldjarn. Reykjavík; 156–62.

Dal, Ingerid. 1938. 'German. *brûn* als Epitheton von Waffen'. *Norsk Tidsskrift for Sprogvidenskap* 9, 219–30.

Damgaard-Sørensen, Tinna. 1991. 'Danes and Wends'. In *Peoples and Places in Northern Europe 500–1600. Essays in honour of Peter Hayes Sawyer*. Ed. Ian Wood and Niels Lund. Woodbridge; 171–86.

Danakonunga sǫgur: *Skjǫldunga saga. Knýtlinga saga. Ágrip af sǫgu Danakonunga*. 1982. Ed. Bjarni Guðnason. ÍF 35.

Davidson, Daphne L. 1983. Earl Hákon and his Poets. Unpublished D. Phil. thesis. Oxford.

De Vries: see Vries

Donaldson, Gordon. 1988. 'Introductory Essay: the Contemporary Scene'. In *St Magnus Cathedral and Orkney's Twelfth Century Renaissance*. Ed. Barbara E. Crawford. Aberdeen; 1–9.

Dronke, Ursula (ed.). 1969. *The Poetic Edda* I, *The Heroic Poems*. Oxford.

[*Edda, Poetic*]: *Edda, die Lieder der Codex Regius* I–II. 1962. Ed. Gustav Neckel. 4th edition, revised Hans Kuhn. Heidelberg.

Edwards, Diana C. 1979. The Poetry of Arnórr jarlaskáld: an Edition and Study. Unpublished D. Phil. thesis. Oxford.

Edwards, Diana. 1982–3. 'Christian and Pagan References in Eleventh-Century Norse Poetry: the Case of Arnórr jarlaskáld'. *Saga-Book* 21, 34–53.

Edwards, Diana C. 1983. 'Clause arrangement in skaldic poetry: I Clause arrangement in the *dróttkvætt* poetry of the ninth to fourteenth centuries; II Clause arrangement in the poetry of Arnórr jarlaskáld'. *ANF* 98, 123–75.

Egils saga Skalla-Grímssonar. 1933. Ed. Sigurður Nordal. ÍF 2.

Einar Ól. Sveinsson. 1947. 'Dróttkvæða þáttur', *Skírnir* 121, 15–20. Reprinted in same author's *Við Uppspretturnar*, Reykjavík 1956, 46–51.

Engster, Hermann. 1983. *Poesie einer Achsenzeit. Der Ursprung der Skaldik im gesellschaftlichen Systemwandel der Wikingerzeit*. Frankfurt am Main.

Fagrskinna. 1902–3. Ed. Finnur Jónsson. STUAGNL 30.

Fagrskinna. 1984. Ed. Bjarni Einarsson in *Ágrip af Nóregskonunga sǫgum. Fagrskinna - Nóregs konunga tal*. ÍF 29. [Edition cited throughout.]

Falk, Hjalmar. 1912. *Altnordisches Seewesen*, in *Wörter und Sachen* 4, Heidelberg. [Separate reprint available.]

Falk, Hjalmar. 1914. *Altnordische Waffenkunde*. Oslo.

Falk, Hjalmar: see also under Shetelig.

Faulkes, Anthony. 1964. 'The sources of Specimen Lexici Runici', *Íslenzk Tunga* V, 30–138.

Faulkes, Anthony (ed.). 1988. *Snorri Sturluson, Edda: Prologue and Gylfaginning*. London. [Reprinted from Oxford 1982.]

Faulkes, Anthony: see also *SnE* (*Faulkes 1979*).

Festskrift til Finnur Jónsson. 1928. Ed. J. Brøndum-Nielsen et al. Copenhagen.

Fidjestøl, Bjarne. 1974. 'Kenningsystemet: Forsøk på ein lingvistisk analyse'. *MM*, 5–50.

Fidjestøl, Bjarne. 1979. 'Kenningsystemet'. *MM*, 27–29.

Fidjestøl, Bjarne. 1982. *Det norrøne fyrstediktet*. Øvre Ervik.

Fidjestøl, Bjarne. 1984. 'Arnórr Þórðarson: Skald of the Orkney Jarls'. In *The Northern and Western Isles in the Viking World*. Ed. Alexander Fenton and Hermann Pálsson. Edinburgh; 239–57.

Fidjestøl, Bjarne. 1985a. 'On a New Edition of Skaldic Poetry'. In *The Sixth International Saga Conference, 28. 7. – 2. 8. 1985, Workshop Papers*. Copenhagen; 319–331.

Fidjestøl, Bjarne. 1985b. 'Skaldestudiar: eit forskningsoversyn'. *MM*, 53–81.

Fidjestøl, Bjarne. 1989. 'Ekspletivpartikkelen som dateringskriterium. Forsøk i filologisk statistikk'. *Festskrift til Finn Hødnebø 29. desember 1989*. Ed. Bjørn Eithun et al. Oslo; 46–64.

Fidjestøl, Bjarne. 1993. 'Pagan Beliefs and Christian Impact: The Contribution of Scaldic Studies'. In *Viking Revaluations. Viking Society Centenary Symposium 14–15 May 1992*. Ed. Anthony Faulkes and Richard Perkins. London; 100–20.

Finnboga saga. 1897. Ed. Valdimar Ásmundarson. Reykjavík.

Finnbogi Guðmundsson. 1967. 'Orkneyinga saga'. *KLNM* 12, 700.

Finnbogi Guðmundsson: see also *Orkneyinga saga*.

Finnur Jónsson. 1901. *Det norsk-islandske Skjaldesprog*. STUAGNL 28.

Finnur Jónsson. 1921. *Norsk-islandske Kultur- og Sprogforhold*, Det Kgl. Danske Videnskabernes Selskab, Historisk-filologiske Meddelelser, II, 2. Copenhagen.

Finnur Jónsson. 1920–24. *Den oldnorske og oldislandske Litteraturs Historie* I–III. 2nd edition. Copenhagen.

Finnur Jónsson. 1927. 'Flateyjarbók'. *ANO*, 139–90.

Finnur Jónsson. 1934. *Textkritiske Bemærkninger til Skjaldekvad*. Det Kgl. Danske Videnskabernes Selskab, Historisk-filologiske Meddelelser, XX, 2. Copenhagen.

Finnur Jónsson: see also *LP*, *Skjald.*

First Grammatical Treatise, The. 1972. Ed. Hreinn Benediktsson. Reykjavík.

Flasdieck, H. M. 1950. 'The Phonetic Aspect of Old Germanic Alliteration'. *Anglia* 69, 266–87.

Flat: *Flateyjarbok* [sic] I–III. 1860–68. [Ed. Guðbrandur Vigfússon and C. R. Unger]. Oslo.

Flo, R. 1902. 'Arnor Jarlaskald'. *Syn og Segn* 8, 264–75.

Florence of Worcester: *Florentii Wigorniensis Monachi Chronicon ex Chronicis* I–II. 1848–49. Ed. Benjamin Thorpe. London.

Fms: *Fornmanna sögur* I–XII. 1825–37. [Ed. Sveinbjörn Egilsson et al.] Copenhagen.

Foote, Peter. 1955. 'Notes on the Prepositions *of* and *um(b)* in Old Icelandic and Old Norwegian Prose'. *Studia Islandica / Íslenzk Fræði* 14.

Foote, Peter. 1978. 'Wrecks and Rhymes'. In *The Vikings, Proceedings of the Symposium of the Faculty of Arts of Uppsala University, June 6–9, 1977*. Uppsala; 57–66.

Foote, Peter. 1984. 'Latin Rhetoric and Icelandic Poetry. Some Contacts'. In Foote, *Aurvandilstá. Norse Studies*. Odense; 249–70. [Previously published in *Saga og Sed* 1982, 107–27.]

Fornaldar sögur nordrlanda I–III. 1829–30. Ed. C. C. Rafn. Copenhagen.

Fourth GrT: [*Fourth Grammatical Treatise*:] *Den tredje og fjærde grammatiske Afhandling*. 1884. Ed. Björn Magnússon Ólsen. STUAGNL 12.

Frank, Roberta. 1978. *Old Norse Court Poetry. The Dróttkvætt Stanza*. Islandica 42. Ithaca and London.

Frank, Roberta. 1981. 'Snorri and the Mead of Poetry'. In *Speculum Norrœnum*. Ed. Ursula Dronke et al. Odense; 155–70.

Frank, Roberta. 1985. 'Skaldic Poetry'. In *Old Norse-Icelandic Literature. A Critical Guide*. Ed. Carol J. Clover and John Lindow. Islandica 45. Ithaca and London; 157–96.

Frank, Roberta. 1994. 'When Poets address Princes'. In *Sagnaþing helgað Jónasi Kristjánssyni* I–II. Ed. Gísli Sigurðsson et al. Reykjavík; 189–95.

Friesen, Otto v. (ed.). 1933. *Runerne*. Nordisk Kultur 6. Stockholm.

Fritzner: Johan Fritzner. 1886–96. *Ordbog over det gamle norske Sprog* I–III, 2nd edition. Oslo. Reprinted 1954. Supplement, by Finn Hødnebø, Oslo 1972.

Fsk: see *Fagrskinna* 1984.

Gade, Kari Ellen. 1988. 'The Concept of a Syntactic Caesura in Old Norse Dróttkvætt Poetry'. In *Semper Idem et Novus: Festschrift for Frank Banta*. Ed. Francis G. Gentry. Göppingen; 3–25.

Gade, Kari Ellen. 1989. 'Hans Kuhn's *Das Dróttkvætt*: Some Critical Considerations'. *JEGP* 88, 34–53.

Gade, Kari Ellen. 1993. Review of Kristján Árnason, *The Rhythms of Dróttkvætt* (1991). *JEGP* 92, 273–79.

Gade, Kari Ellen. 1995. *The Structure of Old Norse* Dróttkvætt *Poetry*. Islandica 49. Ithaca.

Gísli Sigurðsson. 1994. 'Ólafur Þórðarson hvítaskáld og munnleg kvæðahefð á Vesturlandi um miðja 13. öld'. In *Samtíðarsögur / The Contemporary Sagas: Forprent (Níunda alþjóðlega fornsagnaþingið)*. Akureyri; 220–32.

Gödel, V. 1897–1900. *Katalog öfver Kongl. Bibliotekets Fornisländska och Fornnorska Handskrifter*. Stockholm.

Grettis saga. 1936. Ed. Guðni Jónsson. ÍF 7.

Guðbrandur Vigfússon. [1853–]1856. 'Um tímatal í Íslendinga sögum í fornöld'. *Safn til Sögu Íslands* 1. Reykjavík; 185–502.

Gudbrand Vigfusson (ed.). 1887. *Orkneyinga saga and Magnus saga*. Rolls Series 88, I. London.

Gurevitsj, Elena A. 1993. 'Om skaldespråkets *viðkenning* : Til problemet om rekonstruksjon av betydningen'. *MM*, 1–11.

Gurevich, Elena A. 1994. 'The System of Kennings'. In *Samtíðarsögur / The Contemporary Sagas: Forprent (Níunda alþjóðlega fornsagnaþingið)*. Akureyri; 274–85.

Hafstað, Baldur. 1994. 'Er Arinbjarnarkviða ungt kvæði?'. In *Sagnaþing helgað Jónasi Kristjánssyni* I–II. Ed. Gísli Sigurðsson et al. Reykjavík; 19–31.

Hákonar saga Hákonarsonar. 1977. Ed. Marina Mundt. Oslo. [Also *Rettelser til Hákonar saga Hákonarsonar*, by James E. Knirk, 1982.]

Hálfs saga ok Hálfsrekka. 1981. Ed. H. von Seelow. Stofnun Árna Magnússonar á Íslandi, Rit 20. Reykjavík.

Hallberg, Peter. 1978. 'Kenningsystemet: Några reflexioner'. *MM*, 18–25.

Halldór Halldórsson. 1965. 'Hjarta drepr stall'. *Íslenzk Tunga* 6, 38–70.

Hallfreðar saga. 1939. Ed. Einar Ól. Sveinsson in *Vatnsdœla saga*. ÍF 8, 133–200.

Hars(H-Hr): [*Haralds saga Sigurðarsonar* in *Hulda-Hrokkinskinna*]. 1831. In *Fms* VI, 125–432.

Hars(Hkr): *Haralds saga Sigurðarsonar* in *Heimskringla*. 1951. Ed. Bjarni Aðalbjarnarson in *Heimskringla* III. ÍF 28, 68–202.

Heggstad, Leiv. 1930. *Gamalnorsk Ordbok*. Oslo.

Heiðreks saga: *Saga Heiðreks konungs ins vitra / The Saga of King Heiðrek the Wise*. 1960. Ed. C. Tolkien. London.

Heilagra manna søgur I–II. 1877. Ed. C. R. Unger. Christiania.

Heimskringla I–IV. 1893–1901. Ed. Finnur Jónsson. STUAGNL 23.

Heimskringla I–III. 1941–51. Ed. Bjarni Aðalbjarnarson. ÍF 26–28. [Edition cited throughout.]

Helgi Guðmundsson. 1972. *The Pronominal Dual in Icelandic*. Reykjavík.

Hellberg, S. 1981. 'Om inskjutna satser i skaldediktningen', *MM*, 1–24.

Helle, Knut. 1991. 'Tiden fram til 1536'. In *Grunntrekk i norsk historie*. Ed. Rolf Danielssen et al. Oslo; pp. 13–106.

Heusler, Andreas. 1925–29. *Deutsche Versgeschichte* I–III. Berlin and Leipzig.

H-Hr: see *Hars(H-Hr)*, *Magns(H-Hr)* and *Ólskyrra(H-Hr)*.

Historia Norvegiæ: in *Monumenta Historica Norvegiæ*, 69–124.

Hkr: see *Heimskringla*.

Hødnebø, Finn. 1966. 'Morkinskinna'. *KLNM* 11, 705.

Hofmann, Dietrich. 1955. *Nordisch-Englische Lehnbeziehungen der Wikingerzeit*. BA 14.

Hogan, E. 1910. *Onomasticon Goidelicum*. Dublin.

Hollander, Lee M. 1942. 'Arnórr Thórdarson jarlaskáld and his poem *Hrynhent*'. *SS* 17, 99–109.

Hollander, Lee M. 1949. 'The Rôle of the Verb in Skaldic Poetry'. *APS* 20, 267–76.

Hollander, Lee M. 1953. 'Some Observations on the *Dróttkvætt* Meter of Skaldic Poetry'. *JEGP* 52, 189–97.

Hollander, Lee M. 1963. 'For Whom Were the Eddic Poems Composed?'. *JEGP* 62, 136–42.

Holtsmark, Anne. 1960. 'Grammatisk litteratur'. *KLNM* 5, 412–19.

Holtsmark, Anne. 1965. 'Líknarbraut'. *KLNM* 10, 553–54.

Holtsmark, Anne. 1967. 'Ólafs saga helga'. *KLNM* 12, 546–50.

Hougen, Bjørn. 1974. 'Den Havdjerve'. *Viking* 38, 10–29.

Hreinn Benediktsson. 1963. 'Phonemic Neutralization and Inaccurate Rhymes'. *APS* 26, 1–18.

[Icelandic Annals:] *Islandske Annaler indtil 1578*. 1888. Ed. Gustav Storm. Oslo.

IEW: Alexander Jóhannesson. 1956. *Isländisches Etymologisches Wörterbuch*. Bern.

ÍF: Íslenzk Fornrit. Reykjavík.

Íslendinga sögur I–XIII. 1946–49. Ed. Guðni Jónsson. Reykjavík.

Íslendzk Æventyri I–II. 1882–83. Ed. Hugo Gering. Halle.

Jakob Benediktsson. 1960. 'Um tvenns konar framburð á *ld* á íslenzku'. *Íslenzk Tunga* 2, 32–50.

Jakob Benediktsson. 1981. 'Hafgerðingadrápa'. In *Speculum Norrœnum*. Ed. U. Dronke et al. Odense; 27–32.

Jakobsen, A. 1968. 'Om forholdet mellom Fagrskinna og Morkinskinna'. *MM*, 47–58.

Jansson, S. B. F. 1977. *Runinskrifter i Sverige*. 2nd edition. Stockholm.

JEGP: *Journal of English and Germanic Philology*. Urbana / Champaign, Illinois.

Jesch, Judith. 1993. 'Skaldic Verse and Viking Semantics'. In *Viking Revaluations. Viking Society Centenary Symposium 14–15 May 1992*. Ed. Anthony Faulkes and Richard Perkins. London; 160–71.

Johnsen, O. A. 1969. 'Harald Hardrådes Død i Skaldediktningen'. *MM*, 47–50.

Johnsen, O. A.: see also *Ólsh(Sep)*.

Jón Helgason. 1928. 'Bæn Glúms Þorkelssonar'. In *Festskrift til Finnur Jónsson*; pp. 377–84.

Jón Helgason. 1950. 'Planer om en ny udgave af skjaldedigtningen'. *APS* 19, 130–32.

Jón Helgason. 1966. 'Verse auf der Laufás-Edda'. In *Festschrift Walter Baetke*. Ed. Kurt Rudolph et al. Weimar; 175–80.

Jón Helgason. 1969. 'Höfuðlausnarhjal'. In *Einarsbók*. Ed. Bjarni Guðnason et al. Reykjavík; 156–76.

Jón Helgason: see also *Ólsh(Sep)*.

Jónas Kristjánsson. 1988. *Eddas and Sagas*. Trans. Peter Foote. Reykjavík.

[Kålund, K.] 1888–94. *Katalog over den Arnamagnæanske Håndskriftsamling*. Copenhagen.

[Kålund, K.] 1900. *Katalog over de oldnorsk-islandske Håndskrifter*. Copenhagen.

KLNM: *Kulturhistorisk leksikon for nordisk middelalder*, 1–22. 1956–78. Copenhagen.

Knytlinga saga. 1919–25. Ed. C. af Petersens and Emil Olson in *Sǫgur Danakonunga*. STUAGNL 46.

Knýtls: *Knýtlinga saga*. 1982. Ed. Bjarni Guðnason in *Danakonunga sǫgur: Skjǫldunga saga. Knýtlinga saga. Ágrip af sǫgu Danakonunga*. ÍF 35. [Edition cited throughout.]

Kock, E. A.: see *NN*, *Skaldediktningen*.

Konráð Gíslason. 1866. 'Forandringer af "Qvantitet" i Oldnordisk-Islandsk'. *ANO*, 242–305.

Konráð Gíslason (ed.). 1875–89. *Njála* I–II. Copenhagen.

Konráð Gíslason. 1877. *Om Helrim i förste og tredje linie af regelmæssigt 'dróttkvætt' og 'hrynhenda'*. Copenhagen.

Konráð Gíslason. 1879a. 'Bemærkninger til nogle Steder i Skáldskaparmál'. *ANO*, 185–202.

Konráð Gíslason. 1879b. 'Et par Bemærkninger til et Vers af Arnórr jarlaskáld'. *ANO*, 154–60.

Konráð Gíslason. 1889. 'Ældre og nyere Böining af første Persons Plural-Possessiv i oldnordisk-islandsk'. *ANO*, 343–65.

Konráð Gíslason. 1895–97. *Efterladte Skrifter* I–II. Copenhagen.

Krause, Arnulf. 1990. *Die Dichtung des Eyvindr skáldaspillir. Edition — Kommentar — Untersuchungen*. Altnordische Bibliothek X. Leverkusen.

Kreutzer, Gert. 1977. *Die Dichtungslehre der Skalden*. 2nd edition. Meisenheim am Glam.

Kristján Árnason. 1991. *The Rhythms of Dróttkvætt and other Old Icelandic Metres*. Reykjavík.

Kristján Árnason. 1994. 'Hrynjandi Höfuðlausnar og Rímkvæðið fornenska'. In *Sagnaþing helgað Jónasi Kristjánssyni* I–II. Ed. Gísli Sigurðsson et al. Reykjavík; 505–13.

Kuhn, Hans. 1929a. *Das Füllwort of / um im Altwestnordischen*. Göttingen.

Kuhn, Hans. 1929b. Review of Reichardt 1928. *Göttingische Gelehrte Anzeigen* 191, 193–202.

Kuhn, Hans. 1936. 'Die Negation des Verbs in der altnordischen Dichtung'. *Beiträge* 60, 431–44.

Kuhn, Hans. 1937. 'Zum Vers- und Satzbau der Skalden', *Zeitschrift für deutsches Altertum u. deutsche Literatur* 74, 49–63.

Kuhn, Hans. 1969. 'Die Dróttkvættverse des Typs "brestr erfiði Austra"'. In *Afmælisrit Jóns Helgasonar*. Ed. Jakob Benediktsson et al. Reykjavík; 403–17.

Kuhn, Hans. 1971. 'Das älteste Christentum Islands'. *Zeitschrift für deutsches Altertum u. deutsche Literatur* 100, 4–40.

Kuhn, Hans. 1983. *Das Dróttkvætt*. Heidelberg.

Lækningabók Íslenzk. 1931. Ed. H. Larsen as *An Old Icelandic Miscellany*. Oslo.

Lange, Wolfgang. 1958. *Studien zur Christlichen Dichtung der Nordgermanen 1000–1200*. *Palaestra* 222. Göttingen.

Larsson, Ludvig. 1891. *Ordförrådet i de älsta isländska Handskrifterna*. Lund.

Laufás Edda: see *SnE(Faulkes 1979)* and *SnE(Svb.Eg.)*

Laxdœla saga. 1934. Ed. Einar Ól. Sveinsson. ÍF 5.

[*Legendary Saga of Óláfr helgi*]. *Olafs saga hins helga. Die "Legendarische Saga" über Olaf den Heiligen*. 1982. Ed. and trans. Anne Heinrichs et al. Heidelberg.

Letter of Alexander the Great to Aristotle. 1924. Ed. Stanley Rypins in *Three Old English Prose Texts*, Early English Text Society O.S. 161. London.

Lexikon des Mittelalters, Munich and Zürich 1977–.

Lidén, Evald. 1928. 'Gullvarta - Síbilia'. In *Festskrift til Finnur Jónsson*; 358–64.

Lie, Hallvard. 1952. 'Skaldestil-Studier'. *MM*, 1–92.

Lie, Hallvard. 1954. 'Naglfar og Naglfari'. *MM*, 152–61.

Lindow, John. 1982. 'Narrative and the Nature of Skaldic Poetry'. *ANF* 97, 94–121.

Lindquist, Ivar. 1928. 'En fornisländsk sjöterm *skokkr*'. In *Festskrift til Finnur Jónsson*; 385–94.

Ljunggren, Karl Gustav. 1939. 'Anteckningar till Skírnismál och Rígsþula'. *ANF* 54, 9-44.

Louis-Jensen, Jonna. 1977. *Kongesagastudier. Kompilationen Hulda-Hrokkinskinna*. BA 32.

LP: Sveinbjörn Egilsson, *Lexicon Poëticum Antiquæ Linguæ Septentrionalis*, 1860; 2nd edition, revised by Finnur Jónsson, Copenhagen 1931, reprinted 1966.

Magerøy, Hallvard. 1957. *Studier i Bandamanna saga*, BA 18.

Magns(H-Hr): [*Magnúss saga góða* in *Hulda-Hrokkinskinna*]. 1831. In *Fms* VI, 3-124.

Magns(Hkr): *Magnúss saga góða* in *Heimskringla*. 1951. Ed. Bjarni Aðalbjarnarson in *Heimskringla* III. ÍF 28, 3-67.

Malm, Mats. 1990. 'Sannkenningars egentliga egenskaper'. *ANF* 105; 111–30.

Malmros, Rikke. 1994. 'Det sene hedenskabs samfundsideologi: Kan en historiker bruge hedenske fyrstekvad?'. In *Samtíðarsögur / The Contemporary Sagas: Forprent (Níunda alþjóðlega fornsagnaþingið)*. Akureyri; 535–49.

Marianus Scottus, *Chronicon*. 1844. In *Monumenta Germaniæ Historica*, gen. ed. G. H. Pertz, V. Hanover.

Maríu saga, ed. C. R. Unger. Christiania 1871.

Marold, Edith. 1983. *Kenningkunst*. Berlin.

Marold, Edith. 1990. 'Skaldendichtung und Mythologie'. In *Poetry in the Scandinavian Middle Ages. Atti del 12° Congresso Internazionale di Studi sull' Alto Medioevo*. Ed. Teresa Pàroli. Spoleto; 107–30.

Martin, John Stanley. 1972. *Ragnarǫk*. Assen.

Meissner, Rudolf. 1921. *Die Kenningar der Skalden*. Bonn.

MM: *Maal og Minne*, Oslo.

Mohr, W. 1933. *Kenningstudien*. Stuttgart.

Monumenta Historica Norvegiæ. 1880. Ed. Gustav Storm. Oslo.

Morkinskinna. 1932. Ed. Finnur Jónsson. STUAGNL 53.

Morris, Christopher D. 1985. 'Viking Orkney: a Survey'. In *The Prehistory of Orkney*. Ed. Colin Renfrew. Edinburgh; 210-42.

Msk: see *Morkinskinna*.

Munch, P. A. 1852-63. *Det norske Folks Historie* I-VIII. Oslo.

(*Brennu-*) *Njáls saga*. 1954. Ed. Einar Ól. Sveinsson. ÍF 12.

NN: Ernst A. Kock. 1923-41. *Notationes Norrœnæ*, in *Lunds Universitets Årsskrift*, NF XIX,2-XXXVII,5.

Nordal, Sigurður (ed.). 1913-16. *Orkneyinga saga*. STUAGNL 40.

Nordal, Sigurður. 1914. *Om Olaf den helliges saga*. Copenhagen.
Nordal, Sigurður. 1931-32. 'Icelandic Notes'. *APS* 6, 144-49.
Nordal, Sigurður. 1938. 'Sturla Þórðarson og Grettis saga'. *Studia Islandica* 4, 12-17.
Noreen, Erik. 1921-23. *Studier i fornvästnordisk Diktning* I-III. Uppsala.
Noreen, Erik. 1923. *Altnordische Grammatik*, I *Altisländische und altnorwegische Grammatik*. 4th edition. Halle. Reprinted Tübingen 1970.
Nygaard, M. 1906. *Norrøn Syntax*. Oslo. Reprinted 1966.
Ólafia Einarsdóttir. 1964. *Studier i kronologiske metode*. Stockholm.
Ólafur Halldórsson. 1964. 'Nokkrar spássíugreinar í pappírshandritum frá 17. öld'. *Skírnir* 138, 131-55.
Ólsen, Björn M. 1903. 'Til versene i Egils saga'. *ANF* 19, 99-133.
Ólsen, Björn M. 1909. 'Om nogle vers af Arnórr jarlaskáld'. *ANF* 25, 289-302.
Ólsh(Hkr): *Óláfs saga helga* in *Heimskringla*. 1945. Ed. Bjarni Aðalbjarnarson in *Heimskringla* II. ÍF 27.
Ólsh(Sep): [The Separate *Óláfs saga helga*] *Den store saga om Olav den Hellige*. 1941. Ed. Oscar Albert Johnsen and Jón Helgason. Oslo. [Edition used throughout.]
Ólsh(Sep): [The Separate *Óláfs saga helga*] *Saga Óláfs konungs ens helga*. 1853. Ed. P.A. Munch and C.R. Unger. Oslo.
Ólskyrra (H-Hr): [Saga of Óláfr kyrri and Magnús Haraldsson in *Hulda-Hrokkinskinna*]. In *Fms* VI, 435-48.
Ordbog over det norrøne prosasprog: Registre / A Dictionary of Old Norse Prose: Indices. 1989. Copenhagen.
Ordericus Vitalis, *Ecclesiastical History*. 1969-78. Ed. M. Chibnall. Oxford.
Orkns: *Orkneyinga saga*. 1965. Ed. Finnbogi Guðmundsson. ÍF 24. [Edition cited throughout; see also under Nordal].
Petersens and Olson: see *Knýtlinga saga* 1919-25.
Poole, Russell. 1987. 'Skaldic Verse and Anglo-Saxon History: Some Aspects of the Period 1009-1016'. *Speculum* 62, 265-98.
Poole, R. G. 1991. *Viking Poems on War and Peace*. Toronto etc.
Pulsiano, Phillip and Kirsten Wolf (eds.). 1991. *Medieval Scandinavia. An Encyclopedia*. New York and London.
Ragnars saga loðbrókar: in *Vǫlsunga saga ok Ragnars saga loðbrókar*. 1906-8. Ed. Magnus Olsen. STUAGNL 36.

Reichardt, Konstantin. 1928. *Studien zu den Skalden des 9. und 10. Jahrhunderts*. *Palaestra* 159. Leipzig.

Reinskou, Finn. 1922. 'Olav den helliges vimpel?'. *MM*, 32–36.

Roskilde *Chronicon*: *Anonymi Roskildensis Chronicon Danicum*. 1772. Ed. J. Langebek. Scriptores Rerum Danicarum Medii Ævi 1. Copenhagen.

Saga-Book: *Saga-Book of the Viking Society*. London.

Saxo Grammaticus, *Gesta Danorum* I–II. 1931–57. Ed. J. Olrik and H. Raeder. Copenhagen.

Schofield, Guy. 1966. 'The Third Battle of 1066'. *History Today* 16, 688–93.

Schreiner, Johan. 1927–29. 'Magnus Olavssons hjemkomst fra Gardarike'. *Historisk Tidsskrift* (Oslo) 28, 519–24.

Schreiner, Johan. 1928. 'Harald Hardråde og Oplandene'. In *Festskrift til Finnur Jónsson*; 157–72.

Schreiner, Johan. 1930–33. 'Magnus Olavsson og Danmark'. *Historisk Tidsskrift* (Oslo) 29, 37–42.

Scott, Forrest S. 1953–57. 'Valþjófr jarl: an English earl in Icelandic sources.' *Saga-Book* 14, 78–94.

Seafarer, The: in *ASPR* III, 1936, 143–47.

See, Klaus von. 1967. *Germanische Verskunst*. Stuttgart.

See, Klaus von. 1980. *Skaldendichtung*. Munich and Zürich.

Seip, Didrik Arup. 1954. *Palæografi B: Norge og Island*. Nordisk Kultur 28B. Uppsala.

Seip, Didrik Arup. 1955. *Norsk Språkhistorie til omkring 1370*. 2nd edition. Oslo.

Shetelig, Haakon and Hjalmar Falk. 1937. *Scandinavian Archaeology*, trans. E. V. Gordon. Oxford.

Sievers, Eduard. 1878. 'Beiträge zur Skaldenmetrik', in *Beiträge* V, 449–518.

Sievers, E. 1889. 'Nordische Kleinigheiten'. *ANF* V, 132–41.

Sievers, Eduard. 1893. *Altgermanische Metrik*. Halle.

Skáldatal: In *SnE (Arnamagn)* III 259–69.

Skaldediktningen: Kock, E. A. (ed.) 1946–49. *Den norsk-isländske Skaldediktningen* I–II. Lund.

Skírnir: *Skírnir, Tímarit hins íslenzka Bókmenntafélags*. Reykjavík.

Skjald: *Den norsk-islandske Skjaldedigtning*. 1912–15. Ed. Finnur Jónsson. A I–II Tekst efter Håndskrifter, B I–II Rettet Tekst. Reprinted 1967–73. Copenhagen.

Smirnickaja, Olga A. 1992. 'Mythological Nomination and Skaldic Synonymics'. In *Snorrastefna*. Rit Stofnunar Sigurðar Nordals 1. Ed. Úlfar Bragason. Reykjavík. 217–25.

SnE [*Snorra Edda*:] *Edda Snorra Sturlusonar*. 1931. Ed. Finnur Jónsson. Copenhagen. [Edition cited throughout.]

SnE(Arnamagn): *Edda Snorra Sturlusonar* I-III. 1848-87. Ed. Sveinbjörn Egilsson et al. for Det Arnamagnæanske Legat. Copenhagen. Reprinted 1966.

SnE(Faulkes 1979): *Two Versions of Snorra Edda from the 17th Century. I Edda Magnúsar Ólafssonar (Laufás Edda)*. 1979. Ed. Anthony Faulkes. Stofnun Árna Magnússonar á Íslandi, Rit 13. Reykjavík.

SnE(Svb.Eg.): *Edda Snorra Sturlusonar*. 1848-49. Ed. Sveinbjörn Egilsson. Reykjavík.

SS: *Scandinavian Studies* (formerly *Scandinavian Studies and Notes*), Lawrence, Kansas.

Steinmeyer, E. von, E. Karg-Gasterstädt and T. Frings. 1968-. *Althochdeutsches Wörterbuch*. Berlin.

Stephens, John. 1971. 'Is the Skaldic *Dróttkvætt* Metre Trochaic?'. *JEGP* 70, 76-85.

Stjórn. 1862. Ed. C. R. Unger. Oslo.

Strayer, Joseph R. (ed.). 1982–. *Dictionary of the Middle Ages*. New York.

STUAGNL: Samfund til Udgivelse af gammel nordisk Litteratur. Copenhagen.

Sturlunga saga I-II. 1906-11. Ed. Kr. Kålund. Copenhagen.

Sveinbjörn Egilsson (ed). 1828-46. *Scripta Historica Islandorum* I-XII. Copenhagen.

Sveinbjörn Egilsson. 1860. *Lexicon Poëticum Antiquæ Linguæ Septentrionalis*. Copenhagen. [For 2nd edition, see LP.]

Sven Aggesøn, *Historia Regum Dacie*. 1916. Ed. M. Cl. Gertz in *Sven Aggesøns Værker*. Copenhagen.

Sven Aggesen, *Works*. 1992. Trans. and introd. Eric Christiansen. London.

Sverris saga. 1920. Ed. Gustav Indrebø. Christiania.

Symeonis Monachi Opera Omnia I-II. 1882-85. Ed. Thomas Arnold. Rolls Series 75. London.

Tate, G. S. 1978. 'Good Friday liturgy and the structure of *Líknarbraut*', *SS* 50, 31-38.

Taylor, Alex. B. 1931. 'Some Saga Place-Names'. *Proceedings of the Orkney Antiquarian Society* 9, 41-45.

Taylor, A. B. 1937. 'Karl Hundason, "King of Scots"'. *Proceedings of the Society of Antiquaries of Scotland* 71, 334-42.

Taylor, A. B. (trans. and ed.). 1938. *The Orkneyinga saga*. Edinburgh.

Theodrici Monachi, *Historia de Antiquitate Regum Norwagiensium*: in *Monumenta Historica Norvegiæ*, 1-68.

Third GrT: [*Third Grammatical Treatise*]: see *Fourth GrT*.

Thomson, William P.L. 1987. *History of Orkney*. Edinburgh.

Thorkelsson, Jón. 1884. *Bemærkninger til nogle Steder i Versene i Heimskringla*. Copenhagen.

Torp, Alf. 1963. *Nynorsk Etymologisk Ordbok*. Oslo.

Trubetzkoy, N. S. 1969. *Principles of Phonology*. Berkeley.

Turville-Petre, [E. O.] G. 1953. *Origins of Icelandic Literature*. Oxford.

Turville-Petre, E. O. G. 1968. *Haraldr the Hard-ruler and his Poets*. London.

Turville-Petre, E. O. G. 1976. *Scaldic Poetry*. Oxford.

Turville-Petre, J. 1969. 'The Metre of Icelandic Court Poetry'. *Saga-Book* 17, 326-51.

Vigfusson, Gudbrand: see Gudbrand / Guðbrandur.

Vita Ædwardi Regis / The Life of King Edward. 1962. Ed. and trans. Frank Barlow. Edinburgh.

Vogt, W. H. 1934. 'Aldartryggðir og Ævintryggðir'. *Beiträge* 58, 1-66.

Vǫlsunga saga / The Saga of the Volsungs. 1965. Trans. and ed. R. G. Finch. London.

Vries, Jan de. 1952. 'Über Arnórr Jarlaskáld'. *ANF* 67, 156-75.

Vries, Jan de. 1977. *Altnordisches Etymologisches Wörterbuch*. 2nd edition. Leiden. ['De Vries' throughout.]

Whaley, Diana. 1991. *Heimskringla. An Introduction*. London.

Whaley, Diana: see also Edwards.

Willelmi Malmesbiriensis Monachi De Gestis Regum Anglorum Libri Quinque I-II. 1887-89. Ed. William Stubbs. Rolls Series 90. London.

Wolf, Alois. 1965. 'Zur Rolle der *Vísur* in der altnordischen Prosa'. In *Festschrift Leonhard C. Franz*, ed. O. Menghin and H. M. Ölberg. Innsbrucker Beiträge zur Kulturwissenschaft, 11; 459-84.

Wood, Cecil. 1960. 'The Skald's Bid for a Hearing'. *JEGP* 59, 240-54.

Wood, Cecil. 1964. 'Skúli Þorsteinsson'. *SS* 36, 175–88.

C. Note on Further Bibliography

For further bibliographical material relating to skaldic poetry and other Old Norse-Icelandic literature, see Lee M. Hollander, *A Bibliography of Skaldic Studies* (Copenhagen 1958); Hans Bekker-Nielsen, *Old Norse-Icelandic Studies: A Select Bibliography* (Toronto, 1967); *Bibliography of Old Norse-Icelandic Studies* (Copenhagen 1963–83, and currently continuing in electronic form); and the essays in *Old Norse-Icelandic Literature. A Critical Guide*, ed. Carol J. Clover and John Lindow (Ithaca and London 1985), especially Roberta Frank's 'Skaldic Poetry'. See also entries in *Kulturhistorisk leksikon for nordisk middelalder* I–XXII (Copenhagen 1956–78); in *Medieval Scandinavia. An Encyclopedia*, ed. Phillip Pulsiano and Kirsten Wolf (New York 1993); and in the more general works *Lexikon des Mittelalters* (Munich and Zürich 1980–) and *Dictionary of the Middle Ages*, ed. Joseph R. Strayer (New York 1982–).

Index

THE index covers the principal people, places and literary works relevant to the study of Arnórr jarlaskáld's poetry, together with the more frequently cited modern scholars. All Old Norse-Icelandic poems cited are indexed, and abbreviations explained, even when they are only mentioned in passing as sources of parallel usages to Arnórr's. All Eddaic poems and anonymous skaldic poems are entered under their title, together with a few non-anonymous skaldic poems whose titles are particularly distinctive and well-known. Otherwise, skaldic verse is indexed under the name of the poet to whom it is traditionally attributed, with abbreviations where necessary. References to Arnórr's own extant poems are too numerous to be usefully included here, and references to prose sources for Arnórr's verses in the Diplomatic Text and Commentary section are only indexed if of particular interest; they can be located through the tables in Appendix A. The Bibliography is not routinely indexed and topics can best be traced by reference to the Contents. In the alphabetisation, Þ, Æ, Œ, and Ö/Ǫ/Ø follow Y; long (accented) vowels follow short vowels, e. g. Á follows A.

Adam of Bremen 29, 199, 332–335
Akv = Atlakviða 60, 161, 188, 213
Alexanders saga 264
Alfaðir (Óðinn) 123
Alfífa, mother of Sveinn 159
Am = Atlamál 188, 270, 296
Annals of Tigernach 335
Anon XI 334
Anon XII 205
Anon XIII 282
Arbj = Arinbjarnarkviða (Egill) 147, 349
ASC = Anglo-Saxon Chronicle 285, 333, 334
Atli Buðlason (Attila) 75
Atli skáld 60
Austri, dwarf 74, 128, 265, 266

Á Ket = Ásgrímr Ketilsson 222
Ágrip 331, 333
Álfhildr, mother of Magnús góði 332
Árni Magnússon 20
Áróss (Århus) 171, 172, 205, 209, 211, 288, 332, 333
Ásgeir Jónsson 10, 11, 13, 14, 19
Ásta Guðbrandsdóttir 333
Ástríðr Óláfsdóttir 154
Ástríðr Sveinsdóttir 174

B dr = Baldrs draumar 210
B krepp = Bjǫrn krepphendi 61
Baldr, god 74, 126, 246–248
Balti = Bǫðvarr balti 38
Baltic / Eystrasalt 114, 149, 331
Bandamanna saga 46, 354
Battle of Maldon 290

Bára, wave / goddess 74, 75
Beowulf 293, 306, 309
Bergr Sokkason 23
Bersǫglisvísur (Sigvatr) 332
Bj H = Bjarni Hallbjarnarson Gullbrárskáld 160, 257, 264, 332, 335
Bj hit = Bjǫrn Hítdœlakappi (verse) 188
Bjarkamál in fornu 58
Bjarnar saga Hítdœlakappa 41, 42
Bjarni Aðalbjarnarson 9–12, 50, 138, 163, 172, 183, 186, 195, 196, 201, 207, 210, 211, 218, 277, 286, 338
Bjarni Einarsson 3, 5, 13, 339, 344
Bjarni Guðnason 19, 341, 352
Bjǫrn Hítdœlakappi 42, 43
Bjǫrn Ulfsson 122, 210
Blágagladrápa (Arnórr) 27, 35, 45, 134
Bragi, skald 20, 59, 63
Bretar, brezkr / British 125, 126, 239, 246–248
Brúsi Sigurðarson 133, 302, 335, 336
Buðli, legendary king 75
Bugge, Alexander 62
Byzantium 301, 333
Bǫlv = Bǫlverkr Arnórsson 161, 210, 313, 333, 334

Caithness / Katanes 228, 251, 335
Christ / Kristr 32, 248, 299, 300
Clunies Ross, Margaret ix, 66, 74
Constantinople / Miklagarðr 151, 333
Copenhagen / København 10, 18, 171, 337

Davidson, Daphne 74, 102, 193, 221
Denmark / Danmǫrk, Danir etc. 18, 19, 26, 29, 32, 34, 35, 46, 52, 75, 115, 119, 120, 122, 128–130, 134, 148, 150, 158, 159, 162, 163, 166, 171, 181, 192, 193, 195, 197, 198, 200, 215, 216, 251, 268, 269, 272, 278, 296, 309, 310, 332, 333, 346
Donatus 23
Drv = Draumvísur 224
Dublin / Dyflinn 128, 263, 264
Duncan 231
Dúfa, wave / goddess 74
Dýrnes (Deerness) 36, 124, 230, 242, 335

E Sk = Einarr Skúlason 75, 163, 170, 245, 257, 282, 283, 332
E viðs = Eiríkr viðsjá 238
Eg = Egill Skallagrímsson 26, 30, 58, 222; see also Arbj and Hfl
Egils saga 18, 224, 307, 355
Eilífr Goðrúnarson x, 233
Einarr rangmuðr 124, 230, 335
Einarr Skúlason: see E Sk
Eiríkr Hákonarson 41
Eiríkr Sveinsson 26
Eiríksdrápa (Markús) 80, 93
Ekkjall (Oykell), river 54, 125, 238
Endill, legendary sea-king 75, 133, 306, 307
England, Englar / English 43, 58, 92, 126, 127, 130, 131, 159, 174, 177, 192, 248, 251, 252, 254, 255, 279–281, 283–287, 289–291, 296, 332, 334, 335, 356
"Erri" 171
Eysteinn Ásgrímsson 80
Eystrasalt: see Baltic
Eyv = Eyvindr skáldaspillir ix, 52, 174, 197, 352

Fagrskinna: see Fsk
Falk, Hjalmar 149, 151, 161, 271, 273
Falstr (Falster) 122, 212, 214, 215, 333
Faulkes, Anthony 18, 21, 22, 246, 316, 341, 342
Fidjestøl, Bjarne ix, xi, 27–31, 51–53, 59–62, 66, 79, 81, 86, 88, 93, 106, 141, 184, 240, 297
Finnboga saga 293

Finnbogi Guðmundsson 17, 18, 138, 233, 236, 248, 252, 254–256, 263, 305, 307, 340
Finnur Jónsson (incl. Skjald B) x, xv, 4, 9, 12, 15, 18, 20, 21, 25, 27, 30, 32–34, 103, 138, 143–145, 155, 170, 174, 180, 186, 188, 196, 199, 201, 204, 209, 210, 213, 214, 217, 224, 226, 233, 235, 236, 238, 240, 247, 257, 259, 261, 268, 273, 280, 282, 283, 285, 288, 297, 299, 300, 308, 309, 325–327, 338–342
First Grammatical Treatise 186
Fjón (Fyn) 122, 128, 129, 171, 216, 268, 269, 332–334
Flat / Fl = Flateyjarbók 3, 9, 12, 14–19, 25, 26, 32, 39, 41, 44, 102, 150, 158, 159, 170, 179, 189, 200, 202, 209, 214–217, 246, 269, 273, 277, 308, 320, 326, 331, 333, 340, 341, 348
Florence of Worcester 334
Foote, Peter xi, 80, 106, 151, 227, 352
Fourth GrT = Fourth Grammatical Treatise 23, 146, 323, 343
Frank, Roberta ix, xi, 66, 74, 147, 150, 221, 359
Frankish 120, 201
Freyja, goddess 36
Fsk = Fagrskinna 5, 9, 10, 13, 14, 17, 26, 38, 102, 158, 212, 214–217, 223, 320, 326, 327, 331, 333, 339, 340, 346, 347, 351
Fulford 71, 130, 285, 334

G Súrs = Gísli Súrsson (verse) 258
Gade, Kari Ellen 80, 84
Gamli kanóki 80
Garðar (N. W. Russia), Russian 50, 52, 75, 76, 113, 118, 132, 137, 139, 140, 150, 161, 182–184, 300, 301
Gautar 282
Gd = Guðmundardrápa (Árni Jónsson) 30, 250
Geisli (Einarr Skúlason) 75
Gellir Þorkelsson 28, 35, 46, 134, 190, 191
Girkir / Greek(s) 75, 132, 300, 301
Gísl Illugason 60
Gjúki, legendary king 76, 115, 161, 209
Glammi, legendary sea-king 70, 75, 120, 197, 200
Gldr = Glymdrápa (Þorbjǫrn hornklofi) 198
Glælognskviða (Þórarinn loftunga) 63
Glǫð, bell 170
Gráf = Gráfeldardrápa (Glúmr) 293
Grett = Grettir Ásmundarson 144
Grettis saga 18, 42, 155, 255, 355
Grí = Grímnismál 36, 145, 170, 229, 282
Gríp = Grípisspá 225
Gudbrand Vigfusson / Guðbrandur Vigfússon x, 25, 27, 46, 256, 259, 266, 283, 345, 348
Guðr II = Guðrúnarkviða II 180
Guðrún Gjúkadóttir 148, 161
Gullvarta, gate 151, 353
Gunnarr Gjúkason 161, 209, 270
Gunnlaugr ormstunga 41, 46
Guttormr Gjúkason 161
Gǫndul, battle / valkyrie 74, 139

H harð = Haraldr harðráði (verse by) 186, 333, 334
H Hj = Helgakviða Hjǫrvarðssonar 177
H ókr = Halldórr ókristni 154, 166
H-Hr = Hulda-Hrokkinskinna 9, 14, 15, 26, 27, 30, 41, 44, 149, 150, 152, 159, 168, 179, 200, 201, 218, 223, 271, 279, 283, 289–291, 294, 295, 320, 326, 331, 333, 340, 350, 354
Haðaland (Hadeland) 277
Hafgerðingadrápa 79, 93, 233, 351
Halfdan svarti 13
Halland 129, 270
Hallar-Steinn 30, 31, 183, 184
Halldór Jónsson 6

Hallfreðar saga 45
Hallfreðr vandræðaskáld: see Hfr
Halli stirði 69, 208
Hamð = Hamðismál 282
Hamðir, legendary hero 161
Haraldr Guðinason (Harold, son of Godwine) 289, 291, 334
Haraldr harðráði Sigurðarson ix, 3, 9, 13–16, 27, 28, 30, 32, 33, 35, 36, 44–47, 50, 54, 55, 75, 128–132, 134, 137, 142, 148, 175, 180, 181, 186, 223, 268–301 passim, 311, 333, 334, 358
Haraldr hárfagri 222, 224
Haraldr Knútsson 62
Haraldsstikki 334
Harð = Harðar saga (verse) 247
Harkv = Haraldskvæði (Þorbjǫrn hornklofi) 176
Haukr Valdísarson 30
Haustlǫng (Þjóðólfr ór Hvini) 20
Hák = Hákonarmál (Eyvindr) 52, 224
Hákon Ívarsson 277, 334
Hákonar saga Hákonarsonar 263
Hálfs = Hálfs saga (verse) 148, 215, 283
Hárb = Hárbarðsljóð 144
Hást = Hásteinn 282
Háttatal: see Ht
Háv = Hávarðr Ísfirðingr 139, 193
Hebrides: see Suðreyjar
Heiðmǫrk (Hedemark), Heinir 55, 130, 277–279
Heiðreks saga 271
Heimdallr, god 170
Heimskringla: see Hkr
Heiti, legendary ancestor 113, 140
Hel, goddess / realm of death; axe 74, 121, 202, 203, 298
Helgakviða Hundingsbana I 62
Helganes (Helgenæs) 32, 33, 36, 53, 67, 117, 121, 122, 171, 173, 174, 205, 206, 208, 209, 333
Helgi trausti Óláfsson 247
Helsingjaland (Hälsingland) 152
Hermundr Illugason 28, 35, 46, 134, 311
Herv = Hervarar saga (verse) 271
Heusler, Andreas 80, 82, 86, 93, 147
Hfl = Hǫfuðlausn (Egill) 30, 59, 283
Hfr = Hallfreðr vandræðaskáld x, 45, 52, 61, 62, 183, 184, 218, 229, 233, 261, 265, 266, 296, 299
Hildr, battle / valkyrie 74
Hítarnes 41
Hjaltland / Shetland, Hjaltar 125, 126, 133, 222, 239, 243, 262, 263, 307, 308
Hkr = Heimskringla 6, 9–12, 15, 26, 38, 50, 102, 159, 160, 163, 172, 174, 182, 192, 200, 201, 203, 222, 271, 275, 287, 319, 325, 326, 331, 333–335, 338, 339, 350, 358
Hl = Háttalykill (Rǫgnvaldr - Hallr) 168
Hlýrskógsheiðr (Lyrskovheden) 116, 121, 170, 172, 200, 201, 203, 332
Hlǫðvir Þorfinnsson 125, 239
Hlǫkk, battle / valkyrie 74, 117, 172
Hnikarr, Hnikuðr (Óðinn) 145
Hofgarða-Refr 151, 180
Hofmann, Dietrich 177, 178, 194, 296, 308
Hollander, Lee M. 41, 62, 84, 91, 96, 359
Holtsmark, Anne 5, 23, 177
Hólmgarðr (Novgorod) 137, 332, 336
Hringaríki (Ringerike) 277
Hrokkinskinna 3, 15, 26, 27, 150, 159, 209, 285; see also H-Hr
Hsv = Hugsvinnsmál 226
Ht = Háttatal (Snorri Sturluson) 20, 30, 83, 139, 151, 186, 207, 240, 273, 277, 283, 285, 342
Huginn, mythical raven 228, 229
Hulda 3, 15, 26, 27, 198, 326; see also H-Hr
Húsdr = Húsdrápa 35, 170, 205
Hǫgni Gjúkason 75, 121, 161, 209
Hǫrða-Knútr 62, 159, 192, 251, 332

Hǫrðaland (Hordaland), Hǫrðar 52, 114, 118, 121, 122, 148, 183, 184, 202, 213

Icelandic Annals 29, 46, 172, 230, 245, 331
Illugi Bryndœlaskáld 333
Ireland / Írland, Írar etc. 126, 236, 239, 244, 246, 248, 251, 262, 264

Ísldr = Íslendingadrápa 30, 213, 238

Jaðarr (Jæren) 119, 187, 189
Jarizleifr (Jaroslav) 137, 332, 336
Johnsen, O.A. 5, 6, 15, 301, 337
Jóansdrápa (Gamli) 80
Jóm 29, 52, 116, 120, 165, 168, 172, 199, 200, 332
Jómsv = Jómsvíkingadrápa (Bjarni Kolbeinsson) 314
Jón Eggertsson 10
Jón Hákonarson 15
Jón Helgason xi, 5, 6, 15, 22, 36, 37, 59, 159, 316, 337–339
Jón Vídalín 20
Jón Þórðarson 16
Jór = Jórunn 60, 147
Jutland / Jótland, Jótar etc. 67, 114, 120, 122, 129, 146, 148, 150, 174, 195, 196, 200, 211, 212, 274, 275

Kalfr Árnason 260, 268, 303, 306–308, 335
Kalfsflokkr (Bjarni Gullbrárskáld) 257
'Karl Hundason' 32, 124, 230, 231, 234, 236, 239, 335, 358
Katanes: see Caithness
Ketill Jörundsson 22
Knútr inn helgi Sveinsson 26
Knútr inn ríki Sveinsson 28, 35, 43, 61, 62, 134, 150, 158, 174, 178, 258, 308, 309
Knýtls = Knýtlinga saga 19, 20, 27, 102, 171–173, 210, 321, 325, 331, 333, 341, 346, 352

Kock, E. A. x, 25, 27, 103, 138, 144, 152, 155, 163, 164, 166, 170, 188, 191, 193, 194, 196, 199, 204, 207, 209, 210, 214, 217, 224, 226, 236, 238, 240, 247, 252, 256, 273, 280, 282, 283, 285, 293, 297, 299, 305, 309, 313
Kolb = Kolbeinn Tumason 226
Kolbeinn Þórðarson 42
Kolga, wave / goddess 74, 156
Kolgr = Kolgrímr litli 332
Kolli prúði, skald 38
Kolli Þórðarson 42, 43
Konráð Gíslason 145, 150, 152, 159, 163, 170, 178, 186, 207, 226, 241, 250, 277, 279, 305
Korm = Kormákr 41, 240
Kreutzer, Gert ix, 30, 31, 147, 172
Kristr: see Christ
Krm = Krákumál 154
Kuhn, Hans ix, xv, 30, 80, 82, 84–88, 91, 92, 106, 141, 174, 226, 266, 296, 301
Kuml = Kumlbúa þáttr (verse) 229

Laufás-Edda 21, 22, 34, 36–38, 227, 246, 308, 314, 316, 323, 342, 352
Laxdœla saga 28, 35, 191, 231
Legendary Saga 336
Leiðarvísan 30
Letter of Alexander 280
Liðsmannaflokkr 248
Lilja (Eysteinn) 80
Líkn = Líknarbraut 177, 226, 351, 357
Lok = Lokasenna 139, 170, 309
Louis-Jensen, Jonna 6, 10, 11, 13–16, 152, 340
Lækningabók Íslenzk 283

M berf = Magnús berfœt(t)r (verse by) 61
MacBeth 231
Magnús Erlingsson 10, 13, 14

Magnús góði Óláfsson ix, 5, 9, 10, 12–16, 23, 26, 29–33, 35, 36, 44, 46, 50–53, 59, 62, 63, 67, 72, 74, 76, 79, 95, 114–123, 142–219 passim, 226, 258, 275, 290, 299, 304, 306–308, 331–333, 335, 336
Magnús Ólafsson of Laufás 18, 22, 245, 252, 314
Magnús Þórhallsson 16
Magnússflokkr (Þjóðólfr Arnórsson) 160
Marianus Scottus 283
Maríu saga 77, 233
Maríudrápa 250
Mark = Markús Skeggjason 26, 61, 80, 93, 167, 168, 197, 245
Marold, Edith ix, 66
Málskrúðsfræði 23, 142
Meissner, Rudolf 36, 66, 69, 71, 144, 161, 207
Meiti, legendary sea-king 73, 75, 118, 179
Melkómr, king of Scots 228, 231, 334
Mgr = Máríugrátr 299
Miðgarðr 74, 132, 298
Mikjáll (Michael), saint 35, 63, 134, 312
Miklagarðr (Constantinople) 151, 333
Msk = Morkinskinna 3, 9, 10, 12–16, 26, 27, 41, 44, 210, 218, 223, 248, 269, 280, 288, 320, 326, 327, 331, 333, 339, 350, 351
Mærr (Møre), Mœrir 115, 148, 158, 159, 222
Mǫn (Man) 127, 251–253
Mǫrukári / Morcere 279, 285

Nesjarvísur (Sigvatr) 162
Nið (Nid), river 132, 294
Niðaróss (Nidaros, Trondheim) 170, 203
Niz (Nissan), river 129, 269–271, 295, 334
Nizarvísur (Steinn) 334
Níkdr = Níkolásdrápa 312
Nj = Njáls saga (verse) 189, 197
Njáls saga 143
Njǫrðr, god 74, 113, 137–139, 247
Nordal, Sigurður 9, 17, 30, 41, 42, 340–342
Noreen, Erik 69, 103, 105, 106, 174, 242, 248
Norway / Nóregr, Norwegian etc. ix, 9, 11–13, 41, 44–46, 54, 59, 62, 72, 114, 115, 118–120, 148, 150, 154, 155, 158, 159, 170, 184, 188, 190, 192, 196–198, 207, 268, 269, 274, 285, 287–289, 291, 293, 303, 306–308, 331–333, 336
Nygaard, Marius 221, 254, 297, 300, 305, 309

O kík = Oddr Kíkinaskáld 63, 171, 288, 332, 333
Oddi lítli 250
Oddný eykyndill 42
Orderic Vitalis 334
Orkneyjar (Orkney), and jarls of ix, 5, 17, 25, 29, 43, 44, 50, 53, 54, 61, 133, 140, 174, 178, 222, 223, 233, 234, 251, 262, 268, 303, 304, 307, 308, 331, 335, 336, 346, 347, 354, 358
Orkns = Orkneyinga saga 5, 10, 12, 16–18, 29, 32, 34, 38, 41, 44, 50, 102, 140, 226, 231, 233, 239, 240, 253, 254, 257, 264, 268, 303, 307, 308, 321, 325, 326, 334, 335, 340, 341, 344, 349, 354, 355, 358
Ormr inn langi 271
'Ormr jarlaskáld' 26
Orms Eddu-brot 21, 323, 342
Oykell, river: see Ekkjall

Ód = Oláfs drápa Tryggvasonar 259
Óðinn, god 66, 74, 123, 133, 145, 150, 153, 154, 156, 173, 193, 205, 220–222, 229, 248, 282, 288, 306, 307; see also Yggr
Ól helg = Óláfr helgi (verse by) 221

Ólafur Halldórsson 19, 235, 236, 338, 341
Óláfr helgi Haraldsson 5, 9, 15, 16, 63, 75, 117, 119, 122, 154, 160, 164, 165, 170, 171, 187, 188, 221, 226, 275–277, 332, 333, 335, 336
Óláfr hvítaskáld 19, 23, 66, 80, 93, 142, 143, 349
Óláfr kyrri 9, 13, 15, 28, 47, 223
Óláfr Tryggvason 15, 16, 45, 184, 265, 271
Ólsen, Björn M. 144, 146, 170, 219, 229, 233, 235, 242, 304, 305, 307, 308, 343
Ólsh(Hkr) = Óláfs saga helga, Heimskringla 9–11, 17, 38, 275, 334, 335
Ólsh(Sep) = Óláfs saga helga, Separate 5–9, 11, 12, 15–17, 27, 30, 38, 137, 152, 161, 275, 318, 325, 326, 334, 335, 337, 338, 355
Ólskyrr = Óláfs saga kyrra 9, 13
Ótt = Óttarr svarti 31, 38, 61, 295, 296, 335

Páll Þorfinnsson 257
Peita (Poitou) 76, 115, 160, 162
Péttlandsfjǫrðr (Pentland Firth) 43, 68, 127, 128, 230, 260, 261
Plác = Plácitúsdrápa 188, 215, 299
Poole, Russell ix, 33, 76, 248

Ragnarr loðbrók 245
'Ragnarr', skald 26
Ragnars saga loðbrókar 18, 245
Ragnarsdrápa (Bragi) 20, 59, 63, 209
Rauðabjǫrg (Roberry) 25, 34, 36, 43, 44, 53, 54, 127, 258–260, 301–304, 307, 308, 335, 336
Raumaríki (Romerike), Raumar 130, 277, 278, 301
Refr: see Hofgarða-Refr
Rekstefja (Hallar-Steinn) 30, 31, 139, 186, 297
Revelation, Book of 63
Ré (Rügen) 120, 172, 200, 201, 332
Rogaland, Rygjar 207
Rome 46
Roskilde Chronicon 332
Rst = Rekstefja: see above
Russia(n): see Garðar
Rǫgnvaldr Brúsason ix, 29, 34, 35, 43, 44, 50, 113, 127, 133, 137, 139–141, 239, 246, 251, 253, 259, 260, 264, 301–303, 306–308, 335, 336
Rǫgnvaldr Eysteinsson, Mœrajarl 123, 127, 140, 222, 253, 268
Rǫgnvaldr kali 38, 174
Rǫ́n, goddess 75, 156

Sandvík (Sandwick) 124, 125, 230, 234
Saxo Grammaticus 332–334, 356
Scotland, Scots / Skotar etc. 32, 95, 124–126, 228, 230–233, 236–238, 240–242, 246–248, 251, 263, 335, 346, 358
Seafarer, The 306
See, Klaus von ix, 80
Selund / Zealand 332
Sexstefja (Þjóðólfr Arnórsson) 30
Shetland(ers): see Hjaltland
Sievers, Eduard 82, 85–88, 91, 104, 105, 255, 305
Sigrdr = Sigrdrífumál 197
Sigsk = Sigurðarkviða in skamma 294
Sigtún 119, 154, 185
Sigurðr, legendary hero 75, 180, 294
Sigurðr digri Hlǫðvisson 232, 334
Sigurðr sýr Halfdanarson 333
Sigv = Sigvatr Þórðarson x, 31, 41, 61, 62, 88, 91, 154, 160–162, 164, 186, 194, 201, 208, 210, 224, 229, 240, 256, 290, 302, 308, 313, 332
Sindr = Guthormr sindri 188
Skarpåker 148
Skáldatal 26, 28, 41, 43, 178, 309
Skáldskaparmál 20–22, 74, 220, 322, 323, 342, 345, 352

Skáney (Skåne), Skǫ́nungar 34, 35, 122, 134, 200, 205, 210–213, 309, 310, 333
Skí = Skírnismál 297, 354
Skjǫldr, mythical ruler 150, 168, 181
Skotborgarǫ́ (Kongeå) 93, 116, 168, 169, 332
Skúli Illugason 26
Skúli Þorsteinsson 26, 359
Sn St = Snorri Sturluson (verse by) 197
SnE = Snorra Edda 8, 20–23, 25–31, 34, 37, 38, 60, 66, 72, 74, 75, 104, 150, 155, 156, 167, 181, 185, 188, 191, 220, 232, 242, 249, 250, 266, 267, 275, 278, 279, 300, 322, 325, 327, 341–343, 347, 357
Snorri Sturluson 5, 9, 10, 19–21, 30, 31, 35, 43, 50, 66, 72, 75, 83, 104, 152, 159, 163, 168, 172, 310, 311, 337, 345, 348; see also Hkr, Ht, Ólsh(Hkr), Ólsh(Sep), SnE and Sn St (verse)
Sogn, Sygnir 120, 130, 148, 196, 284, 285
Specimen Lexici Runici 18, 325, 341, 347
St = Sonatorrek (Egill) 222
St Michael: see Mikjáll
Stafangr (Stavanger) 52, 115, 162, 163
Stamford Bridge 131, 285, 286, 294, 334, 345
Steinn Herdísarson 26, 279, 280, 334
Steinunn 207
Steinþórr 288
Stiklastaðir (Stiklestad) 137, 332, 333, 336
Stjórn 280
Sturl = Sturla Þórðarson 61, 75, 80, 186, 231, 254, 283, 288, 290, 292
Sturlunga saga 138, 148
Stúfr blindi, Stúfsdrápa 9, 32, 282, 287, 301, 333, 334
Suðreyjar (Hebrides) 61, 251, 262
Sveinbjörn Egilsson 30, 145, 150, 204, 290, 342, 348, 354
Sveinn Alfífuson / Knútsson 62, 95, 115, 119, 157, 158, 188, 190, 191, 332
Sveinn tjúguskegg (verse by) 145
Sveinn Ulfsson (Sven Estridsson) 35, 36, 117, 121, 122, 129, 171, 173, 174, 200, 205, 210–212, 214, 258, 269, 274, 275, 332–334
Sven Aggesøn 333
Sverris saga 189, 261
Sweden / Svíþjóð, Svíar etc. 52, 114, 119, 148, 153, 154, 185, 187, 205, 262, 282
Sygnir: see Sogn
Symeon of Durham 334
Sǫrli, legendary hero 161

The Skerries 263
Theodoricus 203, 332–334
Third GrT = Third Grammatical Treatise 22, 23, 27, 34, 66, 142, 143, 146, 315, 323, 325, 343
Tindr Hallkelsson 154
Torf-Einarr Rǫgnvaldsson 128, 267, 268
Torfnes (Tarbatness) 54, 125, 236, 237, 242, 268, 335
Tósti Guðinason (Tostig, son of Godwine) 289, 291, 334
Trøndelag: see Þrœndalǫg
Turville-Petre, E.O.G. ix, xi, 50, 66, 80
Tyrfingr, sword 68, 76, 271

Ulfr Sprakaleggsson 174
Ulfr stallari 334
Ulfr Uggason 35
Ulfsflokkr (Steinn) 334
Unnr, wave / goddess 75
Upplǫnd, Upplendingar 55, 75, 129, 276–278, 334

Úsa (Ouse), river 130, 279, 280, 283

V Gl = Víga-Glúmr 231

V St = Vǫlu-Steinn 314
Vafþr = Vafþrúðnismál 222
Valg = Valgarðr á Velli 69, 333
Valþjófr / Walþeof 279, 284, 285, 356
Varðrún, troll-woman 291
Vatnsfjǫrðr (Loch Vatten) 43, 53, 126, 243, 244, 246, 335
Vell = Vellekla (Einarr skálaglamm) 59, 193
Venðr: see Wends
Vestland 67, 120, 200, 201
Visundr, ship 29, 71, 115, 117, 120, 160, 162, 164, 175, 195, 196
Vita Ædwardi Regis 334
Víkingarvísur (Sigvatr) 31
Vries, Jan de 61, 75, 144, 154, 165, 166, 170, 172, 184, 188, 210, 218, 229, 245, 247, 271
Vsp = Vǫluspá 60–62, 255, 261, 266
Vǫlsunga saga 60, 148
Vǫlsungr, legendary king 75, 294
Vǫ́r, goddess 170

Wales 248, 335
Wends / Venðr 29, 63, 116, 120, 121, 165, 166, 168, 169, 198, 199, 203, 332, 346
William of Malmesbury 333, 334
Worm, Ole 18, 341, 342; see also Orms Eddu-Brot

Yggr (Óðinn) 66, 74, 109, 114, 117, 121, 153, 156, 173, 205, 247
Ymir, mythical giant 74, 123, 219, 220
York 284, 285, 334
Yt = Ynglingatal (Þjóðólfr ór Hvini) 314

Þ fagr = Þorleikr fagri 332
Þ flekk = Þorgeirr flekkr 332
Þ hreð = Þórðar saga hreðu (verse) 259
Þ loft = Þórarinn loftunga 63, 292
Þ Skegg = Þórarinn Skeggjason 333
Þ Sær = Þórðr Særeksson 61, 139, 313
Þjóð A = Þjóðólfr Arnórsson ix, 30, 33, 38, 39, 59, 61, 69, 70, 94, 147, 157, 160, 186, 194, 196, 197, 203, 205, 209, 211, 212, 218, 258, 269, 271, 282, 290, 293, 295, 313, 332–334
Þorbjǫrn svarti 151
Þorbjǫrn þyna 256
Þorfinnr Sigurðarson, jarl ix, 29, 32, 34–36, 43, 44, 46, 50, 54, 75, 95, 123–128, 151, 221–268 passim, 301–304, 307, 308, 334–336
Þorkell Ámundason 230, 335, 336
Þorkell hamarskáld 37
Þorm = Þormóðr Kolbrúnarskáld 207, 218, 240
Þórðr Kolbeinsson ix, 41–43, 46, 52, 139, 177
Þórsdrápa (Eilífr) x, 233
Þróttr (Óðinn) 133
Þrœndalǫg (Trøndelag) 114, 156, 332
Þul = Þulur 69, 76, 77, 140, 144, 145, 151, 154, 191, 207, 229, 259, 271, 273, 291
Þursasker 128, 263

Ægir, god 75, 156, 250

Ǫrv = Ǫrvar-Odds saga (verse) 196, 231